PENGUIN BOOKS

AN EYE FOR THE DRAGON

Dennis Bloodworth has been Far Eastern Correspondent for the *Observer* since 1956. He was born in London in 1919 and left school at the age of seventeen to become a pigfood analyst, press photographer, junior reporter and sub-editor in succession. After serving in the army during the war he finally joined the staff of the *Observer* in 1949. He spent five years in Paris and was then transferred to Saigon. He now lives in Singapore with his Chinese wife and three adopted sons. His first book, *Chinese Looking-Glass*, was a big success both in Britain and the United States, where it was Book-of-the-Month Club Choice, as is *An Eye for the Dragon*.

AN EYE
FOR THE DRAGON

South-east Asia Observed,
1954–73

DENNIS BLOODWORTH

PENGUIN BOOKS

Penguin Books Ltd, Harmondsworth, Middlesex, England
Penguin Books Australia Ltd, Ringwood, Victoria, Australia
Penguin Books Canada Ltd, 41 Steelcase Road West, Markham, Ontario, Canada
Penguin Books (N.Z.) Ltd, 182-190 Wairau Road, Auckland 10, New Zealand

—

First published by Secker & Warburg 1970
Revised edition published in Penguin Books 1975

—

Copyright © Dennis Bloodworth, 1970, 1974

—

Made and printed in Great Britain
by Hazell Watson & Viney Ltd
Aylesbury, Bucks
Set in Linotype Pilgrim

120711

FOR PING

When you have heard you must listen; when you have seen you must judge in your heart.

(*Lao Proverb*)

Contents

Acknowledgements

I WOULD like to acknowledge my debt to the writers, translators and publishers of works from which I have quoted or taken extracts. These include *Sinister Twilight* by Noel Barber, published by Collins, from which I have condensed material and quotations about the fall of Singapore (pp. 34–7), *The Golden Chersonese* by Isabella Bird, published by the Oxford University Press (pp. 29–32 and 336), *A History of South-east Asia* by D. G. E. Hall, published by Macmillan and Co., Ltd (pp. 21–3), *The Travels of Marco Polo* translated by Ronald Latham and published by Penguin Books Ltd (pp. 22–6), the *Encyclopaedia Britannica* (Introduction: p. 13), and *The Edge of Tomorrow* by Thomas A. Dooley, published by Farrar, Straus & Giroux. I am also indebted to David Condé and the *Far Eastern Economic Review* for some of the material on 'Japlish' (p. 390), to Estelle Holt for permission to use two anecdotes about Laos (pp. 127–8), to Bernard Kalb, now of CBS, for permission to use his Bali anecdote (p. 86), and to Mark Frankland and John Stirling of the *Observer* and Stanley Karnow, now of the *Washington Post*, for their permission to use quotations from their files.

I would further like to thank Stanley Karnow, Hugh Mabbett of the *Straits Times*, Harvey Stockwin of the *Financial Times*, and the two freelance journalists, Alex Josey and Ramsay Williams, for reading parts of the book and for making many valuable suggestions and corrections. My debt to the *Observer* and the *Observer Foreign News Service*, acknowledged with gratitude in the Introduction, should again be registered here. Finally I must express my sincere thanks to my assistant, Edward de Souza, who typed and checked the MS so efficiently and conscientiously.

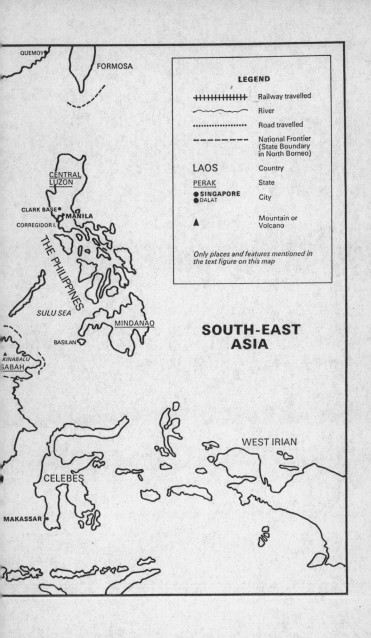

QUEMOY

FORMOSA

LEGEND

++++++++++++ Railway travelled

〰〰〰 River

•••••••••••••• Road travelled

- - - - - - National Frontier (State Boundary in North Borneo)

LAOS — Country

PERAK — State

● SINGAPORE — City
● DALAT

▲ Mountain or Volcano

Only places and features mentioned in the text figure on this map

CENTRAL LUZON

CLARK BASE ● MANILA

CORREGIDOR I.

THE PHILIPPINES

SULU SEA

MINDANAO

BASILAN

KINABALU
SABAH

SOUTH-EAST ASIA

WEST IRIAN

CELEBES

MAKASSAR ●

Introduction:
The Taste of the Durian

THERE are many excellent works on the history, the geography, the cultures and the current political problems of the countries of South-east Asia. Moreover, a good encyclopedia will cover every aspect of the region from philosophy to fruit.

Take, for example, the durian. *Durio Zibethinus*, you may read,

is of the family *Bombacaceae*, and can grow to a height of eighty feet. It is found in Sumatra, Celebes, and Java, and is cultivated in Malaya and Thailand as far north as the 14th Parallel. The fruit is spherical, measures up to 8 inches in diameter, and may weigh eight pounds. It has a hard green external husk armed with pyramidal tubercles terminating in sharp points. Inside, it is divided into five oval compartments, each filled with glutinous pulp and containing up to five large edible seeds. Of exceptionally high protein value, it is noted for its delicious flavour and for its offensive odour.

Now you have been told all about the durian, and you know nothing. For you have neither smelled nor tasted it. In the words of someone who did so one hundred years ago, a 'rich, butter-like custard, highly-flavoured with almonds gives the best idea of it, but intermingled with it come wafts of flavour that call to mind cream cheese, onion sauce, brown sherry'. Let me add that the smell is sweetly fetid, a loathsome compound of rotten onions and rotten meat. But men cheat and steal and fight over durians, as I know, for a big durian tree overhangs my garden in Singapore, and every year thieves smash down the fence to get at the stinking fruit.

South-east Asia is like the durian – prickly, strange, smelly and beautiful, revolting, enchanting, an offence and an addiction. I

am not an academic with all the facts and figures at my fingertips, and my fingertips eight thousand miles away from the
reality. But I have made the Far East my diet for sixteen years.
My object, therefore, is not to measure it and weigh it and put
it into Latin, but to break it open for the ordinary reader who
has never seen it, and to offer him a taste.

This book was originally published in 1970, and I have therefore amended and added to it in order to bring the reader up
to date as painlessly as possible. But it is not a country-by-
country analysis of the region, with a chronological account of
postwar political developments. I have in fact provided a
separate synopsis of the plot at the end, so as to free the text
itself from the burden of narrative form (to paraphrase from
Lawrence Durrell's *Justine*).

I have tried, rather, to explain the nature of the East through
the eyes and experience of a minor character (myself), and to let
the contemporary drama of South-east Asia emerge naturally
from the beliefs, customs, prejudices, and traditional patterns of
thought of the principal players – the peoples themselves.

The book is mainly about South-east Asia, although there are
asides on Korea, Japan and, of course, the great cultural god-
fathers of the subcontinent – India and China. It attempts to
bridge the generation gap between the old established Asia and
the new, emerging Asia, and also to describe the sometimes
clumsy love-hate-play between East and West. Much of the
material has been drawn from articles I have written in the
past, and I am particularly grateful to the Editors of the
Observer and the *Observer Foreign News Service* (OFNS) for
allowing me to take extracts from them.

My references are those of a Far Eastern correspondent, not a
research scholar, and my target is not the Asian specialist, but a
far more important person in the West – the man who does not
know Asia at all. And since the book must have more to it than
the dry bones of academic study if it is to be fit for human
consumption, I make no excuse for the colour and comic relief.
There are no footnotes or acknowledgements in the text to
worry the reader, quotations have been condensed, and the
number of names – whether of eastern politicians or of western

journalists – has been kept to a minimum. As in the case of *Chinese Looking Glass*, this book has been designed for reading.

Certain Chinese artists, it is said, put the eyes in last when they painted a dragon, for this brought the formidable creature to life. Others have drawn the outline of the region for the Western world; I would like to try to give it an eye in which the reader may glimpse, if dimly, something of its awakened spirit (leaving the reader to paint the other one in for himself).

Singapore, October 1973

I

As the Curtain Rises

LIKE all the best cables, this one arrived at Singapore at two o'clock in the morning. Couched in the usual sybilline idiom of the editorial staff, it read:

COULDST INFIT QUICK TRIP MACAO VIEW FILE COLOUR-FUL BACKGROUNDER GOLD SMUGGLING RACKET FOR SWEEK-ENDS PAPER QUERY CHEERS NEWSEDITOR

Two can play at this game, which depends on the seven-and-a-half-hour time-lag between Singapore and England and is contested with the politely-concealed malice of club croquet. It was not until eight o'clock, therefore, that I propped my dog-eared school atlas against the marmalade and prepared to send my opponent on the desk in London an urgent telegram which, I calculated, would get him out of bed at about 0230 hours the previous night.

Not only time, but space was on my side, moreover. Macao, the tiny Portuguese colonial 'province' that protrudes from the gross abdomen of Communist China like an insignificant wart, was fully five and a half inches from Singapore according to my map, or one thousand seven hundred and fifty miles as the crow flies. But it was only forty miles from Hongkong, where my colleague Rawle Knox was then based. Accordingly, I wired briefly:

WHY SEND ME AND NOT RAWLE QUERY BESTEST BLOODWORTH

To which I received the unnerving, even briefer reply:

BECAUSE YOU ARE NEARER LUV FRED

A further exchange of sardonic endearments revealed that someone in London had confused Macao with Malacca, on the west coast of Malaya, which was a little like mistaking Buda-pest for Bristol. There was nothing really startling about this, however. People in the West still send letters to 'Hongkong, China', even to 'Singapore, China'. Men may know something of the Further East, a relatively simple affair dominated by easily-recognizable geographical clichés like China and Japan. But the states of South-east Asia appear to the stranger as an ambiguous, almost obscene muddle of shapes dangling from the world's bulkiest continent and then trailing off vaguely into an untidy mess of ten thousand tropical islands. Africa may have renamed its component parts and disconcertingly changed all its postage stamps, but Africa at least has always been Africa. In the mind of any man west of the Indian Ocean, however, South-east Asia did not even exist thirty years ago. It had to be invented.

Early mapmaking of the region was understandably hit-and-miss, but the cartographical squint that put the 'Stretto di Anian' – and so today's Vietnam – to the north of China in 1562, instead of to the south, would not have raised the well-tended eyebrows of the special envoy from Washington who arrived in Saigon nearly 400 years later during a tour of South-east Asia. While she was being escorted by an American em-bassy official from the airport to a room reserved for her in the Hotel Majestic, this lady (for such she undoubtedly was) commented affably : 'My, it certainly feels good to be in Indo-nesia.' 'Excuse me, Ma'am,' corrected the other, 'but this is not Indonesia, this is Indochina.' 'Jesus,' breathed Her Excellency, visibly moved by something, 'Where the hell have I just come from, then?' Later rioting Vietnamese, although ignorant of this conversation, broke into her hotel bedroom. 'But I am your friend,' protested the anguished ambassadress to the mob. 'I am an American.' Thus goaded, they threw the furniture out of the window.

How does that contradiction in terms, the Western Far East correspondent, explain the one unknown world to the other? Between chains of theatrical mountains, a simple, often indo-lent civilization graces rich rice-growing flatlands veined with waterways and bisected by the great yellow Mekong River.

The golden-tiled temples, with their fantastical upcurling roofs, tower over settlements of little wooden houses on stilts. The mop-headed palms and shady tamarinds stand motionless under a steamy sky. Sarong-clad women bicker in the market place. This may seem to be no more than the setting for the Coke signs and the Cadillacs and the TV commercials, the flashing jets and mechanized armies and student strife, for mushrooming hotels and mushrooming high explosive. But the comforting familiarity of all that shiny western veneer does not help.

For the dubious purpose of writing these reflections I have lined up seventy old notebooks, and now, picking one at random labelled 'Laos, July 1957', I find myself staring, appalled, at a page of almost incomprehensible scribble reading: *'Democrats angry Leuam not retained by Katay as Min. Fin. Also brother murdered in mistake for Phoui (plot with Pau and Bong) and tend blame Sananikones. Prog. party vote 8 K, 5 SP, 4 abstained. SP and Pet not deputies. Vorovong says Katay must fail. Nou Ing also left out last cab.'* Pages of it. What does it, or did it ever, mean? Yet on some sad and sweltering evening in the rapidly receding past, I must have unpicked the tangle and knitted it into 600 words gently explaining the vital importance of this whole grisly oriental vendetta to unconvinced *Observer* readers 8,000 miles away in Windsor Castle and Wormwood Scrubs. How else would I have received in Vientiane an acknowledging cable from London saying:

THANKEST YOUR LUCIDEST LAOS REGRETFULLY OUT-SQUEEZED LATER EDITIONS OWING NEWS PRESSURE CHEERS NEWSEDITOR.

I could hardly blame him. It became an exacting task to try to explain clearly in half a column a series of obscure crises in which, for a start, the name of the neutralist leader Prince Souvanna Phouma appeared to be a deliberately contrived anagram of the name of his 'pro-American' rival, General Phoumi Nosavan. Anyway, as some mythical ambassador is said to have declared of every capital from Saigon to Djakarta: 'anyone who thinks he understands the situation here simply does not know the facts.'

The ignorance cuts both ways. In Phnom Penh once a young Cambodian Buddhist bonze with shaven head and begging bowl stopped me under the shadow of the sunbaked wall of the Royal Palace and in stilted English asked for a light for a cigarette, which he fished from somewhere under his saffron toga. 'And you are what nationality?' he demanded, with cool monastic insolence. 'British,' I replied defiantly, and almost without a moment's hesitation. The naked face sharpened with faint puzzlement, so I repeated: 'British – you speak English, you must have heard of it?' The monk shook his head disdainfully. 'No,' he answered, and left the monosyllable hanging limply in the air as he shuffled on, puffing. I watched him go, consoled by the memory of the chagrined Washington diplomat who discovered that a Malay he was talking to on the island of Langkawi had never heard of the United States. It might be difficult to put Laos across in Lambeth, but at least I was spared the frustrations of putting Lambeth across in Laos.

Too much language and too little learning make an unstable compound for human relationship, for they produce a synthetic sense of understanding which can be as dangerous as dynamite. Thomas Stamford Raffles, the liberal and humanitarian founder of Singapore, discovered this to his cost when in 1811 he wrote to the Sultan of Palembang urging him to force the local Dutch garrison to leave. His scribe translated this into Malay as 'beat them out conclusively' and the Sumatran potentate, adapting it to his own vocabulary of violence, thereupon had the Dutch massacred to the last man. Very wisely my Chinese wife, Ping, refused to teach me any Mandarin before she had first put me through a crash course in Chinese history and philosophy (as well as the Singapore Registry Office). But knowledge limited to acts and facts can be as hazardous as knowledge limited to mere words.

There is an elusive, now-you-see-it-now-you-don't character to man's similarity to man that can be almost shockingly deceptive. South-east Asia can only be interpreted in terms of the mental idiom peculiar to its peoples, the idiom that has evolved over the slow centuries and the fleeting years.

An old philosophical limerick best poses the initial puzzle:

> There once was a man who said 'God
> Must find it exceedingly odd
> That that sycamore tree
> Continues to be
> When there's no one about in the quad.'

Before *The King and I* and *The Ugly American*, before Joseph Conrad and Somerset Maugham, and before the first western tradesman set his big round eyes upon it and staked the first colonial claim, this obscure subcontinent must have existed. But what was south-east Asia before it was ever 'South-east Asia'?

Like spectral figures that materialize in a gloomy corner of the canvas when a masterpiece is cleaned, the outlines of old, lost kingdoms emerge slowly from the dark, featureless map as a century of scholarship begins to dissolve our ignorance.

'The people of Funan are cunning and astute,' mumbles a Chinese chronicler, bent over his brush fourteen hundred years ago.

They trade in gold, silver and silks. When the king travels, he rides on an elephant, and women may do the same. For distraction, the people arrange cock-fights and pig-fights. They have no prison. They judge by heating a chain red-hot which must then be carried seven paces. The hands of the guilty are scorched, but the innocent man is not hurt. Or else they duck one in deep water. He who has right on his side does not sink, he who is wrong, does.

The people lived in thatched wooden houses with tall palisades, but the king reigned from a storied pavilion, possessed many gold vases, incense burners, and foreign slaves.

Only dimly perceived from this distance, Funan dominated the subcontinent for 500 years after the death of Christ, and at the zenith of their power its kings were overlords from the Mekong Delta in the east to the Malay Peninsula in the west. But all that has been found of it has been a few gold and

bronze objects, some of them inexplicably inscribed with the
name of the Roman Emperor Antoninus Pius – as was the wall
he built between the Forth and the Clyde in Scotland.

To the north lay Champa, its kings masters of the littoral
that now includes Central Vietnam. First glimpsed in the days
of Marcus Aurelius, Champa survived seventeen centuries of
uneasy and fluctuating fortune. 'You must know that in this
kingdom,' relates Marco Polo, 'no pretty girl can marry without first being presented to the king for his inspection. If he
is pleased with her, he takes her to wife. If not, he gives her
a sum of money appropriate to her station so that she may
take another husband. I assure you that when I was in this
country the king had 326 children . . .'

The Chams built grand and durable temples as smooth as
sandstone, for they used no mortar but baked the bricks after
they had been laid, as part of a process now lost, so that a
knife cannot be inserted between them even today. The men
themselves proved less durable, however. The great realm, its
centre earlier in the region of Hue, gradually shrank southward
like a fizzling balloon, and finally disappeared into the swamps
west of Saigon.

By the time Champa sank into history, Funan was long
gone, overthrown in the sixth century by a Khmer power
which China knew as Chen-la, and which extended in its heyday to the Chinese border in the north, to modern Tonking
in the east and modern Cambodia in the south. Its royal
palace may well have been at Vientiane, the bucolic temple-
strewn little capital of Laos, but if so, its former magnificence
is lost in the drains and dust.

'Every three days,' wrote a Chinese during the seventh
century,

the king goes in solemn procession to the Hall of Audience and
seats himself upon a bed made of five sorts of perfumed wood and
decorated with seven precious things. Above the bed rises a pavilion
of magnificent materials, of which the columns are of veined wood
and the screens of ivory sewn with flowers of gold. A golden incense-
burner, tended by two men, is placed in front. More than a thousand

guards clad in mail and armed with lances are ranged at the foot of the steps to his throne, in the halls of the palace, at its gates and peristyles.

Men always go about armed, and a simple tiff may lead to a bloody fight, he goes on, but: 'They wash every morning, brush their teeth with small pieces of wood, and do not fail to read their prayers.' They write from left to write, not from top to bottom as in the Celestial Empire itself, it is noted later disapprovingly. But they also hold firework displays on new year's eve, honour twelve signs of the zodiac, and observe leap years, 'for their men are learned in astronomy, and able to calculate eclipses of moon and sun'.

In the ninth century a new master of Chen-la moved the Khmer capital to a new site at which, for nearly 400 years, a line of prestigious kings was to direct the work of thousands of elephants and hundreds of thousands of men in the construction of one of the most awesome man-made wonders of the world, the gigantic complex of stone and tombs, temple-mountains and intricately sculptured memorials of Angkor. For half a millennium after the final decay of the kingdom these fantastic monuments of Kambuja slowly crumbled and sank into a greedy sea of encroaching jungle whose banyan trees crushed whole shrines to rubble between the muscular thighs of their monstrous roots. But in 1863 a French naturalist uncovered a corner of the colossus, and since then his compatriots have painstakingly rebuilt much of it in all its magnificence.

Angkor Wat, tomb and temple for a god-king who personified Vishnu on earth, was surrounded by about four miles of moat, and is still approached by an immense, paved causeway. The structure itself, its successive tiers of terraces and cool colonnaded galleries, pavilions and steep stairways surmounted by five tall towers, was made without mortar, every stone being set precisely on the next, and the whole marvellous artifact is a running riot of bas-relief, of gods and heavenly dancing girls, battle scenes and naval pageants. The first gallery alone has an inner wall of polished sandstone carved into a brilliantly executed frieze seven feet tall and more than 600 yards long.

The kingdom, which straddled the subcontinent of South-east Asia by the eleventh century, declined as inexorably as the waning moon. Harassed by vigorous Siamese newcomers from the north, it collapsed beneath the weight of its own monuments and the exhausting effort required to build them. By 1431 the time had come for the Khmers to move south and soon they abandoned the whole gorgeous growth to the weeds.

There were nevertheless men across the uneasy seas that separated the mainland from the fragmented jigsaw of islands to the south who had looked upon Chen-la as little more than a vassal. The Indonesian archipelago had thrust up its own great realms, and in the manner of arrogant islanders from Cornwall to Kyoto, they regarded the adjoining continent as their footstool. In the sixth century Srividjaja emerged as an ambitious maritime trading empire whose hegemony extended to the coastal corners of Malaya, Cambodia and the Philippines, and 600 years after that a visitor to the capital at Palembang in South Sumatra remarked that it was still a thriving centre of sea power in which, rather typically, 'eight hundred moneychangers are busily engaged'.

Two centuries later, however, the might of Srividjaja was only a memory, eclipsed by the new, formidable Javanese empire of Madjapahit which claimed suzerainty over Siam, Cambodia, Annam and Malaya and also – if with questionable bravado – the entire Indonesian archipelago. It was to hold sway until after Columbus had discovered America and Bartholomew Diaz had sailed around the Cape of Good Hope to put the white man and his white ships into the Indian Ocean for the first time.

Nevertheless, just as the pressure waves in Europe flowed in from the east and finally petered out on the beaches of the British Isles to the far west, in a supine South-east Asia overhung by the mass and might of China, the main pressure flowed from north to south.

The light yellow men who compelled the Khmers to abandon Angkor had been unceremoniously pushed out of their own private kingdom in South China by the Mongol hordes of Kublai Khan in the thirteenth century, and had therefore pioneered all the more boldly into the ill-lit subcontinent to their south. They were the Thais, who became known as the Shans when they overran North Burma, the Laos when they dominated what is now Laos, the Siamese when they obliterated the memory of Angkor and later established the kingdom of Siam. (But they remained the Black Thais and White Thais in the mountains of North Vietnam where they preserved their simple hill-tribe habits and their respect for formal, traditional dress.)

Other small, pale northerners edged down the Indochina littoral, the name of their state changing as they crept southward – 'Nam Viet', 'Dai Viet', 'Annam'. In some ways reminiscent of the conquest of the west in a newer continent, their armed migration was to obliterate the Chams as a nation, but they themselves were again to lose an old identity in order to gain a new one, finally emerging as the people of 'Vietnam'.

Meanwhile, as the deep dyes of Graeco-Roman and Christian culture seeped across the fabric of primitive Europe, colouring earlier patterns of repulsive custom and improbable belief, the East was absorbing spiritual light and shadow from two great presences on the frail fringes of the subcontinent : China and India.

Confucian China offered no gods, but the down-to-earth ethics of a benevolent society. Harmony with the universe depended on harmony among men, and so salvation lay in the careful study and emulation of ancient sages in whose goodness and wisdom lay the secret of human and cosmic concord. The Chinese therefore bequeathed to their Korean and Vietnamese vassals the concept of an empire administered not by blue-blooded dunces but by a civil service of scholar-mandarins steeped in improving reading.

China's suzerainty was inspired by a philosophy which taught that there was no other civilization but the Confucian state and that its Emperor was not only vicar of Heaven but viceroy of all the earth. Other rulers were not fellow-princes, but mere feudatories. They must at least go through the motions of swearing loyalty and sending tribute to the Son of Heaven, and so spare a sometimes embarrassingly weak Celestial Empire the undignified necessity of proving who was the master.

China conquered Tonking a century before Christ was born and kept it for a thousand years, and during His lifetime a usurper on the Dragon Throne sent an expedition as far as North Sumatra to acquire a rhinoceros for his zoo. The impression it made is not known, but twelve centuries later Marco Polo had occasion to describe its Javanese cousin, for the armies of Kublai Khan not only invaded recalcitrant Burma and Annam, but crossed the seas to Java to teach a temerarious king that he could not expel the Son of Heaven's ambassador with impunity. ('These unicorns,' he relates disgustedly, 'have the hair of a buffalo and feet like an elephant's. They have a single large black horn in the middle of the forehead. They are very ugly brutes to look at. They are not at all such as we describe them when we relate that they let themselves be captured by virgins, but clean contrary to our notions.') Later the eunuch-admiral Cheng Ho, castrated commander of China's greatest fleets, seized 'rebel' kings in South Sumatra and Ceylon and removed them to Peking to encourage a proper respect for the Emperor in others.

The Confucian view of Heaven as an enigma about whose nature it was obviously absurd to ask at all complemented, if a little uneasily, the smoky imagery of Hindu and Buddhist mysticism that curled upward from a philosophical conviction that, on the contrary, a sensible man should devote his attention to a metaphysical cosmos whose story was to be measured in 'kotis of kalpas' (tens of millions of cycles of 4,320 million years each). It was the world that was a waste of time.

Appropriately, Indian suzerainty over South-east Asia was spiritual, for the cults of Buddhism and Brahma–Vishnu–Siva, the trinity of Creator, Preserver and Destroyer, had been brought by the Brahmins from India and the Indies. They held in their many-armed embrace almost all of the gorgeously-named kingdoms of the region – Funan, Champa, Chen-la, Angkor, Srividjaja, Sailendra, Madjapahit – and Sanskrit was to the learned of South-east Asia what Latin was to the prelates of medieval Europe.

In Funan, inscriptions recorded the legends of North India, and today Hindu epics still provide the themes for Indonesian shadow-plays, for the dances of Bali and Bangkok and the Royal Cambodian Ballet. Their mythical half-worlds are endlessly re-created wherever Javanese puppeteers perform to village audiences, and Thai dancers, sewn into their scintillating confections of gold and silver brocade, arch their long-nailed fingers in the curlicued gestures of a wordless dialogue.

But as one coat of lacquer is laid on another, new faiths coloured the map of South-east Asia, half obscuring the old, and leaving only Bali as the last stronghold of the earlier Hinduism. The teachings of the Prophet Mohammed spread to South-east Asia as converted Indian merchants from Gujerat sailed to Sumatra and Malaya and the further islands, until the powerful Hindu Madjapahit Empire was overthrown in Java, and two new Muslim kingdoms arose in its place. They were just in time to face the Protestant Dutch in Java, as the Moros faced the Catholic Spaniards in the neighbouring Philippines to the east. The Christians had arrived to save the Orient from itself.

2

The Contract Breakers

WEST and East do not speak the same language, even when it is English. To the half-educated half-heathen product of the British school system medieval 'Islam' evokes a vision of Holy Wars, of flames, scimitars and angry young men in turbans slaying infidels from one end of the Mediterranean to the other in their earnest and impartial attempts to propagate the Word of the Prophet. Early 'Christianity', on the other hand, is St Augustine and the humble hermitage of Iona, the soft progress of peaceable bare-foot friars opening the eyes of the ignorant to the glory of Heaven, and their nostrils to the rather objectionable odour of sanctity.

In much of the Malay world of South-east Asia, however, Islam meant the sufi, the emotional yet gentle missionary who sailed through the islands, adapting the sharp edges of his faith to the curves of the cults he found, and reconciling them through their common denominator of medieval mysticism. Christianity, on the other hand, was carried to the East with the cutlass and cannon, and if the white men that so unfortunately seemed to go with it were not gratuitously bullying the benighted, they were using any local display of enmity towards their priests as a pretext for laying violent hands upon kings and their countries. In this way the persecution of Christian missionaries by two Emperors of Annam lit a powder train of events which ended with Paris writing 'French Indochina' across the entire eastern half of the South-east Asian mainland. This was an age in which even de Gaulle would not have been an anachronism, for French nineteenth-century colonialism was characterized by a chauvinistic hysteria and greedy obsession with Gallic *gloire* which was further stimulated by a perfidious British presence in the western half of the subcontinent.

First in the field, however, were the Portuguese, who seized Malacca in 1511 in order to stop the spread of Islam and Arab trade. Their methods were inspired not so much by the teachings of St Francis Xavier, who rode through the streets of the port ringing a bell and calling on all to pray for 'Jews, Turks, infidels and heretics', as by the exacting example in savagery set by Vasco da Gama when he encountered an unarmed Arab ship in the Indian Ocean a little earlier.

This was found to contain many pilgrims from Mecca among the 300-odd men, women and children aboard. So after carefully removing the cargo, the Portuguese locked all the passengers in the vacated hold and set fire to the ship. And when the hapless inmates obstinately broke out on deck again and tried to beat back the flames, the great navigator sailed his squadron around and around the floating bonfire, bombarding it with cannon while women held their babies up in their arms in an absurd attempt to wring a little Christian mercy out of him. With sour if saintly humour St Francis himself wrote that the knowledge of the Portuguese in Amboina seemed to be confined to the verb *rapio*, in which his countrymen demonstrated 'an amazing capacity for inventing new tenses and participles'. The Spanish, who landed in the Philippines later in the century, showed the same deadly diligence in pursuing their colonial crusade against the Muslim Moros in the southern islands of the archipelago.

'If the Portuguese were little better than buccaneers, the Dutch who drove them out were little better than hucksters,' was the uncharitable verdict of one of those intrepid middle-aged English ladies who always seemed to be penetrating jungles in the nineteenth century when they were not presiding over tea and thin-cut sandwiches on the lawn.

This conclusion of Miss Isabella Bird was presumably based upon accounts of the way in which, with the commendable thoroughness of the Dutch burgher, the Netherlands exploited the Indies. The Dutch founded Batavia in Java and seized Malacca from the Portuguese in the early seventeenth century, and thereafter systematically fleeced the sprawling dependency which is today the Republic of Indonesia. The principle was quite simple. The native farmer was told what to grow on much of his land, and was obliged to deliver the crop for a fixed price to Dutch merchants who held a monopoly on its fantastically profitable export to the Netherlands. Since local chiefs also took their cut, it has been estimated that during the eighteenth century a Javanese planter had to supply double the quantity of coffee that was actually shipped, for which he would receive little more than one twentieth of the sale price in Holland. This 'coffee culture' racket was still operating during the First World War, and ten years after it Dutch Government monopolies in pawnshops, opium and salt in the Netherlands East Indies were still bringing the Hague a respectable revenue of more than £8,000,000 a year.

Like the French, the Dutch were reluctant to groom their golden-brown wards for authority, and when the Japanese invasion of Java in 1942 brought them their first false scent of independence, there were fewer than 250 Indonesians holding senior posts in the civil service throughout the entire archipelago, against nearly 3,000 Dutch.

To the British, one of the most irritating characteristics of the British is the irresponsible fashion in which they will invent something and then leave others to exploit it on a mass-produced basis (tanks, jet aircraft and counter-insurgency all immediately come to mind). But colonialism is the exception. The British left the Portuguese, the Spanish and the Dutch to do the pioneering, and only then went into the business seriously themselves, emerging with a controlling interest in the biggest cartel of all. By 1824 they were still limited to modest beginnings in South-east Asia – Penang, Malacca, and a spit in the ocean off the point of the Malayan peninsula called Singapore. The robust and enterprising spirit of the men on the spot, however, was exemplified by the official of the East India Company who had acquired this 225 square miles of unprepossessing jungle and mangrove swamp with little more than a handful of primitive Malay fishermen clinging precariously to its malarial fringe. Thomas Stamford Raffles, finding the sultanate which controlled Singapore in dispute, installed a dispossessed claimant on the island and at once concluded an agreement with its new, grate-

ful, but impecunious master whereby the Company would pay
him $5,000 a year for the right to establish a settlement. For
he foresaw that this mudbank in the gullet of the Straits of
Malacca, commanding the strategic water-gate between East
and West, would one day outstrip all neighbouring territories
in importance. And he was right.

The coy attitudes of British officialdom towards the acquisi-
tion of empire were also reflected in the Company's reaction
to the Singapore take-over. Raffles was castigated for exceeding
instructions and for annoying the Dutch, and when he died
the Company dunned his impoverished widow for £10,000 to
cover various expenses he had incurred, including those of his
original mission to the island. The same spirit diluted the policy
of the government of British India towards Burma, which was
only acquired piecemeal after the initial moves had been provoked by the repeated threats of an ill-tempered Burmese
monarch to take over bits of India. (This characteristic of
grasping more power under protest has been complemented
by the deceptive aggressiveness of Peking, which many believe
to be no more than a well-developed defensive reflex thoroughly justified in a world in which three out of four people
are not Chinese. The Reluctant Lion, it could be said, has been
matched by the Reluctant Dragon.)

Piracy along their trade routes, and the routine state of
'robbery, battle and murder' in the interior behind their finger-
holds down the steep Malayan coast, drew the British into
pacifying and accumulating more and more territory un-
willingly in accordance with some sort of Imperial variation
on Parkinson's Law, it is claimed. And there is certainly evidence to support the contention. When a British Resident experimentally appointed to the Malay State of Perak in 1875
was promptly murdered, and the Governor in Singapore
launched a sharp 'little war' of reprisal, there was uproar in
England, and irresponsible colonial officers who added to the
burden of empire by conquering territory without parliamentary approval were roundly condemned.

Despite all the ostensible timidity in London, however, it is
to be remarked that with the passage of healing time Britain

found herself virtually in possession of the whole of North Borneo and the peninsula of Malaya. The British Resident to a Malay State, originally sent as an 'adviser' to the ruling native prince, became the government itself. 'Captain Murray,' Isabella Bird tells us briskly of one Resident, 'is Judge, Superintendent of Police, Chancellor of the Exchequer, Surveyor of Taxes, besides being Board of Trade, Board of Works, and I know not what besides.' Local rajahs attended by such Residents she describes as being virtually 'pensioned off'. But in a fetid and lawless land in which personal feuds and rival claims to power were summarily settled with the snake-bladed *kris*, white protection could be a serviceable counterbalance for the blackest reputation. In Perak the British upheld as ruling prince an unamiable fellow who is said to have poured boiling water over the back of a runaway woman slave and then put a red ants' nest on it. Generally detested by his fellow-Malays, he not unnaturally turned out to be 'a proved man as to his loyalty', records a tongue-in-cheek British official.

Striving to run their states on a sound financial basis, Residents relied upon well-tried and conventional sources of wealth like farming, taxes and licences. They needed no knowledge of agriculture, however, for the 'farmers' were enterprising businessmen who were sold monopolies in such estimable services and commodities as gambling, drink, and opium (happily for the exchequer, 'every coolie smokes his three whiffs every night'). It would nevertheless be grossly unjust to suggest that there was no other farming. Plantations were not, on the face of it, unattractive investments, for coolies were paid a shilling a day and it only cost five pounds to build a barrack into which you could cram fifty of them.

This was no continent of primitive jungle-dwellers, however, and what the white man was rearranging to suit his own convenience, much as one may convert an elephant's forefoot into a wastepaper basket or a Chinese bronze drum into a barbecue, were the shards of great civilizations with intricate administrative systems as well as profound religious beliefs. At Angkor the enormous hydraulic network that irrigated the country had in its own way been as wonderful as the monuments to its god-kings. The whole region of more than 12 million acres, served by ingenious devices for controlling the movement of water from and to reservoirs of immense capacity, was squared off into rice fields capable of yielding three and even four crops a year.

The European was constantly to be astonished, and on first seeing the Shwe Dagon Pagoda in Rangoon 400 years ago, a British merchant-adventurer wrote, 'It is called Dogonne, and is of a wonderful bigenesse, and all gilded from the foot to the toppe. It is the fairest place, as I suppose, that is in the world : it standeth very high, and there are foure ways to it, which all along are set with trees of fruits, in such wise that a man may go in the shade about two miles in length.' The arrogant Spanish were chastened to observe not only the excellent craftsmanship of the Filipinos, who built galleons for them of up to 2,000 tons out of splendid hardwood, sailcloth and manila hemp rigging, but also what masterly seamen they were when they handled them.

To these peoples western conquest brought not only war but peace. The mayhem subsided and across the face of South-east Asia there slowly crept an unaccustomed expression of catatonic calm, broken by an occasional nervous twitch here and there but utterly unlike the jerky fits expressive of greed, treachery, violence and hatred that had convulsed it before. This was the hypnotic imperial pax imposed by the new white masters of the subcontinent. But the first catch in any colonial contract is the *noblesse oblige* clause in small print which stipulates that the superior must be seen to be superior, and the right to plunder must be matched by a readiness to protect. In 1941 this clause was invoked, and the West was exposed as a common cheat.

The Admiral, who had studied aboard the training ship H.M.S. *Worcester*, showed the usual national genius for copy-ing others and on the eve of battle dispatched the signal : 'The destiny of the Empire depends upon this action; you are all expected to do your utmost.' This Japanese Nelson then en-gaged the Russian Baltic Fleet which had come half-way around the world to challenge him in the narrows of Tsushima, and sank, captured, or disabled every one of its thirty-eight ships.

Admiral Togo's decisive victory at sea in 1905 and the defeat of the Tsar's armies in the Russo-Japanese war sent a faint quiver of expectancy through the Far East, for an Asian power had for the first time whipped the whites at their own wargame. But although in the thirty-six years that followed twinges of nationalism animated the subcontinent's soporific countenance – there were riots in Burma, and bloodshed in Tonking and Indonesia where uprisings were suppressed with nervous brutality – the domesticated dragons of tropical South-east Asia for the most part remained reassuringly tame.

When for the second time the Japanese displayed the same military vices and virtues by attacking without declaring war and then crippling an enemy fleet with praiseworthy economy, confidence in western supremacy at first remained unshaken. Nowhere was this more true than in Singapore. The Japanese, having struck the first blow at Pearl Harbor in December 1941, lashed out in all directions at bewildering speed and within three weeks had taken Wake, Guam and Hongkong, had landed in Thailand and Indochina, invaded the Philippines, Burma, Bali and Sumatra, sunk the *Prince of Wales* and the *Repulse*, and established a beachhead in North Malaya.

Lolling in the rattan chairs of Singapore clubs while forty-year-old Chinese 'boys' sidled up with the day's first iced *stengah*, a man of the right creed and colour could nevertheless scribble his name on a chit and see things in their proper pink perspective. Singapore was an impregnable fortress. Hills had been flattened and rivers deflected to build the mighty £63,000,000 naval base, with its twenty-two square miles of anchorage, its giant floating dock and seventeen football fields. The island was defended by 88,000 troops, and the RAF were operating from four airfields in machines which, it had been solemnly promised, were 'more than a match' for Japanese Zeros. To reach Singapore, the enemy had to fight his way through 400 miles of impenetrable jungle against British defending forces, and it simply could not be done, old boy.

In fact, the indefatigable little men from Asia's off-shore

islands covered the distance in just over two months, and were decapitating their first Chinese victims on the Singapore waterfront under the eyes of the helpless British by mid-February 1942. The naval base had proved a fabulously costly white elephant, for, as it was belatedly remarked, its 15-inch guns pointed 'in the wrong bloody direction' and could not traverse enough to bear fully upon an army invading overland from the north. In any case they had no high-explosive ammunition suitable for the task of mincing up men, but only armour-piercing shells for knocking holes in absent enemy warships. The RAF's ageing collection of aircraft was soon shot out of the air, leaving one squadron of Hurricanes to face more than 200 Japanese planes. When it was all over bar some defiant shouting that 'There'll always be an England', the Japanese had lost 10,000 men (and the British 139,000 one way and another).

Some of the besieged fought brilliantly, above and below, and many British men and women acted with a gallantry that matched the stoical courage shown by the Asian poor amid the wreckage and mangled horrors of devastated Chinatown. But as morale crumbled and the dispirited and defeated army filtered down from Malaya to join the final dregs of the defence in Singapore, the island stood exposed, both naked and ashamed. And when orderlies piling corpses into a 40-foot trench outside the General Hospital put Asians at one end and white men at the other, it was somehow symbolical. Not all were brothers even now, and the men were still to be separated from the 'boys', it seemed.

First the white wives began to leave – two of them successfully insisting that their cars must be loaded on to the same ship with them, although every inch of space was precious. Next, Harbour Board officials and naval technicians were furtively evacuated, and finally a 'secret' operation to slip out 3,000 'key young men' who must run away to fight another day was mounted on Friday 13 February. The definition was liberally interpreted, and an incongruous flotilla of forty-four boats sailed for Java, carrying among others eighty-seven members of the Public Works Department headed by a man who had been expressly ordered to stay behind – and his wife. They were to be followed within forty-eight hours by Lieutenant-General Gordon Bennett, Commander of the 8th Australian Division, who crept away without permission, having issued a last order to his troops to stay staunchly at their posts before he made for the docks.

In the heavily-bombed and shelled General Hospital Asian civilian nurses, who could have faded back into their *kampongs* without trace, were firmly told that neither their civilian director nor the British Army sisters were going to leave, and chanted 'Then we stay too.' And they did – working with a marvellous devotion to duty. But a few days later the British Army sisters nevertheless silently disappeared. Abandoned by the absconding white man to a yellow conqueror with the leniency of a locust, the island's immigrant Chinese, Malays, Indians and Eurasians stayed put, for they had nowhere to go.

'Don't worry about me – I'll become part of the scenery,' smiled a Eurasian journalist as his white colleagues took off. He did – but he also operated a short-wave radio and smuggled thousands of messages to British internees in Changi gaol, using a Chinese plumber as his courier. Finally betrayed from inside the camp, he was seized, beaten, starved and sadistically tortured over a long stretch of months but never gave away a single accomplice. Eddie de Souza, my Eurasian assistant, who could also have melted into the shadows easily enough, refused to discard his uniform as a volunteer and was duly taken prisoner and sent to work on the infamous 'death railway' the Japanese were building from Siam to Burma.

First known as Timasek, then as Singapore the Lion City, the island was called Syonan by its new Japanese proprietors. There never had been any lions, people realized, and the settlement was now insecure, unsure of its identity, in shock after its traumatic experience. If the British could return to Malaya and Singapore without blushes or bloodshed in 1945, it was because the Japanese had not only behaved so atrociously, but had opened the bidding in brutality on arrival by butchering with bayonets nearly everyone they found in the British military hospital on the island, and the Asian observed in time that the white man was to suffer with the yellow and the brown after all. In work camps, on the death railway, men of all shades perished of starvation and the systematic savagery practised upon them by the dreaded *Kempetai*. The Japanese beat prisoners until they were 'as raw as liver', made them kneel and then jumped on their exposed soles with army boots until the fractured bones appeared, or with fiendish simplicity denied them all food and all sleep for days on end. 'We suddenly feel the British are not bosses but human beings like us,' a Chinese woman told me. A common suffering and a common hatred blurred the colours and brought the races closer.

But the white man had forfeited his right to rule. For to Asian nationalists who had by now had quite enough of brick-faced barbarians from the West, the ugly Japanese had held out one beautiful promise – the magic Malays call 'Merdeka' and Vietnamese 'Doc Lap' and which smells as sweet by a hundred other names : independence.

Since this promise must be made to come true whoever won, however, nationalists supported first one side and then the other as the fortunes of war fluctuated, and sometimes divided the labour between them and backed both at the same time. In Burma the sarcastically self-styled 'Thakins' ('Sahibs') first helped the Japanese and harassed the British, and then backed the British once it looked as if the Japanese would lose the war. In Indonesia, Sukarno and Mohammed Hatta collaborated with the Japanese and were made responsible for recruiting 120,000 men into auxiliary forces which ostensibly served the ends of Tokyo but in fact became the core of the Indonesian People's Army. Other nationalist leaders were simultaneously organizing resistance against the invaders in accordance with the sound principle of heads-I-win-tails-you-lose.

Peace came like the last, revealing chapter of a farcical who-dunit, with the glaring suspects unmasked as sound security risks after all and the crime pinned firmly on to the hero's best friend. The chapter begins with a comic semantical misunderstanding, the Americans and British calling anyone who backed the Japanese 'collaborators' and 'quislings' while Asians are calling them 'patriots'. General MacArthur swears he will run 'every disloyal Filipino' to earth, and in Burma General Slim reminds the Thakins, who are asking London to recognize their provisional government, that they are nothing but traitors under British law.

This makes for a strong dramatic opening, but the reader must not be misled. MacArthur proceeds to give a certificate of good conduct to Manuel Roxas, who served Tokyo's puppet government in Manila by procuring rice for the Japanese, and in the year after their surrender he is elected President of the Philippine Republic and hailed as a loyal friend of the United States. In 1948 he proclaims an amnesty for all 'traitors' who have not committed serious crimes. Marshal Pibul Songgram, who declared war on the Allies and allowed the Japanese to use Thailand as a springboard for their assault on Malaya, is back in power by 1947 and assiduously courted by the Anglo-Saxons. The British recognize an interim government of Burma dominated by the Thakins, just eight years after these gentlemen have been taken to Japan for military training and have returned to Burma with the invading Japanese army.

Magnanimity cannot safely be extended to all those who showed themselves 'pro-allied', however, for they are now politically suspect. MacArthur's disapproval is deflected to the Hukbalahap movement – the People's Anti-Japanese Army whose 30,000 guerrillas, supplied with American arms by submarine and parachute, successfully sabotaged Japanese administration in many provinces of the Philippines, but also sovietized them as a sideline. In Bangkok Pridi Panomyong, Pibul's rival who led the anti-Japanese 'Free Thai' underground, is out in the cold and will end up as a permanent guest in Communist China. At this moment the lesson of the whole absurd paradox is: we can deal with our former enemies, and their possible role in the future deserves sympathetic perusal. But Heaven preserve us from our friends. Most of them may have to be taken as Red.

3

The Carbon Copies

As they marched past the general, the two tall Indian officers, their moustaches as stiffly horizontal as the swagger sticks tucked neatly under their rigid left arms, threw up a clock-work salute in perfect unison as if they were Grenadier Guardsmen crossing a barrack square. They were, in fact, crossing Rue Catinat on their way to the terrace of the Hotel Continental in Saigon and a lanky glass of *citron pressé soda*. 'Crumbs,' said a British correspondent rather nastily (he had served in the Royal Navy), 'Look what a marvellous bunch of carbon copies we've made of ourselves.'

It was 1955 and high summer, and he should have saved his breath to cool his beer, for he was talking about the new lords of Asia, the western-educated élite who had so naturally assumed the mantle of the outgoing white master. They were often few, but by 1963 they were running every ex-colony east of Persia, and the most important oriental languages for any Far Eastern correspondent to know were English, French and Dutch.

The chanceries of Indochina rang with their voluble if slightly glottal Parisian. The flamboyantly patriotic Sukarno signed his name in Dutch fashion 'Soekarno' to the end of his days. When he met Tengku Abdul Rahman of Malaysia, the two champions of Malay culture dropped quite naturally into English (which they both used again when they criticized each other fiercely in separate private conversations with President Macapagal of the Philippines, the third Malay power in the region). Mutually hostile ministers from opposite ends of the continent belong to the same exclusive club of those who took their law or leisure at Oxford and the Inns of Court, their economics at London.

The products of cultural cross-pollination are sometimes singular mutants whose voices and faces do not match. Introduced one day in Formosa to an elderly Chinese with an ivory skin and eyes like ebony splinters, I felt my hair rise on my scalp as the idiom of a dead tongue rolled from his mouth in the accents of Bertie Wooster. 'Howd'yedo, my dear fellah,' he said pleasantly enough. 'Nice runnin' into you. By Jove, isn't it simply rippin' weathah we're havin'?' Medium? Ventriloquist? Fiendishly possessed puppet? He actually said 'Well, pip-pip, cheerio,' when he left, and I learned that he had come down from Oxford nearly half a century before and had not been back to England since.

He was a well-adjusted old gentleman, however, versed in the history and art of his own country, and therefore equally at home in East or West – the East of 1968, and the West of 1923. But when a group of Russians visited the University of Singapore shortly afterwards, they at once created a crisis in communication by innocently addressing a Chinese member of the staff in fluent Chinese. For she belonged to the sad band of English-educated who cannot speak their own language and who, in terminal cases, not only know nothing of their own history, but would rather eat bangers and mash and raspberry jelly than a curry or Cantonese rice.

The French and Dutch failed miserably to train their subject-peoples for administration against the day when they must rule themselves, for they had no intention that such a day should come. The British have a brighter record, but they stand accused of educating nations of dusky clerks into whose minds has been crammed an indigestible porridge of alien fact and fiction like the dates of Wellington's victories and 'Oh to be in England now that April's there'.

In stove-like cities they talk of 'being snowed under' and 'walking on thin ice', and when the anti-colonialist People's Action Party came to power in Singapore in 1959, its official organ, the authentic voice of equatorial nationalists sweating happily for the first time over the problems of self-government, could only say 'The dark stormy nights of winter are passing away, the clean, keen scent of spring begins to fill the air' in a land that knows neither winter nor spring, and in which night falls like a cloak at about seven o'clock all the year round. I pick up a little book entitled *Malayan Songs for Malayan Children*, and find that the first page carries the words and music for 'D'ye ken John Peel', not one line of which could possibly mean anything to any child in the country.

Not all transplants are incongruous, however. The oriental judge in robes and wig may look ridiculously hot, but the equitable law which the British originally imposed on Singapore and Malacca soon had immigrants streaming into these settlements from Malay states where justice was often as uncertain as it was sudden. It was the British Residents who later introduced prisons in the interior, where formerly culprits were just shot, krissed or flogged to save house-room.

From common law to cricket, and from equitable government to driving on the left, the British – as did the other colonial powers in their territories – cut a new and exotic pattern into the original design of South-east Asian society. And their western-educated heirs, hesitant to indulge in too much freehand drawing at the outset, usually begin by following the grooves. In consequence, he who runs 8,000 miles from the freezing rigours of British taxation may read on his first Singapore assessment form familiar-looking crossword clues like 'An individual who is resident for the basis year for a year of assessment is ordinarily resident for that basis year unless he is not ordinarily resident for that basis year.'

Faced with a similar brain-teaser in Vietnamese financial regulations in 1955, I took the trouble to see the minister in Saigon and ask him what it meant. 'To tell you the truth,' he replied at length, avoiding my eye and grinning frantically at a hideous lacquer mural on the far wall, 'I don't really know myself. But it was in the original French document, it was well phrased, and so when we drew up our own laws we thought we had better include it in case it was important.' I slunk out, feeling like a man who had addressed the wrong Chinese in Chinese.

Paradoxically, it was the colonial powers themselves that schooled their Asian wards in the elements of nationalism, and so signed their own expulsion orders. At Oxford and Cambridge, Indians and Malays and Burmese were conscientiously instructed in those ideals of freedom inherent in a sceptred isle that 'never did, nor never shall, lie at the proud foot of a conqueror'. At the Sorbonne young Vietnamese and Cambodians (along with Chinese like Chou En-lai) were inspired by the French revolution but noted that 'Liberté, Egalité, Fraternité' stopped at the Suez Canal. At Leyden thoughtful Indonesians began to realize that there were lessons to be learned from the fine tale of the rise of the small but sturdy Dutch Republic among the bullying monarchies of sixteenth-century Europe. From a continent in which men hardly understood the concept of nation, the young flocked to the capitals of the West to hear for the first time of nationalism, revolution, and a man buried at Highgate called Karl Marx.

And while white men in Europe were teaching the western-educated Asians to throw them out of the East, more white men in the East were literally digging the grave of colonial domination. For archaeologists and scholars from the West drew from the forgotten recesses of Asian history the splendours of Angkor and the might of Srividjaja which were to fire the Khmer and the Malay with their intimations of glorious national heritage. Before they came with their spectacles and spades, Angkor was no more than a fleet of stone wrecks in a Sargasso sea of jungle, and nothing was known of Srividjaja but its name – in 1908 one Dutch scholar still believed it was an historical person, not a power, and no Indonesian contradicted him.

In Dutch Indonesia and French Indochina men newly armed with ancient pride and modern liberal ideas fought their colonial tutors to a standstill after the Second World War, and then negotiated their independence. Yet by virtue of their western education, they were often isolated from the millions.

In 1956 I moved house (two maltreated suitcases and a middle-aged typewriter) from Saigon to Singapore because, incredible as it now may seem, the story in South Vietnam had gone as flat and damp as one of its own paddyfields, while in swinging Singapore the current chant ran: 'See you later –

Agitator,' to which the with-it response was: 'When it's quieter – Rioter.' First deflected to cover right-wing secret society disturbances in Hongkong before covering left-wing anti-colonial disorders in Singapore, I found myself flying from one British colony compounded of barbed wire, broken glass and burning cars, to land punctually in another British colony of barbed wire, broken glass and burning cars. But by the time I could pick up the contacts warmly recommended to me by my predecessor, the Singapore Special Branch had flung nearly all of them into the same, historic Changi Gaol where the *Kempetai* had practised its plastic arts on an earlier generation of prisoners.

I nevertheless managed to meet one disconsolate anti-colonial mobster whom the police had ruthlessly left at liberty. 'They know that what I should like now would be a year or so in clink, and so they won't arrest me, confound them,' he ground out venomously, as if that, too, must be added to the long list of their towering crimes. I murmured a few words of polite condolence, for this was like failing an entrance examination or being dropped from the team. Few who did not qualify for a colonial gaol today could hope to qualify for a cabinet seat in the independent Asia of tomorrow. A man who was denied the accolade of arrest and was allowed to slink about the city in dishonourable freedom might even be suspected of being a police informer.

'You see, if I don't have a year's peace and quiet I shall never find time to learn Malay,' he went on. He had another point there. Chinese and Malay were taught in Changi five times a week, and his great handicap as an Asian nationalist was that he was English-educated, a suspect carbon copy of the colonial master, and he could not hope to enjoy real communion with the uneducated masses of this stirring subcontinent until he could speak to them as a fellow-Asian in the language of a fellow-Asian.

He was far from being an exception. Lee Kuan Yew, Singapore's youthful and astute Cambridge-educated Premier, who is only rarely anyone's fool, long ago threw himself into the task of learning fluent Mandarin and Malay in order to persuade the

Asian populace he was one of them. His problem was brutally simple. The Chinese-educated Chinese, soaked in tea and Mao and a 3,000-year-old tradition of contempt for foreigners, saw him as a beer-drinking, golf-playing barbarian despite his Chinese face.

Nationalism is not rationalism, and its devotees will practise its rites without counting the cost. The compulsive urge to have a national language where the country's nerve-systems have hitherto functioned in English, or French, or Dutch, has prompted the new masters of the East to embark eagerly upon the endless hazards and complications and disadvantages of enshrining Malay in Malaysia (where the Malays are in a minority), Hindi in India, and 'Pilipino' in the Philippines as the shibboleth of the patriot. This nevertheless involves adapting foreign words in order to update their somewhat basic vocabularies and the results are not always felicitous. 'Taliveshen', 'talipon', 'ofis', 'chek' and 'teksi' get by in Malay, but 'semen' is a little unfortunate for 'cement'. There has been much minting of words, of indiscriminately mixing Malay, English and Arabic into philological alloys, until some so-called Malay has become incomprehensible to Malays themselves. In Pilipino, we have 'telebisyon' and 'bespol', but apparently it was unpatriotic to borrow 'cher' for 'chair', and so the word 'salumpuwit' has been coined, a good, earthy phrase derived from the native Tagalog which Filipinos more addicted to English say means : 'something to stick your ass on'.

In the fifties the signboards began to change all over Asia. In Saigon and Phnom Penh the streets called after the tongue-twisting but musical names of the heroes of the French empire – Chasseloup-Laubat, Lagrande de la Liraye, Doudart de Lagrée – gave way to Vietnamese monosyllables set to three-four time like Phan Thanh Gian and the rolling gong-like Khmer notes of Norodom and Monivong. But for years this bedevilled circulation, for even the skinny, knot-calfed drivers of the ubiquitous *cyclopousses*, or pedal rickshaws, stuck treasonably to the old names and did not recognize the new.

The first elected mayor of Singapore, Ong Eng Guan, attempted to make sure that freedom would mean confusion by exuberantly planning to rename all streets that 'perpetuate the memory of ex-governors and colonial officials', and since the most sacred word at that moment was 'Merdeka' (Independence) which had already given the island Merdeka Bridge, there would also have to be Merdeka Circus, Merdeka Highway, Merdeka Way, Merdeka Quay, and others. Those with a smattering of vulgar French voiced their own terse comment on these proposals which in any case quite unsuitably aped the infuriating inability of the British to think of a name, so that in the same area of London there will be Belsize Park, Belsize Gardens, Belsize Lane, Belsize Crescent and so on *ad nauseam.* (He was fortunately restrained.)

Nationalism, like yawning, is highly infectious. The mood was established in Singapore in 1959 that would later prompt a mild, somewhat inexperienced party official to pronounce the best howler of the academic year. Told that a patient he saw during a tour of the General Hospital was to be given a local anaesthetic, he remarked approvingly: 'Excellent, let us rely on our own rather than on foreign resources wherever possible.'

But for many the phase passed. For as knife sharpens knife, nothing quickens mutual understanding better than a long, thoroughly abrasive relationship, and once the new nations of South-east Asia had joined the none-too-amiable club of sovereign states on an equal footing with all others, it was often a relief to their western-educated leaders to see the familiar faces of their former colonial *bêtes-blanches.* Their souls, however different, were at least clothed in the same ill-fitting cultural uniform that they had been unceremoniously thrust into at school, and they enjoyed a certain rough-and-ready understanding, even mutual regard. The horrors of their prefect-and-fag days were over, and they were both old boys of the same alma mater in an alien world.

Sutan Sjahrir, the Indonesian revolutionary leader, expressed the sweet-sour taste of the West on the tongues of Dutch-educated Indonesians when he recommended the 'forceful, dynamic and active life' of European civilization, despite its 'brutality and coarseness'. After two bloody 'police actions', the Round Table Conference at which the Hague grudgingly relinquished Indonesia to the Indonesians in 1949, and the ignominious expulsion of all Dutch from the Republic in 1957, the Hollander whom the Javanese had earlier found such heavy going was given the warmest welcome when western influence filtered back into Indonesia in the mid-sixties. Here was a foreign devil they knew, and he was trusted more than those they did not for everything familiar about him from his aspirates to his aspirins.

In Indochina, where the blue-blooded nationalist movements of royal princes had been inspired by dreams of independence and not the damnation of the French, leaders like Souvanna Phouma in Laos and Norodom Sihanouk in Cambodia sent their children to French schools once they were kings of their own castles, the French planters remained, and the French professors poured back into the lycées of Vientiane and Phnom Penh. When in November 1963 Sihanouk announced that he was kicking the Americans out of Cambodia, he told me that French experts in the fields of education, administration, justice, and even national defence could all stay. 'We are rejecting all American aid in future,' he said a little shrilly, but added in a confidential tone: 'However, if Washington wants to send us money through the French, as representatives of the West here ...' But the Americans did not avail themselves of this unique opportunity to give something for nothing.

No one has personified the post-colonial kiss-and-make-up more than Lee Kuan Yew of Singapore. This English-educated revolutionary was in close contact with members of the Communist-led Anti-British League in 1951, and went puce as if the venom were in his very veins when I first heard him inveigh against the iniquitous white man before a multi-coloured mob of trade unionists in 1956. But thirteen years later he was telling the entire Commonwealth that Britain was not unnaturally frustrated by 'the attitudes of European countries she helped save in the last war and the querulous colonies she nurtured to independence ... and in return received churlishness and sometimes abuse.'

My irrepressible Indian friend James Puthucheary, three long spells of political detention for left-wing activities behind him, watched his anti-colonialism fall out of fashion from behind the wire. He has since taken his own revenge on the treacheries of passing time by qualifying as an advocate and joining a prosperous partnership in Malaysia. 'For law,' he explained to me happily, 'is the last resort of the scoundrel.' Harry Lee Kuan Yew reversed the process by moving from law to politics, but he also has come to terms with his former white tutors and tormentors. Except that you do not call him 'Harry' these days. You must call him 'Kuan Yew'.

His equilibrium is nevertheless denied to men in whom the clash of cultures provokes that most harrowing of all questions: 'Just who am I, anyway?' And these are to be found in quantity in the Philippines.

4
God's Other Country

His name is Gonzalez. He wears a gold medallion of the Virgin Mary, a gift from cousins in Madrid whom he visited two years ago. But it is partly concealed by his *barong tagalog*, the embroidered cream shirt of pineapple fibre which is the Filipino national dress. From his beringed hand dangles a leading Manila newspaper. A headline is visible: 'Cops Air Meal Pay Gripe.' He ignores this mystery, however. 'Don't kid yourself,' he says in his Spanish-American English. 'All this trouble will blow over. The Philippines and Indonesia and Malaysia are gonna be friends. We Malays have to stick together.'

The Philippine Republic consists of forty million Asians sitting on 7,000 Asian islands whose pressing postwar problem has been to prove that they are Asians at all. It has not been easy. Four hundred years ago the Spaniards began colonizing the archipelago, and although they were obliged to chasten the Muslim South with the sword, they found that they could carry most of the rest with the Cross. But in 1898 the Americans took over, and a new army of missionaries preaching private enterprise, democracy, and the virtues of rye whisky swarmed over the land. From this confusion of Madrid and Manhattan, the Philippines emerged in 1946 as an independent republic, an ostensibly Asian nation of Malay stock which took its very name from a dead European monarch.

Nor is that all the Spaniards left behind them. During Holy Week the Catholic churches of Manila are crowded and penitents parade the streets, flagellating themselves with whips laced with ground glass and carelessly splattering the bystanders with blood. The language and the literature of the older generation are Spanish, so are most of the traditional dances, like the formal *rigodon de honor*, performed by ladies whose national dress belongs to eighteenth-century Castile.

It is upon a gracious if politely corrupt Iberian foundation that this most distant outpost of twentieth-century America has been erected. After 400 years in a convent and fifty in Hollywood, as some wag once observed, the Filipino raised on Spanish, English and his native Tagalog and surrounded by bananas is ever fearful that his country will be dismissed as a displaced South American republic out of an O. Henry short story. He is eager above all to be taken for a regular member of the all-Asian anti-colonial team, and although full of much misleading American sass, he is in fact seismographically sensitive about his equivocal identity and his national dignity.

In 1968 President Marcos was urged to cut short his visit to the United States when the Americans treated him 'like a vassal' by sending only a 'second-rate dignitary' to meet his plane. Marcos himself was drubbed by his opponents in Manila for describing President Johnson as the 'Liberator of Asia', for this added dimension to the grinning little image of the Philippines as a sycophantic satellite of the West populated by cut-price Americans.

Fury is aroused by the 'special relationship' between the two countries which enables American soldiers to shoot a Filipino or two from time to time and get away with it, thanks to their extra-territorial rights in the Republic. In 1965 thousands of torch-bearing demonstrators burned Uncle Sam in effigy outside the United States Embassy in Manila, after marching through the streets bearing thirty-two cardboard coffins symbolizing the alleged victims of an American's inalienable right to the pursuit of trigger-happiness. This hateful manifestation was provoked by the killing of a fourteen-year-old Filipino boy caught scavenging for scrap metal at Clark Air Base, nerve-centre of the United States 13th Air Force north of Manila, and the street was filled with placards reading 'Go Home Yankee Dogs,' 'Go Home White Monkeys.' In early 1969 the scene was repeated, with the placards saying 'Johnson is a murderer', after an American court-martial had acquitted a lance-corporal of killing a Filipino inside another US military establishment. The United States authorities have been known to pay compensation to a victim's family, but this has inspired the steely Manila headline: 'Shoot a Filipino for $787.'

From the very beginning of their relationship the Americans showed their new Asian friends that they were up against commendably sharp minds, for their first act was to relieve the Filipinos of the Philippines. During the Spanish–American War of 1898, anti-colonial revolutionaries under General Emilio Aguinaldo rose against their Spanish masters in the Philippines in secret agreement with the United States, on the understanding that they were fighting for Philippine independence. Once the war was won, however, it transpired that the Filipinos had been labouring under a slight misapprehension. The white man's burden was shifted straight from Spanish to American shoulders, and the United States proceeded to suppress a revolt by Aguinaldo, who had been sworn in rather forlornly as first president of a sovereign Philippine republic at his headquarters north-west of Manila.

Forty-eight years later the Americans did indeed grant the Filipinos their freedom, but, true to their own exotic tradition of equality, bound their two countries together with constitutional provisions and reciprocal agreements which gave Americans the same rights as Filipinos in the republic until 1974, allowed the United States to maintain military bases in the islands in exchange for defending them, and provided each country with a duty-free market in the other. The golden handshake had become an iron grip.

By May 1973 President Ferdinand Marcos was already talking about closing down the bases well before the scheduled deadline in 1991. However, if imitation is the sincerest form of flattery and not just the lowest form of humour, no one can doubt that beneath the stinging spindrift of anti-American agitation that blows fitfully over the surface of Philippine life lies an ocean of harmonious fellow-feeling. Manila in the sixties is still a city of cheeseburgers and backyard barbecues and hot-dog stands, of motels and curtained day clubs with soft lights and soothing singers for businessmen prone to fatigue at two in the afternoon, of memorial parks in Californian style where mortal man may buy his plot, erect his own engraved mausoleum, and have nothing left to do but die. Its money looks like the American dollar, and its newspapers use typefaces once dear to Times Square.

A reverence for the past is always touching. A sensitive Chinese delights to find in Japan ancient customs borrowed from his own country more than a thousand years ago but long since abandoned in China itself. An Englishman in New York is refreshed to be addressed in the archaic argot of the First World War by some native joker who fondly believes he is mimicking contemporary British slang and would get along splendidly with my venerable Chinese friend in Formosa, I mean to say, old chap, what? In Manila the happy American finds himself nostalgically reminded of his own great heritage of the twenties.

'Two Cops Slay Four at Fiesta,' scream the streamers, 'Co-ed Taps Frat Sweetheart.' History in headlines nevertheless tells us that in 1957 there was a municipal resistance to the soft-drink civilization, for we had 'City Dads Cool on Pop Plant Plan.' 'Check your firearms here,' reads a notice at the entrance to Congress, and I duly check with a gentle, corpulent official wearing yellow shoes, an olive shirt, and a small straw hat with a tartan ribbon. 'Deposit your lethal weapons,' says another at the municipal waterworks with its charming children's playground. For the republic is a colourful garden of variegated violence with an average annual yield of from 10 to 15,000 murders.

The administration is only faintly sketched in over much of the archipelago and is hampered by a carefully cultivated contempt for the law common to the city gunman and the flick-knife boy in the shanty-towns of Manila, the Christian and Muslim in the deep south who settle ideological differences in blood, and scantily-clad Igorot tribesmen who develop an urge to collect human heads each year when the flame-of-the-forest blooms again. That does not take into account rival police in neighbouring suburbs, who have been known to shoot it out between them while the hoodlums looked on at this somewhat unusual form of gang war. There are about 320,000 licensed firearms in the country, and perhaps half a million more with which it is not authorized to kill at all. In 1968 a report before Congress disclosed that syndicates would commit a modestly-priced murder to order for as little as £100, and I have even heard £10 mentioned as a reserve.

By August 1973 a blitzkreig on crime and violence launched by President Marcos will have yielded a haul of 523,000 guns, but meanwhile a bulge in the waistband feels natural to many Filipinos who believe that it is up to the citizen to heel himself. At a small but well-thought-out diplomatic dinner in 1963 a bespectacled Filipino academic leaned over a centrepiece of cut-glass palm-trees and inquired diffidently whether I had heard of the *Balisong*, or Batangas butterfly-knife. This, it turned out, was not some sort of lepidopterist's scalpel but a beautiful and ingenious weapon which he pulled from his pocket and forthwith demonstrated to the entire table. No blade was visible, but the silver-studded blackwood handle was split down the middle into two legs, joined by a hinge. Holding one leg, the professor deftly jerked his wrist so that the other swung around fan-wise and back into his hand, leaving exposed five inches of serviceable-looking steel which had emerged in a symbolically phallic fashion from between them. 'Have you a knife with you?' he asked, and when I said no, generously pressed it upon me. 'You may need it,' he urged, 'And I have plenty of others anyway.' He was a professor of English, and a man of unquestioned propriety, soberly dressed but for this one ornament. He was also a small man probably weighing no more than the 110-pound farmer named Benito Fidel who killed four bandits and wounded two more with a ·22 rifle when they tried to steal his only six head of cattle in 1969. Fidel had the same instinct for do-it-yourself protection as the Manila politicians, among whom armed bodyguards – preferably ex-thugs themselves – have become status symbols.

The underpaid and under-educated police have been accused publicly of incompetence, brutality and widespread corruption, and in 1969 more than 1,000 officers and men of the Manila Police Department are at their posts but under investigation for conduct unbecoming to the fuzz, ranging from graft to murder. It is characteristic of oriental thought that opposites are seen to complement each other: there can be no light without dark, no good without evil. Perhaps in accordance with this principle many of the Manila police look upon protection racketeers and smuggling syndicates as natural partners whose elimination would automatically mean their own elimination too, and who must therefore be cherished.

Around the scimitar-like curve of the Manila Bay strip on Roxas Boulevard the supper-clubs rival each other in legitimate luxury, but are flanked by plush little gambling casinos with entrances like double airlocks in an H-bomb shelter. I tap on an outside door and a small panel opens to reveal a pair of half-closed eyes to which I say softly and forgivingly, 'Jesus sent me.' The door opens to let me in, but behind it is a black curtain, and when I have fought my way through that I am in a cubicle about the size of an up-ended cabin trunk facing a very fat man indeed in a *barong tagalog* with much fancy weaving on it, while a small candle-faced accomplice leans against what is left of the space. The fat man frisks me, and I am passed through a sliding door – only to find myself in a second cabin trunk with another fat man who also frisks me. I am then allowed into the club to lose a little money.

A shocked Congress, hearing that one of their number had actually been detained by the National Bureau of Investigation when caught frequenting an illegal gambling house like this, reacted vigorously in 1963 by cutting off the NBI's entire budget allocation. But not far from here the son of the Speaker, José 'Banjo' Laurel, was arraigned in 1969 for allegedly slapping and then shooting a policeman in the chic Bayside night club, while his bodyguards followed up with a fusillade that wounded two others. The Speaker himself had been winged by a bullet in a near-by steak-house two years before.

Sometimes one is tempted to ask what this vast archipelago of thin men and private eyes would have done without the culture and the drama delineated for its inhabitants by Dashiell Hammett and Raymond Chandler, but there is, of course, far more to the Filipino–American love–loathe than that. Manila man in the eyes of an Indian is similar to Madison man in the eyes of an Englishman: they both believe in Dale Carnegie and Democracy *à la mode*, they push the same ballyhoo with the same disarming spirit of dedication, and they also live in the same half-world of man-to-man, dog-eat-dog relationships that the deferential Asian or European, imprisoned by his own caste system, would give much to copy. The Spanish-American mastermix may have given the Philippines flagellating exhibitionists and air-conditioned cells for Dominican monks, but it has also created the charming illusion that human equals human.

I remember my first humiliating and vain attempts to see Vice-President Emmanuel Pelaez in Manila by applying ingratiatingly through the correct official channels, to be rightly regarded with contempt by all the bureaucratic flunkeys in my path. One day I told a Filipino colleague of my problem: Pelaez was giving me the anti-British brush-off. He at once made a telephone call which established that at that very moment the Vice-President was on his way to a private room in a smart downtown restaurant, where he was throwing lunch for most of the senior members of the diplomatic corps. 'Okay,' said Benedicto David. 'We go too.'

Frilly with my old-world servility, I protested that we could not barge in on a formal vice-presidential lunch, but David simply jeered, and before I knew where we were, we were thrusting our way through a phalanx of lackeys and two swing doors into an air-conditioned anteroom full of dignified middle-aged gentlemen conversing politely in subdued tones and conservatively-cut suits. Without hesitation, David dragged me towards a tall, greying figure who was gazing at him rather blankly from the very middle of this concourse, like Nelson in Trafalgar Square. When we arrived before him, however, David said: 'Hi, Mani, I want you to meet Dennis Bloodworth of the London *Observer*.' The Vice-President said, 'Hi there, let's go sit over in the corner away from the mob,' and we were in.

This is free-and-easy catch-as-catch-can democracy, as Manila will know it until 1972. No punch lines are pulled in or out of Congress, and Asia's shrillest, most uninhibited press will call the Head of State a 'liar' or 'a coward and a poltroon'. On weekly 'Common Man's Day' I have watched shabby old peasant women, youngsters in aggressive Hawaii shirts, and personable girls in well-starched cotton frocks as they shuffled forward patiently across the gaudy gardens and the cool, tiled floor of the Malacanang Palace to speak, one by one, with the President. The President sat behind a plain wooden desk, and while some just shook his hand, others would launch into a long winding tale of bureaucratic injustice in their *barrio*. Often the President scribbled a note and handed it to an aide, and a Filipino who had thought himself pitted hopelessly against the inert mass of an uncaring administration would suddenly find that all the corners had been cut and his problem was solved. 'He is an honest man,' said one of his admirers. 'He is atoning for the sins of corrupt governments of the past.' 'Yeah,' cut in a detractor neatly, 'He always did think he was Jesus Christ.'

Diosdado Macapagal, who was then President, had just aroused a little ire in some quarters by accusing an opposition candidate of accepting a million dollars from Communist countries, notably China, to finance his election campaign. No one seemed to think it odd of him to make such a preposterous charge, for in the Philippines money makyth man and anything is just possible. At one end of the scale a Congressional Bill to nationalize the rice industry is held up for twenty-four hours so that desperate private dealers who stand to lose fortunes can be squeezed stone dry when they make their last-minute cash bids to have it thrown out; at the other, Filipino firemen let shops and houses burn while, hoses idle, they haggle with distraught Chinese owners over the prevailing price of water. Why should not Macapagal suggest that a rival had been paid by the Communists? An admirer and well-wisher of his own had ruthlessly eliminated another candidate by hitting him in the hip-pocket with half a million dollars.

A Philippine election campaign has been known to cost four times as much as its American prototype for each ballot deposited. Fat bank-rolls are reserved for the hearts and minds

of those party delegates who astutely hesitate in their choice
of presidential candidate, and rivals who conveniently withdraw their nominations are generously compensated. Voters
are won over by putting them on the payroll, or by feeding
them 'peso sandwiches' at campaign parties consisting of two
thin slices with a banknote in the middle (for, as is well known,
man cannot live by bread alone).

These one-dollar-one-vote elections are a free-for-all fought
with bullets as well as ballots, however. During polling in 1965
troops and constabulary moved into the most inflamed parts
of the country to stop the slaughter on the ground. In the
worst single incident, seven died in a gun-battle when heavily-
armed 'fortresses' were set up only 200 yards apart by hangers-
on of two political rivals in the centre of one town. The rivals
were both Congressmen of the Liberal Party. The opposition
Nacionalistas were merely interested, discreetly approving on-
lookers. During partial elections two years later, nearly 100 un-
fortunates were shot, stabbed or killed with coshes, and in the
presidential elections of 1969 more than eighty died violently.

The temptation to look upon democracy in the Philippines
during this period as a tragi-comic circus inspired by Li'l Abner
is not blunted by the behaviour of Congressmen like the one
who submitted to the Speaker's office a Bill for outlawing
typhoons. But it is noted that the military coups d'état that
shake most of the capitals of the Far East like recurrent earth-
quakes are unknown in this republic, that the peasant in the
barrio is the most politically-aware villager in South-east Asia,
that the parliamentary structure is firmly based on two main
parties, and that – an almost unique phenomenon in the region
– power actually does change hands constitutionally whenever
the ballot dictates. Filipinos enjoy the most exhilarating,
irreverent experiment in freedom in South-east Asia, Manila
may seem to combine Tammany Hall with prohibition Chicago,
but then so did the United States only a few years ago. The
Filipino belief in the almost limitless authority of elective
bodies is succinctly expressed in a Manila headline that appears
the day after an important announcement from the Vatican –
'Sainthood okayed for five.'

Democracy is an American graft on an Asian trunk, how-ever, and it does not mean in Mindanao what it means in Massachusetts. The oriental Filipino often sees political power simply as a means to advance family interests, and to stop short of cheating may be selfishly to deprive one's dependants for the sake of one's own lily-white soul. The men already on top are expected to be grasping, but there may still be a good reason for not voting for the others, since 'the mosquitoes inside your net have sucked your blood, but think how much hungrier those outside would be'.

At the beginning of the nineteen-seventies corruption, con-flicting business interests and pressure groups, political jealousies and a dilatory Congress were still providing enough cottonwool to turn any reforming presidential punch into pat-a-cake. The conditions for revolution were present, and it seemed that, given enough licence, democracy might well talk itself into its own grave.

Perhaps it has. In 1971 mounting unrest and mob violence culminated in a series of bomb outrages in Manila itself, in-cluding an attempt to massacre the opposition Liberal Party chiefs in which ten people lost their lives and some ninety others were wounded. President Marcos suspended habeas corpus, and in September 1972 imposed martial law for the first time in the history of the Republic, claiming that the country was threatened by an armed uprising.

Senators and congressmen were among those immediately detained, and Marcos declared war on Communism, crime and graft. Swinging Manila wilted, the murder-rate fell by three-quarters, 145 'private armies' were disbanded, and the civil service was roughly combed for corruption. To an almost un-believable degree the wayward Filipinos were brought sharply to order.

But a 317-man Philippine convention called in 1971 had broken all precedent by turning its back on American example and opting to convert the Republic to the parliamentary sys-tem of government. By virtue of two referenda held in 1973, Marcos was able to proclaim a new constitution which made him both president and prime minister, to abolish Congress, and to declare a 'political moratorium' for the next seven years. The election schedule was shelved, and the Philippines remained firmly under martial law. The President then set out to create a just 'new society', one of whose central pillars was to be the rural reform that the millions so sorely needed but the millionaires had so successfully blocked in the past. Some 600,000 sharecroppers were given parcels of land to be paid for out of the harvests of the following fifteen years.

If even the Filipinos could not keep faith with democracy, however, what was to be expected of their neighbours?

5

The Mask of Democracy

THE dignified gentleman in the blue mohair suit, the restrained club tie and the well-polished black shoes threaded his way towards me through the mob in the air-conditioned Sarawak bar and we shook hands. He ordered lager, and as he raised his glass to drink, the tattoo marks on his finger-joints told me he was that uncommon type of collector, the successful head-hunter, for each blue knuckle in North Borneo is equivalent to a notch on a gun in Nebraska.

A paramount chief of Sea Dyaks or Ibans, a native people of Sarawak whose otherwise unexceptionable manners have been marred by the pursuit of this regrettable hobby, he had been presented to Prince Philip in Kuching earlier that evening. On the morrow I was to watch one of his colleagues, lightly clad in a straw hat, a khaki jacket and an intricately tattooed bare backside, deliver a Loyal Address before the colony's distinguished visitor in the Legislative Council. It was 1959, and the spread-eagled territories of North Borneo, acquired by Britain in grosser days with the irritating ease of a millionaire making yet more money, were still colonial dependencies. Despite the march of time, it hardly seemed likely that these amiable but illiterate gentlemen with their Beatle cuts and illuminated bottoms would one day sit in the federal parliament of an independent Malaysia. But within five years one of them would in fact be a Minister.

This future lay dark before us, however, and the Duke and I (among others) were able to see tomorrow's electorate without any qualms about the one-man-one-vote system. For from the moment when the first chanting Dyak maiden, dressed in nothing but an elaborate silver tiara and a long flashing fish-scale skirt of overlapping silver medallions, ceremoniously offered Prince Philip a rice beer in a thick-rimmed kitchen tumbler, the people stole the show.

Behind the frill of steaming swamp tacked along the North Borneo coast lies a lunatic interior, an almost impenetrable confusion of rain forest and mountains striated by twisting, rock-strewn rivers on which the hard-drinking Dyaks, Dusuns and Muruts build their longhouses on stilts, hunt, fish and cultivate small patches of rice and manioc. And as the Duke pilots his Heron aircraft from strip to dusty strip across this archaic wilderness, followed by twenty cursing correspondents rammed into two flying biscuit tins, the kaleidoscope spins with gathering momentum.

At Sibu the Iban chieftains line up for his touchdown – gaudy ornithological freaks clad in monkey skins and beads and bangles and stuck all over with feathers, whose bare-breasted womenfolk jingle like caparisoned ponies every time they shift their feet. At Miri the Dyak dancers squirm and yelp endlessly into the night, monstrous black-and-white horn-bill plumes streaming from their hair. In Jesselton the Duke watches Bajau pirates assault the coast, leaping from their prahus with drawn cutlasses, and Dusuns shooting stuffed monkeys out of trees with long blowpipes and poisoned darts. He is asked to celebrate by drinking home-made palm-toddy out of a grimy earthenware jar with all his new cronies, and for the first time he appears to lose a little of his aplomb (he does not know that etiquette allows a guest to appoint some only-too-willing 'Mouth' to do the drinking for him).

The Queen's husband is of widespread interest, especially among the Muruts. The chiefs of this diminishing up-river people, alarmed by their falling birth-rate, discuss a romantic proposal based on their traditions of open and polygamous hos-pitality whose adoption would serve the double purpose of doing honour to the royal visitor and of multiplying their number considerably. The suggestion is put to the women of this tribe and meets with a more than favourable response. But, alas, their paramount chief is dissuaded by some officious British bureaucrat from broaching the subject to the Duke him-self. The Muruts continue to decline.

Many of the natives, brought to the coast to be shown to the Duke, are seeing a water-tap, a bicycle, an electric light bulb, sarsaparilla and the sea for the first time. But the moment is to come disconcertingly quickly when these territories will be faced with the strange business of electing forty representatives to the Malaysian Lower House in Kuala Lumpur. Like most of South-east Asia, they are hardly ready for the experience.

The knowledge of tribesmen in Borneo and Central Vietnam alike is often limited by the distance they can paddle or walk in one day. There are Laotian villages in which even the headman cannot quite remember the name of the Prime Minister, and where the ordinary voter may not know the name of his own country, or where it is, or that other countries exist at all. In Thailand the peasants recognize their king, but may look blank if you mention any 'strong man' who has been bedevilling Thai politics for the last quarter of a century. In Vietnam in 1967 there were isolated villagers who were still unaware that President Ngo Dinh Diem had been butchered four years before, and who knew nothing of their latest rulers. In small, smart-aleck Singapore Ping once asked two women construction workers, in their red head-dresses and faded blue denims, what they thought of Premier Lee Kuan Yew. They gazed at us thoughtfully for a moment, faces of cigar-box wood tilted slightly upward. Then one lifted a hand like an old meat board and asked carefully: 'Do you mean the short fat one or the tall thin one?'

In earlier Singapore elections canvassers were known to have told the illiterate that all they had to do was to put a cross against the second name on the list when they entered the polling booth. This would be their own candidate, and the ruse worked – except when the voter unintentionally double-crossed them by holding the ballot paper upside down. When voting is not compulsory, up to 70 per cent of the electorate may not bother to go to the polls, and democracy becomes the business of sharp professional power-seekers and pressure groups – if it is allowed to survive at all. 'We can't afford it,' a Vietnamese whiz-kid once told me, glaring gloomily at the gun-flashes across the Saigon river over his dry martini. 'It is not just the Vietcong. The peasants are too ignorant, too easily misled.' What he meant was that they were amateurs who should be kept out of the club. The 1967 elections in South Vietnam, hailed as a triumph of the people's will, were in reality a modest mechanical success. Many only voted because they were told to, and then for the man their village heads or religious mentors indicated.

There have been other causes for the demise of democracy in South-east Asia during the postwar years. High on the list must stand man's genius for disagreeing with man, and the popular conviction among politicians that two parties are better than one because then there will be twice as many jobs for the boys. The modest Vietnamese have never had more than fifty parties at a time, and the Thais twenty-five, but in the 1955 general elections in Indonesia 169 political groups formed up to fight for 257 seats, which were eventually shared among twenty-seven of them. Nor have Asia's parliamentary representatives always preserved the dignified mien popularly associated with both Westminster and the Wisdom of the East. In 1966 an elected legislator in South Korea lowered the tone of debate by indecorously flinging a badly-secured parcel of human ordure at the Government benches, while in Malaysia a State Assemblyman brandished a naked *kris* and challenged a colleague to a duel on the floor of the House. At the turn of 1970 a woman deputy in Saigon tried to shoot a tiresome colleague in mid-session.

In 1958 Marshal Sarit Thanarat of Thailand, saddened by the rising price of parliamentarians and the high cost of legislating, suspended the experiment in democracy for ten years by dismissing the National Assembly in Bangkok and ruling through a 'Revolutionary Party' of military officers. Few voters were really outraged. Most of the candidates who had won seats in the previous general election were not so much the people's choice as creditors to whom peasants and shopkeepers owed money. When it looked as if their days were numbered, they hastened their own end by becoming more and more expensive to buy, urged on by the need to make quick profits before they lost their jobs.

In the late nineteen-sixties Sarit's successor, Marshal Thanom Kittikachorn, permitted parliament to open for business again, but when in 1971 the opposition parties had the temerity to forge a united front against the government Thanom abolished the National Assembly, suspended the constitution, and began ruling through a 'Revolutionary Council' wrought from the top brass. This is presumably what social anthropologists mean by a 'behaviour pattern', but a year later Thanom embellished on his predecessor's performance by swearing in a new Assembly of 299 members – every one of whom had been nominated. The stage was then set for the massive student demonstrations of October 1973, which ended when Thanom fled and the new government promised a new constitution within six months.

If the Americans are sometimes blamed for moulding their client states into monstrous mutants of modern democracy, it must be admitted that they have often had poor clay on which to work. The old Vietnamese political parties consisted mainly of sharp little revolutionary splinters engaged in conspiratorial intrigues and an occasional act of slaughter. The intellectual opposition that courageously challenged the oligarchy of President Ngo Dinh Diem and his family in 1960 with the 'Liberty and Progress Bloc' proved to be a different sort of anachronism, however.

Having missed its press conferences in the air-conditioned opulence of the Caravelle Hotel in Saigon, I visited the home of one of its leaders to find myself amid a curio-shop clutter of gorgeous, horribly valuable antiques, listening to a smooth denunciation in well-polished French of the iniquities of the President's land reform programme. These iniquities, it rapidly emerged through the slightly perfumed cigarette smoke and the tinkle of liqueur glasses, had been committed not against the peasant but against South Vietnam's powerful and wealthy landlords, of which he was one. Restore them their land, and the peasant would once again be happy under their benevolent patronage, I was told. As a programme, it seemed a trifle to the right of Magna Carta.

One successful Asian politician with emotions as ungovernable as his thirst attacks his critics with his fists or furniture, has been known to beat up his wife (with the help of his mother), shows all the symptoms of a megalomaniac ('practically certifiable' as one of his friendlier colleagues told me), and only ended up in politics because he was sacked from a minor post in the judiciary for brutally abusing his powers. ('And how lucky I did,' he told us smugly when he became a minister.)

I have seen the Montecittorio in Rome and the Assemblée Nationale in Paris turned into close-packed battlefields as ageing deputies launched themselves at each other, kicking, punching, tearing viciously at each other's throats, and ripping up woodwork for weapons when a whole company of police charged in to quell the riot. Nor are corruption, graft, sex scandals, drug dramas and ballot-fixing entirely unknown among the voting systems of the West. But while Europe acquired democracy, Asia had democracy thrust upon it, and many of Asia's masters look upon a parliament much as their forebears looked upon a well-turned-out elephant: it should be thoroughly domesticated and docile, and there must be no doubt as to who rides whom. It may then be an ornament to the state and a symbol of national integrity and prestige, conveying unquestioned authority. But if it goes wild, it should at once be curbed, and if necessary liquidated.

Having taken brutal, furtive punishment in the back alleys of the subcontinent, democracy is still somewhat unfairly in the dock as a delinquent suspected of breaking the peace in the first place, its egalitarian ethics under gloomy scrutiny. Its most implacable enemy has not been the substance of Communism, but its shadow. By 1959 military leaders had seized power from ineffectual or corrupt politicians in Pakistan, Thailand and Burma, Indonesia was well on the way to becoming a dictatorship, and in Laos a conservative prime minister had armed himself with special prerogatives which reduced parliament to a cipher. General elections due to be held in three different countries of South-east Asia in that year were postponed. And all those responsible had the same ready-made excuse: the threat of red revolution.

Communism wages a far more subtle and effective ideological struggle in the counsels and consciences of its most bitter adversaries than it does in any tangle of jungle or secret city cell. The Communists are dedicated to the overthrow of government by fair means or foul. A young Asian state that tries to fight them with constitutional liberty, therefore, is like an inexpert adolescent who tackles an armed thug according to Queensberry rules, many Asian politicians say, and he should be rescued from his own scruples. Which is worse, they ask, to betray democracy by allowing freedom to those who will destroy freedom, or to betray it by restricting their rights as citizens? The argument provides would-be dictators with respectable reasons for having all their political adversaries eliminated as dangerous subversives, and persuades even honest but prudent Asian leaders to whittle down democracy in its own defence. The Communists do not have to discredit their enemy: the anti-Communists do it for them.

In South Korea a National Security Act sweepingly outlaws any action or speech which 'might lead to results advantageous to Communists', and in 1968 the comfortless gaols of Thailand still accommodated those who had been thrown into prison without trial ten years before on the simple charge of 'hooliganism', as martial law allowed. Moreover, the Thai Constitution that restored democracy to the kingdom for two years in 1969 was also well perforated with funk-holes. It guaranteed the rights of the citizen (except where they affected national security), and it guaranteed freedom of speech (except where the Government ruled that it might be harmful to the national interest).

In an Indonesia still queasy with Communist unrest President Suharto, having armed himself with special prerogatives, repeatedly postponed long-promised elections. The People's Action Party in Singapore and the Malaysian Alliance in Kuala Lumpur have preserved the special security ordinances introduced by their former British colonial masters: in Malaysia hundreds of political suspects are held under lock and key without trial, in Singapore more than fifty leftists still languish in detention. It is not always easy to say whether all these manoeuvres are designed to save democracy, the state, or just the ruling party in each case, but the psychological effect is much the same.

To the western democrat, however, the reaction of many Asians of the older generation might seem as startling as his own inverted image in a concave mirror. For these do not cry out at the bruised visage of democracy; they see it, rather, as a specious papier-mâché mask of deceit which in recent years has often been clamped over the homely, familiar visage of oriental autocracy. 'It is not so much the dictatorship that infuriates me,' one Vietnamese told me of Diem before his death, 'but the hypocritical imitation of democracy we have to conceal it with in order to please the United States.'

For when the free West first peddled a vote for every man as the panacea for past ills, the colonized East had been suffering not from despotism at home so much as domination from abroad. It was not dying for democracy, but living for the day when it would be its own boss. The Americans may have attracted numerous rice-democrats who came to pray so that they could stay to scoff, but the mainspring of Asian ambition was something the East had already learned from the West — nationalism. And this could be 'pro-Communist' or 'anti-Communist', according to taste.

6

Danger: Mao at Work

'WE settled into our ambush positions in the jungle,' the major told me, wiping the beer from his bristle, 'automatic weapons trained on the path, and waited for the Communists to come. Suddenly we heard quick, light steps up the track and' – he paused, banging his pewter tankard down on to his knee with restrained violence – 'Hang it if fifteen chaps in vests and running shorts from the local harriers club didn't come trotting past as if they were on Hampstead Heath.'

I nodded sympathetically, for I too had suffered from the frustrations of this dying war, in which the eager and the bloodthirsty were frequently made to look foolish when dramatic danger zones became disconcertingly peaceable stretches of real estate almost overnight. The Malayan Emergency, declared after Communist killers had tied up three white planters in Perak and then shot them down in cold blood in 1948, was now nine years old and fading before our eyes. With guerrilla forces systematically pared down to fewer than 1,000 men, Chin Peng, Secretary-General of the Malayan Communist Party, was soon to creep out of Malaya and cross the border into the sanctuary of the jungles of Thailand. By 1960 it would officially all be over.

This was the end of another act in the tragi-comedy, whose ironies had so far been well sustained. For just as western ideas and western historians had inspired the Asian nationalist to demand independence, so western military organization and western weapons generously helped the Asian Communist to try seizing it through armed revolution.

Like a man plunging further into debt, the defeated white man armed the Asian and organized him to continue the guerrilla struggle against the Japanese all over the subcontinent after his own conventional defences had crumbled in 1942. In Malaya the Japanese had to cope with the disrupting sabotage carried out by a *maquis* of 7,000 men armed and supplied by the South-east Asia Command in Ceylon. Most of them were Chinese immigrants of whom one British guerrilla officer wrote: 'The rank and file were absolutely magnificent. I can hardly find words to express my admiration for their courage, fortitude and consistent cheerfulness in adversity.' They were members of the Malayan Peoples' Anti-Japanese Army, and when a British party from India, secretly landed by submarine, contacted them in 1943 in order to reach a working agreement against the common enemy, the most cooperative leader they dealt with was this same Chin Peng. For the MPAJA was the military arm of the Malayan Communist Party.

The British airdropped weapons and supplies to these willing fighters, a high percentage of which, however, they were later blandly told had been 'lost'. The MPAJA regiments, preparing for the war that was to follow the war, had carefully buried them for future use against their friends the donors. In Burma the British also armed the Thakins, in Thailand the Americans armed the 'Free Thais' of Pridi Panomyong, in the Philippines they armed the Hukbalahaps, and from Kunming in south-west China, which was still in Chiang Kai-shek's friendly hands, the American Office of Strategic Services supported a growing guerrilla movement in Tonking organized by the League for the Independence of Vietnam, the 'Vietminh'. The leader of this group was a Comintern agent who hid himself behind the name of Ho Chi Minh.

For three years after the war the Communists adopted a smiling and seductive mien in order to form 'united fronts' with non-Communist political organizations which they could 'capture' from within and so worm their way into power constitutionally. But in 1948 the Cominform once more identified the West as the enemy in plain terms and damned the new nationalist governments of Asia as imperialist puppets. Dropping their best Party manners, the Communists turned to violence – and the Allied weapons they had kept for this very day. Within months Sukarno faced an uprising at Madiun in

Java, the terrorists had struck down their first victims in Malaya, and the Burmese Communists were in armed revolt against the new and shaky nationalist administration in Rangoon.

In Malaya the agony was sharpest, and it lasted twelve long years, for Malaya was a British dependency for nine of them, and the struggle was therefore 'anti-colonial'. Two thirds of this country as big as England lay under a rough coat of jungle in which a man might not see more than a few yards ahead of him, and in which it could take him a whole day to hack his way through a mile or two of undergrowth with a *parang*. That jungle was the haven of ten 'regiments' of Communist guerrillas, nearly all of them Chinese, who had moved into hidden forest encampments, some capable of sheltering 500 men. Often living on cassava or wild tapioca, which can be the source of sudden death rather than the staff of life if it is not carefully washed and heated to cleanse it of prussic acid, Communists with campfire in their bellies blew up trains and ambushed vehicles, launched large-scale assaults against rubber estates, or murdered miners, planters, government officials and 'uncooperative' civilians at will. Armed with machine-guns, grenades, and carbines, they could shoot it out with army patrols and military convoys, and burn down police posts.

Paramilitary police and twenty-three battalions of regular troops were deployed on the 'inside', pushed into the heart of Malaya's green hell in small 'jungle-bashing' hunting parties that hit the guerrillas on their own ground. It was coldly calculated that the average British tommy, Malay private, Gurkha, or Fiji Islander would spend 1,200 hours soaked through, bitten mercilessly by leeches, and forbidden to smoke or talk above a whisper before he would get his first shot at a terrorist.

As the maddening hide-and-seek war went on year after year, however, the noose made up of some 360,000 men in all slowly tightened. The guerrillas were isolated from their supply lines, sector by sector, permitted to starve and then trapped as they emerged for food. Police services wove an intricate web of intelligence until they held a dossier on every man and woman on the other side. RAF, Royal Navy, Special Constabulary and Home Guards all played their conventional roles. And then to the long bow and the broadside, which had in other centuries given the British mastery on land and sea in the course of their regrettably lurid island story, was now added another unconventional weapon : independence.

It is the white-hot August of 1957. Architecturally, Kuala Lumpur is a fine example of late Victorian Haroun-al-Raschid, a city rich in bogus domes, in minarets and Caliphate colonnades. Even the railway station looks like a palace in old Baghdad (from the outside), and all would be well if some joker had not put down in the very centre of the town a great rambling country club in glorious technitudor. However, on this auspicious day the focus of attention is the new stadium, which stands aside and aloof from that confused riot of arabesques and old oak beams as it gathers into its great dish the colourful crowds and the actinic rays of Malaya's relentless sun.

The ceremony follows its inevitable course. The brass bands play, the usual soldier faints. Then, one by one, each under a great yellow silk umbrella carried by a gaudy flunkey, the sultans of Malaya are escorted across a red carpet to their special dais in the arena, corpulent gentlemen bobbing along in their gorgeous regalia, chatting in a dignified way on this solemn occasion, doubtless about horse-racing and H.R.H. And when all are in their place the Duke of Gloucester (for it is he) makes a graceful little speech in that high, agonized voice common to so many of the House of Windsor, and surrenders the documentary 'instruments' which confer full sovereignty on to the Federation of Malaya as from midnight. The huge concrete bowl vibrates with the cry 'Merdeka!' as if it would crack. I withdraw to the lobby for lime juice, and run into Hamid.

Hamid is a professional Malay 'student' in his mid-thirties whose normal uniform is a frayed white shirt, an elderly sarong and two bare feet, and whose normal cronies are two baby-faced Chinese Communist militants and a fierce little Indian Marxist tiresomely long in the tongue. I only see him intermittently, for he has a fondness for travelling, his journeys sometimes taking him as far afield as Peking and Moscow. Today, however, his face is split by a melon-slice of a grin, and he is resplendent in a glossy black *songkok* (the short soft Malay fez), a faultless pearl-buttoned silk blouse, and a magnificent brocade sarong in blue and silver. We exchange only a few words, but I somehow sense that for him the fight is over. More than violence or votes, most Malayans had simply wanted their independence. And now they had it.

Terrorism smouldered on like a dwindling fire for three more years, but there were too few to stoke it any more. The Malayans quietly assumed the administration of their country as their own native Paramount Ruler moved into his new palace, a fortress-like mansion which had originally been built for a Chinese millionaire and his thirteen wives. The British expatriates were thinned out of the ranks of the civil service like white hairs, but no conspicuous bald patches appeared.

Communist leaders had meanwhile realized that the struggle for world supremacy had become an exercise in isometrics: neither side could win with brute force in any form, from banditry to the Bomb. However, the western powers could be discredited. Already tarnished by their acquisitive colonialist record, they were now the authors of a series of bellicose acronyms – NATO, CENTO, SEATO – which betrayed their chronic aggressions. It was therefore decided that in contrast to these compulsive gangsters the Communists must emerge as respectable, peace-loving champions of national sovereignty and neutralism. An already suspicious Asia could then be enticed away from the West with a little soothing sympathy (and mugged later). While the Communist states befriended the new nations of South-east Asia, the local Communist movements must once more enter into broad alliances with the local nationalists.

But the Chinese soon abandoned this ploy, and by 1960 quarrelling ideologues in Moscow and Peking were no longer troubling to keep their voices down. Peking condemned all peaceful coexistence advocated by the Russians and upheld the hallowed principle of permanent world revolution. For the young new nations of South-east Asia had formerly been tributaries of the Celestial Empire, and just as Imperial China had brought the word of Confucius to those in outer darkness in this region, so Communist China must now imbue them with the Thought of Mao.

The Chinese would not invade the subcontinent themselves, however, for Mao preached local armed insurrection from within, and this was the gospel that would once more bring the former 'vassal states' under the cultural suzerainty of Peking. Since the Chairman's guerrilla precepts were founded on the conviction that native peoples win 'wars of liberation' when the foreigners and mercenaries are all on the other side, China would not risk an international conflict by pouring her own troops into South-east Asia to fight their battles for them. Communist terrorism had nonetheless won a new lease of death, and what followed was predictable.

On 5 August 1966 Inspector Solomon Samy wrote with brutal irony to his bride-to-be : 'This is probably my last letter to you addressed as Miss Mary Ann Peh.' He was right – not because his marriage took place as planned on the 27th, but because Miss Peh was to read the letter while sitting beside his coffin. For forty-eight hours after he posted it, the Malaysian Special Branch officer was shot dead when thirty Communist guerrillas ambushed a joint security patrol on the Thai–Malaysian border, killing or wounding everyone. At the end of the year it was estimated that there were nearly 1,000 hard-core armed terrorists of the 'Malayan National Liberation Army' lurking in the wild sea of jungle on the Thai side of the frontier. They were being given close support by about 2,000 militants drawn from the younger generation of local Overseas Chinese, who in turn collected dues, food and information for the guerrillas from twice that number of active sympathizers.

For the Malaysians this new 'armed struggle' of the Communists was like the familiar grey opening of a recurrent nightmare. Lacking wide popular support, it was on a reduced scale, and some critics protested that the menace was exaggerated. Others agreed that Mao's theories on peasant revolution could never apply in the game-and-rubber economy of Malaysia's jungles and industrial plantations. But it was obviously time to wake up.

Police were soon to raid the first Malaysian 'People's Commune', organized by local Communists in emulation of those formed in China ten years before, when Mao tried to brigade the peasantry into disciplined self-sufficient collectives in which all property was pooled. The commune threatened to become the wagon-circle of the Maoists in imperialist badlands where Communist writ did not yet run, it appeared, and on the Malayan peninsula militant leftists set out to develop a rash of these small red enclaves across the countryside until the revolutionary moment arrived for 'using the villages to besiege the towns'. They had meanwhile deeply penetrated Chinese schools, at least four big trade unions, and two opposition parties.

The activists took their general directives from Radio Peking, carefully tape-recording broadcasts and distributing them to party cells. The 'Quotations from Mao' were being smuggled into Singapore at the rate of 8,000 copies a month, and they were trickling into the North Borneo states of Sabah and Sarawak, where stubborn Communists among the immigrant Chinese still waged their will-of-the-wisp war.

By the beginning of 1973 there were estimated to be between 1,500 and 2,000 hard-core armed terrorists divided into three 'regiments' on the Thai border, and they were filtering southwards into Malaysia itself in parties up to twenty strong. In the northern states of Perak and Kelantan they had already begun to recruit aborigines and Muslims, and three secret Communist organizations that were furtively supplying them on the ground had been uncovered by the Malaysian security forces.

Peking announced the creation of a 'Patriotic Front' in neighbouring Thailand in 1964, and by the beginning of 1969 subverted Meo guerrillas in the north of the country were using rocket-launchers against the security forces. Taking their cue from Radio Peking, the gunmen of the Patriotic Front numbered between 2,500 and 3,000 men supported by about 25,000 sympathizers. Four years later the number of guerrillas had increased to about 7,000, and Thai officials believed that they hoped to make a bid to take over the whole country in 1976. Over the border in Cambodia Prince Norodom Sihanouk now described the struggle against 'Red Khmer' terrorists as an 'all-out war' against a 'foreign-inspired' enemy within, while his hill-tribesmen to the east were a prey to the bullying and blandishments of the Vietcong next door. As more red patches of Communist inflammation discoloured South-east Asia, pessimists began to prophesy the sepsis of a subcontinent from the wound of Vietnam.

Nowhere did this seem more obvious than in Laos. 'Any settlement over Vietnam reached at the Paris talks must include a settlement here too,' William Sullivan, Washington's supercharged ambassador to Vientiane, told me in 1968. But appearances are deceptive. Sullivan lived twenty-four hours of the day with the nagging knowledge that North Vietnamese battalions already operating inside the country could cut right through to the frontier of Thailand and take the Laotian capital itself within a week. Yet he remained unruffled.

For although Laos was a pushover, Hanoi did not push. Some 40,000 North Vietnamese regular troops and up to 29,000 pro-Communist Pathet Lao guerrillas dominated much of the territory, but they were not deployed to conquer it. Their task was to hold a protective lining of geopolitical fat in the northern and eastern provinces of the kingdom, covering the frontier of North Vietnam and the vital Ho Chi Minh trails that served as a pipeline for men and guns fed into South Vietnam. Their forays into the Laotian plains from the foothills of the high Annamite Chain, through whose vulnerable passes the Communist reinforcements must file, were mainly intended to keep the Royal Laotian army at a safe distance. Moreover in the northern provinces of Laos it was the anti-Communist Meo hill-tribesmen who were the hit-and-run native guerrillas, moving easily among their own folk 'like fish in water' as Mao had taught, and the North Vietnamese conventional troops who were the hated alien intruders. They could fight no 'patriotic' war on this soil yet.

In Hanoi Communist spokesmen have revived the old term 'Indochina', and there can be little doubt that the Vietnamese dream of a day when they can act the big brother to a Communist Cambodia and a Communist Laos. But their first concern will be South Vietnam, not the lands across their border, and although the seepage into the fringes of Thailand looks dangerous, there is in fact a damp-course of devotion to King and Buddha in the interior which may stop the rot. As the Vietminh marched into Hanoi in 1954 gloomy analysts predicted that all South-east Asia would go Communist within ten years. But nineteen years later not a single country had done so (although Cambodia in particular looked perilously unsteady). China, the biggest domino of all, had fallen a quarter of a century before, yet only North Vietnam had been knocked over since.

Maoism was losing its looks. When the 'Great Cultural Revolution' broke out in China in 1966 and Mao Tse-tung loosed the Red Guards on everyone from his own Foreign Minister to foreign nuns, the whole mystifying, domestic upheaval appeared to most Asians to present the unedifying spectacle of a mad dog biting its own tail. They became further disillusioned as the Chinese began to export their ideological convulsions, and the novel diplomatic dictum that any mob wearing Mao in the buttonhole was right wherever it rioted began to reap brusque responses.

Accordingly Burma, Ceylon, Nepal, and Mongolia were all accused of insulting portraits of Chairman Mao, or unwarrantably holding up imports of inflammatory Communist propaganda, or unpardonably stopping 'patriotic' Chinese from rampaging through their respective capitals. In Peking nine foreign embassies were successively besieged by Red Guards, and Indian and Indonesian diplomats were forced to leave China under humiliating conditions. In all, China quarrelled with seven of her immediate neighbours and nearly thirty countries around the world before revolutionary rage gave way to some semblance of reason, and the Maoists began to mend their diplomatic fences. But throughout the area irreparable damage had already been done. For it is enough to see a man foam at the mouth just once.

It is very doubtful whether anti-Communists could have slept as easily in their beds if China and the Communist parties of South-east Asia had everywhere practised the peaceful co-existence which produced such solid dividends in Indonesia. In Djakarta the Communists paid unswerving lip-service to President Sukarno, who needed them in turn to counterbalance the Indonesian army and the Indonesian Muslims. This symbolic relationship between the 'Bung' and the Partai Kommunis Indonesia enabled the PKI to rally some sixteen million people to its front organizations, to penetrate the army and to subvert the air force, to win widespread sympathy in the left wing of the Indonesian National Party, to acquire three seats in the Government, slots in the Supreme Advisory Council, and the ear of the ageing master. Sukarno himself denounced 'Communist phobia' and coined the term NASAKOM for an administration in which Nationalism, Agama (religion) and Communism would all be represented.

In 1963, while plans were being laid that would raze the new British Embassy in Djakarta to the ground in a few weeks' time, I asked M. H. Lukman, Deputy Secretary-General of the PKI, what would happen to the Father of Indonesian Independence 'after the revolution'. He looked around the shabby little anteroom at Party headquarters, sipped his coffee to cover the pause, and said softly : 'The way President Sukarno is thinking now, we don't see why he should not remain in office when we are in power.'

Sukarno was flouting the United Nations and threatening to set up a rival organization for states that resented the prerogatives of the Big Five in New York. He had declared anti-colonialist cold war on the white and wealthy West and might well line up the leaner Afro-Asian nations against Washington and London far more effectively than could a Communist behemoth like China, which inspired distrust and fear in so many. His militant policy of rallying the have-not countries as 'New Emerging Forces' against the 'Old Established Forces' of capitalist and colonial powers promised a new polarization that would isolate the imperialists. The Bung was most conveniently chalking out the pitch for a Communist victory later.

Then, having won all this with their smiles, the PKI threw

it away in an abortive coup d'état on 30 September 1965, in which six Indonesian generals were murdered and mutilated and pitched into a well. A palace colonel ostensibly made this foolhardy, grand-slam bid for power, but it was obvious that he was playing with Party cards, and he later revealed that the Communists, who had been sent arms from China, would only have kept Sukarno as a paper-President once they had taken over. It is believed that Chinese doctors attending the Bung's troubled kidneys in Djakarta had whispered (on orders from masters in Peking over-impatient for revolution) that he would soon die. This supposedly prompted the hesitant Indonesian Communists to rise before he ceased to stand between the PKI and the army, for the generals were reputed to be planning their liquidation. If they were not very quick, ran the argument, they would be very dead.

There had been a gross miscalculation, however. Njoto, Second Deputy Secretary-General of the PKI, once assured me in the same shabby room in which I saw Lukman that eight out of ten soldiers were sympathetic to the Party because they were loyal to Sukarno. This *non sequitur* was now to cost the Communists dear.

The soldiers did not wait for Sukarno to die. All over the Republic the military and the Muslims set about exterminating the PKI (and their own private enemies) with such a show of stamina that everyone soon lost count of the corpses, and vague estimates of the dead still range from 100,000 to half a million. As for the much-subverted Indonesian Air Force, General Abdul Haris Nasution, then Defence Minister, told me in the front lounge of his home in Djakarta (where assassins were to miss him on that black day in 1965 but shoot down his five-year-old daughter): 'I am not afraid of Communist penetration in that quarter. The man who controls the ground troops controls the situation. It is a small matter to isolate a few military airfields, cut off the fuel supplies, and ground the MiGs for good.' And he was proved right.

By 1968 Sukarno was out, the anti-Communist Suharto was in, and the army was patiently winkling Communist guerrillas out of limestone fissures and caverns in East Java. Five years

later there were still left-wing alarms and military excursions
in the archipelago, but most of them sounded a trifle stagey.
Additional army battalions were dispatched to Borneo to seek
out terrorists who in fact were more of a nuisance to neighbouring Sarawak than to Indonesia. A startling statement by
the brigadier-general directing the Security Command in
Djakarta that seven-and-a-half million Maoists and Marxists
were still loose in the Republic failed to startle, for even in the
heyday of Sukarno that figure would have appeared to be over-
inflated and just asking to be pricked with the nearest pin.

The Communists were reported to be regrouping, to be
mingling with the peasants and the poorer workers in order
to form a 'united people's front', to be getting guns from China,
to be planning to sabotage the railway system, to be recruiting teenage 'rural warriors', and to be establishing a base in
Djakarta itself. But whatever the remnants of the hard-core
were plotting, rebuilding the Party from the ground up was
going to be a long and hard task, for most of the original
leaders of the PKI were dead, fled, or behind bars. For at least
the third time in its chequered history, the impulsive Indonesian
Party had tried to jump the gun in 1965, and had taken a bullet
in the back for its pains. Peking was back to square one. Coexistence might pay. Crime had not.

7
The Odd Couple

Mirnoye Sosushchestovaniye. I had learned the Russian phrase that morning, and perhaps learned also a little of its real meaning – a cat-and-dog life without conflict – as I trailed 'Mr Peaceful Coexistence' himself across the volcanic piecrust of Java. It was February 1960, and the second day of Premier Nikita Khrushchev's visit to President Sukarno of Indonesia. At Tjipanas, the mountain resort in the hills south of Djakarta, the principle was expressed in a simple tableau. The two men sat side by side, plump thigh to plump thigh, like an ill-assorted bride and groom at an oriental wedding. Khrushchev was pink, sweating, and glum in his handworked Georgian shirt, his cream-puff suit with its cornucopia trousers, possibly wondering what on earth he was doing in this, the third presidential palace he had visited in twenty-four hours. Sukarno was immaculate in his black cap and beribboned uniform, his fastidious drooping lips and large dark glasses otherwise giving him the air of a slightly *passé* Hollywood co-respondent on the beach at Cap d'Antibes. One had emerged from the grey, winter backcloth of Moscow and mechanistic revolution, the other from the torrid, fleshy riot of a Balinese landscape. They seemed to have little to say to each other.

A radio reporter tape-recording the tinkling Javanese music in the background was nevertheless suddenly accused of trying to pick up their heavily starched conversation, and a few minutes later my arm was also seized as I stood with other correspondents on the steps of the open-sided pavilion to which they had so pointlessly been flown by helicopter, just to sip coffee. I turned, to meet the accusatory glare of a tall young thug with eyes of slate who rapped out something in Russian and jerked his thumb over his shoulder. His meaning was obvious, and it was not Peaceful Coexistence. Harsh words were then exchanged in the language of Lenin and Lady Chatterley with neither of us understanding the other, while Khrushchev watched impassively, his small blue eyes unblinking.

Only afterwards did it occur to me that I had been wearing a rather nasty dacron suit that might have been run up in Bratislava, and the bodyguard had therefore probably taken me for a Soviet or satellite journalist unwarrantably hobnobbing with undesirable western colleagues. But his behaviour was typical of Khrushchev's secret servicemen, who treated Indonesia as if it were an insecure dependency of the Soviet Union and ignored the susceptibilities of their hosts. They persuaded the Soviet Premier that he should not risk travelling around the country in the aircraft Sukarno hospitably put at his disposal, but should fly in one of the Ilyushins that had brought the Russian party from Moscow. They also urged him to reject as unsafe the Indonesian programme for him to travel by road to Bandung (but he overruled them).

Khrushchev had already shown his temper on his arrival in Indonesia, and the sunny atmosphere at Djakarta airport, where a grinning Sukarno planted himself on the rolled-up red carpet ready for the occasion and tilted his black *pitji* to one side of his head like some equatorial Maurice Chevalier, had soon been dispersed. The Russian Premier, it seemed, liked neither the arrangements nor the rumours provoked by his acceptance of Sukarno's invitation, and the first thing he did was to fire the Soviet Ambassador to Indonesia straight back to Moscow. It was a poor beginning for a goodwill visit. Khrushchev did not go to the Indonesians in order to entice them into the Soviet Bloc, but his purpose was certainly to dissipate distrust of the Communists aroused by Peking's aggressive foreign policy at this time, and to depict them as men of probity who had found the formula for making modern powers out of backward Asian nations.

In fact, the meeting of minds was no greater than it would have been if President Eisenhower – whose failure to go to Djakarta Khrushchev was neatly exploiting – had been there in his place. Listless, taciturn, wilting in the heat, the Soviet Prime Minister dutifully played his role of 'Prince of Peace' when he faced Indonesians in the mass, perching himself on the back of an American convertible beside 'Bung' Karno to wave at a populace that waved back a million identical replicas of the Indonesian and Russian flags printed on poor-quality paper. But his welcome was well organized rather than warm, and the crowds were thickened by long lines of shrill school-children turned out in force to greet the latest of a long line of foreign faces. He was no more than that to most. Sukarno's quick succession of state guests somewhat bewildered simpler people, and a correspondent who pointed to a poster of Khrush-chev's head in Djakarta and asked provocatively, 'Who is that fat Dutchman?' was solemnly told by a confused trishaw driver: 'That's no Dutchman, that's the King of Thailand.'

It was small wonder that Khrushchev was displeased with the programme, for he and the Bung seemed to be completely at cross-purposes, and he found himself unfairly trapped on a *de luxe* cultural rubber-necking tour during which he would see no plantations or power stations or other Marxist musts. Instead, Sukarno gave him the standard treatment.

First they set off from the capital for the President's sugar-white colonnaded palace at Bogor, where Sukarno showed the Khrushchev family around the deer park and the botanical gardens, while I contemplated the Bung's private rhinoceros. (The rhinoceros is much prized among the more lubricious Asians for the propensities of the horn which, when ground up and swallowed, is erroneously believed to stiffen the deter-mination of ageing men to show how young they are. I do not know Sukarno's views on these matters, but they would surely be well informed. It appeared to be a Sumatran rhino and therefore originally endowed with two horns. Both were missing.)

Their next stop was Bandung, the city of peaceful co-existence itself, where the Soviet visitors and their camp fol-lowers were dragooned into playing the *angklung*. It was Sukarno's custom to make foreigners perform for him, and at numerous, interminable presidential parties ambassadors have

warbled shakily and counsellors have capered at his bidding.
He could hardly order the Soviet Premier to sing a solo somewhere along the line, but Khrushchev was not to be let off
altogether. The Indonesian *angklung* is like a big bamboo
rattle. Shake it, and it gives off a sweet tremolo of two harmonious notes with a hollow, wooden xylophone quality to
them. Herded into rows of chairs in a hotel ballroom, we were
handed *angklungs* graded to cover the entire scale from A to
G and so converted into a living keyboard. A music-master on
a dais displayed placards on which the chords of some simple
tune were shown alphabetically, and by moving his pointer
progressively from one to the next in correct time, he set us
all jingling in turn as our notes were indicated. Khrushchev
sat well forward in this adult bell-ringing class, attentive to
the conductor's gestures but patently ill-at-ease in so unaccustomed a form of collective.

He then flew to Jogjakarta to address the students of its
old university, and that was the only occasion on which he
woke up with words. 'By 1965,' he shouted, a trifle erroneously,
'the Soviet Union will be producing more than half of the
world's goods. You students should come to Russia to see for
yourself. I will give you a guarantee that no one will be forced
to accept Communist ideals against his will.' Much laughter
and applause. I did not see this, however. A time comes on all
these tours when the wise correspondent opts out, leaves it
to the TV cameramen to record the inch-by-inch progress of
prince or premier, and goes overland instead of flitting across
foreign countries by air. For it is written: 'a rider must dis-
mount to look at the flowers'. With two American colleagues
I had hired a battered old Chevrolet with a sulky carburettor
and a leaking radiator, and we set off across Java by road.

From the terraced rice-fields that provide the West Java
volcanoes with their brilliant settings of jade we headed for
Semarang along the north coast of the island, bouncing over
ribbed and potholed roads through stricken flatlands of scrubby
grey-green fields listlessly manured by skinny cattle. The villages were miserably poor, their streets sullen. This was

Sukarno's other island, which Khrushchev was not going to see, the ugly consequence of economic irresponsibility, inefficiency, corruption and presidential megalomania.

On these roads cautious men travelled with a full car, so that armed hitch-hikers might legitimately be refused a lift with a shout of 'no room' and a shoe on the accelerator. Coughing apologetically, the consumptive Chevrolet struggled over the 250 miles to Semarang where this skeletal scenery vanished, and we took the road south for Jogjakarta. The world tilted over as we climbed, the sun fell from sight, and the dry sky took fire until the whole vault was in flames. Against this lurid light there swung into line the great dark cones of five majestic volcanoes. It was as if this were the hot heart of the world. No one could fail to sense the lush, sweating life in the lowlands below that was Sukarno's vision of Indonesia, and turned even his love of country into a voluptuous passion incomprehensible to men conditioned to the Kremlin and the Caucasus.

On the next morning we followed Sukarno and Khrushchev out of Jogjakarta. To our north, across luscious rice lands fringed with coconut palms, the perfect cone of Merapi rose distantly from the plain like an aloof Vesuvius, a flat sliver of cloud half-severing the summit from the base. Ahead, the Soviet leader stood at the foot of its man-made reflection, the magnificent temple-mountain of Borobodur, and Marxist and monument confronted each other stonily, as if each perceived the challenge of the other.

Borobodur was built during the Sailendra dynasty in the eighth century – 100 years before the Viking chieftain Rurik made his base on the Volkhov, and a primitive Russian state was first founded on a policy of plunder and piracy. Rising to a bell-like summit, this colossal sermon in stone ascends heavenwards in nine narrowing tiers of galleries three miles long and intricately sculpted with bas-reliefs. The whole vast crown of rock symbolizes the Buddhist belief that man climbs through his many incarnations to the perfection whose reward is the bliss of Nirvana. It expresses the hierarchical Hindu–Buddhist society whose principle was the higher, the better, until the King at the apex of the system was the perfect earthly incarnation of Vishnu or Siva.

Excavated on the orders of Raffles when Britain occupied the Netherlands East Indies during the Napoleonic wars, Borobodur was another example of the Asian nationalist's debt to the white archaeologist. But in this case the colonialists had, with unconscious malice, restored to the Indonesians a huge hill of a talisman whose magic impassively repudiated the egalitarian and atheistic tenets of the perspiring Russian visitor. Khrushchev and family gave it their suspicious attention, and then took off for Surabaya.

In Surabaya the Soviet Prime Minister's dull speech received a dull reception from the crowd carefully assembled in the local stadium. But when Sukarno rose to address the microphone and the concourse of 40,000 young people beyond it, describing his guest as 'not exactly tall and a little fat, but the leader of a billion people', and then launching into one of his silver-tongued harangues – violent, simple and repetitive like all war dances – he was given an ovation. Khrushchev sighed, and they went on to Bali.

At Bali airport the Russian was greeted by a great bouquet of bare-shouldered beauties in patterned sarongs of silver and blue and red and purple, their sleek heads crowned with flowers of golden filigree, their delicate hands holding bowls of petals to strew in the path of 'Bung' Karno and the white alien. Running through my slides I see Khrushchev being blessed by some local *guru*. He is bearing up well, grinning gamely, straw hat in hand and a *lei* of red hibiscus about his neck. But in Bali above all the mass of great square men from Moscow boxed up in great square suits, the paper flags and pomp and the metallic blaring of banal national anthems over scratchy loudspeakers were an incongruous affront, and the age of cancer and the coronary suddenly appeared at its very silliest.

Beyond the protocolaire frills and the security fuss the blue breakers rolled timelessly in to a silver shore, and behind the lackadaisical palms and the iridescent rice-fields, the dead volcanoes of the hinterland stood in eternal silence, wreathed in cloud. In villages where palm-thatched pavilions alternated with gracefully worked gateways and temples of rose-red stone, copper-breasted women in peacock-bright sarongs undulated bonelessly as they bore headloads of fruit and rice down the dusty streets, naked children played idly on the verges, and craftsmen squatted to carve somewhat repetitiously from sandalwood, teak and ironwood the elongated deer and elongated women, the demons and angels of this haunted animist paradise.

One night I stood among the crowd in a village square while three gorgeously dressed Balinese girls, their heads capped with tiaras of flowers and golden ornaments, their long-nailed tapering fingers curled back almost to the wrist, twisted and swayed to the measured, limpid beat of a *gamelan* orchestra. But into this idyll there inevitably burst a black American limousine from the palace above decorated with Indonesian and Russian national flags, raising the dust and ripping the velvet night with its insistent horn and headlights. We were back in the twentieth century, and 'back' undoubtedly seemed the right word.

On the next evening we went up to this palace of Tampaksiring to watch Khrushchev watching the *Ketjak*. The *Ketjak* is the famous monkey-dance from the great Hindu epic, the *Ramayana*, which tells how Hanuman, King of the monkeys, helped the good King Rama to rescue his wife from the clutches of the evil ruler of Ceylon. Some seventy half-naked men, their glistening backs almost black in the uncertain, smoky light of flaring torches, sat cross-legged in concentric circles, their hands making a dark forest of fingers as they waved them towards the hub of their human wheel and chanted the chattering monkey chorus in explosive unison. Fantastic figures of fable capered among them, as the voices of the soloists – grating and nagging as if from the grave itself – rose and fell in their narration of the ancient and sinister legend. The *Ketjak*, performed under these optimum conditions, is a weird and wonderful thing, but the elderly Russian gazed fixedly at nothing, hot, tired, and bored.

Outside it was a night of stars, and after the dance Bernard Kalb, then of the *New York Times*, took a stroll in the luxuriant moonlit palace grounds with an impeccably dressed Indonesian acquaintance. Suddenly a Russian security officer stepped out of the shadows and ordered Kalb out of the garden. 'But this is the Chief Minister of Indonesia,' he protested, gesturing towards Doctor Djuanda, who stood at his side. The Russian security officer ignored Djuanda and gazed for a moment at the big American's fine semitic head, so reminiscent of some discredited Babylonian monarch. 'I don't care who he is,' he barked tautly, 'Get out.' In deference to Djuanda, Kalb complied. We were back at the beginning again.

'Who's that fat Dutchman?' As the Khrushchev family, including his daughter and son-in-law, Aleksei Adzhubei, disported heavily in the tepid surf at our beachside hotel they must have looked compromisingly like the former colonial herrenvolk to undiscriminating Balinese. Although Sukarno screamed at Surabaya that Khrushchev could speak for Asia at the next summit meeting, and although the Bung was to borrow a billion dollars from Moscow within the following five years, Russians were forever white men in the eyes of Indonesians and of all the other prejudiced and pigmented peoples of the subcontinent.

Aid and trade did not generate greater affection for the Communist half-world. Soviet earth-moving machinery worked badly in Indonesian soil. Soviet building specifications did not meet local requirements, subsidences occurred, cracks appeared, and tempers frayed. A Czech agricultural machinery plant proved entirely unsuitable for the tropics and Prague could supply no spare parts. A Czech tyre factory turned out to be ten years out of date, and Polish equipment for new shipyards rusted on the site because no local currency was available to pay for construction work.

The Iron Curtain experts were exasperated by inefficient Javanese labour and the impractical ministerial plans of Djakarta, but for the sake of political goodwill agreed to projects which the western powers had turned down as misconceived. In Makassar, the Czechs found themselves trying to build a cement plant at a point where the wharves, the roads, the bridges and the vehicles that were supposed to run on them

were all too small and too weak to carry the machines, which
in consequence remained in their crates for months on end.
Moreover, the cement was not required in Celebes but in Java,
400 miles away across the sea. In order not to offend their
protégés, the Russians also insisted on Indonesian participation
in their engineering and construction projects, and this simply
made for more bad blood, for Javanese civil engineers interpreted Russian plans and work schedules in their own way —
and at their own maddening pace.

The sad story was repeated elsewhere, as sad stories always
are. In 1964, I found that Communist benefactors had initially
given Cambodia a paper factory with the wrong sort of
machinery for making paper out of the ubiquitous Cambodian
bamboo, a sugar refinery with the wrong sort of machinery for
making sugar from the ubiquitous Cambodian sugar palm, a
cement works which was erected on a site twenty miles away
from the nearest water, and a plywood factory whose original
glue came unstuck in the heat.

The white elephant is a royal beast well known to Cambodians, and small ones could always be seen chewing away
meditatively at lengths of succulent sugar cane in the precincts
of the palace at Phnom Penh. They looked harmless enough, but
it was the custom for an oriental potentate to show displeasure
by presenting one of these slightly pink pachyderms to hapless servitors who had incurred his wrath, and this back-
handed compliment spelled ruin. For the beneficiary could not
neglect the animal without committing *lèse-majesté*, but must
keep and clothe it in the style to which it was accustomed, and
in time it simply ate him out of house and home.

'And that precisely defines the generous gifts showered upon
us by our Russian patrons,' one Cambodian minister told me
sarcastically. 'Are they, too, angry with us, then?' It was a
malicious Asian reaction to the munificence of the Soviet
Union, which had presented Cambodia with a 500-bed hospital
and a technical institute, and then left it to the Cambodians
to find most of the skilled staff and the money to run them.
There was at the same time a tendency among Khmers in the
know to find that whatever the Russians gave them free was

embarrassingly expensive, and some were secretly a little
envious of the Indonesians, to whom Moscow had only made
one outright gift of a much smaller hospital.

The Indonesians had their own headaches, however. Capitalist
aid was designed to enslave underdeveloped countries, Khrushchev had warned them. Soviet assistance, on the other hand,
was designed to enable young nations to consolidate their independence. 'Through Communism and Communist friends,
you too can grow muscles like ours,' he seemed to say. It was
in theory heady stuff for peoples sick of having sand kicked
in their faces, and Khrushchev's visit to Indonesia was deceptively productive. By 1965 Sukarno was spending the last of
his billion dollar Russian credits, Djakarta was the proud pos-
sessor of the biggest collection of obsolescent Soviet warships
and jets in Asia, and the Indonesian Government was having
to sacrifice more than 150 million dollars a year – nearly one
third of all national foreign exchange earnings – simply to pay
off the interest on the Russian loans.

By 1969, 115 of the 200 fighters and bombers so handsomely
provided by Moscow were grounded for lack of spares, and
the 19,200-ton Sverdlov-class cruiser renamed *Irian* could not
put to sea because the refrigeration system on which it was
completely dependent had collapsed. Inert Soviet-designed
destroyers, immobilized for want of maintenance and replacements, cluttered up the quays at Javanese ports like so much
scrap metal, and there was talk of towing off some of this out-
dated ironmongery and sinking it to make more space for
calling freighters. At the end of 1971 the Indonesians revealed
that thirteen of their major fleet units had already been knocked
down to knackers in Hongkong, Singapore and Japan for £20
to £25 a ton.

The Republic's military debt to Moscow stood at $800,000,000,
but while the Russians were slow to agree to reschedule it,
Indonesia's western creditors and Japan were quick to come to
the rescue with new loans that totalled half a billion dollars
and more a year. Relations between Djakarta and Moscow fell
towards freezing point. At the end of 1972 the Indonesians
refused to allow the Moscow Norodny Bank to open a branch

in the capital. In March of the following year it was announced
that the Russians would not be completing the huge iron and
steel plant in West Java on which they had suspended work
when Sukarno was eclipsed – a consortium of Dutch and Australian companies would be asked to do the job.

Meanwhile the United States was supplying naval ships and
new weapons, and President Suharto had taken into his
cabinet five American-trained technocrats whom the disgruntled
Sukarnoists referred to as the 'Berkeley Mafia'. The Chinese and
the Russians were going through the bruising experience of
seeing the biggest domino in South-east Asia fall the other way.

But in theory Khrushchev had been right. The generosity of
Mr Peaceful Coexistence had brought Indonesia to the brink
of ruin in 1965. And ruin, of course, means poverty, and Asian
poverty is the friend of Asian Communism – when Communism
is the devil the poor don't yet know.

8

The Millionaire Friends of
Mao Tse-tung

IT was somehow inevitable that while most of the West chose
wheat, most of the East chose rice, since the principle that to
him that hath shall be given applies to toil as well as treasure.
For good rice is first planted in nursery beds, where it must
be constantly manured and watered. But when the monsoon
breaks and the main paddyfields flood, the peasant ploughs
and reploughs them thoroughly behind his water buffalo, and
then tenderly and meticulously pulls up his thousands of
young shoots from the nursery and replants each by hand in
small clumps in these inundated fields. And for this he and his
family will bend day after day in the steamheat of the tropical
plains, standing in a foot or more of water, and patiently thrusting each bunch into the sodden soil beneath.

Like rice, like men. If there is no tender transplant from
colonialism to independence under a native administration that
has been properly prepared to receive and nurture the millions,
stunted nationalism may succumb to Communism, the victim
of neglect and poverty.

In prewar Tonking only four Vietnamese farmers out of ten
owned more than an acre of paddyfield. But most were better
off than their brothers in the Mekong Delta, where the rice-
growing peasant paid 40 per cent of his hard-won crop to his
landlord (in addition to other 'gifts' and services exacted from
him), and up to 120 per cent interest a year on the money
he had to borrow between harvests. These are the sort of statistics that push the poor into the red in more senses than
one. In North-east Thailand, where the left-wing 'Free Thai'
guerrillas first trained during the Second World War and Com-

munist insurgency discolours the map today like a bruise on
a green apple, a man may make as little as £15 a year. During
the wet season half of the villages are marooned by floods
and inaccessible, while in the dry season the mean soil crumbles
to dust and the land is afflicted with drought.

Rising Thai doctors, technicians or agronomists decline to
waste their time and talents on this unrewarding outback, and
it has inspired little interest in its administrators. When the
Communist insurgency began, one loyal village chief went
three times to the district authority to report the presence of
armed terrorists, and was finally assassinated for his pains
before any move was made against them. Isolated and seemingly abandoned, most villagers from this remote rural slum
connived at the Communist insurrection not for love of subversion, but of survival. The first task of the Thai Government,
when it was at last persuaded to stir itself by a grant of special
American aid worth about £40,000,000 a year, was to show
that it existed at all, and to 'do something' when the people
retailed their needs and fears. Only a programme of faith and
works, of protecting the peasant to give him confidence and
providing him with roads and wells and drugs and schools,
could win him back.

In a frustrated world darkened by the proposition that un-
bridled sex breeds overcrowding and undernourishment, however, the prolific poor become poorer, the rarer rich richer. By
the year 2000, it has been estimated, Asia will have to feed
more people than there were in the whole world in 1968. In
Malaysia three babies are born for every two covered by an
increase in the national income, and despite an imaginative
campaign launched in 1969 to sell 600 million attractively-
packaged Government-subsidized condoms for about a half-
penny each in the following four years, the Indian population
itself had reached 600,000,000 by 1973 and may well be a
billion by the turn of the century. Furthermore the most efficient plans for making a 'developing' country richer often widen
the gap between the haves and the have-nots, for in the semi-
automatic world of the supermarket and the super-container,
biggest is thought best, and small shops and ships may be lost

without trace. The same is metaphorically true of small farmers and small cottage industry.

The well-to-do West can afford inequality, because most of the poor can afford to be poor. 'Don't show me more museums,' Ping said to me on her first visit to London. 'Show me poor people. I want to see how poor people in West live.' I showed her – the blackened brick and scrawled graffiti, the dirty concrete stairways, the snivelling brats in mean back-alleys, the blowsy drabs and the rusty railings. 'No,' she said with a sort of exasperated finality. 'It's no good. You don't understand. I mean poor people, *reary* poor people.' I looked down at my shoes in shame and mumbled, 'I'm sorry. These are the best I could find.' I knew what she meant.

Asia cannot afford inequality, for the poor cannot for ever bear to be so poor. The development of miracle strains of seeds like IR-8 in the Philippines may mark the beginning of an escapist from-rice-to-riches fairy tale, but experts have calculated that it would cost a billion pounds a year for a whole decade to make it come true. Otherwise there may still be widespread famine. There was already an acute shortage of food in 1973.

Meanwhile at one end of the region the leaking, crate-sized hovels cling to the steep hills of Hongkong, their flat roofs of tin and tarred paper like tired eyelids on the face of the rock. At the other I have seen the destitute of Djakarta swarming in shantyvilles that looked like oversized rubbish dumps, or bedding down temporarily in highly-desirable four-foot-diameter water-pipes lying at the roadside. Their one mod. con. was the stinking canal, in which they bathed, cleaned their teeth, and washed their sarongs, while others squatted meditatively upstream, waiting for nature to take its course.

Until a few years ago there were only eight fully qualified Laotian doctors in the whole of Laos. But that was already a great improvement, for when the famous and lamented Dr Thomas Dooley first took a medical team into the remote villages in 1958, there was only one, and he was the Minister of Health. Dooley gave crash courses in first aid and hygiene to 'glorified dressers', and Laos made full use of every failed medical student with three years of skipped lectures to his credit who would stay in the country and 'practise'. I have seen wards in Laotian hospitals that would have looked unreassuringly familiar to the *younger* Florence Nightingale, the patients lying on bare boards, sometimes without a stitch of clothing on them, or trussed up in dirty dressings in the usual miasma of urine and stale sweat.

'Fifty per cent of pregnancies do not go to completion,' wrote Dooley. 'Of one hundred babies conceived, only fifty will be born alive. Of these fifty, twenty will die during infancy. Of the thirty left, ten will die during childhood.'

In 1968 bubonic plague was reported in Vietnam, Burma, Thailand, and Indonesia, and was threatening the Philippines, where huge armies of rats had invaded the countryside, consuming millions of pounds' worth of grain. The Filipinos were encouraged to look on rats as a treat, to start eating them in order to supplement their diet and rid themselves of the vermin at the same time. 'If locusts can be made a delicacy, why not rats?' one provincial councillor asked illuminatingly, and a home management expert produced a variety of recipes for dressing them up with sauces and chilli and curry for the queasy.

But all this promotion may have been quite unnecessary. Most Filipino housewives had to cater for seven mouths on a family income of about £4 a week, and some sharecroppers earned as little as £4 a month (if they were not cheated by their landlords). While the big American sugar-daddy bought up the cane crop and kept the consorts of the Philippine plantation barons dripping in diamonds, the small peasant was slightly worse off than his Vietnamese fellow-farmer: he was left with only half of his yield, and often had to pay more than 100 per cent interest on any loan to buy seeds, tools, or fertilizer. Land reform may already have been a grim reality in Communist North Vietnam by 1956, but it was to remain a delectable dream in the free Philippines until 1972.

This is not surprising, for the paper-thin upper crust in the Philippines remains true to those comforting capitalist philosophies which teach that, like *yin* and *yang* and cops and robbers, there cannot be haves without have-nots. In his affable, princely way, Tengku Abdul Rahman of Malaysia once comforted President Macapagal by telling him that Filipinos did not have to be left-wing to become Asians. But it cannot be said that their men of moment have shown much inclination to choose Socialism as a cure for their schizophrenia anyway. The worship of private enterprise and unhealthy competition is as devout in Manila as it is among the million-eyed stone gods of Manhattan that suck in the citizens like plankton at nine and spit out the remains at five. And the distance between the poor and the rich strains the eyes.

In 1945 the Filipino capital was the scene of some of the most savage butchery and ruthless destruction of the Second World War, and by the time peace came, it was a wreck. Today troglodyte communities still live in the black holes that pockmark the crumbling walls of the old Spanish town, cave-dwellers in the heart of the city, while newcomers drifting in from the poverty-stricken *barrios* raise their own hideous shacktowns of packing cases and hammered-out petrol cans and fragments of tarpaulin and tent. Yet in 1968 the Vice-President gave a party for a few friends in Manila which reputedly cost him half a million American dollars. It only lasted one night, but the friends had been flown in by jet from Texas and Madrid to drink his champagne – not by the glass, but by the fountain.

'And here,' one ambassador said, pulling a bottle of whisky out of his desk drawer like any West Coast private eye, 'I have for the first time in my life seen gold bath-taps.' He went on to tell me of a Filipino family of five with sixty servants and thirty-two cars, of a woman whose huge wardrobe, housed in an extensive gallery in her Manila house, could only be used in conjunction with a card-index system which listed hundreds of toilettes and was carefully cross-referenced so that dresses might be matched with the right accessories. That was a few years ago. By now she may have a computer.

The talk that season was of an elegant party thrown to honour an outgoing Portuguese ambassador, for which the hostess had erected seven pavilions to house seven tables, each one recreating a different age in a different country in its furnishings, its tableware, and its food and drink. The guests were provided with costumes appropriate to their time and place, and an authentic and lavish banquet of the period was served in each case. There was a pavilion for the Ming dynasty in China, for which the delicacies of 500 years ago were brought in from Hongkong. There was a table of King Arthur's doubtful days at which guests ate and drank from heavy silver platters and goblets. There was a dinner of the Directoire in Paris, a Russian banquet of the reign of Catherine the Great. Mink trimmings for the Chinese tent had been shipped specially from Japan, caviare was flown from Persia, and the hostess supervised seven teams of seven cooks preparing seven different feasts in seven kitchens, as if some crazy hypothesis of the Walrus and the Carpenter had somehow been given reality. And Heaven knows what else was produced in the 'King Solomon' pavilion.

One fancy dress party may provoke another, however.

The group of rather unprepossessing Filipino ladies, a trifle too thick at the ankle and flat at the thorax, bowled down the road in Central Luzon in two 'Jeepney' minibuses. But although their clothes may have been ill-fitting, and their figures somewhat angular, they were most certainly dressed to kill. As they rounded a blind bend and spotted a checkpoint ahead the drivers accelerated and guns came up from under the drag. The buses crashed through the barrier with a deafening burst of fire that killed one constable and subsequently riddled a pursuing police car with bullets. Tragedy had hit one man and his family, but the incident had the flavour of farce about it, with the 'Huk' terrorists in their borrowed feminine finery bouncing along like characters in a comic film.

It was the sort of episode that conspired with the cry-wolf school of excitable journalism in the Philippines to persuade the sceptical public that nothing serious ever happened there except on paper. If Communist bandits were reported to be active again, it was simply to justify more military expenditure. 'Every time Congress discusses the armed forces budget, the number of top Huk commanders increases geometrically,' a cynical commentator once remarked. But the Huks were more than a hoax.

'Huk' was the first syllable of the Tagalog for 'People's Anti-Japanese Army', the Communist-led Filipino guerrilla movement that the Americans supplied so plentifully with arms during the Second World War. But today it is the first syllable of the Tagalog for 'People's Liberation Army'. Looked upon askance and then cheated of seats in Congress once peace was restored, its leaders took to their weapons again.

In 1970 there is still no shortage of these, I find. The United States has continued to supply the movement, so that it is well furnished with sub-machine guns and Armalite rifles. The difference is that in wartime the Americans delivered the arms, but in peacetime the Huks collect them from store. It is not easy to stop a Filipino once he sets his heart on something belonging to someone else, and on one occasion American officers investigating a theft of arms from the conveniently-located Clark Air Base north of Manila were baffled to find the perimeter wire intact – until one of them counted the gates. There was an extra one, complete in every detail, which had no business to be there at all.

Clark Base also supplies the Huks with much of their money. In near-by Angeles City they are the real rulers of an empire of gambling clubs and girlie-bars, bus services, barbershops and straightforward old-fashioned bordellos that any United States military complex grows like fungus, and from all of which they exact taxes. The Huks run bingo games and boxing matches, cockfights and clip joints and car services for American tourists, and no one knows how much of the £30,000 a day that pours out of the air base and into Angeles City is siphoned off into their 'socialist' movement by shopkeepers and prostitutes and cab drivers ready to pay for a little peace. For in addition to their own potential for punishment, the Huks subcontract assassination to juvenile murder squads on a strictly cash basis.

Operating with a jarring combination of principles drawn from Marx and the Mafia, the Huks blackmail and intimidate politicians and big business, and buy up provincial officials or police, slaughtering the uncooperative where it is sound policy to make an example. They have been known to chasten the neighbourhood by presenting the legs of an enemy to his wife and the head (wearing sunglasses) to his mother. A killer squad known as 'The Beatles' specializes in lethal attacks on police and the liquidation of informers in various distasteful ways.

On the other hand the Huks have been praised as the champions of justice in the past. Not only has their invisible government administered hundreds of villages in Central Luzon, but in Huk territory no man steals a water-buffalo or rapes a girl without risking swift retribution from these friends of the farmers. Their 400-strong guerrilla force in this region has been supported by at least 30,000 peasants ignored by the government, beaten by corrupt police, and robbed by landowners. The Huks charge a modest enough fee for their services as protectors, payable in unhusked rice, and these include helping with the harvest, and reasoning with the more rapacious landlords at gunpoint on behalf of the victimized sharecropper. 'Huk Law' was for long the only equity the Philippines knew.

Luis Taruc, former Supremo of the insurgents who surrendered in 1954, explains the two faces of the movement by saying that there are anti-feudal 'ideological Huks' who should be granted an amnesty, and 'fake Huks' who are common bandits and should be exterminated. A pretty fifteen-year-old Huk amazon, captured at the beginning of 1969 when her teenage husband, two uncles and a grandfather were killed in a clash, described how her group of guerrillas had listened every night to an instructive course in Communism broadcast by Radio Peking in Tagalog, and added that the leader of the local liquidation squad was a graduate from a secret 'Stalin University'. She was proud of the Huks, she told President Marcos personally in Luzon. 'They are the army of the poor, and taught to help the people,' she said simply.

But the Huks cannot be divided so easily into red and rogue. Bandits are as much part of the raw scenery of South-east Asia as browbeaten peasants. In the Philippines as elsewhere, poverty may fuse an incongruous mixture of discontented elements

into an explosive compound. In at least one case in modern
political history a Communist leader has found his early
allies among farmers and footpads. His name was Mao Tse-tung,
and subsequent events in China proved that he knew what he
was about.

Subsequent events in the Philippines have done the same.
By mid-1973 the Communist guerrilla movement had expanded
into a 'New People's Army' of about 1,500 well-armed militant
Maoists who were linked to active urban guerrilla groups in
the towns, supplied with food and intelligence by more than
10,000 supporters, and might count on as many as 100,000 sympathizers. They were officially described as 'tough and dedicated' socialists, and their first concern was therefore to thwart
the land reform programme. For in their book the more Marcos
did men good, the more he would do them harm.

9

The Fallen Domino

AT Saigon Airport in November 1954 I boarded an elderly
Dakota with that unmistakable beaten look about it of those
whom life has treated unfairly, and flew northwards to Haiphong in a desperate attempt to reach Hanoi that same midnight. At midnight all movement into the city would stop, and
thereafter I might never be allowed to go there again. For on
the morrow the French were moving out, the Vietminh were
moving in, and Hanoi was to become the capital of a Communist and possibly unapproachable 'Democratic Republic of
Vietnam'. Stunted nationalism and poverty had claimed their
first victim in South-east Asia.

The eight-year-old Indochina War between the Vietminh
and the French was over. The folly of Dien Bien Phu and the
frustrations of the Geneva Conference were behind us. Vietnam was sawn in half at the Seventeenth Parallel until the day
came when some magician could show that it had only been
an illusion after all. Tomorrow the North would have to be
abandoned to the Communists, except for the port of Haiphong, which the French would keep until April 1955. In two
years' time elections were to be held in both the northern and
southern 'zones' of Vietnam, which would then be reunited
into one country under the government of the party that won
them. But this was not among the best-laid schemes of mice
and men, and the consequences were predictable.

The Dakota was not. Fitted along the sides with green metal
bucket seats like a set of mildewed dentures, it was filled with
displaced peasants who had been packed off to their home
villages in the north before they needed visas to get there. The
centre of the cabin was a mound of those obese cloth bundles
and baskets and bulging paper bags that are Asian for luggage,

the whole straining and groaning and shifting uneasily like some captive beast. Outside, darkness had fallen and like some half-blind old dog the Dakota had blundered into a wall of rain intricately cracked and seamed by glimmering explosions of forked lightning. The plane jinked and bucked in a merciless headwind, and I wondered if God would speak Vietnamese. It was all very ominous.

We crawled out at Haiphong into heavy flapping sheets of rain. The airfield appeared to be in almost total darkness and seemed deserted. Hanoi was about seventy miles inland to the west. These are the moments when the lonely correspondent, typewriter in one hand, hold-all in the other, rain streaming down his neck, enjoys that most reassuring of all human sensations – hitting rock bottom. He will not starve, he will not freeze to death. Somewhere beyond this fifty-acre field of twisted and uneven metal runway on which he has just tripped painfully there is another deadline.

We all trudged off to the car park and there, miraculously, was a glorified station wagon converted into a minibus and a bearded young Frenchman in minishorts asking if anyone with 1,500 piastres (about £7·50) wanted to go to Hanoi. By eleven we were rattling over the one-mile-long Paul Doumer road-and-rail bridge that crossed the Red River and led into the dead city. I found a bed in an empty brothel (all the girls had fled south).

On the next morning I saw *them* for the first time. They moved through the grey streets firmly but softly in their rubber sneakers, their small solar topees covered with camouflage nets, their denim uniforms buttoned-up, and with their packs and blanket rolls and rifles they looked workmanlike enough. Only their enamel drinking mugs, decorated with gaudy Communist flags and Picasso's peace dove, appeared a trifle frivolous. They were little men, their faces were young, drawn, expressionless. They had small delicately-formed hands and wrists like twigs. They wore no insignia of rank. They carried their equipment on bicycles and bamboo poles, their rice in bandolier-like sacks slung around the shoulders of one man in each squad. And there was not an ounce of fat among them.

They were the Vietminh. As they marched into Hanoi through the sad, interminable drizzle, the *crachin* of the Tonkinese winter, with their guerrilla air of neatly-patched military poverty, the booted French marched out about 200 yards ahead of them amid the clatter of armoured cars and half-tracks and overloaded lorries. But this protocolaire distance narrowed as the funeral parade crossed the city, the heavily-armed losers leading the makeshift victors, and by the time the senior French officer bringing up the rear had reached the Paul Doumer bridge, the bayonets of his diminutive adversaries were almost in his kidneys, and the look in their eyes was, for once, quite unmistakable.

The French had not trained the Vietnamese to run their own affairs, for they were not voluntarily according sovereignty – it had been wrenched from them by the wrong group. Before they left, their troops were therefore careful to pack up and take away generators, medical equipment and laboratory instruments, to smash the furniture and unscrew all the electric light bulbs in public offices. Only later did diplomats from Paris make some restitution in a manful attempt to see that the last thread of their cultural influence was not snipped through.

After eight years in the hills and paddyfields the Vietminh found themselves moving doubtfully through this stone jungle festooned with red and gold banners and pictures of Ho Chi Minh but rustling with strange wild life – western correspondents, Indian, Polish, and Canadian diplomats and generals of the International Control Commission, Chinese merchants and shopkeepers, Vietnamese doctors and lawyers with fluent French and sophisticated tastes, taxi girls, street-hawkers, Corsican entrepreneurs and petty adventurers who were sticking their ground, even a complete Filipino cabaret orchestra. They had inherited a new and exotic world with new and exotic problems connected with tramways, timetables and price-control, tapwater and taxes and crime and city sanitation, the railway and the airport and all these damned foreigners.

The Vietminh opened a little press bureau, and eventually we went to them to apply for exit visas. *Visas?* They stared at us

stilly, slowly tasting the word. We showed them our pass-
ports, and they fumbled through them blindly, then took them
into a dusty office at the back. After five days of waiting and
filling in forms run off a jelly pad for which someone had
finally thought up four pages of irrelevant questions, we were
given slips of paper authorizing us to leave for Haiphong. I
complained about the delay to Gaston, but the difficulties of
adjustment from the inhospitable bush to the sophistications of
running a state were legion and started with the concept of
time itself, he replied.

Gaston Pham Ngoc Thuan was a senior official of considerable prestige, but he was also a true Vietminh who preferred
simplicity to ceremony. So for the purpose of this private chat
we sat with our legs hunched up on the grass verge of the
Petit Lac in Hanoi, eating fruit. Gaston gazed over the water,
his thin, bespectacled face simultaneously earnest and dreamy.
'In the resistance,' I hear him telling me in his hesitant, self-
effacing manner, the words coming in short, sharp bursts, 'the
time-unit was the month. You see, it took three months for a
southern cadre like me to work his way from the *maquis* in
the Mekong Delta to the Vietminh zone in the north. And after
we had undergone four months of special training up here in
Tonking, we spent another three getting back to the south
again – clandestinely, through enemy territory, and on foot.
In such circumstances, what is punctuality? What can an hour
or a day more or less mean? Well, now we have got our people
thinking in terms of the week as the time unit, and soon we
will get it down to the day – or even the hour, as it is in
western countries. For the moment, however, you must be
patient with us.'

The advice was good. Off-the-cuff administration which took
no account of time or convenience was the rule. A French
commercial agent, whose head office in Saigon had sent him
a sack of southern piastres by air for running expenses (there
were no transfer facilities), unwisely took them to the bank
and was at once told that he had contravened the law by bringing them into the country. They should have been exchanged
for North Vietnamese *dong* at the airport. He explained that

he had not carried the money in personally, and suggested that he should take it back to the airport and change it. 'No,' the Vietminh cadre in the bank replied, 'you cannot do that from *inside* the country, Monsieur. What you will have to do now is to fly with the money to Saigon on the plane of the International Control Commission, and then fly back here with it, duly declaring it when you come in again from the *outside*.' Since Saigon was a full day's journey and a fare of £30 away (for the ICC plane flew via Laos and Cambodia) the Frenchman very sensibly took his cash around the corner and changed it at the black market rate with some accommodating Indian merchant.

The Democratic Republic of Vietnam was certainly starting from scratch. But after eight years of appalling hardship and sacrifice in their astonishing fight for independence, the Vietminh did not like to be told what to do by others. Later I was able to eat Christmas lunch with the Poles and spend New Year's Eve with the Hungarians in Hanoi, and through the smog of socialist solidarity there would gradually filter the exasperation of foreign Communist technicians too often faced with an infuriating combination of ignorance and conceit in the Vietminh. And since when did debt breed love? The Vietminh owed much to Chinese instructors and experts – 'But how we resented them,' a Vietminh field officer at Ho Chi Minh's personal wartime hideout once told me. 'We resented them for their better uniforms and higher pay, for their servants and their cigarette ration and even for their playing cards, but above all we resented them for their *advice*.' He might have been echoing his southern cousins talking about the Americans.

A scribbled half-page of dog-eared notebook, once carried in the pocket of some long-forgotten bush jacket, suddenly evokes a vivid picture, a small sharp image seen down the wrong end of a telescope in time. It is the summer of 1957. Pham Van Dong, Prime Minister of North Vietnam, sits with me on a red plush settee in a palace in Hanoi, pouring out a French aperitif with the grave attention he pays to all his actions, his full lips fixed in a motionless pout beneath the drawn, hollow cheeks. Dressed, as usual, in a blue tunic and slacks, he sips

experimentally. A little speciously, I praise something about
the administration. The expression of disbelief on his face does
not change: anyone who could drink this could say that, it
seems to imply, and he answers rather wryly: 'I find it particularly difficult to credit. We are struggling against so much
ignorance, and our organization leaves so much to be desired. I tell you frankly, I am a very worried man. There are
so many difficulties ahead, and we may face very tough
opposition from the South.' He looks up at me suddenly and
adds: 'But make no mistake about this. We are going to see
that Saigon sticks to the Geneva Agreement, however long it
takes, and that the elections which it provides for are held
in the South. North and South need each other, for we are too
poor. There can be no question of perpetuating partition.'
Unification, or else. It is a warning of the war to come.

Later I hear him saying, 'but we have no intention of slav-
ishly emulating China. We must examine all new steps that
Chairman Mao takes in the light of our own situation. This is
Hanoi, not Peking.' Pham Van Dong picked his way carefully,
like a man moving through a minefield, but subordinates who
followed in his footsteps at a distance then knew the path
was clear and showed less caution. Communist officials privately condemned 'China's dangerous experimental deviations',
and praised Khrushchev's predilection for open diplomacy and
peaceful coexistence. There was unquestionably a pro-China
seam that ran through the younger generation in the administration and the army of North Vietnam, but of all 'friendly'
foreigners in Hanoi at that time, the Chinese were the most
self-effacing, and perhaps the most ill-at-ease. And I remembered Pham Van Dong's words when in the following year
Mao threw China into the 'Great Leap Forward' in industry
and agriculture which in fact broke the legs of both, and
then created his 'People's Communes'. Hanoi did not follow
either example.

History, being the record of a marathon rat-race, is a constant embarrassment to neighbours. China lorded it over Tonking for a thousand years until the tenth century, and thereafter
treated the territory as a vassal. But reluctant subservience was

always interspersed with bitter fighting. Vietnam's greatest historical heroes are those who raised the banner of revolt against
the Chinese and gave them a good trouncing, and their names
adorn the squares and streets not only of Saigon, but also of
Hanoi to this day. The love–hate that the Vietnamese atavistically feel for the French, they atavistically feel for the
Chinese.

Moreover, unlike Mao Tse-tung, Ho Chi Minh himself was
no smash-it-and-see sectarian about the existing order of things,
and did not fire a single shot in anger in his life. 'Uncle Ho'
consistently advocated a two-stage revolution for Vietnam – a
bourgeois nationalist struggle for independence, and a Communist take-over later. His prewar platform was a beguiling
promise of universal suffrage and of mild land reform ('It's like
hot soup,' he once said. 'It should be taken slowly.') One day
Mao will call him 'Russian revisionist', if only under his breath.

No one distrusted Ho's agreement to open negotiations with
the Americans in Paris more than the Maoists in Peking, who
began by treating these peace talks like a swear-word dropped
in church and at first did not even tell their 700,000,000-strong
flock of fellow-Chinese that they had started at all. For Mao
was the champion of the long-drawn-out anti-Imperialist guerrilla struggle in underdeveloped continents, since he invented
the formula, and his bid to become undisputed leader of the
world revolutionary movement might depend on its successful
application in Vietnam. A fundamental difference of outlook
between a big, bellicose, but back-room China and a Communist Vietnam fighting in the front-line for the freedom to
reject 'freedom' inevitably clouded their relationship further.
The Chinese 'Cultural Revolution' was unwanted in war-torn
Tonking, where the enemy was no vague, ideological 'revisionist' bogy, but real and round-eyed.

In 1966 a senior member of the Vietnamese Politburo attacked those who 'mechanically copy the past experience of
foreign countries'. The Chinese retorted that 'acting contrary
to Mao's theory would only lead to defeat', and deplored the
way in which Hanoi had escalated the war from its simple
stick-and-karate beginnings by pouring regular troops into

South Vietnam and provoking the Americans into bombing the North. This had made the Vietnamese increasingly dependent on sophisticated Soviet weapons whose 'false comfort' Peking condemned as 'sugarcoated poison'. The Vietnamese leaders were torn this way and that between Russians who used words like 'negotiate' in mixed company, and Chinese who staunchly supported a 'people's war' which by definition meant fighting to the last Vietnamese. Nowhere else did the Sino-Soviet quarrel bring such schizophrenic anguish, for the Vietnamese were themselves divided between the two camps yet dependent upon both, and their subsequent oscillations prompted much fruitless speculation in the outside world.

But their fierce national arrogance is far stronger than any ideological sympathy for this or that Communist patron. It was impossible to listen to the war stories of Vietminh veterans in Hanoi in the nineteen-fifties and not sense their moral degeneration through hard-won victory, the corrupting pride and joy of terrible sacrifice. I met husbands and wives who had been imprisoned by the French and treated like mangy dogs, and who had not seen each other for nearly twenty years; radio news-readers who had performed their prim and peaceable quotidian task up to their necks in swamp water, with a microphone balanced on a bamboo raft and the enemy almost within earshot; fighting footsloggers who had defeated the French on a handful of rice a day despite the armour and the artillery and the bombers and the napalm and all the other musts of gracious modern dying. The Vietminh had no intention of buying a better life with the coinage of national sovereignty. When Russian wives moved to the head of the vegetable queue in the Hanoi market, the outraged Tonkinese monosyllables clicked back down the line: 'What! We might as well have the French back. Who fought for freedom, us or all these foreigners?'

A few days after I heard this remark (translated to me by my dentist), I was on the Bay of Along in the Gulf of Tonking. This bay belongs to the realm of our dreams. It is as if half of the great wall of eccentric limestone peaks that swings up to the coast from the north-west had tumbled across the foreshore and into the green, translucent waters. The sea is studded with hundreds of huge, grey, skull-like outcrops of rock capped with shrubs and stunted trees, past whose sheer faces red-sailed junks ply like tiny bright toys. Great sponges in stone, these mountains-in-the-sea are fissured and hollowed by grottoes, some of which we visited by launch, clambering through narrow slits in the cliff-walls to enter some tremendous, dripping cathedral thronged with stalagmites and hung with vast tinkling chandeliers of stalactite. And it was in one of these that someone had painted in gigantic letters : 'Long live Poland!'

It was like a distorted echo from across the world of the prayer of these small yellow people, who were every bit as jealous of their independence under the shadow of Big Brother as were the men of Warsaw or Lodz. The Communist solar system has since exploded and even the East European satellites, sputniks thrown up by Stalin, begin to radiate from the Soviet sun. North Vietnam, a self-made socialist state like Yugoslavia, would never willingly become a political appendage of China or the USSR.

If the second Indochina War compelled Hanoi to lean increasingly upon both of them for military support, it simply meant that the unfortunate Vietnamese Communists had become involved in a struggle for independence not only with the Americans, but with the Russians and the Chinese. It was a struggle that threatened to continue after the peace, moreover, for by the middle of 1973 high-powered delegations from Hanoi visiting Peking and Moscow were eagerly received by rival benefactors suspiciously anxious to play a major role in putting poor bleeding North Vietnam on its feet again.

10

Poverty's Child

THE petite Vietnamese dentist who told me about the indignation in the vegetable queue received me in a room that was uncurtained and completely bare but for a pedestal drill and one of those green canvas chairs formerly reserved for film directors. It was lit on this grubby morning by a single naked bulb of perhaps forty watts. I handed her my loose crown, sat down in the canvas chair, opened my mouth as if to shout 'cut', and she peered inside. 'I can fix it temporarily,' she said, 'but you'll have to have it seen to when you go back to Saigon. You see, I can't get any of the things I need here in Hanoi, and I have no dental cement. I'll just have to chance it and use the ordinary stuff.' I had a sudden ant's-eye vision of my own mouth as a huge wall of ivory into which great holes were broken with juddering pneumatic drills and then filled again with shovelfuls of concrete. But whatever she used, it lasted three years.

Communism is poverty's child, and therefore poor itself until the day arrives, if ever, that it makes its own million. One year after the Vietminh marched into Hanoi, it was already a city of shortages. Half the shopfronts were coffined up with wooden boards and the other half had the impersonal, empty look of the dying. It was always Sunday, it seemed. Coffee cost the equivalent of twenty-five shillings a pound, petrol twenty-two shillings a gallon. Grain was scarce, for Tonking was now cut off from the main rice-bowl of the Mekong Delta in the anti-Communist south. In the empty streets the traffic was orderly, for there was no traffic.

High and discriminatory taxation was smashing private business, but central cooperatives were filling little retail shops with cheap goods from China – tumblers and matches and pictures of Mao and Ho, vacuum flasks and vodka, shoddy shoes and exercise books and plastic air travel bags – an odd miscellany of bric-à-brac upon which it might be possible to create a new and strange way of living.

Built around an oval lake fringed by tall shaddock trees, its green waters broken by two small pagoda-tipped islands, Hanoi had once been a smiling little place. But in December 1955 it seemed inconsolably mournful. At night the *crachin* slanted down into ill-lit streets whose silence was broken only by the shuffle and the solitary cry of an occasional street-vendor. I lived in an uncarpeted room among a number of cube-shaped Poles who found Vietnam utterly intolerable. The Canadian armistice delegation organized a Christmas service in a tiny chapel, and a club-fisted colonel read the sermon out of *Time* Magazine. *A la guerre comme à la guerre.*

Those seven words summed up the Vietminh, as I had found out when Ho Chi Minh made his first public appearance at a parade on the edge of the town. I had been given a pass to this, together with an orange and one sticky rice cake, and told to be in position by 0830 hours in the morning. My position was a numbered cross, marked in chalk on a wooden platform without seats. There I stood for six slow and solid hours, eating my orange, nibbling unhappily at my rice cake, and watching the Vietnamese army, the workers, the peasants, the women, the youth, the children, and in fact most of the country file by holding their red banners of praise, their great portraits of Lenin and Stalin and Mao and Ho. A guide with halitosis shouted unceasingly into my face that the trucks were Russian but the guns were American and had been captured from the French, and that the peasants were delighted with the new socialist Vietnam. It was well worth while, but at the end of it I felt ready to confess to anything.

Suffering becomes an addiction, however. Sitting sipping warm water in an open-sided thatched hut of bamboo up in the Tonkinese highlands while the flies ate my lunch, I asked another French-educated Vietminh cadre what he wanted. To my astonishment he confessed to a material ambition: he was saving up for another pair of rubber sneakers. Otherwise he owned two cotton uniforms and some miscellaneous underwear, and he was given a rice ration, a cigarette ration (about five a day), and a few dong a week. He was therefore not in need of anything much.

'I suppose you are aware,' I said slowly and deliberately, as we sweated on our rough benches, feet scuffing the dirt floor, 'I suppose you are aware that in Hanoi there are doctors and lawyers and other professional men who never went into the *maquis* but stayed in the city under the French and made money? And you know that they are still earning one hundred times as much as you, at least half of it paid to them by a government that won't give the price of a pair of shoes to a man who fought for Ho Chi Minh for eight years in the jungle' – or provocative words to that effect. It was quite true, and I had met several of these affluent gentlemen. 'How do you accept this?' I demanded.

He did not take it amiss, but looked at me with contemptuous amusement. 'Of course I accept it,' he replied, as if talking to an obtuse child. 'These men are technicians and we need them badly just at the moment, so we buy them with what they want, which is money. But I am a cadre and a Party member, and it is just because I spent eight years fighting the French that nobody has to buy me.' His was the insidious vanity of the élite, that peculiar form of egoism which prompted British guardsmen to scorn wearing steel helmets in North Africa and American marines to fight without their flak-jackets at Khe Sanh – both outstanding instances of bad, thoroughly unprofessional soldiering.

Early government-by-guesswork, woodenly emulated by a great corps of self-righteous cadres, added immeasurably to the weight of worry already laid on the shoulders of the leaders by the terrible poverty of the country. On the road southward to Nam Dinh I saw miles and miles of barefoot peasant women, the bamboo poles across their shoulders slung with shallow baskets, trotting back and forth in their conical hats beneath the persistent drizzle. They were patiently carrying the earth and the clinkers needed to put together the railway track their husbands had blown up or systematically picked to pieces during the Indochina War to annoy the French.

In the cause of victory, the two sides between them had devastated the roads and railways, the few factories and many of the villages, and it was left to the winners to put it all together again with little more than picks, shovels and their own seamed and calloused hands. At wide river crossings the ferries had been sunk, and the ruined highways were chopped into sections by the gaps where sagging tangles of steel girder and tortured concrete were all that was left of the bridges. Like a tattered sole survivor with a crushed leg, North Vietnam was hauling itself slowly and painfully out of the wreckage of the war.

In the summer of 1955 I boarded a stifling train at Wuhan on the Yangtse River which rattled down to Nanning in South China and from there to a small terminus called Ping Hsiang on the frontier with North Vietnam. Here I was switched on to a narrow-gauge Vietnamese train which would take me to Hanoi. The single-track line, which weaved an unsteady course between the improbable peaks of Tonking, had been rebuilt shortly before by the sweat of 10,000 Vietnamese brows, and I was the first western correspondent to travel it. The train was a push-me-pull-you toy, a miniature o–6–o shunting engine back and front with a clutch of six bare wooden carriages caught between, and this contraption jolted and shimmied its way complainingly over the uneven, grass-grown track like a railway in a fun fair.

The inevitable contretemps arose when it turned out that in their slapdash generosity Vietminh cadres had given me a big box-lunch but the train staff had also prepared a solitary hot four-course meal for me in the otherwise empty dining car. They were flabbergasted when I declined to eat both. Vietnamese tightened their belts, yes, but everybody knew what white men were. They themselves managed on a skimpy bowl of rice and a little salt fish while I stuck virtuously to my sandwiches. The banquet in the dining car probably went to waste.

The train finally squealed its way through the outskirts of Hanoi twenty-four hours after it had drawn groaning out of Ping Hsiang – some 200 miles away. This railway was the slender lifeline to China which was to be pulverized once more when the American jets screamed north in 1965. Like everything else reconstructed during the previous eleven years in Tonking, it was again to be cast into the kitty, to be risked in the double-or-quits gamble for South Vietnam.

The stakes lay between the tenuous fingers of a brittle matchstick of a man with a threadbare beard whose eyes were as luminous and blank as polished onyx. Yet once, when Ho Chi Minh courteously lit a cigarette for me and his face was a little more than a foot from my own, I saw beneath their surface a fleeting shoal of expressions – tired watchfulness, determination, irony. 'You can ask me anything you wish,' he said to me, 'but I certainly do not promise to answer you. I know the sort of questions you people like to think up.' It was the perfect pre-emptive strike.

This disarmingly direct approach to men and headaches captivated those who met Ho, but it was the gloss on the cut-the-cant cynicism of a man who had graduated from being a kitchen-hand under Escoffier at the Carlton Hotel in London to becoming a key undercover Comintern agent. He was reputed to have moved around the Far East and conspired under the noses of his enemies dressed as a shaven-headed Buddhist priest in Thailand, a blind beggar in Tonking, a tycoon in Hongkong. He was gaoled by both the British and the Chinese and led his followers through two dirty wars, and he did not go through all this to emerge as the dear old thing some made him out to be. He was tough, disingenuous. He disguised his Communist party in a sheep's-clothing of national fronts just as he disguised himself to fool his foes in his earlier days. He was a patriot who saw Communism as the only salvation of his country, and he would not betray it for instant rice or instant peace.

Fading out slowly towards eternity, Ho left his indelible stamp on the state he founded. Ascetic, celibate, virtuous in his privation, he tried to discipline a whole people to glory in the name of austerity. Ho spoke Russian, Chinese, French and English, as well as Vietnamese, was a painter, a calligrapher, a pleasing versifier, and a defiant chain-smoker, but his main vice was the cult he made of his own poverty and simplicity. His unassuming manner and impatience with formality and appearances were quite genuine, but he developed and exploited them, as a stage mimic develops and exploits his natural talent for mimicry. In short, 'Uncle Ho' went professional.

He made a practice of turning up at places unannounced, perhaps because he 'had just heard' that someone would be there whom he would like to meet. The first time I saw him do this was at a diplomatic reception in Hanoi which was magically enlivened by some unwary cadre who put on to the gramophone a gross product of decadent imperialist culture, and a voice as boneless and sugared as a fried banana squeezed itself out of the disc singing : '*Gonna tay kasennimennal jernee, gonna sed mahar dadeeze . . .*'

The music was cut off, however, when there was a slight disturbance at the door and Uncle Ho shuffled jerkily into the room in a creased, reach-me-down khaki tunic and trousers, a pair of old rubber-soled sandals on his out-turned feet. As an entrance, it was a shade Chaplinesque but very much part of the mystique. He would suddenly appear in a hospital ward in the same way, rallying the patients in a jocular fashion that just stopped short of the objectionably hearty, or he would saunter into the third form during an arithmetic class. But he had a magnetic presence, and in repose his still, carved face and the set of his shoulders expressed a striking poise and calm and authority.

I saw him at it again two years later, when he 'dropped in' on a party given in Hanoi for Anastas Mikoyan. It was a small buffet supper, typical of the admirable informality of the Vietminh as soon as they stopped being bureaucratic and started being simple again. Pham Van Dong introduced me to the unique moustachioed Armenian whom not even Stalin had managed to massacre with the words, 'Now you can ask him all his secrets,' and walked away from us like a matador who has fixed his bull. Mikoyan's affability was up to the occasion, otherwise we could both have looked a little foolish. This

mischievous trick of suddenly embarrassing people was an endearing side of a Vietminh philosophy that taught persons
to be no respecters of persons.

Ho was an impulsive hand-shaker and joke-cracker, and won
hearts quickly. But he began to remind me of one of those
electric heaters built to look like a pile of glowing coals – the
friendly light is real enough but it has nothing to do with the
true nature of the fire. The first time I saw him was at a very
large dinner party. He was at the high table, and I was well
below the fish sauce. But it seems he had 'heard about me'.
In the middle of a course Ho disappeared, and a cadre whispered over my shoulder: 'The President is waiting for you.'
Astonished, I followed him behind a curtain, and was at once
alone with Uncle. The glistening yet opaque eyes appraised me
deliberately as we talked, but he was easy and amiable,
promised to see me at greater leisure, and kept his promise –
again by turning up unannounced for tea when my official
host was Pham Van Dong. But for all the friendliness ('I hope
you will tell us what you don't like around here') Ho dodged
any significant questions and I quickly learned that an off-the-
record interview with Pham Van Dong was infinitely more
rewarding than 'running into' Ho Chi Minh.

It would be a mistake to think that one was softer than
the other, however. When I arrived in Hanoi in the year of
peace 1957 I found that a Catholic revolt had been bloodily suppressed, and that cadres ordered to implement land reform had
tortured false confessions out of men who did not own a square
foot of soil. The atmosphere was such that when over-assiduous
officials started questioning people for the purpose of compiling
a census, the peasants became convinced a mass purge was
coming and many committed suicide or tried to flee across the
frontier to South Vietnam. The National Assembly then in-
dulged in an orgy of self-criticism, and liberalism enjoyed a
short season. Publishers of a magazine critical of the army
and the Government were allowed to produce five issues, but
by the time it had begun threatening Uncle Ho with a
'Hungary' or a 'Poland' if the people of North Vietnam were
not accorded real liberty, the new mood of contrition had

evaporated, the paper was closed down, and its editors and backers fell from sight.

Not before I had met one of them, however, for some comforts I had brought one family from relatives in Saigon opened up for me a secret labyrinth of intellectual society seething with frustration beneath the hard resonant surface of the Marxist régime. He was a tousled, tired man living among a medley of books and papers, and he was not going to enjoy his home for much longer. 'We intellectuals are not in any way in sympathy with the government of Ngo Dinh Diem in the South, or with the Americans,' he told me. 'We simply want to introduce some democratic freedom into our existing system of government here. But we are helpless. We are miserably caught between leaders who want to bulldoze their way to Communism and a mass of peasantry too cowed, apathetic and egocentric to complain.' This was the last despairing voice of protest I was to hear in Hanoi.

At dawn one week later I was driven to Haiphong to see the enthusiastic welcome to be accorded to Mikoyan when he arrived there at 8.30. Compared with Haiphong, Hanoi was a gay and glittering city, for it always seemed in that depressing, grey port that the last flicker of life must die out, leaving it a pallid corpse. There were no political and military leaders here, no diplomatic missions, no signs of the bustle that surrounds the bosses. A dim phalanx of cadres in faded denims ran the empty streets, the empty shops, and the almost empty quays.

Nevertheless, on this morning there was life in Haiphong. The streets were decked with red banners of welcome, Soviet flags drooped in the heat, and the pavements were thronged with pyjamaed workers and peasants mobilized for the occasion. They had been standing there since five o'clock, the mothers comforting their sleepy little children while the cadres trotted up and down in their topees, barking at intervals and pushing people into line. Seven and a half hours after they had been turned out on to the streets, the cadres told the massed herds of humans that they could disperse. Mikoyan was not coming after all. No explanation was offered. A curious sobbing whimper echoed down the streets as, just for one moment, the crowd instinctively raised its voice in anger. But it quickly sank to a mutter that was drowned by the sound of the wretched beast's 20,000 feet shuffling away.

The potter must know the weakness of his clay, and not demand from it the muscle and texture of the stuff from which he himself is made. Perhaps this is what lies between God and man, and it may be that it lay between Ho and the Vietnamese, most of whom are not starry-eyed cadres but ordinary peasants. Communist leaders are not men to be deflected from their threats and promises, however.

'Street-walkers?' Ho had echoed, when he saw Hanoi within his grasp. 'We shall arrange that they walk the streets all the nights of their lives.' And in the lightless capital of 1965 grim, faded Vietnamese women still moved down the avenues in aggressive pairs, never stepping aside for the oncomer. Symbols of the revolution, they had become the city road-sweepers, no longer pushing sex or drugs in the small hours, but heavy brooms. The population had risen to nearly eighteen million, most of it crowded into the Red River Delta, and pretentious plans for raising rice production had failed miserably in practice. North Vietnam had remained obstinately poor and the people were told to take in yet another notch on their belts. Nationwide anti-American demonstrations were now only held on paper, for the country could not afford to waste man-hours on protest.

In mid-1968, however, the North Vietnamese were still energetically digging shelters in Hanoi, convinced that the peace talks in Paris would collapse and the Americans would start bombing them again on a bigger scale. And behind this grim appreciation lay the determination of the North Vietnamese leaders to be tough and take the consequences. Their mood was marked by a kind of serene obstinacy, it seemed, and they only wanted an end of the peculiar miseries of their struggle if it could be bought dirt cheap. Otherwise they would rather soldier on, for they were more fearful of being cheated in peace than defeated in war. Despite much official finger-wagging at faint hearts, most cadres were neither fatalistic nor fanatical, but treated death and destruction from above as quotidian hazards like TB and traffic accidents. 'They plant flower beds, invite foreign lecturers to come and instruct their scattered university faculties in obscure and often rather useless subjects, and they have even asked the French for advice on raising edible snails when the war is won,' a diplomat stationed in Hanoi told me. 'They have plans for bigger and better factories and irrigation schemes to replace what has been destroyed. In short, they live almost uncannily in the future.'

But for millions it was becoming a little difficult to satisfy Uncle Ho's standards of self-abnegation. Crunch-drunk peasants and workers felt their resolution slowly sinking within them by 1969, and even the armed forces were veined with the hair-cracks of 'negative rightist tendencies'. The stony determination to struggle on until the Americans respected the Geneva Agreements and got out of Vietnam was still there, and it endured until they did get out in 1973, but the years of privation in a penurious land had relentlessly worn away at muscle and spirit.

Where callous neglect makes men dream of drastic remedies, Communism may have its own mystical appeal. But where they have roofs and rice and a reasonable relationship with their fellow-men, it has been discredited as something that is no longer social surgery, but social butchery that leaves the patient mentally lame and physically impoverished.

'Communism is for poor countries like China,' a Cambodian officer told me flatly in 1964 as we stared at the damage done to a small thatched village on the border of South Vietnam by a bomber or two. 'It's not for Cambodia – whatever the Americans do. We are royalists in a small kingdom most of whose subjects are happy with their prince.' The Cambodian peasant was prosperous enough by his own standards and had long since fallen victim to the status symbol. Every third family had its first bicycle and its transistor radio. The people lived in a lush, luke-warm land, they had all that they needed of rice and fish and clothing and shelter, and they often owned the fields they tilled. Moreover: 'If Sihanouk made us work as hard as the Chinese,' one Cambodian murmured with a slow shake of the head, 'we should simply *die*.' He was not to know that nine years later his exiled prince would be making common cause with the Cambodian Communists in Peking, and that left-wing forces would control most of the country.

'Overcrowded China may need Communism,' a provincial governor in Laos echoed, 'but we don't need it here. Our people have a warm climate, enough to eat ...' 'The Communist movement in Thailand has to rely largely on foreign subversives,' at least a dozen Thais have emphasized to me. 'Our people are devoutly Buddhist and very loyal to the King. Except in the North-east, they are not poor, and we have far more food than we can eat. Now in North Vietnam, on the other hand ...'

Although events seemed to give them the lie, they were voicing an underlying truth. If democracy often appeared to be a delusion to the educated South-east Asian, Communism was the reflex of despair. He was therefore tempted to turn back to his own past to find the key to his own future – the third system that was not listed among the official solutions.

11

'Bonjour, Altesse'

IT was certainly not beyond his resourcefulness. Necessity being the mother of makeshift, the needy Asian has a flair for improvising unorthodox, string-and-wire substitutes denied to those who can get their arms and institutions off the shelf.

I was to be reminded of this sharply when the Vietcong opened the second round in Indochina, and on my first operation a South Vietnamese officer took my arm solicitously as I was about to step on to a fallen palm-leaf. He lifted the leaf, exposing a neatly-cut trench in which lay a 'spike-mine', a two-foot-long upturned hairbrush of sharpened six-inch nails driven through a base-board. The Vietcong were making bombs out of milk cans filled with rusty nails, bazookas from gas piping, grenades packed with buffalo manure (the ammonium nitrate only needed a small charge to explode it), and in 1968 they came up with the 'flying trashcan'. This was essentially a dust-binful of TNT fired by the motor of a 122-mm rocket but with ten times the kick, and launched from the twin rails of a seven-foot wooden ladder that could be knocked together on the spot.

Down at Sadec in the Mekong Delta I picked up a Vietcong leaflet on how to deal with Imperialist running dogs in the shape of Alsatians imported to track down guerrillas. This also was a model of slightly misguided ingenuity, and read:

To make the dogs lose their sense of direction when they are chasing us, confuse their sense of smell with mixed odours. Garlic, onions, perfumes like eau-de-cologne, and overripe pepper-corns will all make difficulties for them. When we camouflage ourselves, we should use these items, either spreading them on our bodies or over the vent-holes of our underground hideouts. When in close combat, aromatic foods like fried fish and roasted meats can be thrown to the dog to put him off. You should also discard your sweaty jacket or shirt to

distract him. If the dog is up with you, give him your hand to bite
and then stab him. Or use a cloth which he will start to worry, and
then kick him in the belly, when he will instantly die ...

The arresting vision of a Vietcong in his undervest, a fried fish
in one hand and a bottle of Chanel Cinq in the other, kicking an
Alsatian in the crutch as it worries away at his garlic-sprinkled
jacket should not obscure the inventiveness of the Vietcong
provincial commissar who composed these instructions.

Ingenuity was not confined to one side, however. Sitting in a
command post in the swamplands of the South in 1962, I saw
an odd collection of implements in a corner, and a South Vietnamese officer who had followed my eye pulled out a bundle
of piping that looked as if it had come from a South London
scrap-heap. 'It's an exact copy of an American sixty-millimetre
mortar, without the frills,' he explained. 'It works just as well
and costs only 3,000 piastres to make.' Three thousand piastres
was fifteen pounds, but why make copies when the originals
were available? 'We don't have enough,' he retorted, 'and also
there is hell to pay if we lose an American weapon to the Vietcong, although nobody seems to care much if we lose a Vietnamese soldier. So we keep the American mortars safe in a
headquarter store and use these instead. A blacksmith in the
district capital turns them out for us in a converted garage.'

The Asian is often refreshingly free from the bonds of western convention in national and international affairs. Prince
Norodom Sihanouk of Cambodia was therefore able to tell a
startled Washington that he was ready to hand back American
soldiers from Vietnam caught across the border on Cambodian
soil if the United States recognized his frontiers – or alterna-
tively sent him a bulldozer or a tractor in exchange for each
man. Nor could anyone deny that men like Dr Goh Keng Swee
think high, wide and handsomely. In 1965 and at the height of
Indonesia's military 'Confrontation' of Malaysia we sat together
in a corner of the Adelphi Grill in Singapore, and as the island's
Finance Minister bent his puckish face over the roast pork and
baked potatoes, he suggested how he might bring President
Sukarno to his knees. It was all quite logical really (mustard,

hm?), he said in his gentle, rumbling rock-a-bye tones. Indonesia had to import about one million tons of rice a year to
feed the population. He, Dr Goh, would therefore corner the
rice market and cut off every possible source of supply to
Djakarta (apple sauce?). The corner would leave Indonesia im-
possibly dependent upon an overstrained Communist China.
The rice would be immobilized in Bangkok, Rangoon and other
capitals, and could be sold off cheap later, Mmm? I gazed at
him with reverence, but shortly afterwards Singapore was dropped from the Federation of Malaysia and virtually out of the
conflict.

A knowledge that outrageous fortune can only be challenged
with outrageous nerve animates Asians who come up with the
off-beat answer, or casually shrug on a new role. Sinnathamby
Rajaratnam now performed this impressive quick-change act,
for Singapore had become an independent republic overnight
and he found himself Foreign Minister.

I first knew Raja as a leader-writer on the *Straits Times*, and
even after he became local Minister of Culture my mental
portrait of him did not change. He was still a sandalled figure
in a Hawaii shirt, sipping a slow beer after an unfairly canny
game of badminton and kicking some subject around in a dis-
cursive way, while his eye rested half-seeing on the predatory
dendrobium orchids cultivated by his Hungarian wife in the
sun-bitten garden of their bungalow down the road.

But on 10 August 1965, Raja was suddenly His Excellency –
immaculately turned out in a sober, well-cut suit, shooting his
gleaming cuffs, the touch of distinction at his temples adding
to the impression of a well-poised brown man grey at the edges,
in agreeable contrast to so many of his new calling who manage
to look undistinguished grey men already brown at the edges.
From the outset, his words matched his appearance. His first
policy statements showed a fine regard for the niceties of diplomatic compromise, and a good eye for the cover offered by a
well-grown thicket of generalizations. 'Do not ask us to take
your friends as our friends,' he appealed to other countries, 'or
your enemies as our enemies.' It was the perfect expression of
Singapore's desire to be little pal to all the world. Yet when

Raja became the world's first instant Foreign Minister he was without an office, without a staff, and without a known policy. 'He makes it up as he goes along,' someone said without malice, completing the picture of His Excellency wandering around, looking for somewhere to sit and someone to give him a sharpened pencil or a cup of coffee.

Accommodation was not the only problem. Singapore had no Foreign Service, no passport office, and almost no French-speakers. Rajaratnam had to filch the Prime Minister's protocol expert, since nobody else was familiar with procedure. But no one flapped his hands in horror because there was no precedent for this particular nightmare. Unorthodox problems simply called for unorthodox solutions. For many Asians, niceties of procedure and principle are academic luxuries that it is not always possible to afford. And since this is true of American democracy as well as American 60-millimetre mortars, oriental leaders have also exploited their talents for confounding convention by dreaming up their own substitutes for God's Own Constitution.

Asians are nevertheless fettered by their own traditions, and these may have nothing in common with the moral and egalitarian principles of Jesus, Jefferson and Karl Marx.

In the Malay world, the sacred oriental principle that all men are unequal was challenged by the teachings of Mohammed, but with indifferent success. Under its thin flaking coat of Islam, Malay society retained an exquisitely intricate pecking order in which differences of birth and rank not only determined the elaborate etiquette but the form of speech, for there were quite different languages for talking 'upwards' or talking 'downwards'.

The traditional Javanese would have been repelled by Christian principles of 'good' and 'evil', as a democratic American is repelled by the very thought of Mao Tse-tung, for the reprehensible idea of an abstract 'goodness' which anyone from prince to pauper could acquire with a little practice would seem to strike wickedly at the whole hierarchical structure of society. The Javanese moral measures were *alus* and *kasar*, which carry implications of 'gracious' and 'ungracious', even 'smooth' and 'rough'. And these attributes, like the uniforms and insignia, went with the rank. Kings were gracious, of course, and yokels were rude.

The Javanese village child acquires his pattern of conscience while sitting wide-eyed before the *wayang kulit*. The *wayang kulit* is the travelling puppet theatre, at which coconut-oil lamps throw on to a screen the shadows of grotesque figures fashioned from polished and gilded buffalo-hide as they play out stories from the great Hindu epics. These are ostensibly moral tales, but the characters are not judged by their actions as much as by their fidelity to their caste and their predestined role. Perhaps the greatest hero of all in the *wayang kulit* epics is a man who deliberately kills his own brother in battle, after flinching from the act. If he had dodged his disagreeable destiny, he would no longer be a hero at all. The young prince who shies away from butchering a beloved servant (in order to end a plague) is contemptuously dismissed for his failure to be princely. Men must above all do what is appropriate to their station.

Once, therefore, that the play-actor reads murder into his role, 'Thou shalt not kill' becomes a counsel of deceit, even if he has it on the highest authority. A Javanese can easily short-circuit his own conscience, and this partly explains how the abortive Communist coup of 1965 in Indonesia was followed by a bestial blood-letting in which hundreds of thousands were slaughtered. It was all in the script, so it was all inevitable anyway.

Since there was no conception of equal rights but only of unequal roles, it was hardly surprising that British officials in Malaya a century ago found that Rajahs were justifying everything they did as 'Malay Custom', and rewriting it to suit their own convenience as they went along. Peasants were forced to work for local chiefs for as much as three months of the year, and a prince could oblige parents to present him with their children simply by sending a messenger bearing a *kris*. The terrible system of debt-slavery permitted a creditor not only to seize the man who owed him even a trifling sum, but to take his wife and family and even unborn offspring into bondage also – and the Rajah was the one major creditor in any region.

It was left to the unbelieving British to put an end to these abuses, for Islam recognized bondage, and Muslim teaching dovetailed neatly enough with earlier practices.

In Chen-la wealthy families might have a hundred slaves who lived below the floorboards and among the stilts supporting their masters' houses. They were not called 'man' and 'woman' but equivalents of 'bull' and 'cow', and had to kneel and bow their heads to the floor on entering the door. The tradition clings stubbornly to life. Interviewing a leading Democrat in Bangkok the first time that I went to Thailand, I was startled during our conversation to glimpse, out of the corner of my eye, some poor legless creature hauling himself across the floor towards us with a tea tray held above his head in one hand. But he was not legless, and he was not hauling; he was crawling. It was the servant's normal way of approaching his master. Dr Dooley records that since no simple Lao might hold his head higher than that of a mandarin, he sometimes found himself chasing his patients down to the very dirt floor in order to listen to their heartbeat.

The Laotians may say : 'The lotus flower grows at the level of the lake water,' but they are sticklers for servility, and touchy about their dignity, and if a Lao talks to a superior, he refers to himself as 'Little slave'. It is unsafe to call a stranger 'Monsieur' in Cambodia and Laos, and when a British diplomat had the temerity to use this humble form of address to a rather seedy-looking individual chalking a cue in the Phnom Penh Sporting Club whom he took to be a billiard-marker, he was at once corrected with a haughty : '*Altesse!*'

In a feudal society it is not unnaturally a small aristocratic clique that provides the political yeast, and the postwar anti-colonial movement in Laos was led by three Royal Princes, among whom were not only the future neutralist prime minister, Prince Souvanna Phouma, but his half-brother and leader of the Communist-directed Pathet Lao, Prince Souphannouvong. My happiest memory of the hierarchy, however, dates back to 1962, when the right-wing Royal Laotian Government of Prince Boun Oum in Vientiane was being challenged by a left-wing rebel 'government' at Khang Khay, where the neutralists loyal to Prince Souvanna Phouma and the Pathet Lao loyal to Prince Souphannouvong maintained an uneasy alliance.

It was possible to fly over the non-existent front line, and one glorious morning in March I climbed into a light plane clutching an overnight bag and a bottle of Scotch for Prince Souvanna Phouma, for his headquarters was out on the bare, parched Plain of Jars to the north, and I had been told he would appreciate a little spiritual comfort. The aircraft having been loaded with leaking tins of kerosene for delivery to the enemy, an unshaven Corsican pilot climbed in beside me with a half-smoked Gauloise between his lips, and we soared above the great heaving stone rollers that rear, wave after wave, over Northern Laos and into the blank blue stare of the Indochinese sky.

We landed on a dusty patch of burned plain, and I cadged a lift in a Polish jeep which was calling at Khang Khay. The seat of Prince Souvanna Phouma's government was an old French outpost on a hill. The floor was of stone, the walls of plaster and whitewash, and most of it was divided into rather small bare rooms like cells in a particularly comfortless monastery. Each wooden door was labelled with a magnificent legend like *Ministère des Affaires Étrangères, Cabinet de Son Excellence le Ministre, Commandant-en-chef des forces armées, Président de l'Assemblée Nationale*, and so on, until I began to be afraid to go through any of them, in case on the other side I suddenly found myself looking on to the Place Bourbon in Paris, or the Quai d'Orsay, or the Invalides, as in some nightmare provoked by a surfeit of science fiction. Finally I found one marked *Président du Conseil: S.A.R. Le Prince Souvanna Phouma* (or words and initials to that effect). Inside was an anteroom, empty but for a decrepit chaise-longue, two trestle tables, and a number of not very new cobwebs. Here I was asked to wait. His Royal Highness was out.

The two princes finally returned together, Souvanna Phouma looking, as usual, startlingly like Edward G. Robinson and smoking the inevitable cigar, while the stocky, moustachioed Souphannouvong with his oiled wedge of beard had the air of a Ruritanian forester, so that I half expected him to be wearing leggings and a frogged and fur-collared jacket. I gave Souvanna Phouma the bottle of whisky, for which he thanked me gravely. 'We live simply here, under campaign conditions,' he said. 'However, your kindness reminds me. As it happens, we are having a reception tonight for the delegation from North Vietnam. I hope you will stay, but I must just put some things out ...' He wandered into his bed-sitter next door and presently returned, his arms embracing half a case of Scotch (of a better brand than I had bought him) and a small trunk of best-quality Burmese cheroots. The contents of these he placed at intervals on the trestle tables, which orderlies then loaded with Laotian delicacies while Souvanna Phouma poured lethal measures of liquor for the three of us.

The party itself was undoubtedly the event of the Khang Khay season. The princes turned up for it impeccably dressed, and set the tone for the diplomatic corps – the Russian Embassy, the Chinese Cultural Mission, the Vietnamese Communists and the Czech and Polish delegates. The Chinese and the Vietnamese formed their own drab little coteries in the corners, but otherwise it was one of those loud, confident affairs and I had to keep my eyes upon the stone floor, the naked bulbs, the bare bucolic walls and the cobwebs to stop my four-dimensional nightmare from recurring. Sound parted company agonizingly with sight, for while the scene was a drab fort at Khang Khay, the voices belonged to the elegant chancelleries of Europe. Glasses clinked cheerfully and fragments of French conversation straight out of *Congress Dances* rode the storm of polite chatter : 'His Royal Highness has just been telling me ...' Heels click : 'Excellency, allow me to present ...' 'I assure you, my dear General ...' A little ripple of laughter : 'But certainly you are joking, Highness ...' There was not a mister in the place except me, for even a rather gloomy-looking Slovak was apparently a *Conseiller* and had to be addressed ceremoniously as such. 'We want to get this war over with, you know,' Souphannouvong said to me over his scotch and cigar. 'Stop all this nonsense and get back to some good hunting.' I swear if he had been speaking English, he would have dropped the final 'g'. I left eventually, consoled by the thought that if I stood nowhere on the Laotian ladder, at least my name was more than twenty years old.

The Laos had had little to do with names; they had dealt primarily in titles. As men climbed, new titles smothered the old, and also obliterated any rudimentary sobriquets they might have been given by misguided parents when young. These would almost certainly have been derogatory, for worried fathers deceived the evil spirits that might be greedy to possess their offspring by calling them by such unattractive labels as 'Stinky', 'Monkey', 'Bitchie'. It was only in 1943 that a law was passed compelling all Laotians to have names; they themselves were only interested in honorifics.

As in other parts of the world, classes have become confused in South-east Asia. But the old arrogance still subtly poisons political relationships. Malay critics of Tengku Abdul Rahman, the former Prime Minister of Malaysia, stress that he was a prince as well as a premier and had emerged from a feudal society founded on the subservience of the inferior and the patronage of the superior. In his hierarchical mind men were either above or below each other. They could not be equal. He therefore regarded Lee Kuan Yew of Singapore as beneath him, and when Lee claimed equality, the Tengku found it an impertinence.

Sukarno looked down his broad nose at President Macapagal ('his wife had to teach him how to use a knife and fork'), and Sihanouk despised Sukarno as a *parvenu* ('he has the manners of a peasant'). The frail unity of the Laotian neutralists was constantly endangered by Prince Souvanna Phouma's patrician disdain for General Kong Le and his somewhat frayed French. Meanwhile on the anti-Communist side the bulky Boun Oum, Prince of Champassak, Lord of Southern Laos, is a true *seigneur*. He has been known to draw a revolver and shoot at drivers who had the effrontery to fail to pull over and let his car pass, but he doses his despotism with a kindly condescension. 'We must not be nasty to them,' he once remarked fruitily of his plebeian Marxist enemies. 'They are only *pauvres types*, there is no real evil in them, and anyway you can get medicine even out of a poisonous mushroom.'

Boun Oum is at his best in his own great domain, moving ponderously among his peasantry, yet indulging his own aristocratic whims – like making fish drunk on whisky-soaked bread, catching them when they pass out and float to the surface, and throwing them back to recover from their hangover when they come to. A good-natured elephant of a man, latest of a long line of autocrats, he dresses deceptively simply. I see him lolling on the terrace of the Settha Palace in Vientiane in an open-necked shirt and white slacks, sandals on his feet and around his magnificent circumference a leather belt whose cheap brass buckle is inscribed in large letters with the single, evocative word: *Giant*.

Perhaps that one word said all that Prince Boun Oum wanted to say about himself, doing duty for ceremonial dress and a galaxy of tinkling decorations. He was who he was, he did not have to prove anything to anybody. But most Asians turn everything into a uniform and a status symbol, and the region is already full of them: the Chinese *amah* proudly wears the white coat and black trousers of her sorority, the Singapore heavy construction worker her red head-dress and blue denims, the Burmese his *longgyi*, the Malay his *sarong*, the Vietnamese peasant her pyjamas (black in the south, brown in the north) and her teeth (white in the south, black in the north).

The Malay head-dress may appear to be a glorified handker-chief to the uninstructed eye, but like a damask napkin it can be folded into dozens of different shapes – some with delightful names like 'eagle in the wind' and 'fighting elephant' – which reveal the class of the wearer and his position in society. In Indonesia there are so many uniforms and insignia of rank that even the Indonesians themselves are bewildered and may mistake a tax collector for a colonel or a postman for a public prosecutor, but each is content that he is wearing the appropriate emblems of his station in life.

It follows that men who change may be cheats. When Tengku Abdul Rahman was invited to Tokyo by President Sukarno, ostensibly to negotiate a peaceful settlement of their dispute over the formation of Malaysia, he went hoping for the best. But with a musing, faintly aggrieved air he told us afterwards : 'Every day he changed his uniform. Sometimes he wore white, sometimes he wore black, sometimes blue, sometimes khaki. Here we were discussing a vital issue, and there he was changing uniforms. Now he says whoever is friendly to Malaysia is his enemy. This is how a man who changes his uniform from time to time behaves.'

A change of uniform has nevertheless provided one of the colourful 'third solutions' to the problem of government in Asia, where a flair for improvisation and despotic habits of thought have usually combined to ensure that their highest common factor shall be the power of Number One.

The time-honoured device of restoring law and order once the politicians have made a mess of things is, of course, the military coup, and this is a favourite alternative to democracy and the dictatorship of the proletariat among less imaginative Asians. The coup is habit-forming because in many countries the army has not only held the gun, but has been the only disciplined organization capable of shaking up a slothful state wallowing in its own incompetence and corruption. When the soldiers took over South Korea in 1961, therefore, they very typically began by treating the place like a mutinous infantry depot, and draconian decrees were at once issued to curb every evil from Communist subversion to overeating. But it was in Korea that the first variation on military dictatorship was played, when in 1963 General Park announced that he and other officers of the ruling military junta would don mufti and stand for election as members of a new Democratic Republican Party. The blood-and-iron hand was still there, however, if concealed within the velvet glove of civilian government. Suitable constitutional amendments were introduced to ensure that no undesirable could be voted into parliament or the presidency, which would be reserved for Chung-hee ('call-me-mister') Park. The Democratic Republican Party was crammed with colonels who fought their way into lounge suits for the hustings, and in 1969 Korea was still being governed by men with curiously familiar faces and tell-tale ramrod backs.

General Ne Win's rule by a Revolutionary Council of colonels in Burma has a different flavour, however. At Rangoon Airport the immigration officer records not only the date of my arrival, but also the hour. 'You must be back at this desk, ready to leave the country at exactly this time tomorrow,' he warns in the clipped tones of the efficient bureaucrat – and then writes the wrong date of departure under his entry stamp in my passport, inadvertently extending my twenty-four-hour transit visa for a further nine days. The non-committal mask, the nervous inflexibility, the fluster leading to the silly mistake, and the fact that the Government would not allow a foreign journalist to spend more than one day in the country all belong to the new Burma of the nineteen-sixties – a socialist state ruled by a left-wing military junta that has its own civil service running scared.

Ne Win had done more than change the régime by changing his clothes. He had been striving for a new form of Marxism so Burmese that it would make Titoism look as orthodox as a black bowler hat. After he seized power for the second time in 1962, he introduced his own philosophical formula for running the lives of his 25,000,000 fellow-citizens – the Burmese Way to Socialism. The doctrine condemned man's exploitation of man and all systems based on self-seeking, and advocated the nationalization of everything as a panacea for economic ills. So far, so socialist. But the *Philosophy of the Burma Socialist Programme Party* attacked 'dogmatic leftist imperialism with its quasi-despotic relations with the masses', allowed a place for individual initiative, and was shot through with humanistic Buddhist teachings about respecting the dignity of man. It was poor commons for the Maoists.

While Ne Win may have made concessions to Buddhism, however, he made none to democracy at that stage. For the first six years of his rule the list of political prisoners he held in gaol read like *Who's Who in Burma*, all political organizations were abolished, except for his own official party, and the Government armed itself with an act that empowered it to suspend or extend any law as it pleased.

The press was 'guided' rather than censored, but the trade unions were replaced with 'People's Workers Councils', all shops and wholesalers were absorbed into the 'People's Stores Corporation', fourteen foreign and eight Burmese banks became 'People's Banks', pharmacies became 'People's Drug Stores' and the rice industry – responsible for 70 per cent of all foreign exchange earnings – was also nationalized.

Unfortunately the administration was simply not built to take the load. Rice and cooking oil were soon in short supply, a severe rationing system covering most everyday needs from soap to sarongs was introduced, and the bureaucracy seized up. For lack of official sanction to distribute them, umbrellas remained in warehouses until the rains stopped. Grown men applied for permission to buy a toothbrush or a pair of trousers or a bicycle tyre and waited six weeks for it to be granted, while toothbrushes and trousers and tyres rotted in the Rangoon depots. The country drifted gently towards ruin. In a friendly game of political poker Ne Win had proved that an officer's well-filled holster beat a politician's well-filled pockets, and had introduced his own alternative to parliamentary democracy and Communism. The only trouble with it was that it did not work.

The General then began cautiously loosening the strait-jacket. He freed his most important political opponents, converted his party into a mass organization, took four genuine civilians into his cabinet, and in October 1973 announced that a new constitution would be put to the vote in a public referendum. Burmese Socialism continued to wreak havoc on the economy, however, and when he also announced a new twenty-year plan to raise living standards, a tremor of fear rather than expectation ran through the country.

In Saigon President Ngo Dinh Diem was not worried by the socialistic itch among his entourage that prompted Ne Win's to-each-according-to-his-labour-while-stocks-last offer, for the Ngos – six brothers in search of absolute authority – came of a family of autocratic mandarins. Discarding democracy as 'the wrong tool' for Vietnam, Diem substituted his own political philosophy of Personalism. This provided that while the personal freedoms of the individual were sacred, he should not be trusted with political freedom until he was morally educated to handle it with safety. The would-be parliamentarian, in short, must first be House-trained. His own system was based on an inner, secret political party for his trusties and an outer 'Revolutionary Movement' for the *hoi polloi*.

While hunting trophies snarled at us from the walls, Ngo Dinh Nhu, the President's brother and 'Political Counsellor', explained this plausible paternal nasty-matches-let-daddy-do-it philosophy to me on the top floor of the presidential palace, and excused the most authoritarian régime in South-east Asia by pointing out that South Vietnam was engaged in a life-and-death struggle with Communism and claiming that 'only a revolutionary party can fight a revolutionary party'. The best weapon against the horrors of subjection by a ruthless, fanatical, totalitarian, brainwashed robot of a political organization was a ruthless, fanatical, totalitarian, brainwashed robot of a political organization. He made it sound very convincing, we drank tea to stifle our yawns, and in November 1963 Diem and Nhu were violently depersonalized themselves.

The God-Kings

IN Cambodia Asian invention had meanwhile produced a more exotic political hybrid whose name suggested that Prince Norodom Sihanouk had successfully crossed three philosophical concepts simultaneously, for he called the result Royal Buddhist Socialism.

Few eyebrows were raised. Little seems strange in a land whose main river flows upstream at New Year (which falls in April) and where fish can be dug out of the ground or searched for in the trees after the floodwaters subside. The 'socialist' state of Cambodia had its typically untypical origins in 1955, when Sihanouk abdicated the throne in favour of his own father and proceeded to run the country under the title of 'Monseigneur' (since not even Cambodia could bear both a monarch and a president). On the death of his father, the royal seat itself remained vacant and merely symbolized the monarchy. The prince was the living power. His method of establishing popular opinion was to organize a referendum whenever it looked as if someone really did not like him much after all, but until 1970 the response was always a roar for more Sihanouk.

Nearly seven centuries ago a peripatetic Chinese wrote of the customs of Chen-la: 'Twice each day the king holds an audience. Whoever desires to see the king – either officials or any private person – may approach and sit down on a lion's skin. When all matters are disposed of, the king retires.' But I see the Prince across only a handful of dusty years, standing in the palace courtyard in Phnom Penh before a great mob of Khmers. 'Buffalo tax in Battambang Province?' he is shouting at some sweating peasant. 'No, I can't lower it without knowing more about this. Here,' (this to some cringing court lackey) 'where's the Finance Minister? He's supposed to be here – go and fetch him.' Sihanouk mops his face, while the crowd surges around in the sticky heat. This is a Popular Audience, the Khmer tradition which still brings the ruler of Cambodia face to face with his subjects, to listen to their complaints about lazy and corrupt officials, nose-high seed prices, or the iniquities of the local soldiery. The prince talks it out with a line of indignant plaintiffs, and the dialogue is broadcast live to the nation in cacophonous Khmer. Later a special complaints bureau will handle most of the moaning, but the tradition remains very much alive.

'Monseigneur' will be overthrown early in 1970 while he is away in France, but observe him in the setting of the sixties, the autocrat of today who does not know that he is the exile of tomorrow. Ex-King, Head of State, semi-divine, Sihanouk is also the President of the Popular Socialist Community, a mass movement that includes the government and the civil service and almost everyone in the country with a political thought in his head, so that all differences of opinion are kept in the family and not allowed to give rise to anything so unhealthy as inter-party strife.

Cambodia nevertheless provides some of the liveliest democratic give-and-take since the days when any citizen of the Roman Republic could stand up and abuse his betters in the Forum. The Community holds a congress twice a year at which members and provincial delegates may castigate the government, lay charges publicly against any official or even minister, and ask to see the nation's accounts. The Cabinet must be present to face the music. The hero of the day is always Sihanouk, who may dress down his administrative aides there and then if untimely revelations bring a blush to the cheek. In Cambodia all is done by mirrors – the mirrors of a million dusky faces that reflect the will and the wishes of Monseigneur back upon himself, investing him at these congresses with the collective authority of the nation. Royal Buddhist Socialism adds another remarkable Cambodian paradox to the upswept rivers and the treed fish – one-man democracy.

Vox Dei Vox Populi Vox Dei. At Angkor the monarch was

the Devaraja, the king who was worshipped as a god, the master of the world below who held all justice and authority in his holy hand, and who would be immortalized in stone as Vishnu or Shiva or Brahma. Not surprisingly, Sihanouk enthusiastically identifies his Cambodia with the glories of Angkor, and takes every distinguished visitor to see its marvels, from Princess Alexandra to Premier Chou En-lai. 'See how smooth the stone has been worn,' he says lovingly, inviting the Chinese Prime Minister to stroke the more tempting rotundities of a heavenly dancing girl in bas-relief. 'Many people have done the same before you.' Chou En-lai complies, and a lucky photographer gets a unique shot of the gentleman from austere Peking in the act of forgetting his austerity and being not quite a gentleman.

A few weeks after this episode I stood with Ping amid the broken and tumbled stone of the temple-monument of Preah Khan at Angkor, a complex of long, gloomy corridors and great, still courtyards split and burst by the obscene roots of the giant banyan and silent now under a siege of jungle vegetation. As we stumbled out to the entrance, the clammy air closed over us like a soft unseen hand and the sky went black. Abruptly a thousand forest cicadas set up their sharp, shrill whistle of warning, the first heavy drops fell through an unnatural dusk that had turned the whole world to carved grey stone, and then the storm broke in a rolling sea of rain. It was impossible not to feel the spell of something dark and ancient and alien in the drowned ruin, far removed, it seemed, from the plump, smiling prince in the city suit whom I had left perched on a red plush sofa in Phnom Penh the day before.

Sipping his champagne as we talked, Sihanouk had once again reminded me of some middle-aged gossiping dandy in a Sheridan play or a Mozart opera, for his large, glossy eyes, his flamboyant gestures and his carrying upper-register voice with its stage-French enunciation hold his audience in the same way, so that I miss the wig and the waving lace, the silken hose and buckled shoes. He had discovered that Ping and I were driving to Angkor after I had cabled my interview with him to the *Observer*, and had at once summoned aides and given orders that the provincial dignitaries there should be told to look after us when we arrived. Later, a peremptory telephone call from Phnom Penh instructed those responsible that all our bills would be met by Monseigneur personally.

Correspondents should pay their own way, but this invitation to be the guests of the Prince amounted to a royal command. When we returned, wet and tacky from our visit to Preah Khan, waiters were obsequious, and we were served a creditable dinner. It was as we were drinking an excellent wine at the Prince's expense that someone switched on the news. This included an acerbic commentary inspired by Monseigneur himself on the scurrilous and tendentious inaccuracies about Cambodian policy published by the *Observer* of that day's date. These had been contained in a dispatch cabled from Phnom Penh by the newspaper's Far East correspondent, Dennis Bloodworth, and must be categorically refuted as totally false. My glass half-way to my mouth, I felt the wine slowly turning sour in my hand. It was time to pack and go.

The unshaven comments of foreign reporters regularly provoke the sore and sensitive Sihanouk to the vexed protest of a girl who gets a rasping every time she gets a kiss. He wants foreign publicity, but it makes him gasp with pain, for even the most friendly article will contain at least one observation or descriptive epithet that any right-thinking Cambodian ruler must regard as *lèse-majesté* if not blasphemy. A man of boundless vitality, he spends an inordinate amount of time personally contradicting the calumnies published against Cambodia and himself.

Everything is sacrosanct. When I described an Independence Day parade in Phnom Penh, and remarked that the troops carried an assortment of French, Chinese, Russian and Czech weapons but marched in American boots, the national news agency accused me of 'ridiculing and insulting' Cambodia. There was no doubt about the exalted origin of this attack which solemnly concluded: 'There are, even so, things that our troops owe to no foreign country and to no foreign aid – their blood, their bodies, their hearts, their lives and their unshakeable will to do their duty, *even in bare feet.*' (My italics, for once.)

In November 1964 I wrote an article which was largely devoted to supporting Sihanouk's contention that he was not deliberately helping the Vietcong. But I also listed some of the absurdities of Communist aid to Cambodia, and referred to the well-organized veneration which Monseigneur enjoyed. This was evidently intolerable. On 4 December I was sent a letter embossed with the Royal Cambodian coat of arms and signed 'N. Sihanouk' which began: 'I have learned with profound disappointment of your article on Cambodia published in Hongkong. I have accorded you my confidence and my friendship and had the right to hope for your comprehension or at least your objectivity.' He regretted to see, however, that I had 'rejoined the cohort of American journalists who dishonour their country'.

I wrote back to the Prince, explaining what I and my colleagues understood by 'objectivity', and this drew another royal salvo six weeks later – five pages of single-spaced typing which analysed what the Prince took to be every treacherous line I had written. For example, I had described him as 'flanked by Marshal Chen Yi and the Soviet ambassador' on Independence Day although the French ambassador had also been close to him: this was a dishonest distortion intended to show him up as a pro-Communist. His letter concluded with a sharp twist to the conventional French ending: 'Veuillez agréer, Monsieur, l'expression de ma déception' (the last words added in his own handwriting).

I then served three pages explaining that the point I was making was that the Anglo-Saxon powers had lost ground heavily to the Eastern Bloc in Cambodia through their own clumsy policies, and moved up to the net to meet his other criticisms. In April 1965 back came yet another missive in which the Prince wrote: 'I see no object in replying again, for I do not wish to poison matters further – and for the rest, we shall never finish, each of us not believing himself in the wrong.' Deuce. But later that year I did a television commentary on Cambodia in Singapore, reiterating much that I had said in my articles about the Prince and the Vietcong. This earned me a 161-word cable from Sihanouk thanking me 'very sincerely for the objectivity you have manifested towards my country and myself ...' and ending 'with all my gratitude and my cordial memory norodom sihanouk head of state cambodia.' I was, it seemed, back among the blessed again.

But for how long? If, as our forefathers believed, our personal devil stands behind our left shoulder to tempt us, while our personal angel stands behind our right shoulder to admonish us, Sihanouk's eternal problem with correspondents was that he could not give a visa to the angel without letting in the devil. And while one might have a tongue of sugar, the other was constantly tasting spilled salt.

It was enough to describe Cambodia as a little country with a population of 'only' seven millions to rouse the royal wrath, and among other effusions of Monseigneur's spiky and prolific pen was a publication entitled *Open Letter to the International Press* in which he not only made the point that there were forty countries in the United Nations which were smaller than Cambodia, but listed them all, giving the precise area of each down to the last square kilometre.

It might be protested that with so prickly a prince you could not win, but much of his malice was provoked by a doltish diplomacy which earlier failed to recognize in him the godking to whom no slight should be offered. His favour sanctioned all, his fury forbade all. To court him was to court Cambodia. Yet the first American ambassador to Phnom Penh took his dog with him when granted an audience by Sihanouk, and a high-ranking British official once presented him with a couple of LP records in a paper bag with the bill still inside it. He does not forget these things, and it is not surprising if we find him writing venomously: 'The USA and the West will always symbolize in my eyes, until I die, injustice, inequality, discrimination.' He might well have added 'and downright bad manners'.

On the other hand, all is permitted to the Prince. He will betray diplomatic confidences to the world at large when it suits his convenience, insult envoys in public speeches, insinuate on the radio that a British ambassador drinks too much. But this also has its lighter side.

Diplomats are accustomed to glancing at the bottom corner of any official invitation cards they receive for the words *tenue de soir* or *tenue de ville* which tell them how they should dress for a function, but in 1960 the ingenious Sihanouk introduced a new and ominous variation of this theme – *tenue de travail* (working clothes). Since no power had offered to construct it for him, the Prince had decided to build a railway from the capital to the new port of Sihanoukville with Cambodian manual labour, and to augment his work-force of unskilled hands by inviting the heads of some sixteen diplomatic missions in Phnom Penh to join him in laying the foundations of the track.

Every so often, therefore, an impressive convoy of shining limousines set out from the capital, carrying these polished gentlemen from their embassies to their unusual place of work. Shortly afterwards sweat-stained ambassadors, wearing anything from khaki shorts and bushwhacker hats to Savile Row slacks and Charvet scarves, could be seen shovelling earth into baskets which were then passed down a human conveyor-belt of senior Khmer officials. Loudspeakers filled the air with jazz, while Sihanouk himself, a round figure in shorts and white singlet, dug away briskly. At lunchtime, all retired to a marquee for a superb French meal washed down with champagne. But cynics alleged that urgent coded diplomatic messages were soon flashing to Washington, London, Moscow and Peking, exhorting governments to present the exigent prince with his new railway as part of their foreign aid programmes.

Squashed in an old notebook I find a colour slide of Sihanouk, taken at the palace. Clad in a white tunic and *sampot* with the ribbon of some intimidating oriental order across his chest, he is smiling affably as the entire Cabinet crouches before him in full ceremonial dress, heads humbly bowed, hands joined in prayerful greeting. Scribbled beside it is part of a eulogy by one of his ministers which calls him 'Our August and Infinitely Engaging Leader, Worthy Descendant of the Kings of Angkor ... Young, Dynamic, Supremely Intelligent.' In 1964 he opened a museum to himself, and when he drove through Phnom Penh, sirens wailed to warn the populace and pedestrians hastened to the edge of the pavement to clap gently as he went by.

In 1963 Sihanouk gave up all United States assistance in mid-project, announced that foreign commerce and banking would be nationalized, and brought his country to the very brink of economic catalepsy. It was a personal decision, taken by a man who looked upon the national income as his private purse. A year later he came back from a visit to Peking bubbling over with new, ambitious schemes. Everyone in the country was to be taught to read Cambodian within five months – except for the sick, the dying, the insane, and the diplomats – and the whole population was to be mobilized to plant trees. His mind was full of much else besides, from plans to socialize the entire wholesale trade to designing uniforms to be worn by all waiters, barmen and hotel servants through the kingdom.

Sihanouk has only had four wives, and when in power he lived in a bungalow complex on the edge of Phnom Penh, not in the royal palace. His hobbies ranged reasonably enough from model warships to playing the clarinet and directing his own films. As a host he was careful and attentive, capable of personally arranging even the bowl of flowers in your room, or inquiring anxiously about your favourite dishes. But the whole court might be drafted into the cast when he made his movies, and portly ministers were pressganged into volley-ball teams to play against Monseigneur.

Excitable, voluble, inexhaustible, Sihanouk was a beloved prince who would dig with the peasants and share their most unsavoury food and jokes, and who talked and talked and talked to the masses with frankness and spontaneous charm. It was useless to judge his prima-donna whims or patent egoism by the measures of the West, for he was king in another context. 'It is Cambodia they insult when they insult me,' he cried of the more denigratory newspapers in the new world. He was a royal patriot, and if there had been no Sihanouk, in all probability there would have been no Cambodia today. He was only in his forties then, but it was said that he observed the Hindu–Buddhist rites of his forebears, and in 1969 many still believed that we might see more stone gods erected in his country, bearing a new yet familiar face. If he charmed peasants, however, he exasperated politicians, generals and ambitious young men frustrated by a 'socialist' system run on patronage and a prince's caprice. In 1970 he was duly deposed in a right-wing coup, and set up a government-in-exile under the aegis of 'socialists' of a different definition in Peking.

As Sihanouk reached back to the customs of Angkor, so Sukarno found in Javanese tradition his own alternative to the liberalism and licence of parliaments. For the democratic system, it seemed, only encouraged further fragmentation of an Indonesia already divided by ethnic differences, by 3,000 islands and the seas between, and by the three philosophical streams of Islam, Communism and Nationalism. The proliferating political parties prevented each other from ruling effectively, and cabinets flitted in and out of power every few months in the inglorious fashion of the French Fourth Republic. By 1956 the army was sick of them all, and Sukarno was able to tell them to go and 'bury themselves'. By 1959 he was talking of 'the devil of liberalism', and announcing jubilantly in his new Political Manifesto that Indonesia had now been 'completely divorced from western democracy'.

This raised relatively few hairs, for definitions of fairness change with lines of latitude. Western prejudice may demand a vote for every man : Javanese prejudice demands *Musjawarah* and *Mufakat* – prolonged palaver ending in a unanimous decision when the last dissenter is too hoarse or exhausted to argue further. It is a method whose origins lie buried with a million forgotten wrangles in the ancient soil of every Javanese village.

Even under the mystical hierarchs of their early Hindu kingdoms, Javanese peasants had jealously guarded their own communal custom whereby the head of a family discussed a local problem with the rest of its members until they all reached agreement, then heads of families met in council to talk themselves into a consensus in turn. This practice enabled the village chief to make up his mind without a voice being raised when he had the last word, and it prompted Indonesians to applaud when Sukarno condemned the West's '50 per cent-plus-one' vote as 'the tyranny of the majority', a deplorably unfair way of making policy which ignored the wishes of up to 49 per cent of the people. Moreover in Java, where the land originally belonged to the entire community and the family worked together as a team under its *bapak*, or 'father', the individual was nothing and the principle of *gotong royong* or mutual cooperation was the basis of society. The articulation of Sukarno's dog-French formula for government, *Socialisme à la Indonesia*, came from these village principles of consultation, consensus, and cooperation.

In 1960 Sukarno dissolved the elected legislature and replaced it with an appointed *gotong royong* parliament which included not only politicians but representatives of functional groups – farmers, workers, soldiers, religious bodies, and so on. He then invented a People's Consultative Congress, a Supreme Advisory Council, a National Front, and other high-sounding instruments of 'guided democracy' whose main characteristics in every case were that Sukarno was the President, there was no voting, they arrived at their conclusions by talking things out until all agreed with him, and the members swore fealty to the political manifesto of the great Bung above them all in his glistening white palaces. The ultimate acrological expression of *gotong royong* was NASAKOM – collaboration within all these organizations of the Nationalists, the Muslims, and the Communists.

Among the picturesque horrors of the exotic orient the *kalis*, the evil brown canals of Djakarta, enjoy a proud place. But it is recorded that when an Australian bacteriologist tested samples of *kali* water he could not find a single germ. 'They all eat each other and so cancel each other out,' someone suggested to him. This was a true 'Indonesian solution', with all warring factions brought together so that the prejudices of one neutralize the prejudices of the other. It enabled Sukarno to make the Communists and the anti-Communist generals 'cancel each other out' for so long, and to remain above them at the apex of the state as the supreme *Bapak*, the lone father-figure to end all father-figures whose authority was absolute.

But there was more to it than this. For the fertile coupling of earlier ancestor worship with Hindu–Buddhism bred the same supernaturally sanctioned tyranny in Java as it did in Cambodia. Hindu kings were gods incarnate and possessed mystical powers. Sukarno, some whispered, had been clairvoyant at seventeen, and when he went to Bali, he brought rain. He had healing powers, his bathwater would cure the sick, the dish from which he ate ended barrenness. There are men who still think he is Vishnu and women who have paid for sharing that belief too enthusiastically, and in various parts of the Indonesian republic people say they have seen his profile in the moon.

His basic urge to be Superman titillated by adorers and sycophants from Sumatra to Celebes, Sukarno was not slow to answer the call of Nietzsche, and we see him become Lifelong President, Supreme Helmsman, Great Leader of the Indonesian Revolution, Supreme Builder, Supreme Fisherman, Supreme Guardian of the Muhammadiyah, Supreme Educator, First Pioneer of Freedom in Africa and Asia, and Honorary Chairman of the Indonesian Rat-killing Action Campaign of 1964. On one occasion he appeared to western correspondents fully dressed but in bare feet, explaining that a violent storm was brewing and he had been warned that he was so charged with mystical energy that he might draw down the very lightning (without his shoes he was satisfactorily earthed, he implied).

He described his repetitive speeches to the millions of Indonesia as 'a two-way conversation between Sukarno-the-man and Sukarno-the-people, a two-way conversation between two comrades who in reality are One'. 'I have been accused of megalomania, the sickness of greatness,' he confessed with enormous satisfaction in 1966. 'Yes, I am a great man and my power is the biggest, the biggest, the biggest.' When Djakarta acquired West New Guinea from the Dutch, the main town in the territory was renamed Sukarnapura, and the Bung had the two highest mountain ranges called after himself.

He subsequently revealed that the Prophet Mohammed had inspired his decision to take Indonesia out of the United Nations. The only great leaders were Mao, Ho Chi Minh and

Sukarno, said Sukarno. Something of a name-dropper, he also remarked with approval that Hitler, Christ and Mohammed had shared with him his own secret of success – they had all promised something to the masses. 'Paint a brilliant picture of your aims,' he urged his subordinates – whether these were to be the Third Reich, the Kingdom of Heaven, a Paradise full of houris, or Indonesian 'guided democracy'. From this it may be seen that critics who accuse Sihanouk of delusions of grandeur are simply avoiding taking on someone their own size.

Sukarno promised Djakarta the biggest mosque in the world, and then built its biggest phallic symbol – a 400-foot pillar in Italian marble capped with a flame contrived out of half a hundredweight of real gold and designed to 'stand for a thousand years'. He treated national income like mad money, flew around the world with a personal suite of thirty, moved about Indonesia in a £10,000 air-conditioned Mercedes 600 equipped with a cocktail bar and push-button gadgetry to make hypnotic speeches about hardship and austerity : 'Do you and you and you and you,' he barked at one open-mouthed mob with harsh overtones of well-simulated hysteria, 'do you consider yourselves as Bearers of the Message of the People's Sufferings? Do you really feel to the marrow of your bones that you are Bearers of the Message of the People's Sufferings? The Message of the Sufferings of the Indonesian People is part of the social consciousness of Mankind!'

But Sukarno, of course, was not just of Mankind. There was one law for him, and another for his nation of 105,000,000 debtors. When he was urged to cut his overstaffed *de luxe* government of about 100 ministers down to a utility cabinet which would concentrate on bringing food and clothing to the suffering people, he contemptuously rejected the appeal with the phrase : 'not if it's just to fill empty bellies'. No rice? The Bung said 'Let them eat corn,' promised the hungry a nuclear programme, exhorted the penurious peasantry to 'Love outer space'. He operated in accordance with the finest traditions of ruthless Javanese statecraft which taught the omnipotent monarch that true power depended upon a rigorous self-denial of ethics or scruples, and the Supreme Court was told to rule that the judiciary should be ready to break the law at any time in order to further his Indonesian revolution.

The Bung personified Indonesia as Churchill personified war-time Britain. But Sukarno was no more like Churchill than Bali is like the Isle of Sheppey. And Bali, where the bemused Gauguins of the early sixties would paint the bare-breasted girls carrying baskets of luscious tropical fruits like over-ripe bunches of swollen genitalia – Bali explained the lust of this energetic Sultan, with his moist eye for almost any well-turned ankle.

Counting his wives is like solving one of those irritating mathematical conundrums in week-end magazines. You start off confidently enough with a total of five, of whom three are still at least theoretically in play. But then a corruption trial reveals a sixth for whose house in Djakarta the Bung has set aside £14,000 out of public funds. The books are then balanced, until suddenly there is a report of two further women to whom Sukarno is alleged to be secretly married, and before you have had time to feed these into the computer, the Indonesian press lists a ninth wife, presented to Sukarno as a gift by a proud father, and well-informed sources say that he in fact grosses eighteen marriages (from which divorces are de-ductible). This does not, of course, take into account the casuals for whom he combed continents, both developed and underdeveloped, and much local talent in Indonesia itself. His answer to indignant parents or reluctant subjects was to wed the girl for the sake of form and divorce her the next day, which in turn confuses the marriage count.

The President's will was above the law, but as with Sihanouk his love of personal power was inextricably entwined with his passionate, chauvinistic love of country. It was inevitable that, like the god-kings before him, Sukarno should dream of Em-pire. 'God has determined that certain parts of the world should form units,' he once cried. 'When I look at the islands situated between Asia and Australia I understand that they are meant to form a single entity,' and he announced that in future the Indian Ocean would be called the 'Indonesian Ocean'. From this it was only a step to his self-appointed role as god-given champion of the underdog nations, the 'New Emerging Forces' of the have-not continents. 'We want to create not only a new Indonesia,' he thundered, 'but a new Asia, a new Africa, a new World!' And this was precisely what the Communists wished.

The Bung was finally compromised in the abortive Communist coup of 1965, and evicted from office. But did he jump, or was he pushed? He called himself 'pro-Communist', but his answer to PKI demands that he form a real coalition NASAKOM Cabinet and include them in it was the royal evasion 'I am NASAKOM'. He was confident that he could string along the army, the Communists and the Chinese, but he was stringing them along on a swaying slackwire. The powerful PKI was able to put pressure on him, its mass organizations manipulating the mounting unrest and land-hunger in the underfed republic. In 1963 the Chinese Embassy in Djakarta made a direct, undercover approach to the President, warning him that right-wing parties were plotting against his life. Tengku Abdul Rahman of Malaysia disdainfully flouted him, provoking him to even more vainglorious and venomous speeches, full of sound and fury, dignifying nothing.

And beyond all this was his genuine hatred for 'Imperialism' and 'Neo-colonialism', his fear of 'encirclement', of the destruction of the fragile entity of 'Indonesia' which he had created out of a broken necklace of equatorial islands. Coaxed, cajoled, tricked and tripped by his own blind pretensions, he simply lost his balance, slipped, and fell. And there was no net.

Yet there had been method in his megalomania.

A Question of Identity

DUTCH DOGS! *Get out of West Irian.* It was crudely painted on a high wall in the centre of Djakarta. But there was something written underneath in smaller print : *Rice – seven rupiahs. Rice – seven rupiahs. Rice – seven rupiahs.* And there was the whole sad story, I thought, as I stood teetering somewhat uneasily on the hem of a hostile mob for whom any fair foreigner might be a hated Hollander in December 1957. The Bung was in full frenzy, leading the Indonesian millions in a violent anti-colonial crusade against The Hague for refusing to surrender to him the neighbouring territory still so tauntingly known as Dutch West New Guinea, which lay only 100 miles east of the last of Sukarno's coral strands. Eagerly abetted by the Communists, he tried to bully the Netherlands into relinquishing it by confiscating all Dutch estates and enterprises throughout Indonesia, expelling all 48,000 Dutch subjects still in the country, repudiating all previous agreements with Holland, severing diplomatic relations, and starting a surreptitious war for the conquest of West Irian with the Russian arms that Khrushchev had given him power to sign for in the Soviet supermarket.

The effects were to be foreseen. The Dutch had run 600 rubber, coffee, tobacco and tea plantations in Indonesia, against thirty-five managed by the State Agricultural Service. Seventy-eight freighters of the Dutch KPM line had provided the main links between island and island in an archipelago which straggled across 3,000 miles of sea. Holland had bought one fifth of all Indonesian exports. *Rice – seven rupiahs?* The price trebled in the following four years and trebled again in the next three months, so that by January 1962 it was costing sixty rupiahs a litre. Exports had dropped by one third in the preceding year, and foreign exchange reserves were down to a ridiculous ten million dollars.

But Sukarno got his 'West Irian' in 1963, and thereupon ploughed his poverty into a new venture – the military 'Confrontation' of 'Imperialist' Malaysia. This extension of the Bung's guns-before-butter routine cut the republic off from the free ports of Singapore and Penang which normally processed and sold three out of every four pounds of Indonesian rubber and two thirds of all Indonesia's oil products. The rupiah broke into a canter and the cost of living doubled in a year. In the summer of 1963 I ordered a modest enough supper in the Hotel Indonesia in Djakarta – soup, cold platter, coffee, no drinks – and felt virtuously thrifty because it had cost me no more than an Indonesian colonel's pay for a whole month. The black market value of the American dollar in this meaningless money was now thirty times the official rate of exchange. Two years later all foreign companies were placed under Indonesian 'supervision and control', and the oil output fell sharply. *Rice – seven rupiahs?* In 1965 it was costing 200 rupiahs a litre, by 1966, 5,000 rupiahs a litre. But in 1966 the joke was over, Sukarno was finished. Confrontation had petered out, and new men were running their fingers through their hair in Djakarta at the sight of the outstanding bills – two and a half billion dollars in foreign exchange.

While solid citizens of the West countersunk in their own confident logic may write off the Bung as an irresponsible lunatic, however, many perceptive Asians would sympathize with his basic quandary.

As with all other continents, South-east Asia's molten surface sluggishly rippled with the ebb and flow of conquest for centuries until frontiers finally began to settle along firm lines. Vietnam materialized only 150 years ago. The borders of 'Laos' were bulging and collapsing for century after century as Thais, Burmese or Annamites invaded or withdrew, and at times it was two and even three kingdoms.

Then came the western colonialists like rival land development sharks, ruthlessly ripping out the original topography without regard for nature or the natives, and neatly redrawing the maps to mark off their own concessions. The British took four provinces from Siam and added them to Malaya, while the French took a fifth one for Cambodia and more miscellaneous territory to lump together with Laos. The new synthetic Laos included territories which were not ethnically Lao, and left out other territories which essentially were. If it were only possible, the answer for this tormented country would be a geopolitical sex-change operation whereby the north-east of Laos would be grafted on to North Vietnam and the north-east of Thailand would be added to Laos, altering the shape of the kingdom from phallic to oval.

The British mapped out the lots known as 'Burma' (sixty different language groups with cultures as far apart as Scot and Slav), and 'Malaya' (excluding four Muslim provinces in South Thailand), a vertical straight line with only one kink in it was drawn 400 miles down the centre of New Guinea, and the Dutch were given the western half. Later Korea and Vietnam were to be bisected by horizontal lines, and the British were to invent 'Malaysia' so that they could tack on to the now sovereign Federation of Malaya the island of Singapore and a 1,000-mile-long strip of real estate in North Borneo which they were anxious to unload. But all this neat cut-and-paste cartography was apt to leave the local inhabitant confused.

The Straits of Singapore and Malacca are narrow drains up which the British and Dutch drew a line in 1824, leaving one side under the flag of the Netherlands, the other under the Union Jack. And since none of the earlier indigenous kingdoms had conformed even vaguely to the new divisions these red-faced carpet-baggers now dubbed 'Malaya' and the 'Netherlands East Indies', traditional identities became blurred. When in 1945 the losing Japanese encouraged the emergence of an 'independent' Indonesia, the sixty-four Indonesian leaders whom they called together to define its frontiers were quite unable to agree what they should include in it.

Sukarno knew that the fragile unity of his new republic, which lumped together more than a hundred different ethnic groups, rested paradoxically on centuries of common colonial subservience. Indonesia did not lack substance, but identity.

Seven out of every ten men lived a simple kampong existence on these fertile, sunlit islands and the greatest danger was not famine, it seemed, but fragmentation. So turning his back on economic problems, the Bung set out to weld his assortment of sturdy but mutually distrustful gold-brown men into an arrogant, fiercely chauvinistic nation. Believing that a chip on the shoulder was worth two in the hand, he did not give them bread, but loud, angry words and the largest armed forces of all South-east Asia.

Imaginary external threats and proud answering challenges from Djakarta were written into his script for postwar history to divert the masses from the sorry state of affairs at home, and to make not only men of them, but Indonesians. The Bung was determined to build a nation on hatred and anger, moulding his bricks with a thick stook of last straws. The Dutch presence in West Irian was a national insult. Malaysia was a 'neo-colonialist' creature under western protection that had 'committed an act of aggression against Indonesia' by acquiring former British dependencies on the otherwise Indonesian island of Borneo.

Malaysia was more than that: it was a living menace to the precious unity of Sukarno's archipelago republic. For its government left others to trail clouds of glory, and pursued happiness with the aid of all that the Bung had condemned – foreign bases, foreign advisers, foreign capital – and nobody was nationalized. Prosperous, pragmatic, the young federation threatened to make Indonesia look like a neighbouring slum, to lure away not only the best brains in outer islands of the republic restless under the ruinous hegemony of Djakarta, but possibly some of the islands themselves. Malaysia subverted a vainglorious but threadbare Indonesia simply by existing at all.

Man may not live by bread alone, but he certainly cannot live without it, and although it has been said of many Asians that if you offer them rice or an idea, they will take the idea, the idea is very often about rice. With this nagging knowledge in the back of his mind, Sukarno became 'obsessed with the frailness of Indonesia', as one of his cronies told me. And the more obsessed he became, the more he fought against the demons of division by playing dictator.

The obsession was not just the byblow of his fevered imagination. In 1950 there had been rebellion in the South Moluccas at the south-eastern edge of the republic, and in 1953 there had been an insurrection in Atjeh, at its north-western tip. Then, five years later, the 'Revolt of the Colonels' had exploded into civil war in Sumatra and Celebes, and I had found myself going into battle on a dining-room chair.

The men who split Indonesia open in 1958 were the men who had wrenched the archipelago from the Dutch in the first place: the officers of the Indonesian People's Army. Having freed the country, the soldiers not unnaturally claimed as much right to a say in its destiny as any caucus of conniving civilians. But they belonged to territorial contingents which had mainly fought the colonial enemy in their own home islands – in Java, in Sumatra, in Celebes and Borneo. Once independent, therefore, Indonesia fell naturally into a pattern of military regions, in each of which the local commanders held the ultimate source of local power – the gun.

By 1956 the incompetence and corruption of the successive governments in Djakarta, the capital of the republic on the central island of Java, had made regional military commanders in the outer islands increasingly fidgety. For overcrowded Java was not only the seat of the administration, but the home of six out of ten Indonesians. It earned only a small fraction of Indonesia's foreign exchange, but it absorbed most of the national income. To the Sumatrans, therefore, Java was a cuckoo in the nest. As a shock-haired politician once told me over a disgracefully early highball at Palembang in South Sumatra: 'In 1956 this island earned five times as much as Java, but the government spent six times as much on the damned Javanese as it did on us. Well, as far as we are concerned, it's a case of "no money, no love".' Scottish nationalists would doubtless have sympathized.

Neglected by Djakarta, the outer regions developed a thriving barter trade of their own, shipping thousands of tons of rubber, copra, coffee and spices directly to Singapore and

Manila in exchange for everything from rice to road-building equipment that the Central Government now failed to provide. And when Djakarta outlawed this commerce, it was transformed into a gigantic smuggling operation.

The disastrous economic consequences of throwing out all the Dutch, and Sukarno's first open steps towards a *gotong royong* administration which would logically include the Communists, further enraged the commanders on the richer islands of the republic and framed their mundane grievances about lack of money and local autonomy with a new and shining halo of anti-Communist resistance. Slowly but surely the revolts of individual colonels who now assumed absolute power in their respective regions were knitted into a pattern for national rebellion, and in February 1958 a rival 'Revolutionary Government of the Republic of Indonesia' was proclaimed in Central Sumatra.

The Rebel 'Government' was an impressive board of directors, calculated to inspire confidence in the foreign political investor. It included not only some of the ablest officers of the Indonesian army, but three former prime ministers and the republic's most brilliant economist, Dr Djojohadikusomo Sumitro. In Celebes, 1,700 miles away to the east of this core of insurrection, other colonels with 12,000 men under command were conducting their own branch revolution in co-ordination with the Sumatra office. The 'Government' was meanwhile negotiating a wary but useful alliance with the somewhat murderous Darul Islam rebels in North Sumatra and West Java who had been fighting for a Muslim Indonesia for several years already. Sukarno's fears about centrifugal force appeared to be justified.

At this point Singapore became the neutral bottleneck through which the traffic of all sides passed – the freighters loaded for Djakarta, the rebel blockade-runners, the money, the men and the secrets. A hundred ships rode at anchor in the harbour, their masters often tight-lipped about their destinations.

The working day was not without incident. One of the more dilapidated fixtures in an otherwise well-appointed bar might suddenly lean across to whisper, 'We'll pay twenty-five bucks an hour to any ex-commando type who knows his stuff and can run a small school for our boys. You know, old man – booby traps, limpet mines, sand in the petrol, all that. These Indonesian government gunboats are frightening off our Chinese shippers.' There was almost a scandal when ten obsolescent British armoured cars were driven straight through the city and down to the docks for forwarding f.o.b. to the revolutionaries. At night blacked-out bombers from Clark Base in the Philippines, filled with American small arms from Okinawa and heading for Sumatra, droned in softly to refuel. The rebels needed rice, vehicles, machinery and guns, and they had rubber and copra to sell. The town was full of couriers and agents with ready cash, false papers and false information.

But one story was not false: Djakarta had thrown paratroops and a seaborne mobile brigade against the east coast of Sumatra, seized the oilfields and forced the rebels back into their mountain fortress to the west. The fight was on. Robert Pepper Martin of *U.S. News and World Report*, Keyes Beech of the *Chicago Daily News* and myself decided to pool our plans for reaching the war. Pepper is a rumbling mountain of middle-aged man with hair and moustache indignantly *en brosse* and Keyes is a trim specimen of American Marine biology with a lightly frosted head and the collected air of a fight veteran. Together we boarded a little coaster and sailed for thirty hours across a sea of smoked glass, to Palembang in South Sumatra.

Once the heart of the mighty Srividjaja empire, Palembang was the headquarters of a 'neutral' colonel who stayed out of the fight himself, but provided a port and pipeline to the rebels for fuel and volunteers and other much-needed strategic commodities through the 500 miles of swamp and jungle and mountain to his north. Our object was to get ourselves fed into this pipeline, and by devious Indonesian means we were told how to do so. We crossed the swamplands of the south concealed in the back of a plain lorry, and after ten painful hours found ourselves in a market town tucked into the shadow of the tremendous, overgrown and crumbling wall of mountain that guards the 1,200-mile littoral of western Sumatra. Through this range was stitched the tenuous thread of road which Government troops advancing westwards out of the ooze of the east were undoubtedly bent on cutting.

Within an hour we were seated in a decrepit green and yellow bus, its roof piled high with tin suitcases and fraying wicker baskets bulging with edibles dead and alive, its interior stuffed with twenty-four assorted and good-humoured Sumatrans and three correspondents. A diminutive driver climbed up into the cab, the sodden stub of a cigarette stuck obstinately to the corner of his mouth. He started the engine with an ear-splitting roar, and began jolting us through the sudden potholes that combined in their tens of thousands to make up the road to the heart of the rebellion at Bukit Tinggi.

He was to keep us reeling on recklessly for forty-six hours without once pausing for sleep. Only at sundown would we stop for half an hour to swarm into some village eating-house for the first meal of the day, for this was the Muslim fasting month of Ramadan. Seven times we crossed muddy, palm-fringed rivers on flat ferries that tilted and wallowed as the bus was eased down on to them, the sun burnishing the crocodile-ridden waters or our headlights probing at the farther shore through spiteful curtains of rain. Every few hours we would jerk to a halt as police and military emerged from the veranda of some dim-lit attap hut and laboriously checked all our papers but never held us up.

When the sun rose on the second morning we found ourselves roaring through a spectacular gorge choked with unkempt jungle that thinned out to bony peaks nearly 9,000 feet up. We were already within the rebel stockade.

Sumatra is a long shark of an island nosing up into the Indian Ocean and the Revolutionary Government was defying Djakarta from what might be called its underbelly – the midwest coastal area and its spectacular hinterland. The zone included the port of Padang, and also, sixty miles in and 8,000 feet farther up, the hill-town of Bukit Tinggi into which our bus snorted like a bull plunging into the arena. At such heights men may see visions and dream intoxicating dreams and this perhaps explains much. The grey-haired Prime Minister of the Revolutionary Government, the pragmatic ex-Governor of the National Bank of Indonesia, told us confidently two days later : 'the dislocation of normal commerce and sources of revenue, caused by our resistance, will bring Djakarta to its knees very soon. In three months' time we shall reach the turning point – and time is on our side.' Within three months, in fact, the Central Government would have its hands on Bukit Tinggi. The rebels did not dispose of more than 3,000 regular troops, and although the stockade was full of cheap rice and fat buffalo, prices were already beginning to rise and petrol was in desperately short supply.

An ancient 15-cwt army truck was finally lent to the eight foreign correspondents in Bukit Tinggi together with a driver and a listless young lieutenant. A great rusty drum of petrol, purchased at killing cost, was manhandled into the middle of the back and as this only left room for three men along each side, we borrowed two flimsy dining-room chairs from the rest house which we now dominated, and tied them to the tailboard with rope. Perched on one of these, I set off to see the war. The truck jounced past Lake Singkarak, an eleven-mile-long eye of still, mist-laden water just south of the Equator, and after ten hours of erratic driving swung left on to an uninviting track that disappeared into the grim mountain fastnesses to the east. Somewhere down that green gulch, Central Government troops advancing from the oilfields were working towards us to cut the north–south road to Palembang and invest the rebel stronghold.

As night fell, we pulled up in the shadow of a big, wooden house on high stilts, the headquarters of the rebel regiment that had been pushed steadily westwards by the oncoming Government troops and was now holding a river-line farther down the road at a place called Lubukdjambi. 'Our commander at Lubukdjambi, Captain Azwar, has recrossed the river and driven the enemy back about ten miles,' the second-in-command told us jubilantly. 'We shall now go forward and retake the oilfields.' Why were they lost in the first place? 'Our men panicked when Government planes came over bombing and strafing,' he replied slowly. He reflected for a moment, and then burst out sorrowfully: 'We never expected Djakarta to behave like this. We never thought they would make war on us as a country makes war on an enemy state.'

The Javanese were not playing fair, he implied. The whole business was supposed to be an Indonesian charade leading to an Indonesian compromise, but Sukarno had lost his temper and pulled a real knife. In this very civil war he was not talking things out in accordance with the principle of *Musjawarah*, but behaving as if all were over bar the shooting.

On the next morning we found Captain Azwar at a command post still on the hither side of the river. Characteristically, he flatly contradicted his superior at regimental headquarters. The opposite bank was still in enemy hands. 'But you have seen what fantastic country lies behind us,' he went on hopefully. 'If the enemy tries to advance further he will find this road impassable.' The men from Java nevertheless crossed the river, thrust Captain Azwar off his perch two days later, and pressed on towards the Palembang road-junction. Shortly afterwards a swaggering staff officer told me that Azwar had nevertheless killed 150 of the enemy in a counter-attack. When we checked with the regimental commander, he silently lifted three fingers. The whole rebel zone was a minefield of misinformation.

The Central Government, having scraped together a motley collection of ships and aircraft, finally launched a successful sea-and-air assault on Padang which was only briefly opposed. But meanwhile there were reports of fierce rebel resistance against Government troops advancing down the 600 miles of road that led to Bukit Tinggi from Medan, the loyalist capital of the north. And this news attracted Keyes, who kept repeating disgustedly: 'I shan't believe there's a war on till I see a body.' We therefore hired a small bus so that we each had a whole bench to lie on and set off one evening in this luxurious way for the battle. For fifteen hours the bus fought the ridged and rutted road through the thickly matted mountains. The night was fine, and once a flock of vampires, their great jagged wings black against the moon, flapped silently over us like a migration of demonic umbrellas. By high morning, however, the malicious wilderness had given way to calm green plains flanked by smooth rolling hills. It all looked very peaceful.

'But you cannot go all the way north by road,' a rebel major warned us. 'You must cross Lake Toba by boat. Carry a big Red Cross flag, whatever you do, and go by daylight. The Central Government troops will fire on you as you approach Prapat. And take care in Prapat, because they are fighting there.' This was another stale slice of misinformation. We climbed into our bus, and a few hours later the country coarsened equatorially again, the hills rose sharply at our approach, and suddenly before us lay the fabulous mountain lake, sixty miles long and encircled by high cliffs and escarpments. We boarded a ferry that had no Red Cross flag and after five hours of violent tropical storm it deposited us on the north shore of the lake in darkness without a shot being fired.

On the next morning we took off for Medan in yet another hired bus. 'Watch out,' we were admonished by well-meaning Indonesians. 'Central Government troops hold Siantar but are fighting off heavy attacks by the rebels. The hospitals are full of wounded.' In Siantar we had a glass of beer in the somnolent main street with a bored army sergeant, and so bowled on up an excellent road to Medan, lunch, and a post-mortem.

We had chalked up 100 hours of travelling by bus and truck from one end of Sumatra to the other. We had not seen a dead, wounded, or really frightened man. We had been through a dozen military and police checkpoints – Government, neutral, rebel – and nobody had questioned our dubious itinerary, our right, in fact, to drive a bus right through the whole war.

I booked the one empty seat left on the Garuda Airways plane flying to Malaya. At Medan airport a Javanese immigration official asked me where I had been in Sumatra. 'Just Prapat,' I lied, foreseeing last-minute trouble. The loyal servant of President Sukarno looked shocked. 'And you a journalist? In your shoes I would have gone to see the rebels in Bukit Tinggi,' he said reprovingly. 'I'm really surprised at you.'

It should be added that once the Government forces controlled the main towns, the rebels took their war into the hills

and their guerrilla sorties and ambushes began for the first time
to give their enemies a taste for aspirin. Early in 1961, therefore, Sukarno offered a free pardon to all who surrendered before October, and by August most of them had 'returned to the
republic'. In Sumatra those killed in action officially numbered
193.

An old agency message before me reports that a provincial
governor is defying Djakarta's ban on the export of unprocessed
or low-grade rubber from Sumatra. This is not a flashback to
Sukarno and the revolt of 1958. The message is dated ten years
later. The President of Indonesia is now Suharto, and the Trade
Minister who imposed the ban is the brilliant Dr Sumitro,
quondam financial wizard of the rebels. But when the safety-
catches are off the real masters of the archipelago are still
some fourteen regional military commanders.

However, if Suharto sometimes appears to be the sort of soft
tough who would drink tabasco through a straw, his intelligence and determination should not be underestimated.
No one was naïve enough to be surprised in 1971 when the
'Sekber Golkar', the Joint Secretariat of Functional Groups
backed by the Army, won a resounding victory in the general
elections for a 460-member parliament in which 100 seats were
already automatically reserved for military nominees of the
Government. But Suharto had meanwhile trimmed the army
structure severely in order to protect ambitious provincial warlords from any distressing temptations in the future. In 1973
a major reshuffle put all the key commands into the hands of
a new generation of professional officers at the expense of
the old politically-minded generals of the revolutionary era,
and the defence ministry tightened its grip on the dispersed
armed forces. Politicians and parliaments might be a pest, but
in any Asian situation Suharto knew where the real danger
to unity and peace – and President – really lay.

14

The Sweet Smell of Corruption

LIKE the rigged packs of some celestial card-sharper, most Asian communities can be cut neatly into the rulers and the ruled, however much they are shuffled by well-meaning westerners. For the oriental answer to imperfect government has not been argument, but insurrection, since he who challenged absolute power with soft words in earlier centuries was simply asking for an excruciating end. The more dictatorial powers an Asian gives himself, the more he convinces malcontents that they can only overthrow him by force, and the more he is aware of the threat they pose, the more tyrannical he becomes, and the more desperate he makes them. This is the oriental equation whose normal solution is an act of violence that simply replaces one clique with another.

By the time Sukarno was finally supplanted he had survived two attempted coups d'état by two different Chiefs-of-Staff, five major uprisings, four or five miscellaneous assassination attempts, a palace bombing, and the Tjikini Affair. On Saturday, 30 November 1957, Darul Islam fanatics threw five bombs at the Bung as he emerged from a fund-raising fête at the Tjikini School in Djakarta. Nine toddlers and a pregnant woman died, and in all forty-eight children fell critically wounded as the blood began to mingle sluggishly with the steadily falling rain. Sukarno was protected by two military aides, both of whom were severely injured. He was shaken but unhurt. I was the only British newspaper correspondent in the city and I had an edition going to press within a few hours. But my exclusive story rated just two column-inches in the *Observer*. Distance lends no enchantment to the news, and foul play in the Far East was as common as dog bites man.

A correspondent coursing around a subcontinent of eleven

Asian states cannot always be in the right place at the right time to cover every coup or killing, but he may sometimes be fortunate. One fine sunny morning in March 1962 I was working my way through coffee and croissants in my air-conditioned hotel bedroom in Saigon, and glanced idly out of the locked window to see an aircraft dive silently into view and then climb out of sight again. I paid no attention, for the Vietcong had no planes, and therefore all were friendly. I was deservedly shaken out of this facile syllogism by a muffled, rumbling roar, and as I put down my cup and jumped to my feet a second aircraft dipped noiselessly across the airspace framed by my window, there was a second juddering explosion and from below the sill a cloud of very dirty smoke began to rise hesitantly into view. The circus proceeded, the planes bobbing quietly across my vision at regular intervals as if I were counting them to cure insomnia. But it was all so dream-like that I felt sure I was already asleep.

It was no dream for the Diem family. Two young Vietnamese air force pilots were giving a very suitable signal for a coup d'état by divebombing the presidential palace. Operating with commendable accuracy, they half-wrecked the huge colonial structure, but failed to pin down the President himself. One pilot was shot down and captured. Twenty officers were arrested, and loyalist tanks began to clatter once again through the streets of Saigon to take up position in the park-like palace grounds.

This was the sequel to an abortive thirty-hour revolt in 1960 when 700 paratroops surrounded the palace, and were quickly joined by infantry, marines and artillery units in and around Saigon. But I had already ducked instinctively as the mortar bombs shrieked overhead to hit that same palace as early as 1955, when Diem's enemies had first tried to liquidate him. Later the Buddhists explored their own strange corner of the Asian map of violence by burning themselves alive in the streets of the capital in order to rouse men to bloody rebellion against him. They were to succeed where others had failed, and on 2 November 1963 Diem and his brother Nhu were unceremoniously butchered in the back of an armoured personnel-carrier in Cholon, the sister-city of Saigon.

To renounce the howitzer and the half-nelson in favour of dependence upon such dubious devices as the rule of law and the polling booth calls for a stupendous act of faith on the part of the millions. For most start by regarding a hovercraft society held up by nothing but an air-cushion of civic responsibility and loyalty to the constitution as no more feasible than a flying carpet. In much of Asia the contract between men and government has been a loose, low-geared agreement-in-principle, with little obligation on either side. The government has not cared much for the people, and the people have cared little or nothing for the government. As an old Burmese saying has it, a man has five enemies – fire, water, the king, robbers, and 'the one who hates him'. The king is placed, it will be noted, while ordinary criminals and murderers are among the also-ran.

Moreover, dumb insolence towards authority acquired the aura of heroic national resistance once the struggle against the white colonial boss was joined, so that by the time the countries of South-east Asia became independent sovereign states, the old habits of defiance had been consecrated, and today it is ironically the new native governments that are their target. Even when a régime conscientiously tries to sweep up the sociological mess, it is liable to be discouraged by the ingratitude of a sceptical public.

The diminutive conductress in her high-necked Burmese blouse and longgyi blocks the gangway as I move to get off the bus. 'Back door for exit,' she says accusingly. 'The front door is for the entrance.' This orderly canalizing is a confusing novelty in Rangoon as far as I and a million-and-a-half Burmese are concerned, but then so is the new, shining bus, and the smooth road on which it runs, even the fact that the conductress takes the trouble to collect all the fares.

General Ne Win has been in power for nearly eighteen months, and has given a convincing demonstration of the orderliness and punctuality that a little barrack-room barking can achieve. The streets are clean and 100,000 mangy stray dogs have been systematically destroyed, Buddhist tenets not-withstanding. The railways run on time, the passengers pay for their tickets, and trains are only occasionally blown up by frustrated insurgents. Prices of staple commodities are fixed and shopkeepers must tag their goods and not haggle. Rackets in trading licences have been suppressed, speculation curbed.

That was in February 1960. But the stiff and scarifying mili-tary broom had already swept itself out of favour. A few days later the voters returned with an overwhelming majority Prime Minister U Nu and the party 'hagridden by prejudice, jobbery and nepotism, muddle, delay and corruption' which Ne Win had originally replaced. The General had made the mistake of putting the intensely individualistic Burmese through a crash course in social discipline under the erroneous impression that they would be happy if it gave them a richer, more reliable and cleaner commodity. The Burmese preferred the old scramble, the dogs, the pedlars and the garbage in the streets, so that Ne Win felt constrained to seize power again in 1962 for their own good and to inaugurate rule by 'Revolutionary Council'. And this established new standards in mutual mis-trust between people and potentate.

In lands where the central government is a dubious source of comfort or protection, men naturally depend on other men of the same clan, village, class, or profession. Charity begins at home, and so does everything else. Even the Asian Christian has a somewhat clouded sense of sin, adulterated by his far greater sense of shame. He is more anxious for the good opinion of his grandfather than the good opinion of God.

Loyalties and feuds alike are determined by family rather than by moral relationship. It is hopeless to try to separate out party rivalries in a country like Laos with the conventional political prism, for even mass movements with resounding titles like 'The Rally of the Lao People' turn out to be the instru-ments of some cosy clique within which everyone of note has the same name. Perhaps the most important single fact that any correspondent must bear in mind, when unravelling the contents of the bag of gentle vipers that is Vientiane, is that in the mid-fifties a man named Ou Vorovong was assassinated

while sitting in the house of another man named Phoui Sananikone.

The Vorovongs are a southern family into which the former
Laotian 'strongman' Phoumi Nosavan is married, and Phoumi's
father's elder sister was the aunt of Marshal Sarit Thanarat, the
former 'strongman' of Thailand. Their link with the Nosavans
has enabled the Vorovongs to acquire numerous posts of power
in the past from government ministries to the receipt of customs. But their bitter vendetta against the Sananikones has
brought them little joy, for the hated Sananikones are also great
landowners, brother Phoui is a former prime minister and president of the National Assembly, brother Ngon has held every
ministry but two in the succession of cabinets since 1954, and
nephew Oudone is at the apex of the Laotian army. More
than this, Phoui's sister was the first wife of Khou Abhay, and
Khou Abhay's son, Major-General Kouprasith, is Commander of
the Fifth Military Region which includes the capital of Vientiane. Meanwhile *Nhouy* Abhay was married to the sister of
Prince Boun Oum, Lord of the former kingdom of Champassak.
Now Boun Oum . . .

At this point we drop our programmes on to our laps in dis-
gust and wait for the singers themselves to unravel what is
obviously one of those dire nineteenth-century operatic plots
that so unaccountably inspired Mussorgsky and Verdi to com-
pose relatively comprehensible music. That, nevertheless, is
Laos.

Turn the coin over and on the back of Vendetta (you lose)
we find Nepotism (we win). In 1961 at least six members of the
sixteen-man Laotian cabinet were relatives of Prince Boun
Oum and all but two came from his home town. The Minister
of the Interior was his brother-in-law, the Minister of Finance his
nephew, another nephew was Minister of Public Works, and
a rather backward brother was given the Ministry of Cults.
Moreover, since General Phoumi Nosavan was Minister for
Defence, it naturally followed that one Ngon Nosavan should
be Director of Customs. Boun Oum, of course, was Prime Minister.

Seven years later most of the pieces were still on the board, although in different positions. The commanders of the five military regions remained semi-independent warlords who ran their own profitable fiefs, only intermittently scorched by the conflagration in Vietnam that was searing their eastern flank. This layout resembled the pattern in Indonesia and Vietnam, but takeover bids by military tycoons were unlikely, for the King (who commands great traditional veneration) was said to have declared officially : 'All coups are banned.'

The fine fretted screen of narrow allegiances and obligations through whose obscuring lattice alone Asia can be seen as Asians see it is no decoration, but part of a functional structure that stiffens even the modern political party – sometimes to a point of paralysis. For every postwar group is saddled with old-guard revolutionaries whose parochial minds are rooted in the past but to whom loyalty must be given in return for long-standing loyalty. And this can produce remarkable perspectives of judgement which leave an unwary western observer cross-eyed.

In 1964 a member of the Malaysian opposition accused the Minister of Education of embezzlement and corruption. The Minister sued his opponent for libel and lost the case with costs. The implications were obvious. But when the Minister reluctantly resigned, Tengku Abdul Rahman wrote to him with a royal disregard for the courts which can only be described as princely in its generosity : 'I very much regret that you consider it necessary to take this step. I would like to assure you that your colleagues and I are convinced of your innocence, having known you for this number of years. I would like to take this opportunity also of thanking you for the service that you have rendered to our party, our people and our country . . .'

Nor was that all. Parliament was asked for a supplementary vote of £10,304 7s. to meet the legal expenses of the unlucky Minister's case, the Tengku explaining patiently to indignant critics of his open-handed gesture with the taxpayer's money that after all ministers' salaries were 'small' compared with the earnings of business executives.

A modern Asian dictator must also reward all those who so

wisely assisted him when he mounted the coup d'état that put him into power in the first place. In South Korea General Park promoted no fewer than fifty senior officers to the rank of general for their selfless services to the state on the day he seized control of the country from its lawful civilian government. In Thailand, Marshal Sarit Thanarat paid 'coup money' to the officers who helped him to take over, and thoughtfully provided his generals with unique opportunities for land speculation, smuggling, and other profitable business enterprises. These in turn allowed money-making options to percolate down through the ranks to their own loyal subordinates until it looked as if Thailand might die the death of a thousand cuts.

Limited loyalties encouraged unlimited corruption, but in the minds of many prominent men in South-east Asia what the unsubtle West calls graft is a natural process with an honourable history. Air Marshal Nguyen Cao Ky, when Vice-President of South Vietnam, startled the Americans by saying that nine out of ten Asian politicians were corrupt, adding 'and the fact that I am one of the corrupt is obvious'. He did not hang his head in shame, however, and then resign. He grinned engagingly, and got on with his work as he saw it.

Official squeeze is a custom that dates back to the days when men appointed to senior posts were expected to finance their administration by milking the millions, and were regarded as feckless failures if they asked to be given a budget to help them out. Since the millions paid few if any other taxes, this was regarded as equitable. In order to avoid the dunning that would have been beneath the dignity of the panjandrum, those seeking preference would present him with gifts. And these he pocketed.

With a little adjustment of moral focus, public funds and private purse could be made to merge, like the double image in the viewfinder of a camera, until personal expenditure became a patriotic duty. As Laotian Minister for Finance, General Phoumi Nosavan made a fortune in the early nineteen-sixties by smuggling gold into Thailand with the complicity of Marshal Sarit in Bangkok (it will doubtless be recollected that Phoumi's father's elder sister was Sarit's aunt). However,

Phoumi explained that his object was not to fill his wallet, but to pay the troops and the building costs of the 'Monument aux Morts', a sort of stone cruet on stilts, evidently inspired by the Arc de Triomphe in Paris, which stood forlorn and forever unfinished in the middle of Vientiane.

Of the five regional warlords in Laos at the beginning of the decade, one had the Customs service in his pocket and was not getting any poorer, others dealt astutely in rice and timber, and a fourth worked hard selling opium ('It is my duty to dispose of it,' protested this oblong, garishly-decorated general stoutly. 'Otherwise it would fall into the hands of the Communists.') Even the advertised strength of the Laotian army had to be questioned, for commanders normally drew money for far more men than they had. These non-existent troops were called 'spirit soldiers', and the angry Americans accused venal Laotian officers of appropriating their pay and allowances, much as Chinese put food on the altars of their ancestors and then eat it themselves. The Laotians indignantly rejected these charges of dishonesty, and pointed out that this excellent practice enabled them to help families of dead or crippled servicemen, since the army gave dependants nothing through official channels. Laotian officers also exaggerated the poverty of their own equipment or the strength of the enemy in order to wheedle more weapons out of the Americans and more men from the Ministry of Defence. These devious forms of private enterprise were substitutes for equitable and efficient distribution from the centre.

In 1968 the able and youthful Laotian Minister of Finance made himself unpopular by rather prissily declining to give generals money for non-existent private soldiers, a break with tradition widely regarded with disfavour. He told me that modern methods and morals nevertheless paid, for in the old days the Government could only put its hands on 40 per cent of all revenue, as the rest was discreetly drained off into private pocketbooks. By the beginning of the year, however, he had reduced the leak to a mere trickle of 20 per cent. On the other hand, when President Lon Nol of Cambodia was told in 1972 that two million dollars of American aid was disappearing into the phantom pockets of 100,000 'spirit soldiers' he is reported simply to have laughed.

Intriguing details of Sukarno's generosity with cash from the national till emerged during the trial in 1966 of Jusuf Muda Dalam, ex-Minister for Central Bank Affairs in Indonesia, who had been arraigned for manipulating public funds on a colossal scale but declared firmly that he handed out money only on the specific instructions of the Bung. Drab daily existence in Djakarta was much enlivened by the court scenes, in which the action was punctuated by a parade of languorous beauties who provided eye-catching, three-dimensional décor reminiscent of a Ziegfeld Follies production, for the ex-Minister was also charged with polygamy.

A twenty-seven-year-old secretary explained how she escorted five wives and three concubines to his different guest houses. 'How did you have time ... ?' the bewildered court president asked the defendant. 'There is plenty of time after office hours,' Dalam retorted severely. And there was plenty of money too. A raven-haired vision of twenty-six in a white shimmering dress mentioned a novel kind of gift for good girls – a two-million-dollar import licence, granted to her on 'deferred payment' terms. An actress confirmed that Dalam had allowed her another vast sum on the same basis, and a third charmer described how he had given her cheques worth five and a half million dollars to cash. Altogether this fast-moving man-about-town, whose name means 'Joseph Young Inside', was accused of squandering more than two hundred and fifty million dollars by granting import licences and credits to tame businessmen and pet mistresses without guarantees or time-limits for repayment. He said he accepted 'gifts' from grateful merchants in return, 'because my salary was not enough'.

But behind the trial of Dalam was the shadow-trial of Sukarno. One personable young lady confessed that Dalam had allowed her a two-million-dollar loan after she had gone to see the President. The Bung's Japanese wife admitted that she had been given another two-million-dollar credit, and not only a marketful of merchants but a famous woman racing driver chipped in with other stories of presidential thoughtfulness.

Sukarno also accepted 'gifts', and one businessman who had been accorded a ten-million-dollar loan on orders from the Palace was required to pass 600,000 dollars of it back to the President. Small wonder that his successor, President Suharto, ungallantly told a crowd who saw his wife with him in 1968: 'She was fat before I became President – don't think she has become fat since.'

When Marshal Sarit of Thailand died, he was found posthumously guilty of having embezzled state funds to the value of £12,000,000, at least £7,500,000 of which had been diverted into his private account, most of it to be spent on 'minor wives' of whom there always seemed to be a score or so around at any one time. Sarit and his family held the monopoly for importing gold and the concession for the sale of state lottery tickets, and had acquired controlling interests in more than a dozen businesses, including a construction firm much favoured with Government contracts.

The creeping damp of Asian corruption filters downwards from the top. The civil service is regarded as the ideal opening for young men ambitious not so much to slave for their country as to improve their situation and that of their family, and when a Filipino bureaucrat was caught giving special import licences to his wife, the President himself defended him indignantly with the words: 'Is there anything wrong with a civil servant providing for his future?' In 1968 another official in Manila claimed tax exemption for the 'gifts' he had paid out to his own seniors and to useful Congressmen, and listed them all on his assessment form. Five years later a member of the Malaysian parliament protested that the immediate effect of imposing heavier fines for traffic offences would be to oblige motorists to pay heavier bribes to the police.

Generations of exasperated American aid experts in Vietnam cursed mercenary civil servants for filching the medicine and comforts sent down to the villages to win the hearts and minds of the peasants away from the Vietcong. But the resentful petty official saw himself as the victim of a vicious system of western discrimination whereby the peasants got free cloth or choppers or candy, and he got nothing. By helping himself judiciously to the quantity befitting his rank, therefore, he was only ensuring a fairer distribution of foreign aid.

On the outskirts of Saigon lorry drivers with loads of innocent vegetables or concealed Vietcong paid the police to allow them through, and in Manila and Djakarta pointsmen would hold up trucks and cars to exact a little casual tribute from those in a hurry. During the Sukarno era rent-a-rifle soldiers in Indonesia would hire out their weapons to a would-be killer or kidnapper for a modest fee and ask no questions. Bullets came extra at two shillings each. In 1968 Indonesian navy helicopters were still making trips around the capital carrying tourists ready to pay a pound a time, and army trucks ran shuttle services to the suburbs for any grateful commuter with the price of the journey in his pocket.

For countries where the system of taxation is not effective enough to collect sufficient revenue to guarantee government servants a living wage, the private citizen who has put nothing into the central exchequer finds himself paying out to the individual functionary instead. And in Sukarno's day only one Indonesian in every 400 paid taxes, but all needed the signatures of seven officials to be wed, and of five more to be buried.

The more complex the bureaucracy, the more numerous the tollgates and the bigger and the more equitable the graft. In the Philippines this egalitarianism could be seen at its best in the sixties, when a merchant might pass through fifty-four eager hands in the Customs Department before he was free to sell imported goods under a misleading description which would enable him to recuperate his outlay in bribes by paying less duty on them. Within this vicious circle the customs officers made more, but the exchequer made less and therefore paid them less so that they in turn had to make more money still by taking more tips for seeing that customs duties remained unpaid and the exchequer therefore made less.

A simple principle underlies much of the corruption in the East: Time is money. The official will save you precious time by putting your application at the top of the pile, or stamping your licence without delay, or granting your immigration permit, or letting your car through the cordon. But you must pay, for every minute has its price. Western champions of eastern corruption claim that it gives the administration a flexibility which enables a man to get things done without being bogged down in a bureaucratic morass. This comforting theory ignores the fact that the system favours the tycoon who can afford to pay his way through a forest of formalities in which money is cheap and documents dear, while prices are pushed up prohibitively for the small man. The lopsided licensing pattern which then develops inevitably makes for a lopsided national economy.

The managers of the big white companies do not usually soil their hands with all this sticky money, but they may employ a native fixer who knows which waving tropical palms to grease to get what they want. They themselves remain contemptuous of the corrupt oriental, blissfully unaware, it seems, that the man who slips a Djakarta policeman a thousand-rupiah note is as venal as the policeman himself, even in a world in which the cops are the robbers.

The older Asian neither praises nor blames corruption, for its sweet smell is a part of life, like weather and hypocrites. For all his lamentable acquisitiveness Marshal Sarit was genuinely mourned by many in Thailand, his splendid obsequies were attended by the King and the Queen, and an opposition motion to deprive him of his rank posthumously was roundly defeated. He had steered his country through a difficult passage of years, and his peculations must be taken as part of his performance.

A Manila merchant said on the subject in 1969, 'All that worries us now is that here in the Philippines graft has reached such proportions that the government has become *inefficient*.' The citizen in a corrupt society has his own place on the spiral of connivance and confidence. To assure him that he will be more secure if the community is remoulded into a new, exotic shape within which his equilibrium will be maintained by law and not lucre is like telling a nervous non-swimmer that if he just lies still he will float anyway.

The Traffickers

As hallowed by history as corruption, the diligent practice of piracy and smuggling on a grand scale is also part of the pattern of politics in South-east Asia. In 1969, accordingly, Lee Kuan Yew told a slightly surprised reporter in Singapore that perhaps the most useful role the United States Seventh Fleet could play after British forces had withdrawn from the area would be to check the growing piracy in the Straits of Malacca.

This occupation, regarded as reprehensible in the squeamish West by those who think in terms of the haphazard depradations of buccaneers like Blackbeard, Morgan and Kidd, had respectable origins in Malayan waters as a form of systematic taxation. Henchmen of the local rajahs boarded ships when they sailed into the river estuaries bound for markets upstream, and exacted a toll from them. Malacca itself – one-time powerful Venice of the East – held the gorgeous West in fee by forcing ships to put in and pay in coin or cargo for the right to proceed further, while great war-fleets of Muslim rovers, proud of their profession and sanctified by their persecution of the infidel, hovered in wait for them in the South China Sea. Piracy was the flighty sister of commerce, in the tradition of the trade-or-raid policy of Vikings who importuned the English in the eighth century, landing on their coasts with a pair of scales in one hand and a two-edged sword in the other like Blind Justice herself.

Things are not what they were, and the modern Malay, Thai or Chinese pirates make do with modest enough little squadrons. But they operate in fast launches armed with machine-guns or junks fitted with a row of powerful outboard motors, and hijacking smugglers or terrorizing and robbing fishing fleets are routine activities. In the uneasy waters that lie between Borneo and the Philippines, cut-throat raids on coastal towns are one of the hazards of living. In mid-1968 four boatloads of pirates armed with high-powered weapons assaulted Basilan City in the Southern Philippines and fought a pitched battle with troops and police until helicopters flew in army reinforcements. This was no isolated instance, and Lee Kuan Yew's concern was quite natural. For Royal Navy minesweepers working with RAF patrols have in recent years crippled flotillas of marauders infesting the notorious Sulu Sea, but in May 1973 the Malaysians reported that pirates were active again and 'stern measures' might be necessary to suppress them.

Piracy and general smuggling still envenom the sometimes bilious relations between Malaysia and the Philippines, but in the sixties the real poison was provided by the Filipino 'cigarette boats' – long, dainty fingers of open craft capable of skimming over the razor-edged coral at 35 to 40 knots, leaving any revenue cutter or armed hijacker to feel its way gingerly around the hazard. Slipping into the small sun-baked ports of Sabah, the Malaysian state in North Borneo, Filipino cancer merchants could cram 350 cases each containing 10,000 'blue seal' American cigarettes into one of these, and set off safely again across the 800 miles of sea to Manila. Their purchases were not illegal in Sabah, and their re-entry into the Philippines was made as smooth as a well-oiled palm. In this elegant fashion 90 million cigarettes could be smuggled into the republic every month. Until recently Malaysia made a million pounds a year out of the legal 'shipping tax' on all forms of exported contraband, while Manila lost more than forty million pounds in annual revenue. The reluctant Malaysians were finally persuaded to forgo their profit and sign an anti-smuggling agreement with the Philippines in a spirit of goodwill. However, this goodwill, like all spirit, quickly evaporated when exposed to the elements and by 1969 the slim cigarette boats were back in Sabah's harbours, 'smugglers' in the English of the Filipinos, 'barter traders' in the English of the Malaysians.

But in South-east Asia the very word 'smuggle' should be used after careful thought, for impoverished governments must resort to many unorthodox ways of raising cash. When it becomes legitimate, smuggling should be called traffic, and once it is official, it becomes trade.

In 1967 those flying over the lightly grilled Thai plains from Bangkok to Vientiane in the antique aircraft of Royal Air Lao might at any time find themselves sitting next to some unassuming individual whose sole luggage consisted of a bundle of gold bars resting on the otherwise empty seat on his far side. The gold was brought into Laos legally, subject to payment of an 8½ per cent duty. It was then quietly filtered out again with the blessing of the Laotian Finance Minister, mainly to ready buyers in Saigon and Bangkok, and ultimately to India and elsewhere. It accounted for half of all that Laos earned, for it moved at a speed of up to six tons a month, and the price of a kilogram outside Laos – including in Communist Hanoi – was anything from £40 to £140 pounds higher than the price originally paid.

The principal Laotian export of the past decade, however, is not officially listed. From the ideal spring-like climate of the northern uplands the Meo tribeswomen trudge down to the markets in the plains to barter their agricultural produce for gold and cloth and salt. And their main cash crop comes from waving fields of *papaver somniferum* which may yield sixteen pounds of crude opium per acre.

The 'smoking saloons' of South-east Asia range from utility accommodation with wooden benches for trishaw drivers and coolies to the usual plush tourist traps, but ask in any of these where the opium has come from, and the reply will be 'Yunnan'. Yunnan is the mountainous south-western province of Communist China whose government in Peking, filled with sanctimonious ideological scruples, joined North Vietnam in refusing to give any details about national production of the raw material of oblivion to the 'Imperialist' United Nations Opium Board until the People's Republic was itself admitted to the world body. But 'Yunnan', like Cognac', has become a loose generic term. It applies to the opium not only of China, but also of the other countries whose high frontiers converge in the same remote region of tossed hills and lush valleys – the

Shan States of Burma, the northern borderlands of Thailand, the western limits of Laos – where the absurdly-named 'Garden Poppy' flourishes and multiplies.

From this 'Golden Triangle' – the source of half of the world's opium, it was estimated in 1973 – the trail of poison leads southwards to the Thai frontier region, where in crude 'kitchens' in the mountain villages practised hands refine much of it into powder with a morphine content of up to 80 per cent. In North Thailand the commerce is in part organized by remnants of the Nationalist Chinese army which were forced out of Yunnan when Mao's men overran the province in 1950. There is no evidence that China deliberately exports opium, but traditional local enterprise is not easily discouraged. While Peking and Taipei indulge their common talent for mutual mudslinging, therefore, the growers of Communist Yunnan and the former diehards of President Chiang Kai-shek may co-operate – if at arm's length – in a profitable venture in damnation.

The narcotics seep down to Bangkok and from there out into the world – in the tyres of cars, in sacks of fertilizer, even embedded in the flesh of specially-branded cattle. Some pass through Rangoon, or are smuggled overland to Singapore. For a long time an enterprising group of French pilots ran a transport service affectionately known as Air Opium, dropping their cargo at selected points outside Saigon or parachuting it into the Gulf of Thailand to be picked up by waiting ships. But the main centre of distribution is the British Crown Colony of Hongkong.

In Singapore or Hongkong an ounce of white heroin may be worth thirty times its price in the 'factories' of Bangkok, and 150 times that price when it is peddled off Piccadilly Circus. In most countries the traffic is officially illegal, but may nevertheless have powerful protectors. In Laos military aircraft authorized by the top brass have flown the drug, and in Thailand marketing is invariably in the hands of men of distinction. Bribes buy blind eyes, and in some parts of the Far East, in consequence, the arm of the law is more golden than long.

But if minds and movements in modern South-east Asia must

be seen through filters that bring out the gaudy threads of gold and graft, piracy and *papaver somniferum* in the geopolitical design, they must also be observed through the other influences that colour them, from philisophy to superstition. For in an ignorant subcontinent opium is not the only religion of the people.

Mumbo-Jumbo Makes History

WHEN I wrote *Chinese Looking Glass*, certain superficial critics in England sneered at me for suggesting that superstitious belief and religious custom had survived Communism in China itself. (The Chinese Communists, being rather better acquainted with the subject, have repeatedly admitted that the supernatural has been among their most stubborn ideological foes.) But then a common western fallacy until recent years was that the new generation born in Soviet Russia must grow up knowing nothing but Marxism, and would therefore behave like a mindless machine programmed to repeat propaganda only.

Instead, forty years of Communism produced a Russian salad of Communists, drop-outs, teddy boys, dissenting writers, protesting students, and plain ordinary patriotic youngsters, as did forty years of democracy in other countries. In fact, the technological West might have stunned Asia into a state of amnesia more easily than the Marxist East during the same period, for it did not challenge cult with cult, but offered the same collection of distracting gadgetry from the Pill to Pop Music that had emptied the churches and the consciences of the white world with an efficiency Mao Tse-tung himself might have envied.

However, most people in the East are poor and ignorant, and therefore cling to the habits and superstitions of their venerated ancestors. The elaborate graves in a Chinese cemetery are often decorated with photographs of the departed, so that those who cannot read the inscription in stone will nevertheless be able to identify their dead relatives. In Laos seventeen out of twenty cannot write, in Filipino villages only five men in every thousand buy a newspaper. It was not until 1960 that the first Dyak from the longhouses of Sarawak began to study modern medicine. He had been introduced to this strange science when a visiting English missionary had given him a dose of castor oil seven years before. But his regular family doctor had been a *bomoh*, whose stock remedy was to paint his face and chant ferocious incantations. It often worked, for his half-naked patients were no sceptics.

Dress must not be allowed to deceive in such matters, however. A smartly turned-out Lao, sipping his Scotch in the bar of the Georges Cinq in Paris, may be observed with some surprise to be wearing several frayed and rather soiled threads of cotton around his wrist in place of the platinum chronometer one might expect. But the threads serve a purpose almost as important in this brisk age as telling the time: they keep his thirty-two souls inside his body and out of mischief.

When it is suspected that the souls of the thirty-two parts of the human anatomy are straying and perhaps falling in with evil companions, or when someone is sick, or marrying, or about to leave on a long journey, or has just returned home, it is customary in Laos to give him a *baci*. This is a ritualistic party to which the *phis*, the animistic spirits of mountains and flowers and water and trees and dawn and dusk, are also enticed with promises of gifts. Once the presiding sorcerer is satisfied that all are present, he calls back the souls of the guest of honour: 'Be with us, return to your home of flesh, fear not, return to your body,' he wheedles, and when the souls are once more imprisoned he slams the bolt home by tying the first length of cotton twine around their owner's wrist. Others present follow suit, each bestowing a wish upon him. Even Soviet ambassadors to Vientiane have been known to return to Moscow suitably abashed with faces as pale as milk from a non-stop round of diplomatic farewell parties, and body and soul held together only by a thread.

Laos are devoutly Buddhist, Malays are Muslim. But just as the Laos will invoke primitive divinities with names like Sakke, Kamaphob, Attarikhe, and their stilted bungalows have spirit-houses in the garden in which gifts of food may be placed to placate the *phis*, so the Malays believe that a *kris* may be the home of a *kramat* or spirit that could kill a man even if only his shadow were stabbed with it. *Kramats* are common throughout Indonesia and Malaysia, and when a few years ago the Malayan Railway Administration wanted to move an old brass cannon that was holding up the construction of a terminal near Penang, the matter had to be referred to the State Religious Affairs Department. For many believed that the cannon had healing powers, and its caretakers demanded that a medium first obtain its permission for the move.

The West also has its witches and warlocks, but they are not normally hired to keep the pitch dry for a Test Match at Lords, or engaged to find a lost flock of sheep with incantations. The Malay *bomoh*, however, is a versatile fellow who, like Lloyds of London, will insure you against anything. In Malaysia the general practitioner will undertake to locate missing corpses, drive off ghosts, heal the sick, supply love potions, put spells on a customer's enemy, and much else besides. To him the supernatural and natural are all one, and he shows it in his contempt for both, to which headlines in the English-language press bear witness – 'School Ghosts Told: Keep Off Students', one before me reads, and another: 'Spirit in Tree Served Quit Notice'.

Some *bomohs* are not above using their spiritual powers to gain very material ends indeed. They have been involved in crimes from confidence tricks to robbing the Treasury, but their real speciality is rape. Local faith can be only too touching, it seems, and in 1969 the Malaysian Education Minister specifically advocated sex-lessons in school to protect pupils because 'we have all heard of those *bomohs* and religious teachers who have been brought to court for molesting girls'. The record is impressive, possibly a legacy from the ancient days of Chen-la when maidens were ceremoniously deflowered by monks before marriage, for the accent is very much on youth.

One Malaysian medium took away and violated a fifteen-year-old after telling her mother that he was going to perform a ritual which would remove eight lethal needles hidden in her body, and an eighteen-year-old wife was ravished on a beach by a *bomoh* who assured her that this treatment would 'cure her husband's stomach-ache'. Even a blind *bomoh* has been known to take a girl out at night 'to dig for gold' and then outrage her. Another told his victim that he had to see a mole under her left breast in order to forecast her future, and a third raped three fifteen-year-old schoolgirls who were under the mistaken impression that he was making sure they passed their examinations. Age cannot wither them, it seems. In April 1973 an amorous *bomoh* of sixty-nine was finally slaughtered by an irate husband who discovered that he himself had been lying in the same bed all the time while the old wizard, having first used supernatural powers to immobilize his wife, had made love to her on three successive occasions.

Not all *bomohs* are bad, however. The magical healers of Indonesia and Malaysia are often careful herbalists who will charge no fee for their services – they were incidentally the first to use quinine as a cure for malaria. Today *bomohs* trusted by the aborigines in the backwoods of Central Malaya are being given a smattering of western medicine and a compendium of pills to increase their powers. But while many of them are turning towards antibiotics rather than arrowroot plucked by the light of a gibbous moon, western doctors are beginning to study their earlier methods more closely.

In 1968 an opposition MP tabled a written question in the Malaysian Parliament asking the government if it would appoint a national *bomoh*, and also seek the services of other reliable witch-doctors to stop the annual floods in the peninsula. There was nothing odd about this suggestion. When the King of Malaysia (they are elected every five years) paid a state visit to Sabah, a seventy-year-old *bomoh* was flown over the Kuala Lumpur to keep the sun shining, for it had been raining steadily for about a month in North Borneo. His timing was perfect. Everywhere His Majesty went, the weather smiled upon him, but within forty-eight hours of his departure, storms were lashing the streets of the state capital, and a gale half-scalped Sabah's oldest church.

Among educated Malaysians to whom Oxford, Cambridge, or the Middle Temple are alma mater, and whose tastes run to Jaguar cars, the stock-market and golf, far more than would

care to admit call in the family witch-doctor to cure suffering
– or sometimes to inflict it on others. Politicians hire *bomohs*
as they hire bodyguards – to protect them against the *bomohs*
of their opponents. An attempt to liquidate President Suharto
of Indonesia in mid-1968 was ascribed to a witch in the pay
of the equivocal ex-Foreign Minister, Dr Subandrio. Sihanouk
and Sukarno consulted soothsayers, and important if mystifying political consequences might follow when prophetic
words were whispered into their ears by some shabby old
shaman. Warned that he would 'die by the knife', Sukarno
hesitated to commit himself for surgery when his kidneys
rebelled, and drew comfort instead from acupuncture and her-
bal drugs prescribed by Chinese doctors from Peking. This put
the Maoists in an excellent position to spread the rumour
that the President was about to die, and so precipitate the
abortive Communist coup of 1965.

That coup was nevertheless inevitable, and so was the blood-
bath that came after it. Eight hundred years before, the great
seer-king Djojobojo had prophesied a long period of subjection
from which the Javanese would be freed after a yellow race
had driven their white masters away and ruled them 'for as
long as the age of maize'. Liberated Java would then be led for
twenty years by a man with supernatural powers, but 'a time
of madness' would follow, in which half the Javanese would
perish. Only after that would a second superman and a 'prince
of justice' arise to bring prosperity once more to the land. The
Dutch, the Japanese, Sukarno, and the Chinese all played their
roles faithfully in this predestined drama.

That Sukarno was Djojobojo's first 'supernatural' man cannot be questioned, for every Javanese knows that this is why
he survived several particularly distasteful attempts on his
charmed life. In the West he was depicted as a sex-soused
megalomaniac, fumbling compulsively with girls and glory. But
distance plays tricks with values as with light, so that images
may appear upside down, and what marks a man for disgust
in the occident may mark him for distinction in the orient.
Asian peasants, ignorant of nations but loyal to their leaders,
expect divine despots to be demanding and the incarnation of

Vishnu to be virile beyond the potency of ordinary men.

After the 1965 coup, Sukarno was not violently wrenched from office, but stripped of his power excruciatingly slowly, as if it were his own skin. For Suharto, advised by his own *dukun* or medicine-man, suffered keenly from stage-fright. He was reluctant to deface the god-king with whose fate his own seemed so mysteriously linked. Assured, however, that he and the Sultan Hamengku Buwono of Jogjakarta were respectively Djojobojo's second supernatural man and prince of justice who would jointly restore peace to Java, he gained confidence and started to take logical steps to see that the prophecy came true. His predestined running-mate, the Sultan, was made a superminister with nine portfolios under his control, and subsequently told the press that his plans for the economic recovery of Indonesia would start bearing fruit in 1970. Whether this prediction was inspired by a computer or an astrologer is seriously open to question.

Numerology and astrology wield an arcane and incalculable influence over public events throughout South-east Asia, where even house-numbers may be chosen for luck rather than location, and do not always follow each other consecutively. When Sukarno set 270 experts the task of drawing up a National Overall Development Plan he was not so much concerned with the content of its 5,000 pages, as with its form: it had to be divided into seventeen volumes, eight parts, and 1,945 clauses, because Indonesia had declared independence from the Dutch on 17 August 1945. It is now possible to graduate in astrology in Thailand after a four-year course, and it is certainly desirable that this occupation, which regulates the very tempo of life, should be confided to the hands of properly qualified experts and not left, like politics and government, to a haphazard collection of amateurs.

A professional was consulted before the date was set for the formation of President Suharto's cabinet, and many believe that Mrs Bandaranaike lost the general elections in Ceylon in 1965 because her astrologers goofed over the choice of polling-day. The new Thai constitution was originally to have been proclaimed on 9 June 1968, but the stars said 20 June, and 20 June

it was. In the same year the King of Laos was advised to open
the country's new radio station – a gift of the British under
the Colombo Plan – on the first of August. Only at the last
moment was it discovered that astrologers had been using the
wrong calendar, and, to the annoyance of the heavily-engaged
monarch, the inauguration had to be switched to the following
day. They were nonetheless asked to select an auspicious date
for the Royal Government and the Pathet Lao to sign a peace
agreement in September 1973. The Communists did not object,
it seems, to this manifestation of bourgeois-reactionary and
feudalistic superstition.

Astrology and clairvoyance not only time events, but shape
them. Their exponents, when sycophantic or self-seeking, will
promise their clients distinction and glory in the hope that they
will then swagger forward confidently and claim the eminence
predicted for them, whereupon the soothsayer will in turn enjoy even more powerful patronage. Different scheming politicians and ambitious generals, turning to different astrologers,
are in this way driven upward in an ever-narrowing rivalry,
for only in the context of off-peak bus services is there ever
plenty of room on top.

A sibyl in Vientiane went into a trance and shrieked that
Kong Le was the reincarnation of a former king. Could anything more perilous have happened to the inflated ego of the
cocky little captain who had already seized the Laotian capital
with his paratroops? A seer told Chaerul Saleh that he was
destined to reach the highest office in Indonesia, deceitfully
withholding the important rider that he would then be involved in a massacre. This revelation unquestionably fired the
ambition of the arrogant Indonesian minister, who is said to
have forced Sukarno to sign the declaration of independence
in 1945 at pistol point, and who once ferociously felled a
senior Shell Company representative to the green with a number three iron for objecting when he failed to shout 'Fore'. Yet
the prediction obviously clashed with those provided by the
pet prophets of Dr Subandrio, General Nasution, General Suharto, and Sukarno himself.

Mysticism makes its own history. The wife of the Vietnamese

warlord, General Khanh, commissions a geomancer to resite her kitchen so that it will be more fortunately oriented and in harmony with the universe. But word gets out, other generals at once suspect that Khanh is unsure of his ground in more senses than one, and that the moment has therefore arrived to mount a coup against him. Within a few weeks, in consequence, Khanh is out and his emboldened rivals are in. Why did not Kong Le and the Communists attack the Royal Laotian capital of Luang Prabang at the beginning of 1961, as all expected? Because they would have drawn down upon themselves the vengeance of the *phis* protecting the corpse of the late King Sisavang Vong, whose uncremated body was still in the palace precincts, preserved in a large jar of formaldehyde.

Does Prince Boun Oum promise democracy as the antidote for Communism? No one cares. For a Lao villager who knows that there are sixteen hours in the day and the world is flat, the most powerful antidote for Communism is not democracy but Boun Oum's magical amulet. This loathsome fetish, which happens to be a dried human foetus, enables the prince to become invisible at will in spite of his aristocratic corpulence, and is part of the mystique which binds the Champassak peasantry to him in spite of the blandishments of the pro-Communist Pathet Lao. The ease with which magic can beat Marx in the myth-laden lands of South-east Asia must never be underestimated.

Four Thousand Million Born Losers

'How many religious sects are there?' asked a powerful sixteenth-century Japanese overlord when the Buddhists of Kyoto begged him to suppress the new rival ideology that was being so effectively propagated by a certain Francis Xavier. 'Thirty-five, Excellency,' they replied. 'Then it seems to me that one more is not likely to make much difference,' retorted the great magnate, dismissing the plea. The feudal *daimyos* accordingly embraced Catholicism enthusiastically, finding that this act of faith won the hearts of the Portuguese, who would then furnish them with the cannons and muskets they so earnestly desired in order to kill each other off more efficiently.

The world's most dangerous weapon after the megaton bomb and mob oratory is the label, for when it does not destroy completely, it blinds. The peoples of the Far East cannot be tidily docketed Christian or Muslim or Buddhist or 'Commie'. In Java alone 'Islam' covers about 150 varieties of the faith, including one pious group that was found to have killed forty-eight people in answer to somebody's inner voice in 1968, and another that was banned in the same year for ordering its disciples to pray naked.

Every man from Goa to Nagasaki has his own worm's-eye view of God, and his own road to salvation. In Korea 434 couples are married at a mass wedding, and then take off in a fleet of newly-imported Swiss buses for nearly six weeks of celibacy and evangelical work instead of a honeymoon. They belong to the Tongil Church, which was invented in 1944 and requires newly-weds to observe strict chastity for forty days after their marriage. While others whip their way through Good Friday in Manila itself, fifty miles to the north a young Filipino dressed in a purple robe and a crown of thorns has himself impaled annually on a ten-foot cross with stainless steel nails by a crowd of extras dressed as Roman soldiers.

Down in the capital another young Filipino stretches his arms wide as he recites his rosary before a plastercast image of Christ on the Cross. As one member of a team of eight, he has taken the *Cursillo*, a short course in instant salvation that includes a three-day retreat for what detractors have called evangelical brainwashing. From now on he is bound to the brotherhood of his own team, and to the wider Christian fraternity of all other 'Brods', as the cursillistas call each other. He is on call like a member of Alcoholics Anonymous to save any backsliding 'fall-out', perhaps rallying him with the theme-songs of the movement, including its own version of *Colonel Bogey*. The *Cursillo* is a society within a society. It is gradually crystallizing into a political force like the much older *Iglesia ni Kristo*, which was founded as far back as 1914 by a hatter called Felix Manalo and now has more than three million followers.

INK is a high-powered organization for godliness combining business efficiency and political punch with a Communist cell-structure that has defeated the Communists themselves. It preaches popular religion in plush, air-conditioned modern chapels where the faithful may lounge comfortably in well-sprung fauteuils, part of the pay-off from a spectacularly well-run exchequer. The Iglesia operates a system of mutual aid among its units, and this closed circuit of social insurance alone has drawn many converts. But INK also has its own firm doctrine, which demands rejection of the Holy Trinity, of Christ as God, of the Virgin Mary and the immortal soul. The brotherhood achieves emotional unity through the solace of weeping, for its oratorical preachers reduce their congregations to tears regularly once a week.

With its cells and subcutaneous political power, INK is in many ways a Christian parallel of the Buddhist Sokagakkai movement in Japan, but I first encountered modern mutations of Buddhism in Vietnam, and I could hardly have had a more exotic introduction to Asia.

I had never been east of Suez until 1954, when an Air France

Constellation picked me up in Paris and dropped me down two nights later in Saigon. It was pitch dark and pouring with rain. I had no local piastres and my hotel booking had fallen through. A kindly Briton put me up for the night and I found I had flown 9,000 miles to eat a supper of mock turtle soup, bacon and beans. The East was nevertheless at my elbow, and at dawn we drove to the Holy See of the Cao Dai sect at Tay Ninh for the Mid-Autumn Festival. The Great Temple of the Cao Dai was an opium-eater's dream of Westminster Abbey, the two square towers and the ridged roof writhing with multi-coloured Chinese dragons and curling prodigiously at the corners, the pillars entwined by gaudy serpents, the embrasures embellished with giant lotuses. The ceiling was a mass of silver stars, and from above the altar the Eye of the Great Spirit bored down blindly upon the marble floor. But among garish sacred beasts in stone or stucco were also the effigies or symbols of Christ and Buddha, of Confucius and Lao Tzu (the mysterious master of the Taoists), and a painting of saints ranging from the late President Sun Yat-sen of China to Victor Hugo (in the full fig of an *académicien*). For Cao Daism is nothing if not syncretic, and its cardinals assured me that when he died, Winston Churchill would be canonized and reverentially inserted into the holy calendar.

A cocktail of most great needs, the Cao Dai doctrine was inspired by the dreams of a young Vietnamese civil servant earlier in this century, and the Church was first organized in 1926. It was in that year that the elaborate ouija board, which is the means of contact between the faithful below and the rather numerous divinities above who jostle for attention on its pointer, suddenly spelled out: 'I am the Supreme Sovereign. I am the oldest of the Buddhas. I am Jesus Christ. I now take the name of Cao Dai to teach a new religion.' The board was demonstrated to me later by two young mediums, but there were no revelations.

After a vegetarian lunch we stood on the balcony of the Great Temple and watched a long procession of religious floats followed by a march-past of the Cao Dai army. For this Vietnamese Vatican controlled not only the souls of 1,500,000

men and women, but also the rich province of Tay Ninh, and
it was defended by some 20,000 soldiers of the Great Spirit who
had been armed by the French to fight the Vietminh. Across
the years, however, Cao Dai generals have shown the same
genius for reinsurance with governments and guerrillas as their
founder displayed with gods. They have rallied gallantly to His
Holiness their Pope, or retired in revolt to the sacred Black
Virgin mountain that sticks out of their wooded plains like
a vital statistic; they have intrigued against President Ngo Dinh
Diem, submitted on occasion to the indelicate attentions of
the CIA, engineered a tacit truce with the Vietcong in order
to outlive and outlast them.

The Hoa Hao are different. The Vietminh rewarded them for
their initial support by assassinating their beloved Master,
Huynh Phu So (sensibly taking care to cut his body in two
and bury the pieces far apart, in view of his supernatural
powers). Huynh Phu So was a dynamic spiritual leader who
preached a new, simple and ascetic Buddhism, and rapidly
gained renown as a great healer and prophet who foretold
the Japanese invasion and the French defeat. He founded a sect
which may have more than a million devotees, and whose
centre is Hoa Hao village, deep in the Mekong Delta. The Hoa
Hao army was also equipped by the French to fight the Vietminh, and in 1954 joined the Cao Dai in defying Ngo Dinh
Diem. The Hoa Hao believe that the Communists could not
really have killed their Master for ever, and that he will
therefore come again. But hate is long, and in the flooded flatlands of their principal province the Vietcong moved on
tiptoe during much of the Vietnam war.

The Cao Dai and the Hoa Hao sects, like all the strange
progeny of Hindu and Buddhist belief, trace their ancestry back
to the doctrine of Brahman, the All-Pervading spirit of the Oneness of the Cosmos. The monstrous regiment of Hindu gods
and heavenly avatars sometimes makes the devotee of this
mother-religion appear to be a polytheistic pagan, but these
deities simply provide convenient symbols for the many aspects
of the One which a plain man can then see in his mind's
eye or shape into an idol – Vishnu, the Preserver; six-armed

Kali, the Destroyer-goddess of the Thugs; Ganesh, Wisdom with
the head of an elephant. For Brahman is formless, and cannot be
envisaged. Now the Christian is compassionately rescued from
struggling with the concept of a formless Creator by the legend
that God made man in his own image, yet even he must conjure
up the picture of an old fellow with a white beard. But to
mistake this venerable gentleman (whose features can be submitted to anthropometric identification by any reasonably well-
equipped police force) for God, is to take the picture of the
apple for 'A', measurable illusion for immeasurable reality, and
as futile as putting a clock in a crypt.

The reality of the universe is that light and dark, silence and
sound, cold and heat are all part of the One, for they cannot
exist independently of each other. Good and evil are inseparable. All that gives the illusion of individual form or contrast,
therefore, is deceit. When man measures and classifies everything, including himself, he creates an illusory world of false
identities, among which is his own ego.

Buddha was a Hindu, and Buddhism teaches that a sage asked
the Greek King Menander of Northern India who said he had
come to see him in a chariot to 'Explain what "chariot" is. Is
the pole the chariot? No. Is the axle the chariot? No. Is it then
the wheels, the frame, the flagstaff, the yoke, the reins, the
goad? No. Then is it the pole, axle, wheels, frame, flagstaff,
yoke, reins and goad added together which is the chariot? No.
Then is the chariot outside the sum of these things? No. Then
I can discover no chariot at all except for the sound "chariot".
There in fact is no chariot. So of whom are you afraid, Great
King, that you do not speak the truth?' The King replied that
it was the dependence of the parts upon each other which was
the chariot. Similarly, concluded the saga with an approving
nod, there is no enduring ego. What we call 'I' is not a fixed
being but simply a collection of sensations, thoughts, emotions
and wishes. And it is this interdependence of parts that makes
all One.

His obsession with the illusory world of 'ten thousand things'
is at the root of man's suffering. He can only attain bliss by
prising his fingers away from it, whether they are clutching

at riches or reason. Until he withdraws from the mirage, shedding the greed and hatred that it so falsely engenders and that bind him to it, he is chained to the wheel of life. He is reincarnated again and again, and each existence is a new settlement day for the moral debts incurred in all previous ones. It is a terrible world, but he has to live somewhere until he can stop pretending that he is anybody and craving for personal rewards. Right thinking, right speaking, right acting will lead him to right understanding, contemplation and enlightenment – his sudden, final awareness that he is one with the universe. Since at that point he has no further claim to a separate identity, he is excused from further living and the flame of his mind is gently blown out. That is Nirvana.

To the disciple of this Theravada Buddhism, whose yellow-robed bonzes throng the pagodas of Laos and Thailand, Burma, Cambodia and Ceylon, we therefore live in a community of 4,000 million born losers. His creed offers no Messiah, demands stern asceticism, and promises nothing more than blessed oblivion at the end of it all. But farther east among the millions of China and Vietnam the comforting Mahayana Buddhist doctrine, with its gentle saints, its short cuts to a Heavenly 'Pure Land' through simple faith and the calling of Buddha's name, its prophecy of a Buddha that is to come bringing happiness to all, long ago overshadowed the stricter sects. For Asians are not immune from man's most terrible of fears, expressed in the universal silent prayer that no church voices : 'Please, God, Let there be a God.'

At dawn the quavering voice of the *muezzin* replies : 'There is no God but God,' reaching me through loudspeakers plugged into the tape-recorder on the minaret of the stucco mosque near by, and Malays in the kampong next door turn piously to the west to pray. Islam slashes the Buddhist yellow of Southeast Asia with a scimitar of green, its hilt resting on the border provinces of South Thailand, its great curving blade taking in Malaysia and the Indonesian archipelago, its tip lying over the Southern Philippines.

But Islam is more than a faith. The Holy Koran is a transcript of the will of Allah, and since his will cannot be expressed through the fallible sense of justice of mere humans, Islam is not simply a religious congregation, but a society regulated by a legal code which has been divinely inspired. There is no priesthood, and the Muslim is spared the bureaucratic frustrations of going through channels to God. But there are Kathis and Shariah courts to administer Koranic law, working parallel with the secular magistrates and the civil courts of the country.

Sitting with the beauteous Che Rogayah binte Abdul Rahman in a Brunei bar and asking what she would like to drink, I realized that this innocent meeting for an off-the-record interview about her husband (who had been detained for fomenting an insurrection in 1962) could get us both into trouble on two counts. Overzealous police of the Kathi's court in this sanctimonious enclave of Islam on the North Borneo coast could catch us for technical *khalwat* (compromising proximity) and slap a further charge on me for tempting Che Rogayah to alcohol, which is *haram* (forbidden). A couple may be guilty of *khalwat* if they go to a cinema together, or link little fingers in the street, and frequently if somewhat unfairly Chinese bartenders are arrested in Brunei for serving liquor to Muslim Malays who bang on the bar and demand brandy or beer, as if all the weaknesses of the Faithful were the fault of the infidel.

The Muslim may go to the mosque only once a week, as a practising Christian goes to church, but he must pray five times a day, he must fast during the month of Ramadan, and he should make the pilgrimage to Mecca at least once in his life. In Southeast Asia Islam is inextricably intertwined with ancient Malay custom, however, and most Muslims, easygoing by nature, are only ostensibly strict in their observances for fear of the ire of their Kathis rather than of the wrath of their compassionate God.

The flesh is weak. Men drink liquor in private, eat surreptitiously during the fasting month, slip into the cafés on Friday when their employers release them to go to the mosque. Imams are not immune from the more tantalizing temptations, and in 1969 one of these prayer-leaders was arraigned for making love to two of his concubines while his four wives and a third concubine watched. This, it seemed, was against Muslim law, but the defendant pleaded it 'kept household relations harmonious'. The Kathi's courts are busy with divorces – in the fervently Muslim Malaysian state of Kelantan, for example, more than seven out of ten marriages have broken up in the past. In addition the magistrates hear cases involving the abuse of women, the use of alcohol and the eating of pork (mousemeat was also outlawed in Java during the thin year of 1963). In Brunei Muslims are gaoled for adultery.

The orthodox are still strong and the bigots powerful. Some religious teachers in Malaysia insist that even to go near a dog is to be defiled, and in 1962 Muslim leaders urged the government to ban alcoholic drinks throughout the country, to forbid the showing of films on Thursday night before Friday prayers, even to arrest all who failed to attend mosque. One Mufti was obliged to admonish a teacher for calling Muslims themselves infidels if they so much as associated with unbelievers. The Islamic laws of Malaysia discourage wedlock with non-Muslims and still stipulate that the infidel bridegroom or bride must first embrace the Faith. Intermarriage between Malays and pork-eating Chinese has therefore been relatively rare, and these two strong, mutually-suspicious racial groups which dominate the Malayan peninsula cannot blend into one harmonious community. Islam lies between them like a sword.

Yet like the Buddhist Sokagakkai of Japan, the Vietnamese Hoa Hao, and the Filipino Iglesia ni Kristo, Islam still offers a formidable challenge to creeping Communism – despite the common belief of fanatical Muslims and fanatical Maoists in the cleansing properties of that most sinister of self-contradictions: the Holy War.

Wars of Religion

MY first contact with the world of holy wars was Colonel Abdullah Taher Hussein Tyrconnel-Fay, an Irish-Canadian Muslim convert and the liaison agent of Darul Islam in Singapore. 'Turk' to his friends and enemies, a curious blend of the over-precise and the fraudulent that made one think of false teeth, the 'colonel' was a prized acquaintance, for it is one of the pleasures of life to deal with men whom the pious have written off as all rogue.

It is the righteous who are to be distrusted. Ambassadors are professional liars, and no one can be more preposterously dishonest than a second-rate politician, unless it is a second-rate academic. Status is no guarantee of probity. The correspondent who is always talking to well-polished premiers or clean and lightly-oiled four-star generals is simply blinding his editor with giants.

Turk was the perfect example of the deceptively dubious: a long, sallow middle-aged man whose flat expressionless hair and eyes might have been painted on the pockmarked face with lacquer. He spoke with a Canadian burr as soft as a quagmire, but the Canadians like everyone else refused to give him a passport. His background was not only obscure, but shifting, as the tales about him changed. People did not believe him when he said he had been in the Special Air Service and had parachuted into Greece or Albania, that he had become a Muslim in the Middle East and was in constant contact with Darul Islam rebels in North Sumatra. For he cadged drinks and borrowed money, and so he was marked down as an army deserter and a blarneying beachcomber. But his claims were true.

However improbable the colonel might have appeared, he

was the boss of the Darul Islam office in Singapore. He slipped 'Ministers' of the insurrectionist government into the island, and on at least one occasion to my knowledge justified Sukarno's suspicions of Malayan sympathy for the insurgents in Sumatra by taking one of their leaders to meet Tengku Abdul Rahman in Kuala Lumpur in the middle of the rebellion.

A silver-studded black holster hung on a hook behind his door, his drawers were filled with shopping lists for Bren-guns and British mortars, and a large framed map of Indonesia was screwed to the wall. I remember that map well. In unenlightened continents people sometimes stick pins into small images of their enemies in order to torment or kill them by proxy. This map of Indonesia was transfixed by scores of pins shewing the locations of Darul Islam guerrilla forces in revolt against Djakarta. And the magic worked, if in reverse. Every time Turk thumbed another tack through some name on the map, that place in turn suffered the horrors of terrorism, murder and arson, for he was recording the latest focus of Darul Islam interest.

Led by a white-bearded Imam with headquarters in West Java, Darul Islam was virulently anti-Communist. Its followers had risen against Sukarno when he failed to make Indonesia an Islamic State after independence had been proclaimed from the Dutch, and by 1958 their loose confederacy had established the supreme authority of the Koran and the kick of the Lee Enfield rifle over great regions of North Sumatra, Java, Celebes, Borneo and many of the smaller Indonesian islands. Their fanatical hard-core was fringed with thugs, and they burned, ambushed, massacred, and spent money like water abroad in the cause of holy war. It was they who tried to murder Sukarno with a hail of hand-grenades outside the Tjikini School in 1957, and I subsequently met the man who planned this peculiarly repulsive act of piety in Turk's Singapore flat. He was a Darul Islam militant working in the Djakarta headquarters of the youth movement of the legal and constitutional Muslim political party, the Masjumi.

And here lay the heart of the paradox, for the anti-Communist Muslim terrorists defeated their own object in the end. The more that tens of thousands of Darul Islam rebels extended their dominion of violence over the archipelago as disreputable partners of the Masjumi, the more Sukarno and the nationalists were persuaded that Muslim militants were a bigger threat than the Marxists to the secular state of Indonesia. In consequence the powerful Indonesian National Party moved closer to the Communists, the Masjumi Party was outlawed, and a determined campaign launched to stamp Darul Islam into the dust. By 1965 it was just another bloody memory.

Its instruments discredited, Islam lost the leadership of the nationalist movement which had first flickered into unsteady flame nearly 150 years before. By 1964 it was flabby, disorganized, split into factions, victim of its own corrupt political chiefs. By comparison, the PKI looked well knit and invincible. The moment finds its men, however. As the Communists urged Sukarno to arm the workers and peasants and the threat of a left-wing take-over bid increased, a mass movement of Muslim youth rose to challenge them. The orgy of killing that followed the Communist coup in 1965 was for many the latest stage in a *jehad* or holy struggle against Communism which the Rector of Al-Azhar University in Cairo, the highest seat of Muslim learning, had urged upon the Islamic world early in 1959. Although Java, soaked in the earlier dyes of Hindu–Buddhism, was full of permissive 'lapsed' Muslims the faith had thrown up enough militants to fight the 'good' fight.

But in the other, yellow half of South-east Asia, where Buddhist canon and not the Koran is the repository of man's beliefs, it has been otherwise.

Across the Theravada Buddhist lands hundreds of thousands of celibate novices and monks tend the well-kept temples and live on the charity of the people, for they are allowed to own nothing themselves but three pieces of cloth, a mat, a blade, a needle, a water-strainer and a begging bowl. In Laos the housewives kneel humbly at the roadside each dawn to fill these bowls as the bonzes shuffle past in Indian file, for they may eat only one vegetarian meal a day, and that before noon. Throughout South-east Asia it is usual for teenage boys to don the saffron toga and enter the pagoda for anything up to two years, and crown princes are not exempt from this spiritual substitute for the draft. The bonze is the village teacher. He will be consulted over the smallest decisions and he wields a moral influence that rival politicians are always anxious to win for their side.

If the lapsed Muslim is guilty of a tolerance towards his fellow-humans that has tarnished Islam in Indonesia, however, the black sheep of Buddhism that have erred and strayed from the Noble Eightfold Path can be counted in flocks. In 1966 General Ne Win said the body of Buddhism was fouled by 'pseudo-monks' whom he publicly accused of cheating, killing, sleeping around and boozing. Gangsters, fugitives from justice, and common idlers thronged the pagodas in yellow robes which gave them anonymity and sartorial sanctuary. And these were not in all cases euphemisms for men whose real crime was that they had defied Ne Win.

There was nothing new about this defiance. The bonzes of South-east Asia inherit fine fighting traditions that in other parts of the world are normally associated with famous regiments. According to legend it was the unarmed Buddhist monks of China who invented the ancestor of all the more terrifying pugilistic practices of the East, including karate, and one historian remarked nearly forty years ago that in Burma 'no political mob was complete without its saffron-robed leader.'

In South Korea celibate monks, incensed over the authority granted to married men in church affairs in 1960, burst into the Supreme Court in Seoul, smashing windows and sacking offices, and police squads could only quell the rioting after knocking twelve shaven pates unconscious and bundling the rest of the ringleaders off in trucks. Six of the rioters then tried to commit hara-kiri on the spot and had to be rushed to the nearest hospital. This may seem mystifying in the West, for it must be some years since cudgel-toting ecclesiastics took London's Old Bailey apart. Yet only a few months earlier Theravada monks from rival monasteries in Rangoon had gone to war upon each other with bricks, rocks and bottles, and when the police arrived to appeal for a little peace and holiness through loudspeakers, the monks had replied by combining forces to shower the common enemy with missiles for two hours. They only stopped when the riot squad unfairly started firing gas shells into both monasteries.

Nowhere, perhaps, has the potential of the pagoda as a cradle for political rabble-rousers been better exploited than in South Vietnam, where mayhem directed by militant Buddhist bonzes has so often provided a discordant urban antiphony of howling mobs and wailing sirens to the staccato ballad of battle in the countryside. Since 1963, when President Diem fell as their first victim, they have overthrown three governments, and helped to edge three others towards the abyss.

As the smoke and the smell of teargas clear for a moment from disorderly scenes of street power and strife, a man may pause to ask what has happened to the Four Noble Truths of the Lord Buddha, to the belief that all suffering is born of human passions and desires, and that salvation lies in turning the back on worldly things. But just as the casuistical Christian can find excellent reasons for condoning mass killing in wars holy or unholy, so the Mahayana Buddhist in particular has a ready-made rationalization for playing politics or pelting the police with broken glass. He must bring not only himself but all others nearer to Nirvana. If he sees misery and misgovernment thrusting his despairing fellow-men into sin and corruption, he must renounce selfish renunciation which otherwise would keep him aloof from the human tragedy, and pitch in.

Nevertheless, in some respects the cloistered Theravada monk who withdraws from the world is as unstable an element in the ideological struggle as the militant and his mob. He avoids taking sides, for fear of becoming the victim of rage and ambition. He sees capitalism and Communism as crazy if contradictory obsessions with matter. Safe in the sanctuary of his spiritual eyrie, he can coexist with either, and thinks he can be master of both. Western agents who have embarked upon the terrible intellectual odyssey of trying to win Buddhism over for democracy have soon been lost in swirling sea-mists of contradiction. The modern Sokagakkai sect in Japan fights Maoism with its own weapons, and in Burma there has been a defiant revival of worship and ceremony since in 1967 Communist rebels tortured bonzes and trampled on Buddhas. On the other hand there are also Buddhists who hail Marx as the modern torch-bearer of many of their own teachings, and complaisant priests in Communist countries ready to pay lip-service to a Lenin who, after all, is only part of the Illusion. I have clattered through the empty halls of pagodas in North Vietnam to find a solitary Superior who has been neatly inserted into the setting to greet me with bitter tea and tell me of the square deal Hanoi is giving holiness.

The desire for peace has been a passkey to the often baffling complex of relationships between the Buddhists and the Vietcong in South Vietnam. The worst mistake a correspondent can make in Saigon is to look no further than the devious intricacies of the local political weave, thinking that he has now seen everything. It is essential to turn the rug over, not only for the dirt that has been swept underneath, but for the even more unlikely system of knots and link-stitches and loose ends to be found on the side you do not see.

In 1954 Wilfred Burchett, the pro-Communist Australian correspondent and writer, flew down to Saigon from Hanoi to observe how the Fascists were living, and introduced me to an agile young Frenchman with a square face, round spectacles and a thin strip of well-mown moustache who might have been Molotov's favourite son, but whose name was Charles Meyer. A few days afterwards Charlie took me to a certain Mr Tran, who in turn invited me to a tea-party attended by twenty-six Vietnamese intellectuals, all members of the newly-formed 'Vietnamese Peace Movement'. The movement was soon broken up and its leaders arrested as Communist-front agitators, but I never lost touch with Mr Tran, and after Diem's demise in 1963 his peace-loving friends were released. These, in their turn, now introduced me to militant Buddhist leaders whom I had so far failed to meet, for they were as close to the more pugnacious priests as is glue to lacquer. Trudging through the mud of the Vien Hoa Dao pagoda in Saigon, which was field headquarters for the Buddhist offensive against the new régime of General Khanh and looked it, I would sip the inevitable tea with some bonze in his wooden hutch of an office while typewriters chattered indignantly next door, trying to discover when the next riot would be raised and just where the Vietcong came into the matter.

I only saw the master mind, the ambitious, sloe-eyed Venerable Tri Quang, as one of a crowd, but as time passed the tracery of thought beneath that bony skull began gradually to show through, like veins under ageing skin. Tri Quang had been accused of being pro-Communist and of conspiring deviously with the Vietcong. Accordingly, American Quang-watchers were cast down when this powerful prelate castigated their pet Vietnamese governments one after another, but uplifted when he declared staunchly that he hated 'atheistic' Communism, and that it 'could never win'. Yet these two remarks revealed his most perilous conceit – that the materialism of Marx offered no permanent challenge to the teachings of Buddha, and that therefore he could sup with this devil even with a short spoon. He did not denounce the National Liberation Front, for he conceived it to be cleanly divisible into a Communist minority and a 'Buddhist' majority with which he was in touch.

Both parties wanted peace, for the Communists were convinced that they could then take over the country, while the bonzes boasted that they would then unite the Buddhists on both sides and leave the Communists stranded. As one Buddhist politician put it to me: 'We can only lose the war, but we could win the peace.' And this arrogant assumption may yet cost Vietnam dear.

The Catholics of Vietnam do not, it seems, share the Buddhist belief – illusion or reality – that they can spiritually outflank Hanoi, for most of the priests in the South originally fled with their flocks from the Communist North. They are ferociously anti-Marxist, and as far back as 1965 they were already debating what to do if South Vietnam were sold to the enemy, some desperately advocating that they take to the *maquis* themselves, perhaps regrouping all able-bodied Catholics in the southernmost area of the Mekong Delta and fighting off all assailants from there.

I saw their first Exodus, but now there is no further that

they can go. In 1954 nearly a million men, women and children bundled up their poor bits and pieces of pots and pyjamas in North Vietnam, and then crowded on to half-submerged rafts and leaking old tubs in the hope of reaching rescue ships waiting outside territorial waters before their own craft capsized or were shot up by Communist soldiers along the coastline.

Life was little better for them when they reached South Vietnam. From my room in the Hotel Continental in Saigon, I could look down upon the airless oven of the main square with its peeling, fever-yellow theatre, around whose withered lawn and stinking gutters were camped hundreds of Catholic families from the North, their shrill hubbub rising like the morning chatter of migrating birds. They had perched their pitiful little tents of black rags and cardboard wherever they could steal a six-foot square of soil, and there they contrived to cook, to quieten querulous children, to wash themselves and their clothes meticulously in water scooped from the drains, to fight in their misery and squalor and filth and frustration, women shrieking hysterically and tearing at each others' waist-long hair, men kicking their wives mercilessly in the rump.

But then aid began pouring in, and the Government, dominated by the Catholic family of President Ngo Dinh Diem, set the refugees to work rebuilding their lives. All were sorted according to trades, sites were chosen, and neat little brown wood-and-palm-thatch villages, each with its church and school, sprang up around the country. The Catholics were on their feet again, 700 miles from their original homes.

At first the Buddhists watched impassively as the oligarchy in the presidential palace perpetuated the religious favouritism of the Catholic French colonialists. But later they began to complain, for promotions and plum jobs and import licences and foreign aid funds were flowing to this minority of fewer than two million Christians. The schools remained in Catholic hands, and the power went to Catholic heads. When the Buddhists rebelled in 1963, the disdainful Madame Ngo Dinh Nhu, sister-in-law of the President, dubbed them Communists who should be 'beaten three times harder'. After the first bonze had burned himself alive, she complained that the Buddhists had used 'imported petrol' to 'barbecue one of their monks'.

The first outbreak of Buddhist violence was a protest against religious discrimination and organized by bonzes who felt a Christian conspiracy closing in upon them, a Cabal of Catholics on both sides of the world – President Diem, President Kennedy, Cardinal Spellman. With the brutal suppression of Buddhist demonstrations in Hue, Catholic became synonymous with Can Lao – the hated secret Government party within the administration and army – and indiscriminate terror was countered with indiscriminate terror as Catholic villages were sacked and looted and Catholics were killed by Buddhists in their turn. By 1966 the tumult had died down. But a year later the Buddhists were again aroused when general elections threw up forty Catholic senators out of a total of sixty under another Catholic President, Nguyen van Thieu. And then in 1972 President Thieu laid down stringent qualifications for the registration of political parties that quickly reduced their number from more than twenty to three – one of them Catholic, but none Buddhist.

No religion needs Communism as a focus for hatred, for there is always another religion to fight. Little love may be lost between Catholic and Buddhist in Vietnam. But by the same token the harmony of the hammer and sickle is not for the Cross and Crescent (which they so curiously resemble).

When it was rumoured that a Protestant teacher had made disagreeable references to Islam in Indonesia in 1967, several thousand Muslims attacked Christian churches without further ado, damaging nineteen, and Imams in many parts of the republic began making wild speeches in the mosques. The fever recurs like malaria. Two years later Muslims wrecked another Protestant church in West Java, and in 1970 a Catholic school. And when President Suharto introduced a new marriage bill in 1973 which stipulated that difference of race or religion should not be obstacles to matrimony, this incitement to unholy wedlock with the infidel was violently attacked by Muslim scholars as 'disguised Christianization' that would 'destroy the principles of Islam' and legalize 'atheistic' wedlock and free love.

In 1968 the Muslim Moros of the Southern Philippines were complaining that they were neglected by the Christian Government in the capital, fobbed off with meagre funds and empty promises of improvements, and treated like second-class citizens. There were only four congressmen and no senators or generals or police chiefs of their confession, and they were losing their lands to Christian carpet-baggers from the north. President Marcos hastily flew south to meet an ex-Governor of Mindanao who threatened to create an independent Islamic republic, gave the disgruntled dignitary a gold watch, and promised to build a mosque in Manila.

These handsome gestures did not resolve the matter, however. By 1970 Muslims and Christians were butchering each other over land claims, and three years later some 9,000 armed insurgents were fighting to set up a breakaway state in the south. The President claimed that in all the rebels numbered 14–16,000 and were armed with modern weapons provided by foreign states.

Suspicion fell heavily on Tun Mustapha, Chief Minister of neighbouring Sabah, who was accused of training, arming, and dispatching Muslim volunteers to fight alongside their brothers in Sulu. But when plans for an uprising had leaked out in 1968, Filipinos had already blamed the Malaysians, some of whose politicians were at that very moment accusing the Buddhists in Bangkok of discriminating against the Muslim and Malay minority in the southern provinces of Thailand. Once again religious unrest was adding an extra, spicy ingredient to the stewpot of international rivalries in South-east Asia.

Where the world of Islam and the non-world of Buddhism touch there is no meeting of minds, as Sihanouk was distressed to find when he opened the sixth international conference of the World Association of Buddhists in 1961. Declaring that Buddhists held the 'keys to international society' because they were peace-loving, showed tolerance, and knew how to master hatred, he expressed faith in U Thant as Burmese Secretary-General of the United Nations since he was a 'fervent disciple of Buddha'. Nevertheless, on the very evening that Sihanouk spoke four people were killed and more than forty injured when Buddhist monks led anti-Muslim rioters on the rampage through a suburb of Rangoon.

Two months earlier Burma had become the world's first Buddhist state, and the Government had celebrated this pious enactment by closing the Rangoon meat, poultry and fish markets for three days during which the slaughter of animals was prohibited. More than 500 pigs, sheep, ducks and crabs were sent to monasteries for sanctuary. Moreover, ninety-eight humans under sentence of death were also spared, for the devout Buddhist kills no living thing, however lowly.

But the new law at once fired men on all sides with the worldly passions of greed and illwill so strictly abjured by the Lord Buddha. Non-Buddhists objected indignantly to the idea of a Buddhist state religion, and Buddhists were infuriated by riders in the law giving non-Buddhists freedom to teach other faiths. A confusion of righteous rioting and protest followed, with Hindus mobbing Muslims, Buddhists boycotting national ceremonies, and Christian Kachin and Karen guerrillas in the hills fitting more mayhem than ever into their working week, inspired by the earlier teachings of Baptist missionaries.

By 1966 General Ne Win had sapped the power of the native Buddhist hierarchy and its sources of income, but he had also thrown it a sop by flinging out all foreign missionaries, nationalizing their hospitals, and seizing their schools. Like the generals in Vietnam who have for years vied with one another to win either the approval or the healthy fear of the priests, Ne Win had learned the lesson to be drawn from the Judgement of Paris: it is difficult to say which is more dangerous – to arbitrate between gods, or women.

Ladies Only

THE jagged mountains of Central Sumatra are fissured by golden fjords of fertile plain, and in these may sometimes be seen the magnificent houses of the Minangkabau, standing like solitary six-horned cattle amid the growing grain. The eaves of a small home, built of intricately carved wood and roofed with thatch or gleaming corrugated aluminium, sweep upward steeply at each end like the horns of a buffalo, but as the family grows, new extensions are added, giving a second pair of glittering horns, and later perhaps a third. Minangkabau means 'Winning Buffalo', and these people proudly trace their origins to the authors of a thoroughly questionable ruse which is said to have saved them from the hegemony of the Javanese some centuries ago.

It seems that a certain King of Java who claimed suzerainty over a hostile Sumatra ill-advisedly agreed that their dispute could be decided by a buffalo fight, rather than the usual procedure which leaves these valuable beasts safe on the sidelines while the men slaughter each other over such issues. A site was marked out for the match, and in due course the Javanese fielded a herd of enormous males.

The Sumatran entry, on the other hand, raised a contemptuous laugh, for it consisted of the puniest animals the Javanese had ever seen. They looked puny, however, because they were extremely young calves. They were, in fact, sucklings to whose soft noses the sly Minangkabau had attached sharp spikes. The Javanese males, in the gentle manner of lesser species, offered these youngsters no harm, and the sucklings were therefore able to make swiftly and greedily for what they took to be the udders of their elders. After a few excruciating minutes which hardly bear thinking about, both the Javanese king and the

Javanese buffalo knew only too well that they had been licked.

This humiliating legend, with its undertones of sex-war, is symbolical. For the Minangkabau were matriarchal, women wielded the whip, and when an extra 'horn' was built on to one of their houses, it was because a new son-in-law was moving into the home of the daughter, and the young couple would come under the care and control of the mother or grandmother. The Sam Sui women, who go out to work shovelling cement or laying bricks in Singapore, are the mistresses in their families also, and from the Nairs of South India to the Mois of Vietnam there are Asian societies in which the lady inherits the power or at least the purse. But with the demand for sex equality in a modern age and the consequent emancipation of the men, the matriarchs have been losing their mastery as swiftly as their sisters elsewhere have been losing their mystery.

For the rest of Asian womanhood, however, the screw has been on the other thumb, and the lowly female must now fight her way to freedom through a fog of religious and traditional prejudice. For all eastern confessions are marked by that disdain for women which is common among seers and sages. The Catholics do not allow them to be priests but may canonize them once they are safely dead. The Mahayana Buddhists, however, do not usually go so far, and when Kuan Yin, Goddess of Mercy, became a Buddhist saint this unique achievement was nevertheless marred by the fact that she had started out as a male god in the first place. Women may enter the Buddhist Pure Land of Bliss above, but they have to be transformed into men for the purpose. In Burma the glory of manhood must never be tarnished by female disrespect. A wife must be meek, for Buddha himself was born a man. In old-fashioned homes, therefore, it is sacrilege for a woman to touch anything of her husband's with her feet, to use the same jar for bathing, to throw her clothes on to his bed.

In Islamic Malaya wives were formerly 'the mean ones within the gate'. 'Women', the Koran tells the Muslim curtly, 'are your tillage.' A husband may beat his wives, according to the good book, for 'Men have authority over women because God has made the one superior to the other'. Mohammed was married several times – once to a child-bride – and the Koran allows a man four wives provided he can treat all four alike, and unlimited numbers of concubines. Yet Mohammed was a champion of women, it has been said, for to commit polygamy was a charitable act in a society loaded with weak, unwanted girls. Unhappily, the liberalism of great men opens loopholes for the licence of lesser ones, however, and for centuries Muslims have quoted the Prophet himself to justify marrying twelve-year-olds or applying Parkinson's Law to their harems. Until recently a Malay could divorce his wife simply by saying the word 'Talak' three times, and men have been known to acquire a string of forty wives over a few years by starting with two and then divorcing one to pick up a third, and repeating this simple process of marital knitting until they have worked their way through three dozen or so.

Muslim women are not the only ones to suffer in a buyer's market. In April 1972 the High Court of Malaysia ruled that when a young Chinese had formally told an assembly of friends and relations two years before that he was divorcing his wife for showing disrespect to his mother, the proceedings were perfectly legal and he subsequently owed her no maintenance. The Malay judge found that as she had been married according to Chinese customary law, she could be divorced on grounds recognized by Chinese customary law, which are said to predate Confucius (who died in 479 B.C.). And the seven customary grounds for which a Chinese wife can be summarily disowned are showing disrespect to the husband's parents, jealousy, barrenness, theft, serious disease, adultery – and talking too much.

Just as polygamy, condemned as a vice by the outraged West, had virtuous origins in the East, so the arranged marriage now so repugnant to the European was considered a sensible and practical custom, while the white man's freedom to choose his own mate appeared in oriental eyes to produce comically ill-assorted couples and columns of divorce cases. For many Burmese and Laotians, the consent of the fiancées themselves is still irrelevant, and bride and groom often do not speak to each other before their wedding day.

A Chinese schoolteacher in Singapore told a divorce court in

1968 that he had only slept with his wife once, and he had been drunk at the time. His bride had been his mother's choice, not his own. But it is to be remarked that the marriage had lasted twenty years. The West has nothing to say on this subject, for the history of Europe is hideous with the howlings of beaten wives and of daughters sold off willynilly into wedlock. 'For very need,' complains the voice of one impoverished English gentleman down the ages, 'I was fain to sell a little daughter I have *for much less than I should have done by possibility*.' In Europe also, every price had its girl.

South-east Asia is schizophrenic about the solid flesh. On the one hand Muslim leaders wage an unceasing war on lust, it is not uncommon for the authorities in Malaysia and Indonesia to neutralize exotic curves with exotic curbs, and beauty contests always produce their own *crise de conscience*. In 1965 thirteen rather obviously budding Miss Malaysias competing for the honour of representing their country at the Miss Universe contest at Miami Beach were suddenly told that they could not parade in swimsuits, for this would be offensive to both the religious and national culture of the fatherland. They therefore presented themselves before an astonished audience of 8,000 Malaysians in baby-doll nighties (which were a knock-out anyway).

At the same time Rizal Province in the Philippines outlawed bikinis, backless dresses and all garments 'tending to show any part of body from the breast down to the middle of the thigh'. Wearers could be sentenced to between twenty and thirty days in gaol. In Kuala Lumpur, police also insisted on attending an undress rehearsal of the bare-bosomed *Ballets Africains* before sanctioning a public performance to be attended by the Prime Minister, although like honest witnesses testifying at the trial of their traditions the girls swore that they were 'not covering up for anybody'.

Yet the women of Bali have for centuries made do without uplift, and although bare breasts are now banned, they quickly shed the irksome and unaccustomed bra when no one is looking. They will, moreover, revert to their traditional folk costume by whipping off their tops if a tourist with a camera flourishes a suitable banknote. The Mois of Vietnam also concede that one exposure deserves another, and British soldiers fighting in North Borneo during Sukarno's Confrontation of Malaysia collected colour-slides of dusky Dyak women that may have taken some explaining away back at home in Dunstable and Doncaster.

A highly-sauced mixture of poker-faced propriety and tropical heat characterizes Asian morality, tickling the palate of the Anglo-Saxon accustomed to the dull fare of his own workaday hypocrisy. The Vietnamese Secretary of State for Social Welfare, for example, announcing that special brothel quarters would be set up in the main towns of the hard-pressed republic so that soldiers could enjoy proper 'rest facilities', solemnly assured his hearers that the decencies would be strictly observed : no females under eighteen would be allowed into these A-certificate precincts, and gambling would be strictly forbidden. Kissing in local films causes a furore, for it is irreligious and lustful and common, and so only to be done when no one is looking. In Thailand, where 'making love in public is contrary to the national tradition', kissing on TV is not allowed. But the number of girlie-bars, all-the-way massage parlours and bookable premises for private orgies in Bangkok more than doubled between 1965 and 1966 alone.

Which came first, the phoenix or the ash? The moral laws that invite contravention, or the profligacy that calls for moral laws? 'The women of this country are lascivious,' remarked a visitor to Chen-la. 'When a husband does not satisfy their desires, they abandon him. If the husband is called away, the wife will usually say after a fortnight : "I am not a ghost : how can I sleep alone?" ' The enthusiastic amateur is indeed not unknown in South-east Asia, her inclinations sharpened, it is said, by eating the evil-smelling durian. One pound of this large, knobby fruit contains about 600 calories and has a wondrously high protein value. But Asians give it credit for more than that, so that the Malays say 'When the durians are down, the sarongs are up', and the police of Djakarta on occasion find themselves ordered to restrain not only the city's 10,000 professionals, but the so-called 'hiding women' who demand no money, but love for love of love.

The Asian Communists, supposedly dedicated to a continence far removed from the gross excesses of the licentious capitalist, are not immune to the urge. In 1964 it was revealed that the Huks frequently took an extra woman as a paramour 'provided she was within the confidence of the Party and the family'. In both Indonesia and Vietnam, the Communists have not scrupled to recruit and train loose women either to corrupt and suborn officials or to seduce overgallant American soldiers and kill them when their heads were turned.

Certain literary parasites have made large sums of money by depicting the journalist as an alcoholic layabout who invents the news in between rounds of drinking and debauchery. But even in my fancyfree days in Indochina I found myself only too often struggling earnestly to get the story in the face of irrelevant temptations pushed my way by frivolous subversives. I remember the anticipation with which I climbed into a black Citroen in Saigon one night to meet an undercover contact to the Vietcong, only to find that it was also occupied by two giggling little charmers in silk *ao-dais*. 'My nieces,' he explained fondly, while the girls tinkled away at this sally like windbells on a temple roof. 'Look," I protested angrily, 'I came out to talk, not fool around with girls.' 'Of course, of course,' he replied, planting one on my lap, 'but we need them as camouflage. Do you want us to look like a couple of conspirators? This way we are just a pair of husbands on a night out.' But it was soon clear that he was simply making a necessity out of a vice.

It had all happened before. When the highway across South Vietnam was still open, I had joined two left-wing extremists on a trip from Saigon to Cambodia. I knew that the noise inside a two-horsepower Citroen clattering over the roads of Indochina would leave little margin for murmured confidences, but on arrival in Phnom Penh I hoped for an evening of interesting revelations, to be extracted painlessly during a leisurely dinner and a pleasant chat. They had other things in mind, however. After a snatched supper, they collected two girls from a house on the edge of the capital, packed them into the back of their rattletrap on either side of me, and tore off into the countryside while I fought for my composure with both hands.

Our destination was a love-village, a hamlet of thatched wooden houses on stilts which could be hired by the night and were staffed by servants ready to provide drinks and light refreshment discreetly, but were otherwise uninhabited. We were served raw turtle eggs, and I was then invited to hear the musicians in a room at the back. 'But I'd rather have a bit of talk about the recrudescence of guerrilla activity,' I argued despairingly. 'Later, later,' they said. 'First, the three musicians. They're waiting.' I love the liquid soft notes of Cambodian music, and allowed myself to be pushed gently into a small moonlit chamber. I emerged some considerable time later, and borrowed a comb. I had learned what the Vietnamese meant by 'the three musicians', but we never did get around to talking about the recrudescence of guerrilla activity.

It was a pro-Chinese adviser to Prince Norodom Sihanouk who first introduced me to Madame Choum on the pretext that we were going to discuss Monseigneur's last visit to Peking. 'It's the best place to talk,' he said. 'Quiet, discreet, and the opium is of sound quality.' We climbed the steep steps of the huge old stilted house, and were admitted by one or two girls. 'Come and say hello to Madame first,' suggested my companion. We pushed our way down a dim-lit wooden passageway and he knocked on a door. 'Entrez,' answered a quavering voice, and we walked in on Whistler's Mother.

At a secretaire in one corner sat a little old Cambodian lady in black bombazine, wearing a cap over the neat bun of her glossy greying hair, black stockings and buttoned shoes. On her nose rested a pair of round steel-rimmed spectacles, and I was not so much introduced as presented. Madame Choum ran a beady, critical eye over me, and apparently decided that my credit was good. After a little while and one soft drink, we were gently encouraged to run along like good boys and smoke outside. The implication almost seemed to be that opium was a dirty habit and no gentleman lit up in a lady's boudoir. It was a memorable meeting. But matters seemed to be arranged deliberately at Madame Choum's to prove that opium and sex were not incompatible, and I learned little of Sihanouk's visit to Peking that evening. When I mentioned the subject, my companion thrust it aside impatiently, protesting that there was a time and place for everything. Sulking over my notes in a corner, I saw what he meant.

However, it is often in fields unconnected with their natural gifts that Asian women have advanced most swiftly towards freedom. They have burst into the men's league from all sides to become taxi-drivers and trade unionists, moneylenders and real estate manipulators, lawyers and doctors, politicians and even diplomats, so that Filipino ambassadors appealed in 1969 to their Foreign Secretary to stop 'this woman explosion' in the service. The Vietcong may have their female artillery, but the South Vietnamese forces also boast tough and grimy girls in green, and in Laos women make highly-trained police officers and army paratroop nurses who jump with the men. As females fight for their rights with that supple feline ruthlessness and efficiency that is so much part of their make-up, the male retreats, so that in Singapore, for example, women are now comprehensively protected by a special Charter, and are given the same pay as men in the civil service – as they also are in Malaysia.

Women are perhaps regaining their ancient but stolen birthright. Funan was a matriarchal monarchy ruled by a queen until the first century before Christ, the Burmese had their feminine rulers, and the Vietnamese were led against the Chinese in 40 A.D. by a team of warrior-queens reminiscent of Boadicea and her daughters. These Trung Sisters had two spiritual successors in the postwar era. In an isolated house on the rainsoaked border of Cambodia and Vietnam I once met under conditions of uncomfortable secrecy a beautiful tigress in peasant pyjamas, devoid of make-up but possessed of a pair of slim, carefully manicured hands whose short-cut nails would not snag on the safety-catch of a machine-pistol. Her voice was soft and warm, but as she dilated upon the unholiness of the Diem Government she began biting off the ends of her words with a vicious snap, and her eyes lit up with sombre hatred. She was 'Madame Ba Cut', the wife of the last fanatical general of the Hoa Hao sect who continued to fight a guerrilla war against the Saigon régime after all other rebels had been crushed or corrupted, and she was reputed to be a more efficient terrorist than her husband (he was caught and beheaded in 1956).

I talked with her counterpart in the ruling Catholic hierarchy she so detested in Saigon in rather different circumstances. The sad rain had been sweeping the swamps, but brilliant sunshine bathed the presidential palace in the capital. I had met Madame Ngo Dinh Nhu, wife of the President's brother, at one or two diplomatic functions and felt no pain, but this time her beauty half-stunned me as I rose to my feet, like a sudden blow from a low ceiling. She had been lightly but carefully made up and then plunged into a plain scabbard of heavy sherry-coloured silk with a simple collarless neckline. She looked like an enchantress.

She did not enchant, however. She started off softly enough, pouring out tea and assuring me almost girlishly that she left politics to the men of the family, but as I raised this or that little matter of opposition to her will, it was if the steel in her were being screwed into a tight coil. 'Yes, at first the women disagreed with me,' she admitted, speaking of a new ukase she had just imposed upon the community. 'But I called their leaders together, and I listened to what they had to say patiently, and then' – and she fixed me with an eye that was growing cold as fast as dying ash – 'and then I *explained* matters to them, and *told* them what had to be done, and after that, *they – un-der-stood!*' – and the measured monosyllables '*Elles – ont – com – pris!*' came out like four jaw-breaking slaps from an iron gauntlet.

Diem found her unendurable, but he had to accept his sister-in-law as 'First Lady'. She invented the Women's Army and the Women's Solidarity Movement. She gave Vietnam the Family Law, forbidding divorce and polygamy and protecting women from the weaker sex, and the Morality Law that outlawed gambling and dancing and sleeping with strangers, and she was, in consequence, much disliked.

Among her many detractors was the Doctor. The Doctor was physically a tiny man, whose feet dangled childishly if he absent-mindedly sat on a high chair on a low dais, instead of the converse. Husky footballers from the CIA have been known to make the mistake of slapping him on the shoulder in the hearty fashion of such fellows, only to see him skitter uncontrollably across the room with a look of durable fury on his features. The Doctor was not a small man in other respects, however, for he was the master of SEPES, another of those chilling acronyms that hide the more intimidating forms of secret police in the best tradition of the GESTAPO and the OGPU. He would nevertheless wax sarcastic about the power of Madame Nhu in his own field of private public service.

'Her word is the law,' he once told me with a marvellous expression of innocent indignation on his friendly little face. 'She rings up any minister she likes, gives them all orders, and they have to do what she says. But worse than that,' and he wagged a diminutive index finger, 'she uses her Women's Solidarity Movement as a private intelligence service. This movement is a farce, I tell you, for most of these women are simply housewives without an intelligent idea in their heads. In fact, what is happening,' he piped triumphantly, 'is that the Government is being run on female gossip.' But in spite of her own imperial waspishness and the resistance of the outraged Vietnamese male, there is no doubt that Madame Nhu had personified the truth that if every dog could have his day, so could every bitch.

Throughout the subcontinent women are sidling into politics. Six were elected to Thailand's new House of Representatives in 1969, and the Malaysians made one of their three feminine MPs a minister. Wives play a crucial role, and much of the mayhem in Laos may be attributable to the fact that while the neutralist Prince Souvanna Phouma is married to a French bourgeoise, his half-brother the 'Red Prince' Souphannouvong is married to a Vietnamese Communist.

Both Ceylon and India have women prime ministers as I write. But while the encroaching female may seem to upset traditional hierarchies, and to dislodge the pieces from their appointed places on the board, the despot and the dictator remain arrogantly male.

20

The Broken Lands

BEYOND the colourful cast of egotistical overlords and ambitious generals, of corrupt officials and pious bigots, of Communist guerrillas and nationalistic mob-raisers who strut across the screen of memory is a faceless multitude – the two hundred and sixty million extras of South-east Asia. Victims of flat-chested economies, of megalomania and war and racial and religious discrimination, these are the poor and the patient whose needs should be our musts, but whose tears have become a tiresome cliché.

'Want?' asks a Vietnamese, wonderingly, stopping in the middle of a muddy village square. 'What do you want me to want – a world free of Communism? A two-party system of government? A TV in every home? I want peace, that's all. I am twenty-five years old and I do not know what it is. But that's what I want.' It is 1966. His country has known only occupation and reoccupation and civil war and political banditry and more civil war since he was born.

Five years later the small Asian everywhere is still dreaming above all of a little security. His desires are deceptively simple – enough to eat, medicine when he is sick, schools for his sons. He does not ask for an affluent society or a welfare state. He does not know of these tourist traps for the traveller on his way to eternity. But he would like a more equitable administration. He wants fairer shares all round, and a little social justice. This does not necessarily imply that he believes he will achieve final bliss through nationalization – that economic Nirvana in which the ego of personal initiative merges into the Oneness of the state. For nationalization simply offers bigger and better opportunities for official incompetence and what is ironically known as official corruption.

He nevertheless offends an American prejudice that has proved to be Asia's political tragedy. The natural conservatism of the American – his reverence for capital, property and private initiative – have made him recoil violently more often than not from any suggestion of levelling legislation in South-east Asia. A man to whom the scramble for success is sacred can only see the politician who may best reflect the modest dreams of backward millions as a dangerous radical preaching 'something-for-nothing socialism', if not a crypto-Communist. But when those dreams are shattered, only the real Communists may be left to pick up the bits. This has been made all the easier for them by the anti-colonialism of the Americans, which has inhibited them from putting strong pressure on Asian Governments to ensure that the money Washington paid out in aid did not simply slide into the fat wallets of the few, lest they be dubbed interfering 'Imperialists' by friend as well as enemy. Many depairing Asians therefore see the ills of the inflamed subcontinent springing from American hostility towards the Left.

It has meant that Vietnam has not been allowed to go quietly Titoist over the years. Instead, the United States has propped up a series of discredited 'anti-Communist' dictators and warlords in Saigon who have consistently attacked any movement based on concepts of liberty, democracy and equality that has incautiously raised its head. This system of 'dealing with principals only', so reminiscent of Victorians buttering up local despots and calling it the administration of an empire, automatically puts age before beauty, old and corrupt ideas before younger and cleaner ideals. In Korea, Formosa and Vietnam, Washington may most laudably save millions from Communism, but the Asians have not always liked the price.

I have leaned across a green baize table to reach for an ashtray, and found my hand in North Korea without a visa. The green baize table stood in the middle of a modest corrugated-steel hut on the windy hilltop at Panmunjom, and the line which marked the cease-fire boundary between Communist North and Nationalist South ran precisely down the middle of it. Here the

titanic struggle between the two world blocs had reached a
point of inertia. It was the South Koreans who paid for the
subsequent 'peace'. Impoverished, separated from their natural
resources, devoting nearly 35 per cent of their budget to the
maintenance of a very necessary army 600,000 strong, they
could no longer stand up by themselves. For twelve years Washington underwrote the murderous dictatorship of President
Syngman Rhee, until in 1960 the outraged young rose spon-
taneously against his infamous régime. The sickly parliamentary
government that then emerged was killed off by coup d'état
a year later, however, and once again the Americans found
themselves shoring up a military junta.

'If you stretch out your arm,' said the general – bespectacled,
donnish, a product of Cambridge and the Inner Temple – 'you
can almost touch the other side from here.' We were not on the
38th Parallel in Korea, however. We were on the Chinese
Nationalist island of Quemoy, staring at the beaches of the
Communist mainland a mile and a half away. The countryside
of this scorpion-shaped island in the maw of Mao's colossus
looked peaceful and empty. But along the rocky coast and in
the barren boulder-strewn volcanic hills were nearly 100,000
moles in uniform who ate, slept, and manned their weapons in
a labyrinthine warren of tunnels, bunkers, and gun positions
beneath thirty, fifty, even five hundred feet of rock. Their frustration grated like a hangnail on satin – the frustration of exiles
sick of dictatorship, of veterans who wanted to 'return to the
mainland', to go back across that tantalizing strip of water to
homes all over China which most of them knew they would
never see again.

'Germany? What has this situation in common with Germany?' It is not a Chinese Nationalist on Formosa, but a Communist cadre in Hanoi, bitterly resenting my suggestion that the
brutal bisection of Vietnam could be compared with the gentler
Herr-splitting in Europe. 'In Germany the people can move
backwards and forwards across the frontiers of East and West.'
In Vietnam it was very different. There was no commerce between North and South, and travel between the two zones was

strictly forbidden. And this was 1957, by Vietnamese standards a year of piping peace. The Geneva Agreement which ended the Indochina War in 1954 had stipulated that by 1956 the two halves of the country should hold general elections, winner would then take all, and Vietnam would be one again. But the year before I was already writing from Saigon : 'There is much speculation as to whether the USA may not ignore the Geneva Agreement and build South Vietnam into a strong military power.'

Diem duly repudiated the treaty clauses calling for elections, and in October 1956 I watched a phalanx of troops marching smartly through Saigon, boots rapping the road in time to the music, rifles at the slope, glistening black hair permanently waved. This was the women's contingent of the new Vietnamese army, and only a small part of a vast military parade to celebrate the first anniversary of the step which had turned the two armistice zones into two hostile states : the proclamation of the new independent republic of South Vietnam. Seventy-six American jets screamed over the saluting-base. Escalation had begun.

These were the broken lands, in which the extremism of the Communist leadership supported by the Soviet Bloc in the North was matched by the extremism of the anti-Communist leadership supported by Washington in the South. In each case the threat posed by the Communists in one half provided the pretext for the President to overrule his parliament and assume quasi-dictatorial powers in the other half. In each case the Oliver Twists who asked for more for the masses were condemned as Communist dupes or decoys. In each case the 'strong man' – Rhee, Chiang, Diem – was defended by his apologists on the grounds that he was isolated and deceived by ambitious scoundrels in his entourage and did not know of the abuses committed in his name.

'And so we have no political leader or party or front or administration which the people trust to put the people first, and which could therefore offer a serious political challenge to the Communists,' a Vietnamese diplomat said to me sadly. 'Vietnamese want prosperity and a square deal and they get poverty and rule by racketeers until we are all stuck with division and war, because we cannot risk unification and peace.' And they were still not risking unification and peace one year after the peace had been provided for under the Paris Agreement of January 1973.

Our Men in Saigon

THE American choice of Ngo Dinh Diem as Prime Minister and the future saviour of South Vietnam in 1954 was as honest as the word of a computer, and dictated by that iron logic which does not bend, but only breaks. Minister for the Interior in 1933, Diem had resigned from the Imperial civil service in protest against France's refusal to grant his country a fair measure of sovereignty. He had declined to become Prime Minister of an 'independent' Vietnam under the Japanese during the Second World War, and he had declined to take office in a post-war 'provisional' government under Ho Chi Minh. He had been stamped and approved anti-colonialist, anti-Japanese, anti-Communist. Moreover, he did not even have to be dewormed of worldly ambition – Mr John Foster Dulles had had to drag him out of his retreat in a Benedictine Abbey in Bruges and beg him to take the job.

It was not the fault of Mr Dulles that this courageous and honourable patriot had grown up a pious, humourless swot, over-fervently Catholic yet educated to the Mandarinate of an empire which had been the vassal of Confucian China. The Mandarinate was the civil service of scholar-officials, and had been founded on the principle that only the educated could be trusted to subordinate personal freedoms to the interests of society. The ignorant millions, on the other hand, must be re-strained by laws. And it was this tradition of the divine right of eggheads, of the futility of debate with the rabble, that inspired Diem's rule.

After an absence of twenty years Diem returned to a Vietnam at the fag-end of the French era and saturated with the poisons of the immediate past. The residue of the entire colonial power structure welcomed the 'pro-American' exile back to Saigon

with the firm determination to cut him down on the first possible occasion. This included the conspiratorial French themselves, the Emperor Bao Dai, the French-trained generals of the
South Vietnamese Army, the Cao Dai and the Hoa Hao allies of
the French against the Vietminh, and also the Binh Xuyen 'sect'
of whom, alas, more later.

Early in 1955 the Emperor ordered Diem to report to him in
France with his Chief of Staff, and to hand over the army in his
absence to the pro-French operational commander, General
Nguyen Van Vy. This was to be the end of Diem. But Diem did
not go, and late one evening I leaped up the stairs of the Independence Palace in Saigon to find myself gaping at a curious
tableau on the landing, where a group of small and rather scruffy
civilians were holding one improperly-dressed Vietnamese
general at pistol-point, while in the background other generals
lounged in deep fauteuils, smoking and chatting in a desultory
manner like spectators at Balmain. The latest creation they were
being shown was the new 'Revolutionary Committee', a confec-
tion of Diem's astute brother which was defying the authority
of the Emperor and noisily demanding that Diem reconstitute
South Vietnam as a republic. This was the group of scruffy
civilians. The general, his insignia already torn away by their
angry revolutionary hands, was Vy. Bao Dai had lost the round.

Vy was far from being the Emperor's only friend, however,
for His Majesty had shown much kind condescension to General
Le Van Vien (or 'Bai Vien' as he was affectionately called), boss
of the Binh Xuyen sect. Binh Xuyen was an autonomous fief in
the Mekong marshlands, a robber barony in which the rich were
plucked and the poor recruited to swell the purses and the forces
of piracy and the protection racket. The Binh Xuyen had collaborated with the Japanese, the Communists, the Emperor and
the French in that order. In consequence, by the time I arrived
in Vietnam in 1954 Bai Vien was enjoying his just rewards, and
sitting astride Saigon as the master of both its vice and its
virtue.

On the one hand he controlled the brothels, gambling farms,
opium dens and night clubs of the capital (The 'Hall of Mirrors'
alone advertised a cast of a thousand personable young ladies);

on the other, a grateful Emperor had made his brother-in-law Director of the Sûreté Nationale, so that Bai Vien might at the same time control the police and security services in addition to his own private force of 5,000 well-armed thugs. Mortal man could hardly have asked for more.

But this satisfactory state of affairs was not to last, for Diem was determined to put an end to private armies and private provinces, and to confine the sects to their religious function. And since all the functions of the Binh Xuyen were strictly irreligious, that would mean their extermination.

I first saw Bai Vien on the evening Diem closed down the 'Grande Monde', the biggest gambling casino in Saigon at whose twenty-odd tables pin-shanked trishaw drivers and portly French officers rubbed shoulders to lose two million piastres a night. This was Diem's first crack of the whip, and as the last customers trooped out Bai Vien was brooding over it, a middle-aged man in an immaculate white shirt and slacks, leaning against his Cadillac and surrounded by his personal hoods. Under brush-cut hair, his face was pitted and swarthy, his eyes like stones in the lamplight. He had already deployed fighting men in and around the city equipped with armoured cars, mortars and machine-guns. 'We are going to teach Mr Diem the four truths,' his aide translated softly into French. The tenets of Buddhism? I never learned. But the stage was now set for a showdown.

A few yards up the street from the Hotel Continental the Binh Xuyen, barricaded and wired-up within the Sûreté Nationale, their gunners alert behind their sandbags, faced the pro-Diem troops at the Ministry of Defence not forty yards away across Rue Catinat. It was as if the front line ran down Bond Street. The whole town was stippled with redoubts and make-shift fortresses, bristling with weapons of both parties.

Diem, cooped up in his palace and 'advised' by an American colonel named Ed Lansdale, was distributing dollars adroitly, and having persuaded certain of the Cao Dai and the Hoa Hao to accept ministries in his government, he began buying up the rest of their generals. Beneath all their plausible promises of solidarity, however, we the watchers seemed to hear the dry slither of treachery. The generals were watching and waiting too, their loyalty swaying from side to side, like the cobra at La Lania.

It was Charlie Meyer who shot the cobra. Among the imperial concessions granted to the worthy Bai Vien was a large tract of rolling jungle eighty miles north of Saigon, in which he had built a shooting cabin. Here the general would come to hunt, setting out down the overgrown tracks at night in a jeep fitted with machine-guns and searchlights, and blazing away at any pair of eyes that shone. But on this occasion he was not with us.

We were an improbable party of four. There was Charlie in shorts and singlet, now a political agent employed by Bai Vien under the curious cover of a geographer. As a geographer he was supposed to help the second member of our group, Bai Vien's brother-in-law, a gentle old fellow with a soft cello of a voice whose avowed aim was to bottle the spring water that bubbled out of these untidy hills. Next myself, six feet of sweat and apprehension, for I had never been on a tiger-hunt before; and finally Suzie, whose presence proved conclusively that the whole venture was a Bob Hope farce. Suzie was a gorgeous butter-blonde with long French legs, bursting out of an undo-it-yourself shirt that hung loose over the briefest of briefs. Formerly associated with an elegant bar off the Rue du Faubourg St Honoré, she was a complaisant companion to many, for she would take most things lying down.

Thus equipped, and carrying one carbine, two shot-guns and a camera we set off in search of prey in the late afternoon. Monkeys looped and swung along their copperplate courses in the treetops far above, the brother-in-law nearly shot his foot off by mistake, and Charlie killed a cobra that rose three feet out of the jungle grass to strike. This commotion apparently attracted a tiger which kept discreetly out of sight, but followed us all the way back to our cabin on a parallel course about ten yards off to our right, every now and then roaring throaty imprecations just when we thought we had left him behind. He reminded me of the Vietminh, watching the absurd antics of their adversaries in Saigon from the wings.

Other scenes flick through the mind briefly like siesta dreams – the bandit's brother-in-law bending solemnly by an elephant pool, tasting water from its spring and murmuring 'Perrier'; Charlie and Suzie and myself in an opium den, Charlie whispering conspiratorially to a sect rebel who dutifully damns Diem but who is absorbed by his task, for amid the sickly-smoky odour of the pipes he is translating the Cao Dai bible into English; dining off a leg of lamb imported from Singapore in the house of the Australian Military Attaché as the mortar bombs scream overhead like a ragged flight of startled birds to explode with shattering futility in the grounds of the presidential palace across the road. Plaster falls into the peas. Bai Vien has begun teaching Diem the four truths, it seems.

The mortars, I believe, are sited near the Y-Bridge, which is just off the boulevard that links Saigon with Cholon. The bridge crosses a waterway called the Chinese Arroyo but also serves a long slip of an island that splits the channel into two at that point. On this island the defiant Bai Vien has set up the headquarters of the new 'National Front of United Forces' which combines the armed enemies of Diem among the three sects – Cao Dai, Hoa Hao, Binh Xuyen. The front has issued a five-day ultimatum to Diem, demanding a change of government, but Diem has ignored it. The Front has therefore attacked, and the unforgiving antagonists now slog it out with machine-guns and mortars across the city.

A gimcrack cease-fire follows this inconclusive trial of strength, with the legitimate civilian population ebbing and flowing in fright as Binh Xuyen and National Army spar for the best positions. The town is choked with guns, a running fight suddenly develops in Cholon only to peter out, a Hoa Hao headquarters is blown to rubble with plastic explosive. Charlie deposits a large sealed parcel in my wardrobe without asking – 'Books,' he explains, avoiding my eye, 'for safe keeping in case my place is searched.' Suzie finds three of his hand-grenades among her underwear in a chest of drawers.

During this ominous truce Diem seems to be encircled by an elusive smoke-ring of enemies which we can only half-perceive. Ho Chi Minh is flirting covertly with the sects through their tame representatives in the Communist North. Down at Y-Bridge headquarters two supercilious French intelligence officers whisper in a corner to a Hoa Hao general whose magnificent moustaches, it is said, are locked in a frame each night and watched by two wives, one lying on each side of him, to ensure that they come to no harm. Beside me in another corner sits Ho Huu Tuong, his soft hand tapping his knee rhythmically as he murmurs almost hypnotically into my ear. Novelist and poet, this rounded figure with the moon face, the lizard-quick eyes and the flattened iron-grey hair is a Trotskyist in a country in which the Communists and the Trotskyists have made common cause in the recent past. For Bai Vien, under the misapprehension that politics is more respectable than piracy, has been trying to go legitimate, and has acquired a little coterie of 'progressist' counsellors who have drawn up a socialist programme for his National Front.

When it seemed certain that Bai Vien was nevertheless bent on bloodshed, his Trotskyists came to me, covertly. I was the only British newspaper correspondent resident in Saigon, they pointed out. I was therefore a neutral political observer, yet not a diplomat who might be finicky about his friendships. I knew what the Americans thought about Bai Vien. I must tell the general the truth personally: that if he wanted to be taken seriously as a politician rather than a thug by Vietnam's rich foreign patrons, he must not start another shooting match in the capital. I agreed. My first move was to take a *cyclopousse* down to the United States Embassy and talk to one of those tightly-furled diplomats they turn out in Washington. This man finally conceded through a thin pink wound low down on his face that the Trotskyists were essentially right: if Bai Vien attacked, the Americans would be doubly confirmed in their support of Diem, and dollars would win the day.

At ten o'clock the next night a Citroen with three men in it picked me up in the shadows near my hotel, and after racing suicidally through the tense streets towards Cholon, eased past the armoured cars and the sandbagged machine-gun nests of the Binh Xuyen guarding Y-Bridge, and dropped down to the island. Bai Vien's headquarters was in almost complete darkness. His caged tigress, to which the general was said to feed those who displeased him (when in a fractious mood), grunted once off to the right, but otherwise there was silence. I walked warily over a narrow plank bridge above the pool that led to Bai Vien's private office and could just make out three crocodiles below – smallish beasts, but reputedly with the same disconcerting eating habits as the tigress.

In a hut lit only by a flickering oil lamp, I sat down across a small desk from the enigmatic, illiterate general and talked to him for an hour through Ho Huu Tuong. He listened quietly, only moving to scratch one bare arm occasionally, his dead black eyes dancing deceptively in the wavering light. When I flagged, he prompted me with a question in Vietnamese. 'You have impressed him,' whispered the Trotskyist happily, as we left. 'It will be all right.'

For nine days Bai Vien, poised for battle, made not the slightest move. The American ambassador, General Lawton Collins, discreetly withdrew to Washington. Then Diem suddenly attacked Bai Vien. As the machine-gun bullets ripped into flimsy buildings and the mortar bombs whined down once more, the jostling Vietnamese tenements took fire, and hundreds of acres of crowded, miniscule homes were swept away in the flames and smoke. Bai Vien, his headquarters wrecked, retreated into the swamps of the Delta pursued by Diem's winning battalions. Quiet returned to Saigon–Cholon. It was May 1955.

Bai Vien escaped to live in opulent exile in an ever-friendly France, and Charlie Meyer escaped to Cambodia to become an 'adviser' again, this time to Sihanouk. But Ho Huu Tuong was captured, accused of inciting the Binh Xuyen to violence, and condemned to death. Destiny had not done with him, however. After several people, myself among them, had testified that the accusation was false, his sentence was suspended. He was imprisoned on Poulo Condore, the Devil's Island of Indochina, and released when Diem fell. In May 1968 he was again whispering conspiratorially to me as a Buddhist member of the South Vietnamese National Assembly.

By 1956 Diem had bloodlessly eliminated the powerful pro-French generals who at first opposed him, and had won the National Army over to his side. He had used this army to smash the sect rebellion, and when the Emperor himself tried to divest

Diem of power, it was the Emperor who was removed – for Diem rigged a popular referendum and, armed with the authority of its falsified results, was able to declare Vietnam a Republic and become its first President. Diem resettled the Catholic refugees from North Vietnam, introduced land reform, built up impressive foreign exchange reserves. By 1958 he had created a state out of chaos. If they short-listed his achievements and rejected the rest, the Americans could feel proud of him.

Nevertheless, when Ho Huu Tuong was released with other political prisoners from Poulo Condore on a fiery November day five years later, a festive mob armed with banners and garlands roared its welcome down at the docks. Diem was dead. Fourteen generals had overthrown the devout dictator and happy crowds were showering posies on their helmeted and booted troops in the streets of Saigon. The time had come to call at a house I had not visited for three years, the home of Doctor Pham Quang Dan.

Doctor Dan's original sin was that he had been elected as an opposition deputy in 1959. For this affront he was arrested while on his way to the National Assembly to attend the opening session, and after being confined in eight different gaols he, too, was shipped over to Poulo Condore. There he met the only other opposition candidate who had successfully beaten Diem's otherwise impeccably rigged ballot boxes.

Years of discretion have left on Doctor Dan a mask that is almost batrachian in its cool immobility, but as we sat in the shabby little room that makes him one with his poorer patients, the tale he told gained from his detached air and stilted English.

For months he had been shut up in a narrow, dark cell, not knowing day from night. He was interrogated endlessly, and when he protested his innocence he was tortured. They came, in their conventional way, in the smallest hours of the morning to strap him down on a hard bench and connect his fingers and toes to the terminals of a hand-dynamo. Then, as the first waves of electricity throbbed through his pinioned body, they poured water into his mouth and nostrils until he was bloated with liquid through which the current could jump with almost lethal impulse. When he fainted, they revived him and repeated the process.

For women prisoners under the Diem régime, striptease came to have a second, more revolting meaning. For men there was not only the water torture but the agony of the feathers. Their fingers were each pinned separately to a table top with very long fine needles driven through the nails. Feathers were then attached to the needles and an electric fan directed upon them. As the quills twisted and turned agitatedly in the breeze, the needles bent and quivered in the wounds, ingeniously causing excruciating pain. Another prisoner in Saigon had told me how this treatment had at least made a change from the cell into which Vietnamese Sûreté officers had thrown him as a left-wing suspect. The cell measured seven feet by eleven feet in area and was filled in with humanity rather as a hollow block may be filled with rubble. Eighteen men were crammed into it, and however they arranged themselves, two had to remain standing all the time. They did this in turn for three months, the shift on its feet fanning all the others to prevent them from stifling. As they were fed only two bowls of thin gruel a day, there was soon much more space both outside and inside their clothes, whereupon the guards topped the cell up again.

Meanwhile, as the torturers became ever busier, many bathed and talcumed western diplomats in their air-conditioned Saigon offices were sternly warning reporters who criticized Diem not to 'rock the boat' but to 'get with the team'. 'Aw, Diem may be a son-of-a-bitch,' agreed one distinguished American with rugged loyalty, 'but he's our son-of-a-bitch.' Lyndon Johnson called him 'The Winston Churchill of Asia'. (Why not? Richard Nixon was to call the war in Vietnam 'Our Finest Hour'.) Now he was gone. No doubt the new heroes would all sink back to size and perpetrate another ordinary human muddle, but just for this fleeting, golden moment, it seemed as if we had reached a happy ending. Vietnam had been exorcised.

The wretched Far East correspondent who in his day has toiled up the pretentious staircase of the Independence Palace in Saigon, and then wasted two hours listening to the mechanical monologue Diem reserved for such fellows, will agree that absolute anti-Communism corrupts absolutely. Diem was mature, honest, conscientious, celibate, continent, sober, cultivated, patriotic, fastidiously dressed, and both clean and godly – like the citizens of Chen-La, he brushed his teeth and said his prayers every day. But when this good man had reiterated for the fifth time that all opponents of his régime were automatically playing into Communist hands, his victim was praying that South Vietnam would get a scoundrel for its next president, provided he had a pinch of pink in his make-up.

By 1963 Diem's secret police had picked up or pushed into the arms of his enemies nearly every prominent nationalist who had fought for the freedom of his country during the previous twenty years. He and his family suppressed all opposition, filled the gaols, muzzled the press, rigged the elections, and clung to all power, so that at one point no visa for Vietnam could be issued without the President's personal permission. He chose his lieutenants for their yesmanship, and promoted according to political loyalty, not seniority or merit. Vietnam had to be saved from Communism, and therefore the Diem régime must be preserved at all costs.

In Hanoi, it was reported, leaders regarded Diem with almost affectionate approval. His régime had become a better argument for Communism than any they could hammer into the heads of the peasantry. Idling under an awning by a swimming pool in Phnom Penh, Wilfred Burchett appeared to contradict this when he told me in his ironical, gravelly way that the President of the National Liberation Front had described the assassination of Diem to him as 'an unexpected gift', for Diem alone had built a machine of political control and terrorism sturdy enough to enable him to run the country despite the guerrilla war. But that was exactly one year after Diem had died, and there had been time to observe what followed.

Like the jigging scribe of an electrocardiogram or a lie-detector, the reporter's pen tells the story independently of the words. The measured speech of a polygamous minister opening a family planning seminar is recorded in the fine, regular hand we associate with baptism certificates and pawnbrokers' receipts, while an eye-witness account of a riot goes down in an agitated scribble that might well be a sketch of the event, instead of an account of it.

My notebook labelled 'South Vietnam : November 1963', the month that Diem was murdered, is faithful to this law. It is a portrait of a coup, the fighting and firepower and rivalry and disunity depicted in almost indecipherable ballpoint blue, with the names of mutually distrustful colonels and generals inserted into the schizoid order of battle of an army pitted against itself : 'IV corps Bui Huu Nhon', I read. 'Do Cao Tri I Corps. Dinh got els 7th Div. Main force 5 and 6 para bns, one-third marines, one-third armour, 2 regts 5 div (III corps). 400–600 presidential guards surrendered midnight 20 killed 250 pws. 9 p.m. four coys attack with M-113 and 57-mm rec. rifles 80-mm MGs 105-mm Hows et 81-mm mortars. Marines half with Thao, half with Minh . . .' Then a long list of generals followed by 'Dinh treacherous but needed, Minh feels essential oust Mai Huu Xuan. Kim and Don with Minh, Thao pushing Khiem . . .'

It was an earnest of what was to come – Minh, Kim, Dinh, Don, Khanh, Huong, Ky, Khiem, Thieu – the cracked carillon of names rings the changes of régime from year to year as coup follows coup in South Vietnam, and there is always an American on hand to say of the latest leader, 'He's our boy. He may be a son-of-a-bitch, but, by God, he's our . . .' Against a confused background of Vietcong violence in the flooded paddyfields and Buddhist rioting by flarelight in the city, odd, random scenes flick into the mind like illustrations seen when riffling through a Victorian novel, and one half-expects to read an infuriatingly cryptic caption in fine italics underneath the frontispiece : *Colonel Thao unstrapped his belt and laid his pistol on the table.* '*Comme-ci Comme-ça,' he replied.*

We were sitting in the muted, high-walled courtyard of his little house in Saigon with its single, scented Malay-apple tree. The first coup was over, Diem was dead, and the dust was settling. Colonel Pham Ngoc Thao, in fresh-pressed khaki drill, had just answered 'So-so' to my question : was he satisfied with the new government of generals announced that day? The non-committal answer was uncharacteristic, for Thao had a trick of hesitating, taking in a short breath as if he were thinking up an equivocal response, and then coming out suddenly with a flat shocking statement like a resounding slap on the cheek. And this somehow matched the look of blank disbelief forever fixed upon the firm, tanned and youthful face by his wall-eye. He paused for a moment and then, sure enough, sprang a verbal ambush on me: 'But we are organizing another coup,' he added simply.

While the generals had coalesced uneasily to conspire against Diem, Thao had worked energetically to recruit the men who would count when the chips were down – the unit commanders of the infantry battalions, of the marines and paratroops. When the storm broke it was Thao who led a battalion of marines into the radio station in Saigon, proclaimed the coup to the world and then telephoned to the beleaguered President, shouting through the peremptory rattle of machine-guns outside that the palace was encircled and he should surrender.

But now his mind was on the next phase of the plot, the second explosion which would shatter the 'Military Revolutionary Council' that had replaced Diem, and fling to oblivion the old pro-French officers who had seized this chance to creep back into power. Thao was already undermining selected targets among the high brass, planting his charges of insurrection deep among their junior commanders. 'Generals afraid of Thao,' my scrawl of the day reads. 'They begin see his power over tps, his infl among capts, majors.' He was to die for that, in agony, two years later.

Coups breed press conferences. The 'Military Revolutionary Council' assembles on the dais, its four most prominent generals behind a baize table, immaculate, beribboned, speaking out firmly from a tulip-bed of microphones and a haze of cigarette smoke, the new authority, the heroes of the hour. Within months, however, one will be in exile, and the others will find themselves running not a republic, but a restaurant. The second coup came, but not as Thao planned, for in January 1964 Major-General Nguyen Khanh, warlord commanding the Vietnamese First Corps, seized power.

The eighteen chaotic months of rivalry and religious strife that followed have left their own unbeautiful or comic memories : in the market square of Saigon a mob of Buddhists brutally hacks at a Catholic student who staggers forward, his face streaming blood, until a small man drives a knife into his stomach, dropping him dead (Look again. It is not a small man, it is a boy of about ten); five senior generals besieged by Catholic rioters at the headquarters of the Joint General Staff telephone frantically to the Archbishop to come and save them (their bodies, not their souls); the Deputy Premier calls Khanh a madman, a second minister is accused of treason after publishing an article calling him a dictator, and a third minister shaves his head and goes into retreat as a Buddhist; Khanh serves assembled newspaper correspondents a tasteless, indigestible mound of platitudes with the solemn air of a man clowning his way through crises: '... will do all to serve the country, fight the Communist lackeys and also the colonialists and neutralists, carry out the revolution, build the foundations of true democracy ...'

There are more meetings in Thao's courtyard and two abortive coups, but Robert S. Macnamara, American Secretary for Defence, shouts almost defiantly: 'I want to stress ... complete respect and support, economic and military, for General Khanh and for Vietnam ...' There will be no American backing for any man that tries to replace Khanh, and the bearded thirty-seven-year-old is now in the same strong but fatal position enjoyed by the autocratic President Diem.

By 1966 the United States was nevertheless supporting Air Marshal Nguyen Cao Ky with the same obdurate, abiding love for the latest general-on-the-make, but the evanescent nature of these phenomena was now recognized in Washington, it appeared, for when a colleague asked a senior American official what would happen if Ky fell, the man replied instantly: 'Well, I guess we'll just have to deal with the next guy.'

In 1968 I found myself attending yet another press conference in the presidential palace, which had been finally rebuilt after that breakfast bombing attack six years before. Outside, the architecture of the new palace seemed to have been inspired by the old prewar cinema wurlitzer, but inside it was all conventional red carpet and yellow drapes and great dusty chandeliers like frozen fountains of ditch-water. The latest government filed on to the rostrum, natty little men with slicked-down hair, most of them dressed in what appeared to be identical dark suits and ties, for Vietnamese generals had also added this ministerial uniform to the rest of the modern military wardrobe.

President Thieu told us that his government was defending the freedom of Vietnam, and Vietnam was an outpost of the whole free world. The Vietnamese were determined to combat aggression and not give in to the Communists. If the Americans withdrew, they would be avoiding their responsibility to the free world, but the Vietnamese would fight on alone for democracy and so on.

As the familiar jargon rolled on, my eye wandered to a more casually dressed man in a cream suit at the end of the Cabinet line-up, and my mind at once somersaulted back thirteen years to the old palace and this same man in his old identity, the insignia of his uniform torn off, a pistol thrust into his side by a nervous but irate little civilian. It was the pro-French anti-American pro-Bao Dai anti-Diem General Nguyen Van Vy. And he was now Minister for Defence. Beside him sat the man who had been the second Trotskyist adviser to the Binh Xuyen thirteen years ago, Mr Tran Van An, now Minister for Information. 'We're not putting money on any alternatives,' a man from the American Embassy told me. 'This is our team.'

A year later members of an Anglo-American study group visited Vietnam and produced a thirty-eight-page report which found that the South Vietnamese Government relied 'more upon police state tactics and American support to stay in power than upon true representation and popular support ... torture and brutality are widespread in the arresting and interrogation process ... without question the Thieu–Ky Government uses the words Communism, neutralism and coalition to silence dissent and weaken political and religious opposition ...' Palace for palace, torture for torture, Vy for Vy, they were different, only they were the same. Someone had burned the phoenix again. This was where I came in.

Their Men in the Sticks

THE nineteen helicopters whirr high above the watery flatlands of Vietnam's southernmost peninsula like a flight of squat
ducks. Beside me in number eleven an American corporal, helmeted and visored, mans a fifty-calibre machine gun pointed
down through the open doorway towards the sunstroked paddyfields below, where escorting fighters skim at hedgehopping
height. But this is not a major airborne operation against the
Vietcong. It is Robert S. Macnamara, United States Secretary
for Defence, paying a visit to Hoa Hao Village, accompanied by
General Nguyen Khanh and a number of very large and white
men like General Maxwell Taylor and Mr William Bundy.

From a balcony Mr Macnamara beams down on the Hoa Hao
villagers, and the gap-toothed teak-coloured visages of the elders
gaze up inscrutably at his neat chartered-accountant's face. He
makes the same speech that he has made throughout this barn-
storming tour of Vietnam, emphasizing that Washington is supporting General Khanh personally and exclusively. Then he
descends among them and does his stuff. He clasps the hands of
the adults, he clowns with the children, and in a cool, ornate
pavilion he reverently puts his fingers together in a Buddhist
greeting before a tiny, emaciated old lady in a green silk dress.
She is the mother of Huynh Phu So, the mystic master of the
Hoa Hao sect who was murdered by the Communists. Neither
speaks the other's language. The old lady is very deaf. Mr Macnamara ceremoniously presents her with a hearing aid. But then
nobody can make it work, however much they twiddle the
buttons. The lack of comprehension is complete.

It is all fantastically irrelevant. Beyond the bewildering trans-
pacific bonhomie of all these big men and the impressive weight
of aerodynamic hardware in which they have come lies the sad,

flat scenery, as awash with Vietcong as it is with brackish water, into which one of the helicopters crashed just an hour ago. Matters will improve slowly, but at this moment it is not safe to go into more than one village in seven in the area, even in broad daylight and with an armed escort. Once darkness falls, the Vietcong dominate it almost completely. 'The army can move anywhere, but it cannot stay,' an American military adviser tells me bluntly. 'And when it withdraws, the Vietcong come back in. We make about as much permanent impression as a ship sailing through the Red Sea.'

'. . . *no more effective than cutting water with a sword.*' The similarity takes me back to 1962, when Diem was still alive and Colonel Thao was for a time military governor of Kien Hoa province. The colonel had used it while we were on an anti-guerrilla operation that proved a model of military futility.

Thao clung to the wheel as the little launch bounced over the Mekong Delta waterway not ten yards from the opaque fringe of mangrove and latania palms that bordered it. 'Either you race by close to the shore or you keep well over on the other side,' he shouted. 'In mid-stream they get your range and strafe you.' A grenade, fired from behind the screen of tangled water-edge vegetation, thudded on to the swampy bank to our left and exploded. Half-a-mile farther on, another burst ineffectively. 'We have got the Vietcong boxed in here,' he shouted. 'We have flushed 150 of their regulars and I have troops closing in all around them, not to mention' – he cocked an ear to the sudden roar of guns – 'a battery of one-oh-fives to pound their hideouts.'

We were on the tattered hem of Asia, where twisted threads of land reach out for the sea, and the swamps and dense coconut forests are veined with the byways of the Mekong, some of them half a mile wide. We swung left, nosed down a narrow creek, and puttered to a stop beside a command post. A company commander began to report thinly over the field-telephone. Thao cursed, barked urgent instructions into the instrument. The inevitable had happened. The trapped, pyjama-clad Vietcong guerrillas were shedding their battalion scarves, concealing their weapons, and hiding themselves among the local peasants by forcing all the menfolk to accompany them down their escape routes. The enemy was now indistinguishable from the villagers whose sympathy the Government was so anxious to win. It was the loyalist forces, in their American steel helmets and camouflaged uniforms, who appeared to be alien intruders. 'When in doubt,' Thao ordered, 'Don't shoot. Take everyone prisoner.'

The box contracted. Forty men were killed, at least four of them ordinary peasants whose deaths would further inflame resentment against the Saigon régime. More than eighty prisoners were taken, but only eight of these were readily identifiable as Communist guerrillas. Half naked and bound together with cords, the captured for the most part turned out to be innocent villagers. The enemy had melted away.

Covered by the automatic weapons of Rangers, we plunged into the main hamlet of the battle area. In the square stood a wood and plaster building, the propaganda office of the Vietcong. 'We would rather die than live under the domination of American Imperialists,' ran its painted slogan. We were only seven miles from the provincial capital.

An NCO reported with a plastic airbag full of documents taken from the body of a Vietcong political cadre. Thao thumbed through receipt books which showed in detail the contributions to the Vietcong cause that the guerrillas had extracted from every peasant household in the area. Then he ordered a sweep to recover discarded enemy weapons. We stumbled in open order across vast squelching rice-fields under a smouldering evening sky, the stinking mud sucking at our submerged boots to find four rifles and twelve hand-grenades. The place had the hallowed feel of hostile territory, but fortunately the Vietcong seemed to have gone for they could have mown us down in minutes. A residual rattle of distant machine-gun fire faltered and died. The countryside lapsed into sardonic silence.

'You see,' remarked Thao, 'the enemy scatters only to return to dominate the area again once we have left it. These sweeps are no more effective than cutting water with a sword, except where we have good intelligence. And that means that until we can protect and befriend the peasants and so win their support, we will get nowhere.' We listened a little anxiously in the gathering darkness for the reluctant outboard motor of the launch to splutter into life and take us away from this area which the troops had just cleaned up. Then Thao opened the throttle and we roared along between the ragged edge of man-grove that flanked the delta waters. It did not look any more friendly than it had before the operation began.

But when Macnamara speaks to the Hoa Hao we are already two years and four coups further on, and all hopes of a stable central administration that will earn the respect of the Viet-namese peasant by dealing with him fairly are receding steadily into the sunset. The peasant himself – seventeen men out of every twenty in the country – is not worried or excited or elated or downcast when he is presented with a Khanh instead of a Diem. He is indifferent. Too often his district officer is a cheat and a bully, and that is all the government he knows. He owes it neither his trust nor his meagre treasure. It does not protect him from the Vietcong, and it does not provide his simplest needs. It collects taxes and it takes the young men of the village away to fight. As for the riches of all these white men (French-men, Americans, or whatever they are by now) they never filter down to him.

The successive upheavals in the capital threaten to shake into rubble the fragile framework of civil and military defence against Communism. The soldiers become gun-shy and think only in terms of survival, for every time there is a coup, com-manders and administrators are changed, military province chiefs are shuffled around, and no man knows which will last longer – his job or the ephemeral governments for which he is so unreasonably supposed to risk his life. This in turn makes 'pacification' almost impossible.

'Our 1962 pacification plan got going in July 1963,' an Ameri-can staff officer once told me in the deliberate, wry manner of the Vietnam veteran, 'but in November 1963 President Diem was overthrown. The Government changed, the provincial and district officials vital to this effort were mostly replaced, and so the campaign ground to a halt. In December 1963, we rewrote the programme, but it came to grief when General Khanh seized power in another coup in January 1964. In March 1964, we drew up yet another plan, and started executing it in June, but in October Khanh was obliged to relinquish power to Mr Tran Van Huong, and so more wholesale changes . . .' And so it went on through project after project, until the 'Tet Offensive', the powerful Vietcong onslaught on Saigon and other cities at Viet-namese New Year in February 1968, wrecked the sandcastle of trust that the United States was so painstakingly reconstructing once again.

All had long since agreed that the basis of this trust must be the security provided by a fortified village. As early as 1960 Diem had summarily ordered the construction of 10,000 'agro-villes' – new rural centres within which peasants would be protected and given every social amenity. I trudged around several of these, dutifully noting the watchtower and the warn-ing drum that would bring help in case of attack, the first-aid station, the school. But the peasants were sullen. They had been recruited as forced labour to build their own agrovilles, and they would rather have been left alone in the first place.

Two years later I was trudging around the 'Strathams', the new strategic hamlets of the Mekong Delta, their huddles of huts enclosed with a formidable chastity belt of trenchworks and hedges of sharpened bamboo to keep the enemy out and the villagers in. But rape was inevitable nonetheless, for the Viet-cong were already inside the hamlets, 'guerilleros' who supplied the guerrillas outside with food and intelligence and the names of suitable villagers to assassinate. And they normally outnum-bered the Self-defence guards.

While the Government devoted large sums of American aid to flashy projects in and around the capital, the ill-armed Self-defence guard in the hamlet was paid one pound a week for risking his life twenty-four hours of the day, and his wife and children received nothing even when he was killed. The price of loyalty was higher than this, and in one lonely community I visited, perched on the salty fringe of the Delta and only to be approached in a steel-sided infantry landing craft, it had been possible to recruit no more than twenty-five young volunteers out of a population of 1,700. The region was forlorn, remote, almost lost in the everglades, infested with Vietcong. A breeze blew across the stockade from the invisible sea, like a faint breath of freedom from afar.

By the time Diem and Nhu were murdered in November 1963, the whole concept of the village-fortress had been discredited in the minds of most peasants, who in many areas smashed their own bamboo perimeters or carefully picked them to bits on the principle that if you do not lock your door, the burglar will not break it down, or enter in an unnecessarily aggravated frame of mind.

With almost oriental patience, the Americans began again, feeding their ideas through Khanh. The 'New Life' hamlet was introduced for good peasants, while pro-Vietcong villages were in some cases bulldozed flat to teach men a simple lesson in good and evil, cause and effect. Instead of trying to save all the provinces simultaneously, the Saigon government developed the 'oil slick' technique of using regular battalions of troops to establish complete security in a limited area, and then slowly expand it. 'And it works great,' an American official confided to me sarcastically, 'so that out of 218 hamlets in Long An province I am now prepared to sleep in twelve at night, and maybe visit thirty during the day.'

The helicopter had come to the rescue of the Vietcong, for now the South Vietnamese army could commute to and from the war, flying into battle in the morning and back home to barracks after the afternoon tea-break. Air transport, which should have been used to maintain men in the field, was running a suburban shuttle-service with rush hour at about sunset. It was the peasants and the Self-defence corps who had to stick it out in the villages in the dangerous hours of darkness.

South Vietnam had become a disturbing, equivocal land of optical illusion, and it was often as if the Vietcong were only on the other side of the looking-glass. One village would have a headman appointed by the Saigon government. The district chief visited it regularly, it was guarded by a squad of the paramilitary 'Popular Forces'. It had medicines from the provincial capital, a hidden telephone for emergency contact with the South Vietnamese army, three-day-old Saigon newspapers, and American aid in the shape of a lorryload of cotton cloth or a starry-eyed official with an addiction for teaching mildly-surprised peasants how to build windmills.

The next village across the chessboard of rice-fields would mainly be run by a lean-cheeked young man in a buttoned-up denim tunic and slacks, wearing a plastic topee with a yellow star on the front. Behind him was the National Liberation Front. The Vietcong defended the inhabitants but liquidated the unrighteous. They also distributed the rice, collected the taxes, taught everyone to brush his teeth, love Uncle Ho, and observe strict discipline. The village newspaper was *Nhan Dan*, the official organ of the Front.

A Government survey of the intervening fields would show one pattern of ownership and tenancy. But a Vietcong survey of the same fields showed another, for the Communists had redistributed the land among the more pliable peasantry. When the Government ordered a call-up of young men, it was almost as if the Vietcong had done so, for many of those who shied at serving with one side dodged the draft by fleeing to the other. There were hamlets that the Government controlled by day and the Vietcong by night, communities controlled by both at once. The two South Vietnams were almost superimposed upon one another.

The Vietcong were not fighting the war. They were living it. The inability to understand this led to much false analysis by the more optimistic. Whenever there was a lull in Communist activity, Saigon began to brag that pacification was paying off. But on three occasions I was able to discover the truth about these successes. In the first instance the Vietcong wanted the bridge to an isolated village to be repaired. They secretly ordered their own force to observe a local cease-fire, and the South Vietnamese army obligingly took advantage of the break in hostilities to mend it. In the second, the Vietcong were furtively moving large quantities of supplies into prepared dumps within striking distance of Saigon. In order to beguile their opponents, therefore, they stopped all offensive action along the route. On the third occasion everything was quiet because everything was, quite simply, under Vietcong control.

Government officials were rapacious, the police and army brutal; the Americans bombed and shelled and gunned the villages and then made up for it all by being nice to the peasant in some overcrowded refugee camp after his home had gone up in smoke, and perhaps his wife and children, too. The Vietcong gave him free land, treated him with courtesy (if also to much rather tiresome propaganda) when he showed willing, and murdered him when he did not. But the Vietcong also pointed out that if the alien Americans remained a hundred years, the war would last a hundred years. As for themselves, they were fellow-Vietnamese and represented no obstacle to future peace and quiet. The Americans struggled to win the heart and mind of the peasant, the Vietcong his body and soul. It was an uneven contest, for the Americans were playing away.

The failure of the South Vietnamese Government to defend the peasant against himself was matched by its failure to endear him to Saigon in spite of himself by one sure means : nationalization of all land and its redistribution to the men who tilled it. In the early days of Diem the programme introduced by enthusiastic American experts to take surplus acres from the landowner and give them to the landless was converted into a gigantic racket for cheating both parties, and in 1969, fifteen years after it was first mooted, land reform was still being sabotaged in Saigon.

In February of that year the Prime Minister had nevertheless announced yet another pacification drive, designed to win over the entire country within ten months. The looking-glass was well polished at the time, for while Saigon claimed to control 86 per cent of all the people, the Vietcong simultaneously claimed 80 per cent for themselves. But at last pacification slowly began to pay off as more men with better arms were deployed to defend the villages. The anti-Communists greeted the new year in a mood of cautious self-congratulation : Man had shown that he could learn from his mistakes after all, and this was a comfort to many. Except that it was now 1970, and it should have been 1960.

23

Two Buckets of Blood

SLIPPING through the mirror from the Saigon of General Khanh to the Saigon of the Vietcong was a delicate operation, but in late 1964 I arrived at the last of a long chain of shy contacts and walked into a small, excessively untidy radio and electrical repair shop near the Central Market which had been chosen as my particular crossing-point. I murmured a name and was simply given a time to stand on a street-corner after dark. At 8.30 that evening I was picked up in slanting rain and taken to an empty, upstairs room in an Indian restaurant, to be introduced to a middle-aged mouse of a man with a balding head and a missing front tooth through which his breath whistled softly. He was dressed like a slightly ostentatious French-educated clerk in an immaculate white shirt and clip-on bow tie, gold cufflinks and wedding ring, and as we ate chicken curry and drank a glass of red wine, he played his bit part as a petit-bourgeois to perfection. No one would have dreamed that he had just sidled into the city from War Zone D.

This was the first of three meetings with two senior cadres from the Liberation Front in obscure restaurants and a dusty attic above the radio shop. I saw them nearly five months before President Johnson put the first American combat units into Vietnam and nearly five years before President Nixon started pulling them out again, but the view from their side of the glass is not without interest even today.

'We are ready to do everything possible to save Washington's face, so that the Americans can go home,' my clerkish contact told me, sipping his wine expressionlessly as if it were the blood of Christ. 'If we start real trouble in the towns, they may pour fighting troops into the South, or even attack North Vietnam. That's why we have not organized a campaign of intensive terrorism against the American "advisers" already here. You realize, of course, that this is what otherwise we should be doing. We should be killing Americans as fast as we can in order to raise a storm of protest against the warmongering policies of Washington with a few thousand tearful widows and mothers at its centre.' If there were no negotiated American withdrawal, he said, that would have to be the next stage. 'You will know when we are ready for the final push both in town and country,' he added, 'because part of the South Vietnamese army will change sides and fight for us, or simply stop fighting altogether.'

I met my second contact at the beginning of November 1964. He was a long, stick-insect of a Vietnamese in an open-necked shirt, slacks and sandals, cool, collected and contemptuous. He believed that the Americans must either be persuaded to give up the war in Vietnam as hopeless, or 'they must be provoked into acts of greater and more costly terrorism which will bring such an avalanche of condemnation down upon them from their countrymen that the leaders in Washington will be able to back out with a good grace, bowing to *force majeure* at home'.

Sitting and chain-smoking above the radio shop at one in the morning as the street outside fell silently to sleep, he went on: 'After all, what is the danger? The Liberation Front may seem to be no more than an intermediate step towards a Communist South Vietnam which can be united with a Communist North. But the Front is nevertheless mainly made up of southerners, and the common denominator of all its members is not Communism, but nationalism. It will be many years before South Vietnam goes Communist, if it ever does. Meanwhile it will be a democratic, neutralist state, and after eighteen months of hesitation the North has conceded the need for this neutralism, even for a coalition between the Front and a suitable Saigon Government, because with that we make a concession to the Americans and can perhaps persuade them to go away sooner.'

This cadre gave me a second contact address, and I took it down without comment. It was the house of Mr Tran, the 'Peace Movement' leader to whom Charlie Meyer had introduced me ten years before, and who had put me into touch in turn with the militant Buddhists. A few days later Ho Huu Tuong, the Trotskyist adviser to Bai Vien who had been released from the prison island of Poulo Condore, grasped me gently by the elbow in the tiny courtyard of his home and began a long, reasoned exposé in a hoarse mutter, much as he had done at Binh Xuyen headquarters nearly a decade earlier. He insisted that the Liberation Front leaders did not even stipulate that they must be represented in any future coalition 'peace' government in Saigon : they would be content with a neutral, socialist-minded cabinet of Saigonese intellectuals at first, as long as its members were acceptable to them. Elections could come later. They did not want South Vietnam to lose American aid. There could therefore be no question of establishing a Communist régime.

It all sounded like a conspiracy to give the Americans a dishonourable discharge from service in South Vietnam, a neat pretext for begging the whole question of 'Communist containment'. It was obvious that the field for negotiation was sown with mines, and the question that no one in Saigon or Washington could answer for certain was : to what degree was the Liberation Front indeed a 'front', a booby-trap whose lethal charge of Communism was concealed in an innocent can labelled 'nationalism'?

This suspicion reinforced the blind distrust which many responsible Americans reserved for all nationalists who opposed the son-of-a-bitch-of-the-moment in Saigon. Genuine nationalism was the only currency that was valid on both sides in the war, but they hesitated to fit the two halves of the coin together.

I remember congratulating Thao in the Mekong Delta once, as we watched the torn green curtain of latania that screened the Island of Leaves where Vietnamese Rangers attached to him were mopping up the remnants of a Vietcong battalion after a masterly exercise in stealthy envelopment. He rapped the resonant side of our landing craft and shook his head impatiently. 'All this should not even be necessary,' he replied softly. 'Nine-tenths of the men who joined the Vietminh resistance were not Reds. They were nationalists like me who collaborated with the Communists in order to end French domination of Vietnam. These men are the true Vietnamese, the force that can unify the country. Those on the other side never wanted to change French masters for Chinese or Russian ones. Those on this side have no intention of changing French masters for American ones.'

He paused and then went on with a slight smile. 'Look, when I was second-in-command of a Vietminh regiment against the French, the commander of the Vietcong guerrillas we are just defeating over there at this moment' – and he waved towards the subsiding battle – 'was my immediate chief. I know that man as I know myself. He is no Communist. But when I send messages to him these days urging him to rally to us, he thinks it is a trap, that the security chiefs in Saigon will wring him dry of intelligence and then push him in front of the firing squad. So he stays with the Vietcong. He has no choice. If once we had a government that men like him could respect and trust, the Vietcong problem would be solved.'

He knew what he was talking about, but he was also making enemies fast, for the foreign press was beginning to lionize him as the man who knew the answers, prompting dangerous comparisons between Thao on the ground and the powerful armchair strategists in the capital. Sensitive correspondents like Stanley Karnow, then of *Time*, and Robert Shaplen of the *New Yorker* became his personal friends, and he was unfailingly courteous to Joseph Alsop because the President had specifically told him to be ('he's supposed to have Kennedy's ear, you see'). But I had already known Thao for seven eventful years.

Thao was a southern Catholic, born of a well-to-do family from the Mekong Delta. During the Indochina War he had joined the Vietminh, had risen to command a guerrilla regiment against the French in the Delta, had been sent north to Ho Chi Minh's headquarters, and had then returned clandestinely to become Vietminh Intelligence chief for the whole southern region. As a senior cadre but also a Catholic, he had arranged a furtive meeting with his Bishop, and had promised him immunity from the Vietminh guerrillas provided His Grace did not denounce them from the pulpit. Thao kept his word, but he had no means of knowing that the prelate he was protecting would become Archbishop Ngo Dinh Thuc, and that his brother,

Ngo Dinh Diem, would be the postwar President of South Vietnam.

I first met Thao in 1955 as 'Albert' when he was paying a rare night-visit to Saigon, for as a former Vietminh chief his position was still delicate and he was living almost invisibly down in the Delta, scraping along as an obscure schoolteacher. However, the Archbishop was later able to pay his debt of honour, and Thao emerged from his cover to be commissioned as a major in the South Vietnamese army. He was then appointed personal adviser to Diem and his brother Nhu, and constantly toured the country in order to give them first-hand reports about the situation in the provinces. Why did he change sides? Thao was no Marxist, and his ambition was to see a popular and progressive government set up in Saigon which would capture the imagination and the loyalty of all good men in North and South. But as he watched the country on behalf of the palace oligarchy, he watched the palace oligarchy on behalf of the country, and was soon stripped of all hope that it would produce a clean administration to which nationalists on both sides could or would rally.

Thao then ran an erratic but predictable course dictated by the belief that whoever established despotic misrule in Saigon was simply driving good men after bad into the arms of the Communists. A born conspirator with a sweet-tooth for undercover living, he helped organize the successful coup against Diem in November 1963, the coup against Khanh in February 1965, and a third but abortive coup three months later.

I last saw him just before the second coup and ten years after our first meeting. Knowing that Thao was against him, Khanh had first sent him into diplomatic exile, and then recalled him in order to liquidate him. Thao had therefore returned to Saigon secretly and at once gone into hiding to plot Khanh's overthrow. The civilian Prime Minister, Tran Van Huong, had put out an official call ordering Thao to report to the Foreign Ministry, but had sent him a private warning to ignore it. I picked him off a pre-arranged street-corner on a fine night in Cholon, after a double-take at his nocturnal dark glasses and the ridiculous beribboned nylon hat which supposedly disguised him as a Vietnamese teddy-boy. When he took the glasses off, I saw a jaunty, new-old light in his one good eye. He was his own man again – on the run, covertly contacting marine and paratroop commanders in a quest for reliable allies in his hazardous conspiracy for honest government.

As we dined frugally, he told me he had seen Air Marshal Ky, who had wanted Thao to join him against Khanh. Thao had refused ('He's just a warlord'). He had seen General Thi, the corps commander in Central Vietnam, who had made the same proposition. Thao had again refused ('Just another warlord, but that one should be destroyed'). He had seen Thich Tri Quang and other Buddhist venerables, and heard Khanh described as a 'vaurien' and a 'salaud' in round canonical tones. He had in mind two ex-Vietminh generals of good repute to lead the next government, 'and the rest will have to be young men, perhaps unknown but at least unblemished also'.

Thao then confided to me a letter for McGeorge Bundy, President Johnson's special adviser who was at that moment visiting Vietnam. We shook four hands, and left the restaurant separately. I watched his absurd hat bob away among the evening crowds, and then looked back to note the name of the restaurant – *Bahat* – for it was the same one in which I had dined with the Liberation Front delegate less than four months before. But there was nothing odd about that, for the cut-out who took me to my meetings with these two men – one in the service of Saigon, the other in the service of the Vietcong – had been the same.

How lovingly would MI5 or the FBI cross-index a detail like that on the cards, snapping the new and damning link into place like a handcuff. But this syllogistic practice of forging circumstantial chains of guilt can lead to hideous mistakes anywhere in the world, and in Vietnam, where only the dark side of the truth has meaning, it was simply not applicable. Old comrades of Thao's seniority in the Vietminh were not only in the swamps of the South, fighting the forces of Saigon. They were in North Vietnam too, and they included his brother Gaston, with whom I had sat on the grass at the edge of the Petit Lac in Hanoi when he was Director of the Western Department of Ho Chi Minh's Foreign Ministry. Gaston was a thin, staccato edition of Thao in spectacles, and had been a Vietminh political boss of South Vietnam during the Indochina War when Thao was the intelligence chief. At our last meeting Thao spoke wistfully of an imaginary Saigon régime that could rally nationalists from the Vietcong, and Gaston had spoken wistfully of an imaginary Saigon régime with which Hanoi could negotiate, when I had breakfasted with him in Cambodia just three months before.

In 1962 'Gaston' (now only known as Thuan) was the Ambassador of North Vietnam in East Germany, and various scheming minds began to wonder whether 'Albert' (now only known as Thao) could not contact him and try to talk him over to the side of South Vietnam. I knew nothing of this until Thao and I were standing at the window of his headquarters one dusk, looking down on the darkening waters of the Delta. Turning his disbelieving wall-eye towards me, he broke silence with a characteristic gunshot of a statement: 'I have been asked to see Gaston in Berlin.' 'Are you going to?' He paused and then shook his head decisively. 'No.' Gaston was not a hard-core Communist, and if he could be persuaded to rally to Saigon and to participate in a suitable government, the effect among southern nationalists on both sides of the non-existent firing-line would be electric. But it was useless, Gaston would not rally to Diem or any American puppet. He had already told Thao this in a message sent through an intermediary in Paris, and shortly afterwards Gaston was recalled to Hanoi.

Thao never concealed his links with the Vietcong, and in the letter to Bundy he gave me in February 1965 he wrote: 'I have been in districts where officers who are my friends are in charge. With them I have visited the shelters and underground Communist fortifications. The bombs and the type of military operations that we are employing at present have no chance of success.' But five months later it was as if some short-circuit in the agonized tangle of Vietnamese intrigue had blown a fuse, leaving many in darkness. In July Thao, condemned to death in absentia and with a price on his head, was lured into a trap north of Saigon, wounded, seized, and later shot dead. There is a tale that it was the new President Nguyen Van Thieu who enticed Thao into ambush by sending him a message saying that he wanted to rid himself of Air Marshal Ky, and suggesting that they meet in secret to discuss ways and means. But the story is doubtless apocryphal, for it presupposes that Thieu did not in reality want to eliminate Ky.

Thao's letter to Bundy, therefore, rings in the memory like famous last words : 'The Communists do not have entire confidence in the Liberation Front. The southern political cadres who were in the resistance from 1945 onwards have, in the majority, come back. I know them all personally. They are only Communists when occasion demands. They have all suffered from the vexations and sectarian measures of the Communists' – and he names four men who by 1969 were leading members of the Liberation Front and of its 'Provisional Revolutionary Government for South Vietnam'. 'If we establish honest government,' Thao continues, 'and dare to put through profound social and administrative reforms, there is a firm hope that the ex-resistance will follow us and abandon the Communists.' He urges the need for land reform, for a new tactical policy that does not involve slaughtering peasants, for a socialist government that can meet the Communist challenge.

I sealed the envelope and took it to Barry Zorthian, the Director of the Joint United States Public Affairs Office early next morning. 'Oh, Thao,' he sighed, dropping his bulk into a sturdy chair and rolling large Armenian eyes of frozen cognac towards the ceiling. 'Yeah, well, all right, I'll see it gets to Bundy.' And I am sure he did. Thao had timed his appeal well. This was a moment of decision. Bundy was verifying the rival reports of State Department, Pentagon and CIA on the ground, trying to help President Johnson to evaluate the chances of negotiating peace from strength, or of fighting the war from weakness. South Vietnam was groggy, on its knees. If no radical changes were made to the whole rotten structure, the Vietcong would knock it out in a matter of months at most.

Having left Thao's letter with Zorthian I walked circumspectly to the Vietcong radio shop. There are many conditions in life under which a man may suddenly doubt his sanity, and one of them occurs when his eyes simply do not see what his brain is expecting. The whole dusty, ramshackle frontage had gone. It had been replaced by a glossy façade of brass and varnished wood and lattice windows, and a neon sign on which the magic words 'American Bar' flickered capriciously. The interior was decorated with a cluster of duty-free GIs and tired tarts. I stood gaping glassily at the entrance from the middle of the side-street, until watchful eyes within observed me, and a girl in warpaint came out to lean on the lintel and lob me a soft 'Hi, Joe' like an easy catch. This, evidently, was one battle General Westmoreland had won. My Vietcong contact, I later discovered, had fled to the hills around Dalat. Things had become too hot for him. I shook my head, waved vaguely at the girl, and set off to join friends at the Sporting Club.

'You notice something?' asked an American correspondent, his eye swivelling absently towards a passing bikini on the edge of the pool. 'When Uncle Sam was spending one million dollars a day on this war there were about 20,000 Vietcong. But by the time we were spending a million and a half a day, the figure had gone up to about 27,000 Vietcong, and now that we are spending two million a day there are supposed to be 33,000 of them, plus about 85,000 auxiliaries. So maybe the secret of victory is financial de-escalation. By the time we get down to spending a mere hundred thousand bucks a day the Communists will be reduced to a handful and we can buy them out anyway.'

Light, forgivable laughter shimmered for a moment over the sun-flecked water, for no man could live up to the misery of Vietnam every minute. It was Tet – Vietnamese New Year – 1965, but beneath the brittle holiday mood Saigon was a tense, sick city. Nearly 24,000 Americans had been fed into Vietnam, their dollars producing a morbid crop of touts and black marketeers, gimme-five-piastres boys and the world's daintiest whores. There was a faint, persistent racial bitterness in the air, like the taste of almonds. The Vietcong had already launched a spectacular attack against the main American air-base only twelve miles away. The country was meanwhile bedevilled by military coups and kingmakers, violent Buddhist and student riots, a divided army through whose pastry-weak positions the Vietcong might suddenly push a steel fist and so end the anguish.

Most men nevertheless agreed that this was only a displeasing dream compared with the nightmare that would follow if, unthinkably, Washington tried to stave off disaster with a massive injection of American fighting troops – tall black and white aliens strange to the country, pitted against an enemy who belonged. For it could only end in a fury of frustration and indiscriminate destruction, and it must not happen.

But it did. President Johnson duly made his decision, and it cannot be said that he ignored the possibility of uniting all true Vietnamese nationalists, as Thao had urged, for it pushed many of those who had sided with Saigon into the arms of the Viet-cong. On 7 February the Americans began bombing North Vietnam in earnest and in March the US Marines 'stormed ashore', the first of half a million American troops to be thrown into the war to win the South, while back at the ranch President Johnson waited for a 'signal' from Hanoi that would open the way to negotiations. For dread of the ghost, as the Malays say, Washington was clasping the corpse.

More than one thousand days and 21,000 dead Americans later, the President was still waiting for his 'signal'. It was the spring of 1968. There were 500,000 Americans in Vietnam, and my colleague's thesis that Communists multiply in direct ratio to cash invested in their elimination seemed to have been borne out. The war was no longer costing two million dollars a day, but two thousand million a month, and the number of enemy had therefore risen to an estimated 175,000 Vietcong, plus 55,000 North Vietnamese regular troops. Three years before, the distant grumbling of guns could sometimes be heard at night in my hotel, but now the windows and walls shook repeatedly as if with a wasting fever as the dark hours were punctuated by the heavy, flat, supercrump of Vietcong 122-millimetre rockets slamming into the outer skin of the city. Curfew fell like a guillotine at 8 p.m.

The gleaming Saigon of the past had disappeared. During the day the murmur of war, like an unheeded voice of conscience, was drowned in the urgent din that rose with the diesel fumes from the stinking, rubbish-strewn streets of the sun-baked capital – the shrill chatter of the sidewalk black market in stolen army gear and PX goodies, the inferno of traffic in which monstrous convoys of army trucks and ten thousand scooters fought for supremacy. By the end of 1969 North and South Vietnam, whose respective fertile deltas had once earned them the geographical nickname 'Two Baskets of Rice', could more appropriately be called two buckets of blood. The North Vietnamese and the Vietcong had sustained 580,000 mortal casualties, the South Vietnamese at least 100,000 and twice as many wounded. The Americans had lost more than 6,000 aircraft and 40,000 fighting men killed – each one of whom cost an estimated £12,800 to put and keep in the field.

As with all escalators, there had been a mechanical inevitability about the steps that led up to this platform. 'The Viets were extremely difficult to defeat,' I read in an official record.

They did not come out to fight, but hid in their familiar mountains and used the jungle like a weapon. In consequence, neither side could win. The security forces became increasingly fatigued, and the transport problem involved in supporting half a million men with food and arms progressively worsened. The Viets would raid suddenly, rob, and get away fast, so that just as our army obtained its supplies from the home base, the Viets obtained theirs from our army. Permanent garrisons were established, but the administration only effectively controlled the towns, the plains and the roads.

This is not a chilling glimpse at the history books of 1980, but a fair translation of the official account of the first invasion of 'Vietnam' by Imperial China. It does not describe the frustrations of the twentieth century A.D., but of the third century before Christ. Two thousand years later the Indochina War again taught that a heavily-encumbered conventional Franco-Vietnamese army could not crush an elusive Vietminh guerrilla movement that merged with the countryside, any more than a swarm of ants could be exterminated with an iron pickhead. Nevertheless, in 1955 the US Military Assistance Advisory Group in Saigon duly began to build up another heavily-encumbered, conventional army of South Vietnamese on the strictly unilateral understanding that the Communist North would not start a second guerrilla war to gain control of the South, but might march its regular divisions across the Seventeenth Parallel for a good old-fashioned stand-up fight.

The new national army consequently proved incapable of coping with the Vietminh Mark Two – the hit-and-run Vietcong guerrillas. By 1965 victory against the elusive enemy was proving as perishable as birthday cake – all glorious on the day, yet tending to crumble drily between the fingers one week later when it was found that he had filtered back into the conquered area in undiminished strength. But the United States had modern military might and money, and the enemy did not, and these were therefore the weapons that Washington must now logically deploy. I still hear the despairing words of trapped American officials in Saigon explaining as their jets hit out at the North : 'We had to escalate or get out, even if escalation could only lead to a bigger and bloodier stalemate.'

It was not difficult to guess what was to come. The enemy and the peasant soon learned what a B-52 bomber could destroy on a single sortie costing no more than $60,000, what defoliants could do to their crops and napalm to their villages, and just how alike armed guerrillas and old grandfathers could look to undiscriminating troops engaged on a 'partridge drive' for the Vietcong across the farmlands of the Delta. In the holocaust that followed the 'Tet Offensive' of 1968, heavy retaliatory fire wreaked havoc in towns and hamlets, and not long afterwards nearly three hundred peasants were killed and wounded in one village alone when troops turned their flame-throwers on it 'by mistake'.

Yet the war still dragged on. Why? General Vo Nguyen Giap, 'The Tiger of Dien Bien Phu' and anxious father of the 'People's Army of the Democratic Republic of Vietnam', had given me the answer ten years before. 'The men who fought the Chinese two thousand years ago were Vietnamese fighting for Vietnam,' he said simply. 'And so are we.' Relaxing between wars, he greeted me in 1957 in Hanoi with a quick, easy smile that the healing years had at last restored to him since his wife had died in a French colonial prison, and he radiated an intelligent, calculating confidence. His features, taken separately, were softly moulded in the broad face and almost feminine, the lips full, the chin rounded, the eyebrows like black feathers. Put together, however, they became the visor of the soldier, the eyes and facial muscles imposing their own discipline. Giap is unbending on duty, meticulous among the maps, a sagacious organizer, a buttoned-up man in a buttoned-up uniform who watches where he puts his small feet.

He is not infallible, nor are his men. His first premature mass attacks against the French in 1951 earned him a bloody nose, yet his impatience began to creep into his campaigning against their successors in 1968, when Americans sometimes found themselves ploughing into close-packed waves of North Vietnamese foot-sloggers with 105-mm howitzer shells fired at point blank range.

Many of these 'human sea' heroes might have been the dazed products of indoctrination courses which had armed them with a semi-automatic death-wish, or they might have thrown themselves into battle only because they knew that if they dodged their destiny at the 'front' they would get it in the back from their own comrades. But if Vietnamese Communists come in the usual limitless combinations of vice and virtue, patriotism and poltroonery, they nevertheless have an outstanding record for violence and valour. For to the lean and hungry spirits among the mentally recumbent millions that half-loved, half-hated their French masters, Ho Chi Minh's call to revolution in 1946 was like a voice from the honourable past.

Obsessed by their own colonial ignominy, the Vietnamese rebels subsequently showed a masochistic capacity for self-sacrifice that left most of them rake-thin but radiant over their victory at Dien Bien Phu. Then, nightmarishly, the vanquished French were replaced by the Americans. But the Vietcong soldier was like a bird that screeches its defiance and spoils for a fight if any other trespasses on its territory, even when it is caged. Born unfree, the true patriot was driven by a desperate nationalism and could often die with facility. He did not worry that he could not take it with him. He had nothing of value to take. 'I know the Liberation Front cannot gain a purely military victory,' Gaston Pham admitted to me in 1964. 'But you will see. The Americans will have to back down. They do not have the tenacity of the Vietnamese to win, for it is not their country.'

However, it was the country of other Vietnamese who were

mobilized against the Vietcong in the regular army of South Vietnam, in the auxiliary Regional Forces and the Self-defence corps. Yet by 1968 one man in every three was deserting. Even in its extreme youth the army suffered from those afflictions normally associated with ageing bones, for it was stiff with incompetent officers chosen primarily for their loyalty to President Diem, and in 1969 promotions were still political, officers still clung lovingly to their authority, corruption was still rife, and incompetents still commanded many battalions. Moreover, for the Vietcong or the North Vietnamese the American was yet another foreign invader on whom to strop his national will to fight; for the South Vietnamese he was often a hateful ally who contemptuously called him a 'slope', a 'dink' or a 'gook'.

Some units of the National Army fought both ably and bravely, but too many soldiers only wanted to see an end to the struggle. 'How can we win?' as one officer asked me, hopelessly. 'We Vietnamese can only lose, whatever the results. We are a nation divided, we are killing each other, and God cannot save all of us unless we stop.' The whole agonizing business was futile anyway, it seemed to others. 'The Communists will soon take over once the Americans go,' a South Vietnamese minister commented to me bitterly. 'If they cannot do it constitutionally, they will dig up their buried arms in two or three or four years' time, and rise again to seize the country by force as they did after the Geneva Agreement of 1954. It's all been for nothing.' For him, the sum just would not come out. It must always leave a recurring decimal of conflict.

'Peace' came in January 1973, and it only remained to be seen if he was right. In the years between I had known many heroes of the war, but also many villains of the peace – students, Buddhists, Trotskyists, socialists, nationalists, ex-Vietminh, left-wing intellectuals, neutralist monks, 'non-Communists' of the Liberation Front, and men like Thao. They did not all form one vast conspiratorial ring of Marxists. Pawns or patriots, they were Vietnamese expressing Vietnamese ideas. But it was only too easy to dub them 'Commie' and throw them towards the Vietcong, just as American escalation threw Ho Chi Minh back upon the arms of the Chinese and Russians. Ironically, the sal-

vation of South Vietnam will still depend on these twilight men
and their amorphous national spirit when the sound of the last
shot of the 'cease-fire' has died away and the first hopes of long-
term political victory may be nursed. For the nature of Communism is that it only starts to lose after it has won.

The Good Guys

SCRAWLED upon the inside covers of buckled notebooks filled across the years are the most cryptic reminders of all : *'Maurice in gaol Saigon. Raymond no news, believed Hanoi. Michel with Vietcong, putting on weight. Jean captain in South Vietnamese marines at Tu Duc. Jacquot, marine cadet, ordered to Saigon.'* This was the blood and bones of the matter in the form of a sketchy record of five Vietnamese brothers divided by their convictions in a land split between the extremes of Communism and anti-Communism. I collected these scraps of information from time to time for an anxious sister, safe on the outside. To the Americans, Vietnam was the frontier of freedom, to these, a tortured land in which brother killed brother, and classmate classmate. The gap of incomprehension was virtually unbridgeable.

The Vietnamese and the Americans treated each other with the distrust of men with entirely different aims. The American soldier was often conscientious, imbued in the early stages with a sense of mission, machine-turned and impeccable with his weapons and his war-theory. He was exasperated by the sight of the Vietnamese old-soldiering their way through the endless maze of military mayhem – 'an armoured battalion just stayed in a trance, our captain died trying to make them advance', as one bitter librettist put it. The Vietnamese was committed to the long struggle for the duration, and his object was to survive. He looked down on the American as a textbook soldier, a tourist who was committed for a mere 365 days and counted them off eagerly on the pocket calendar that seemed to have become standard equipment, along with his boots.

Mr Tran Van Huong, the Prime Minister of South Vietnam who saved Thao from the vengeance of Khanh, was described in mid-1969 as the indispensable 'darling of the Americans'. But just one year before I had gone to see him in yet another of those small, simple Vietnamese homes that conspire to make the large Westerner feel like an uneconomical dinosaur. He was out of office, his face sick and tired beneath a wire brush of white hair, and he did not talk like anybody's darling.

'The experience of Eastern Europe shows that if you enter into a coalition with the Communists, your country ends up Communist,' he said. 'South Vietnam would go in two weeks. The idea that we would fight on alone against the Vietcong if the Americans left us is just talk. But, after all, we are all Vietnamese. In Eastern Europe the Communist states have settled down to a national life that you could call nearly normal. This could have happened to us, and anyway we could not possibly have suffered so much from the Communists as we have done through this war. The Vietnamese people tend to blame the Americans for all their troubles. And perhaps they are right.'

In the old Imperial city of Hue on the River of Perfume in Central Vietnam men with reason to curse the bigots of both sides might well have agreed. The Vietcong had thrown themselves into the town during the New Year offensive of 1968 and perpetrated a massacre of innocents among the local Vietnamese. But the Americans had blasted them out of it again in accordance with those humane principles of modern attack which prompt commanders to save the lives of soldiers by first pulverizing the enemy zone with bombs and shells, reducing towns to stinking tombs of rubble and plaster commemorating the Unknown Civilian buried beneath.

All is a matter of perspective, however. For many Americans the Vietnam war was a first and last ditch stand against Communism in South-east Asia. Behind Hanoi were the aggressive Chinese sectarians, rogue Marxists preaching a world revolution that would impose their totalitarian dogma on all humanity. Relentless in their conviction that the bloodiest war was 'just' if it advanced the sacred cause of Maoism, they insisted that the ideological end excused the means, for theirs was the only true doctrine. Their visage was a screaming, fanatical face, full of teeth and hatred, glimpsed in a shufflepast of Peking Red Guards.

The urbane Californian lawyer with whom I lunched in Singapore during the early stages of the Chinese 'Cultural Revolution' hardly seemed to belong to the same division of mammals. But he soon proved that he did. Well travelled, well educated, he argued his case in a voice as smooth as sump-oil while easing his way with practised caution through a menu the size of the *New York Times*, and it went like this : the United States had the most perfect democratic system in the world. It was therefore essential that the United States remain powerful and prosperous, so that Washington could see that the American form of democracy prevailed everywhere. 'So the struggle in Vietnam,' he went on, 'is a vital confrontation between the United States and China. It is a struggle for big stakes in which Vietnam and the Vietnamese are themselves of no importance. Even if a million Vietnamese died, it would still be irrelevant.' As for the contention that defending freedom meant defending the right of the Vietnamese to choose their own form of government, 'that's just a lot of semantics'.

This was the kind of talk that made many Asians feel that they were caught between two intolerant, powerful, often ruthless antagonists. The war against the enemies of democracy had become a righteous crusade, leading to the same savage abuses and brutality that had characterized all the other crusades in history. The American who believed that he and only he could build Jerusalem on earth was moving perilously close to the sixteenth-century religious sectarian who called murdering heretics 'holy work'. And no one would have agreed with this general principle more promptly than a Vietcong terrorist.

'*Jacquot*,' records a later notebook, '*gone USA for a course in US Marine School. Jean, now major commanding battalion of SVN marines, usually Tu Duc. Raymond, with VC near Dalat, okay; Maurice, out of gaol, teaching in Saigon; Michel, in Hanoi, rumour may be sent south to fight Americans ...*'

The Vietnamese could scarcely be blamed for beginning to suspect that preserving the American way of life was becoming the Vietnamese way of death. Obsessed with a grand global

strategy, many Americans holding more immediate power than
my Californian acquaintance appeared to be as little concerned
about the fate of the Vietnamese themselves. The Pentagon
used the country as a testing ground for tactics and weapons,
and received news of heavy Vietnamese casualties with impressive equanimity. A proposal that the US Air Force should
drop a line of atomic bombs right across the Seventeenth
Parallel, blasting it into a belt of scrambled radio-active jungle
and effectively separating the two halves of Vietnam, was
among the less lethal schemes kicked around at command
level. But it took a military brain at its most professional and
pure to conceive the brilliantly simple alternative: to start at
the southernmost tip of Vietnam and roll it up systematically,
as it were, destroying everything in the process from the armed
enemy to 'psycho-social' targets like hospitals, schools and
churches, and leaving it all politically decontaminated and fit
for democracy. It was as if the American liberator were toying
with plans for converting this unconsidered trifle of a nation
in the right-hand bottom corner of Asia into a second, slow-
motion Hiroshima.

An outsider might admire unstintingly the American combat
soldier at his best, could recognize that devoted American field-
workers were risking their own lives to improve those of the
Vietnamese peasant, and that in America itself millions were
honestly examining their consciences. But in the minds of
many Vietnamese in the middle, the American who bombed
him and the American who wept over him – the hawkish and
the mawkish – merged into a schizophrenic figure as unnerv-
ingly inexplicable as Jekyll-and-Hyde.

Those who would not plunge after him in his pursuit of the
infidel, however, were made to feel the cutting edge of his
disfavour. During a short hot summer visit that I made to
Washington in 1967, Eugene Rostow, Assistant Secretary for
Political Affairs in the State Department, told me he had found
it extremely odd that although the Australians had come half-
way around the world to help the British twice in two world
wars, the British would not 'go to the aid' of the Australians
in Vietnam. The fact that the Australians had committed

300,000 men to the Second World War and fewer than 8,000 to Vietnam was presumably irrelevant. The struggle had assumed the ridiculous dimensions of a third world war in his mind, and he did not even realize it.

When I asked Dean Rusk, then Secretary of State, whether he thought Whitehall should act on Mr Rostow's stricture, he replied with a quick, cold snap: 'That's up to the conscience of the British Government,' and then added 'We know today who are our friends and who are not. And our friends are the allies who are fighting beside us in Vietnam.' I also asked him whether the United States would consider halting the bombing in North Vietnam. 'To please whom?' inquired Rusk, in a voice like a bastard file, 'The left-wing of the British Labour Party?'

I am sure that Dean Rusk was aware that a nation's first duty was to itself, and that it was this enlightened self-interest that had persuaded the United States to stay out of the First World War until 1917 (by which time Britain had taken more than a million casualties in Flanders alone), and out of the second until the end of 1941 (by which time the City of London had gone up in flames and the Nazis dominated all Europe). Washington had also prudently refrained from throwing in troops to stop the Communists from taking over Cuba, China, Hungary, Poland, Bulgaria, Czechoslovakia, Yugoslavia, Rumania, Albania, half of Germany, half of Korea and half of Vietnam, and in 1963 the Americans made no ill-considered moves when President Sukarno set out to destroy the democratic Federation of Malaysia with the biggest Communist Party in the free world as his ally, and the smiling approval of the Chinese in Peking.

Indonesia had a population ten times that of Malaysia and was ten times as big. Under the Anglo-Malayan Defence Agreement the new Commonwealth state was mainly protected by some 50,000 British servicemen, but the Indonesians had more than 300,000 regulars under arms and the most powerful fleet and air force of any country in South-east Asia, all bought on tick from Moscow. They were well placed to make mischief for the fragile federation whose two halves had only just been joined with little more than faith for a fixative.

One year later Indonesian personnel were still undergoing training in the United States, Washington was still giving Sukarno forty million dollars' worth of 'residual' long-term economic and military assistance. In February 1965 Sukarno inaugurated an atomic reactor at Bandung, built with the help of the US Atomic Energy Commission and a US government grant of $350,000. The United States Government next declared that it had no objection to the sale of an American three-million-dollar, jam-proof Tropospheric Scatter Fixed Communications System to Djakarta, which would provide an up-to-date radio network linking all major military headquarters in the Indonesian Republic. American Armalite rifles began turning up in the hands of Sukarno's guerrillas, and Washington applied diplomatic pressure to stop the British from hitting back at their bases on Indonesian territory.

Mr Howard Jones, United States Ambassador in Djakarta, had apparently convinced the State Department that if the United States embargoed aid to Djakarta, and the British were allowed to be beastly to the infiltration forces that Sukarno was lining up on his side of the frontier to attack Malaysian Borneo, the Bung would lean even further towards the Communists. On the other hand a friendly America could exert a soothing influence over him and might eventually 'swing him round'.

Few Asians were impressed. Most shared the sour conviction that Washington's conciliatory gestures evoked no reciprocal tenderness towards the United States but simply encouraged the Indonesians to think that they could intensify their terrorist campaign against Malaysia with impunity. Their fears were borne out. By August 1965 Mr Jones, the man who 'understood' Sukarno, was being accused in Djakarta of plotting aggression against the Republic, and his successor was greeted with placards inscribed 'Stay away from Indonesia' and a cutting lecture from Sukarno. Despite his many suitable qualifications for the job – his horror of democracy, his autocratic rule, and his corrupt government – the Bung was not to be 'our son-of-a-bitch' after all.

On the other hand, Indonesian Confrontation gave a new

if evanescent shine to the tarnished and blackened British image. Britain had been the victor of the Second World War that had led the way towards the welfare state and had given India, Burma, Ceylon, and later Malaya freedom to follow if they would. But subsequently the evolving political characteristics of the Briton had begun to distort this presentable portrait. His inconstancies blurred its edges, and he became hard on the eyes. He tagged along behind the Americans, joined the South-east Asia Treaty Organization, put troops into Korea – and then sold buses to Cuba and Viscounts to Peking. He was co-chairman of the Geneva Agreement on Indochina and advocated neutralism for Laos – but simultaneously he trained hundreds of Vietnamese officers in anti-guerrilla warfare at his jungle school in South Malaya. Asians understand flexibility, but it must be justified by results. It fascinated them that all Britain's power, perfidy and political wisdom could be ground into meaningless fragments of seemingly uncorrelated action.

By 1966, however, the British had not only slugged it out stubbornly with the Communist terrorists of Malaya for twelve years, but had successfully blocked off the Indonesians as well. As middleweights they had proved that they carried a useful punch. 'We should like the British to keep their military bases here,' Rajaratnam told me at the end of Confrontation, sitting in an expensively panelled coffin of an office whose windows had been walled up against Indonesian terrorists. 'The British are welcome, and for three good reasons: they are not trying to build any more empires, they are not playing power politics in this region, and they want to go home anyway.'

With the lessons of Confrontation behind them, on the other hand, Singapore and Malaysian leaders said to me in almost identical words: 'To the Americans, Indonesia represents more than a hundred million potential anti-Communists. That is all the arithmetic the United States wants to know. If the Indonesians attacked us again, do you really believe that they would back us and risk estranging Djakarta? You saw what happened last time. They would sacrifice us as pawns to win Indonesia's allegiance.'

For Washington there was no right or wrong, it appeared,

only white or red. But most Asians were not susceptible to the mental warp that automatically translated the 'free political education' offered in South Vietnam into 'compulsory brain-washing' when it was given in North Vietnam, or that would damn the New York *Nation* for a rose-red weekly twice as old as *Time* and blacklist its readers as 'Commies'. That kind of blinker-visioned outlook earned the United States, somewhat unfairly, a reputation for exporting more Joe McCarthy than Jefferson.

During the sixties many felt that they were being manipulated for questionable ends. There was a revulsion from the long queue of those who shambled cap-in-hand up to the American pay-desk, and from the type of divisions-for-dollars deal that took 48,000 South Korean troops to Vietnam in exchange for massive United States economic assistance to Seoul. In Saigon men murmured that they were no longer masters in their own house. In Thailand the Foreign Minister remarked waspishly, 'We are not the fifty-first state.' In Singapore Lee Kuan Yew tartly told a television audience in 1967, 'I am not going to be the monkey of the American organ-grinder.' There was a contagious dread that control of events was rapidly slipping out of the small, weak hands of the South-east Asians into the clutches of two Big Brothers, one the unpredictable servant of Mao, the other of the machine.

Nowhere in the entire disaster area, however, was the sense of being prodded and pinched and plucked at by foreign fingers more acute than in Laos. But as the Laotians themselves say: 'When the buffaloes fight, it is the grass that gets trampled.'

Civilizing the Natives

NOTHING could have been more incongruous than that the indolent, sunwashed country of the Laotians should have become the loose hinge on which the fate of South-east Asia was to swing, for Laos is the land of *Bau Pinh Yanh*, the 'never mind' that makes *mañana* sound like *Achtung!*

Bewildered and uncomprehending, the Laos were not cut out for the task of defending the free world against the international Communist conspiracy, especially as most of them had never heard of either. Prince Souvanna Phouma once told me that he did not believe there were more than 100 truly Marxist cadres in the whole of the left-wing Pathet Lao guerrilla movement. Prince Souphannouvong, the Pathet Lao leader, solemnly swore that his Communists were fundamentally loyal to the Laotian monarchy and the principles of neutralism.

Nonetheless, by Christmas 1960 the face of Vientiane was pockmarked with shell-holes and shattered, burned-out buildings, over which festoons of twisted telephone wire hung like uncombed hair. Shops were boarded up, there was no water, and in the Hotel Constellation frayed correspondents groped their way around by candlelight. For the ideological struggle had hit the Laotian capital.

This particular round had opened in April 1960 with an electoral victory for the 'Pro-Americans' which had been so blatantly rigged that the Americans themselves had found it a little breathtaking. 'We did not think our friends would go quite so far,' as one CIA officer said in Vientiane, 'but the main thing is that the right side is in.' When in August, therefore, a neutralist paratroop captain called Kong Le upset this satisfactory state of affairs by seizing Vientiane in a coup d'état, the Americans were displeased. And when the new government under Prince Souvanna Phouma insisted on seeking a reconciliation with the pro-Communist Pathet Lao, they obliged him to forgo further aid.

Instead, American agents in Bangkok and Hongkong began buying up all the available Laotian currency on the market in order to pay the troops of the 'anti-Communist' General Phoumi Nosavan, who was bent upon throwing Souvanna Phouma out of office again. Accordingly Souvanna Phouma, the pay of his troops and police six months in arrears, started taking aid from the Soviet Union in order to offset the American boycott, and the Russians obligingly airlifted to Vientiane not only food and fuel but a battery of howitzers for its defence. The right-wing army of General Phoumi then moved up from the south-east to wrest the capital from Kong Le and Souvanna Phouma, and for four days the two Lao forces hammered away at each other across the town with mortars and artillery.

Caught on the wrong foot by events, I finally reached Vientiane in the monstrous belly of an RAF Blackburn Beverley transport aircraft feeling like some latter-day Jonah, surrounded by eight tons of medical supplies for the choked hospitals of the capital, and hoping that the airfield would be safely in the hands of one side or the other as we lumbered towards it at 130 miles an hour.

In the shell-shocked Hotel Constellation, where the soporific Laotian flies and the low canvas chairs that set one's knees about one's ears nevertheless looked much the same, I learned that my colleagues had only been able to file a short joint telegram to their agencies and newspapers once a day over the radio of the British Embassy. They had, however, seized at least one opportunity to work off their frustrations, for as shells and mortar bombs fell on all sides of their unhappy headquarters in the middle of the town, a thick-skinned Australian Communist writer insulted one of their number in the bar.

While the sky spewed death outside, therefore, those gathered together for shelter within threw themselves into battle against one another. A genial American press photographer laid the Australian flat with a felicitous blow, but within minutes found himself saving the man's life by forcibly restraining him from plunging out into the inferno in the street. A woman went into hysterics and a gallant Frenchman thereupon added a deft touch of comedy amid the pandemonium inside and out by playing the role of the neutralist, reminding the dishevelled Anglo-Saxons in tones of unbelievable pomposity 'Gentlemen, gentlemen, there are *ladies* present.' The scene was like a miniature Laos within a Laos. For although there were 'ladies present' throughout the land, the big alien antagonists were not to be deterred from treating it as their fight-ring.

Phoumi captured Vientiane, and Souvanna Phouma was compelled to make common cause with the Communists to the north. 'The Americans have made me utterly dependent on the Russians now,' he told me, moodily chewing on a cheroot, when I met him subsequently at the rebel headquarters which he shared with the Pathet Lao on the Plain of Jars. The dismal farce was not to lose pace, however. Having suspended aid to Souvanna Phouma because he tried to unite the country by coming to terms with the Pathet Lao, the Americans now began to have second thoughts, and Washington was soon suspending aid to General Phoumi in turn – in his case because he failed to try to unite the country by coming to terms with the estranged Souvanna Phouma. But of course it is misleading to write 'Washington'. 'The trouble with us,' an elderly Laotian statesman said to me with a shrug during those stirring days, 'is that we have three governments and all of them American – the State Department, the Pentagon, and the C I A.'

Phoumi's reaction was to defy the Americans and go on a spending spree, and when I next arrived in Laos the roads of Vientiane were being widened, a set of traffic lights – the first in the country – had been purchased and put up at one arbitrarily-chosen crossroads, and the 'Monument Aux Morts' was being completed with a large quantity of cement originally provided by the United States for the specific purpose of extending the airport runway. But in the unforseeable future Souvanna Phouma was to return to Vientiane as Prime Minister, and Phoumi was to end up plotting in exile in Thailand.

The neutrality of Laos became official under the Geneva Agreement of 1962, and was endorsed by all the powers in play. Promises in writing are only on paper, however, and in 1963 I found Souvanna Phouma still stretched between extreme right and extreme left in a nerve-racking effort to bring them together and so reunite Laos as a neutral state. As I walked into his office in Vientiane a small, boyish figure ran past me – Kong Le, now a general. 'I have just told him,' said Souvanna Phouma a trifle petulantly, 'to go back to the Pathet Lao and start talks with them again. How can we hope for national union when all these people insist on quarrelling all the time?' He looked harassed, a morose honey-bear who knew in his heart that he would never find the sweet ambrosia of peace and unity. 'But what is the good? The Pathet Lao are almost impossible to talk to, because they are creatures of the Vietnamese Communists, behind whom in turn are the Chinese. Meanwhile, now that I am back in Vientiane, my Government is again utterly dependent upon American aid, and so I am labelled an imperialist. There would be no difficulty in resolving the differences between us Laotians – if only all the foreigners would go away and leave us alone.' There were Russian, Chinese, and North Vietnamese missions in the 'neutral' Laotian capital, all accredited directly to the King and therefore free to denounce the Prince and his government as a collection of capitalist puppets. On the way out, I passed the Chinese Ambassador on his way in. Souvanna Phouma was having a trying day.

For the bemused Lao, who was faintly surprised in the first place to find that Russians were white, the struggle of the powers was scarcely comprehensible, but the war had meaning. It meant that more and more young men who should have been behind ploughs were now behind guns. It meant that Laos, which should have been self-supporting in grain, was importing 70,000 tons of rice by 1968, that out of a population of fewer than three million, there were nearly 600,000 refugees, at least one quarter of whom had to be fed and given shelter. The Americans paid for almost everything, but to the Lao it seemed that the Americans were paying him just to suffer, while on the other side the Chinese and the Vietnamese Communists made him suffer without paying. By 1969 there were more than 50,000 Vietnamese troops in the country, and Laos had virtually lost her two northern provinces.

All hope of reconciliation and reunification rested on respect for the Geneva Agreement of 1962. But even this was in turn dependent upon a settlement among nine different kinds of foreigner in an alien land – Vietnam. One thing appeared to be certain : the Laos were not to be allowed to resolve anything for themselves simply by folding their own hands in peace.

However, brother has fought brother with such distressing frequency in Asia that a fine military tradition has grown up, whereby victory and defeat may be decided by simple mathematics rather than unnecessary bloodshed. When warlords contended for the control of China in the twenties, the army which was smaller or had fewer machine-guns or less money often capitulated to the larger force after firing a few shots in the air for the sake of appearances. This civilized custom was honoured by the rebels in Sumatra, and prompted those swift withdrawals that enabled towns and strongpoints to change hands in a peaceful and tidy manner, so that classmate did not kill classmate. For only holy wars flout humanitarian convention today.

In Laos the game was often geared to the movements of the sun during the sixties. If a Laotian detachment heard gunfire at dusk, it would abandon its post for the night; the Pathet Lao guerrillas would then move in, but they would leave at dawn, and the Royal Army would reoccupy the position again (after breakfast). In this way casualties were avoided but stirring communiqués could be issued and profitable indents for expended ammunition filed. When the Pathet Lao threatened the key town of Nam Bac in 1968, the defending troops promptly withdrew from it, the men dispersing in an orderly manner from the battle area and turning up a few days later to rejoin their units once all was quiet. No one was so impolite as to suggest that this was tantamount to desertion in the face of the enemy.

The Laos are not natural soldiers, and their lack of martial aptitude can be measured by the fact that even their

Communist-indoctrinated guerrillas are incompetent. The principal reason for this depressing situation is that the Lao does not like to kill. The devout Buddhist knows that he should not be personally responsible for the death of any living thing – he has no right to change its destiny, and anyway a Pathet Lao (or a pi-dog) may be Grandpa reborn. Even the birds in a Laotian cockfight are not fitted with spurs, so that neither is slain.

The infantrymen that attacked Vientiane in 1960 for the sake of Phoumi and the CIA fired most of their shots into the air, and mathematically-minded American advisers calculated that in most circumstances Laos aimed all small arms upward at an angle of thirty degrees to make sure of missing everything. According to my slightly incoherent notes, few soldiers died in this battle, but there were at least 450 victims among the civilian spectators, and many more lost their homes, for by then a chink had been found in the armour of Buddhist scruple.

The Lao recruit was first persuaded of the essential innocence of impersonal weapons like heavy guns whose shells killed indiscriminately and out of sight, for their crews were not directly responsible for any individual death. And in time he showed that he could progress from that starting point, so that it was later recorded with some satisfaction that he was beginning to adopt a more responsible attitude generally towards the serious business of slaughtering his fellows. I saw Laotian gunners handle 105-mm howitzers in action as far back as 1961 at a place called Phou Khoun, and by the distorted philosophy of the newspapermen considered myself lucky to have done so.

Laos is one of the most frustrating countries in Asia to cover, for the highways are narrow, pot-holed tracks winding through almost impenetrable mountains of steep plaited jungle, hardly any of them are passable all the year round, and much of the countryside is in Communist hands. The reporter may spend most of his time trying to get out of Vientiane, and never more vainly than when his objective is a battle somewhere in the back-of-beyond.

But in January 1961 the rebels, advancing westwards from

the Plain of Jars, took the strategic junction of Phou Khoun and so cut the main road that threads its way northward through the mountains for some 250 miles from Vientiane to Luang Prabang. The Royal Army then set out to dislodge them, and at that moment Fortune turned upon me her brief, meretricious smile. I happened to be on the airfield at Vientiane when a Sikorsky chopper, flown by an under-the-counter American Marine in an anonymous flying suit, dropped in for ten minutes to unload a few wounded and take on a few bags of rice for Muong Kassy, headquarters of the regiment that was carrying out the counter-attack. As no one else was in sight, formalities could be waived, so after a brief exchange of courtesies I climbed up the side of the helicopter into the seat beside the pilot, and fastened the safety straps over my thin tropical suit.

The chopper lurched off the wilting grass in a cloud of dust, fluttered north over the parched floor of the Mekong Valley, and began to weave its way purposefully among the grey ridge-backed heights that rose abruptly from the flat plain on all sides. Deep in the hills, Muong Kassy lay astride the road some 200 miles to the north, a cluster of wooden bungalows on stilts from which there rose into the cold blue heavens thin threads of woodsmoke and the soft, nasal lament of a solitary *khene*, the Lao syrinx that has the nostalgic quality of distant bagpipes. For the rest, the village slept. And so did the regimental headquarters. The regimental commander was a certain Colonel Oudone Sananikone – tall, amiable, agreeably ugly. After his siesta he greeted me with a wry grin. I was in luck, he said, a convoy would leave for the front in the morning. I could go with it.

At dawn next day this convoy, lined up on the stony, rutted farm-track that turns out to be the road, gives food for thought. It consists of two topless trucks, one loaded with fourteen sacks of rice, the other with eight open oil-drums filled with drinking water, for the colonel's troops eighteen miles farther on through the tangled jungle and the limestone gorges are not only desperately hungry, but desperately thirsty. For this pitiful grocery-run we are nevertheless to have an escort of two

armoured cars and two more open trucks mounting Bren-guns
on their cabin roofs and packed with a full platoon of riflemen
in French and American steel helmets.

On the map, the road to the front is a mere kink in a brash
red line. On the ground it proves otherwise. I climb up beside
the driver of the water truck and we jolt into the first deep
ruts, over the first potholes and the first spurts of sharp shale
that make up this section of the 1,000-mile-long Highway Number Thirteen of all Indochina. The track is about twelve feet
wide, and soon becomes a ledge which winds its way along
the steep fall of mountainside. The small dust-stained clutch of
vehicles grates forward, shuddering and dipping and bouncing
at an average speed of six miles an hour, and the water slops
out of the oil-drums at every lurch. A small pig tied to the
side of the armoured car in front of us squeals in a cross
falsetto, and hens in a bamboo basket jammed behind its
machine-gun shift and cluck uneasily. The gunner, dressed in
jungle green with a peacock feather stuck through his beret,
snatches at a tangle of convolvulus and stuffs the stem of one
delicate blue trumpet into the barrel – just as we pass a blown-
up and burned-out armoured car exactly like his. The country
is ideal for guerrillas skilled in ambush, and the enemy has
Chinese mines.

We edge into a clearing and groan to a halt outside a stilted
village. Bare-breasted women are sifting grain. Raw meat hangs
from a tree, dripping blood. It is a peaceful, almost idyllic
scene. Suddenly there is a shout of warning, and a man runs
fast towards the surrounding thickets. In a second our infantry
escort is scattering frantically. To fight or flee? Unhappily, I
think I know the answer. Then there is a laugh, another shout,
and the original runner reappears, holding a squawking hen
by the legs. Soldiers emerge from the underbrush, grinning a
little sheepishly. The convoy comes to order, and we push on.

By midday we can go no further. Half-way around the
haunch of a hillside four howitzers are lined up across the
road, firing over the gorge at the next ridge. Two officers are
squatting with their backs to the mountain wall, one listening
to the snarl of a small radio-telephone, the other working out

coordinates on a map. Sights are adjusted, the motley gun-crews in sneakers and denims, butt ends of cigarettes dangling from their lips, slam home the breech-blocks with almost Gallic panache and the shells scream hysterically over the valley. The target is the T-junction of Phou Khoun further along the winding road.

Half the water in our drums has splashed away. The soldiers tumble out of the trucks and sit down at the roadside to eat balls of rice and play an obscure game of cards as the guns continue to bark from their mountain perch. Happily, the enemy has not brought up guns that can bark back, for the convoy is now an untidy cluster of vehicles and men crowding up against the howitzers. From below us rises the crackle of rifle fire, so I edge apologetically past the four howitzers and set off along the road to find the Lao infantry. But the battery commander takes one look at this chilly apparition in his polka-dot bow tie and chemical city suiting and says no. Neither the water nor the rice nor I get any further, but, armed with the moral superiority of the thwarted, I can now sting him for a briefing.

At dusk the trucks start back towards Muong Kassy with four wounded. It is the first time the army has run a night convoy, for fear of ambushes, and hardly have we completed the first punishing kilometre, sidling forward precariously without lights along the rim of the range, when the armoured car in front opens up with a machine-gun, there is a cry of alarm, and once more the troops are leaping from their lorries with un-Laotian alacrity. The convoy soon comes to order again, however. The machine-gunner fired by mistake, it appears. Three hours later I am back in Muong Kassy, frozen stiff and still streaming sweat. The mission has been accomplished. So much petrol has been wasted bringing a little rice and water closer to the troops that regimental supplies of fuel are now exhausted in their turn, forward units will be without ammunition for half a week, and no more wounded can be evacuated.

At the headquarter bungalow the convoy commander huddles over the maps with his master, but after he has gone off into the darkness the colonel calls me over to the porch. 'Now *you* please tell me what's going on up there,' he says, glancing at the retreating back of the captain. I throw myself into what I hope is a soldierly report, to find myself baffled by something for which Second World War experience has not prepared me: the colonel's two war maps tell two different stories, the one often placing the enemy where the other places own troops, and vice-versa. But I do my best. And so subsequently did he. When I last saw him in 1968 he was not only a general: he was Chief of Staff of the Royal Laotian Army.

On returning to Vientiane in a chopper with the four wounded in order to cable my story, I found that I need not have gone to Phou Khoun at all. For the Laotian Minister of Information had already given my colleagues an admirably clear and authoritative account of how the junction had been captured. This was the war as we usually saw it. Had Phou Khoun really been taken the previous afternoon, as he claimed, I could testify that the Royal Army's victorious artillery must have been decimating the Royal Army's victorious infantry under my very nose. But the neat maps and facts and figures available in the capital would look fine on the pages of the newspapers in London, New York and Paris.

The Minister produced for us a one-man war far more absorbing than the incoherent and pointless plot the opposing armies were unravelling in the field. Shortly after his imaginary fall of Phou Khoun, he disclosed that hordes of Chinese and North Vietnamese had overrun a northern province, with which all radio communication had therefore broken down. But distrustful journalists later established that the army commander in that region had quarrelled with Vientiane and in a fit of pique had just switched off his W/T set for a few days in order to enjoy a little peace and quiet.

I preferred another minister who found a crumpled piece of paper in his pocket while eating lunch after a press conference and remarked gently: 'Oh dear! Here is a list of the army's victories I was supposed to announce. I really have no head for military matters.' That seemed to sum it up. Visiting the headquarters of a Lao general with 10,000 men under command, one third of them élite paratroops, I was struck by a notice on the door of his office. Anywhere else it would have read 'Walls have ears' or 'Know your enemy'. But this one said *'La tranquillité avant tout'* – 'Tranquillité above all'.

If the Lao were an arrant coward, his distaste for war might still be admirable. But he is not afraid of death : he simply does not seek it prematurely for himself or others. The Lao word for 'death' is the same as for Nirvana, and a house bereaved is a 'happy house'. It is dangerous to mourn, for mourning may bind the spirit of the dead to this illusory world. A cremation is therefore an occasion for all-night parties and roystering, the house must be filled with laughter and the family settle down to drinking, dancing and a little gentle gambling. Since final release from a long and wearisome succession of incarnations must be the ultimate object of the human operation, 'Death is the most important event in thy life.' And like all the best things in life, it is free.

However, a man must be sure what he is dying or killing for, the Laos would say. Any heroic impressions gained during the battle for Vientiane may have been obliterated by the spectacle of soldiers rushing into Buddhist temples in full fighting fig, only to emerge again a few minutes later dressed as harmless bonzes in saffron robes. But these did not necessarily lack courage. They simply lacked conviction. And Buddhists believe that fate should not be tempted lightly. You do not play chicken with God.

My Country Right or Left

A PERCEPTIBLE shiver of dismay nevertheless fled through the subcontinent in 1968 when the Americans first showed signs of doing what they had so often been asked to do – go home. For even vociferous critics of Washington among Asian anti-Communists slept easier in their beds behind the shield the Pentagon provided.

Yet local leaders were torn two ways, since Americans not only made dangerously compromising friends, but they came from a considerable distance and would therefore make safer enemies than '700,000,000 Chinese' just over the sill of South-east Asia. America was far, China near. Mao had unified his intimidatingly vast country. By mid-1967 the Chinese had run the nuclear gamut from A to H in the record time of two and a half years. And they were unpredictable.

No Asians were more exquisitely sensitive to the threat they posed than the Burmese, who remembered what happened when their own King Sinbyushin defeated the Chinese nearly 200 years ago. The Chinese sued for peace, and King Sinbyushin demanded the daughter of the Emperor as part of the price. In due course a retinue arrived bearing aloft in a gilt sedan chair a lady of great accomplishments. The court criers went forth and proclaimed that a Chinese princess had been received in the royal bedchamber. But the celestial lady proved to be a member of the oldest profession in the world, dressed up for the part. 'And the moral of that story,' a Burmese editor told me in his rat-ridden office in Rangoon, 'is that with these people you cannot win.'

Rangoon's attitude towards Peking had been determined by the disagreeable knowledge that Burma was an overstretched underdeveloped state of only twenty-five million people which

shared more than 1,300 miles of wild and remote mountain
frontier with the Chinese colossus to the north. From the first,
therefore, Burmese leaders had held out a slightly shaking hand
of friendship to the People's Republic across the fence. The
Chinese might give the 'White Flag' Burmese Communist Party
leaders asylum while their armed guerrillas continued to ter-
rorize the Burmese countryside, and the obstreperous behaviour
of the local Chinese 'Red Guards' in Rangoon in 1967 might
lead to an open breach between the two countries, but in the
last analysis the Burmese knew whose protestations of affection could bring them the most comfort, and at the end of
1969 General Ne Win was begging hotheads 'not to give vent
to anger' against the Chinese.

Malaysian and Indonesian ministers were meanwhile protesting that their governments were ready to be friends with China,
if only the Chinese would just stop fomenting revolution all
the time. In Manila President Marcos said that he was in
favour of establishing diplomatic ties with Peking. In Bangkok,
a two-headed image of Thai policy was already engaged in
crosstalk with itself. Mr Thanat Khoman, the Thai Foreign
Minister, justified a suggestion that Bangkok open the dialogue
with China by saying blandly, 'in a world of changing
allegiances, enemies have become the best of friends, and allies
the worst of enemies'. With his other voice he remained
vociferously hawkish, castigating American 'doves' who 'aspire
to withdraw into their quiet parochial concerns'. For it was
still desirable that the United States defeat Communism at a
decent distance and across two frontiers in Vietnam if possible, and the 48,000 American servicemen in Thailand had not
yet ceased to be an asset and started to become a political embarrassment. 'But that day must inevitably come, my dear
fellow,' a close aide of the Foreign Minister once told me coolly
in the impeccable English they cultivate there. And it soon did.

Michel, no news, Raymond, okay, now with V C in the south.
Maurice, still teaching in Saigon. Jacquot, still on a course in
America ... I jotted it all down. 'Would you say Jacquot was
pro-American?' I asked their old father as we sat by his fish-
pond in Saigon, sipping lime-juice and soda. 'Pro-American,' he

scoffed. 'Pro-western, pro-Communist, anti-Communist. How can you presume to label us all? There are a hundred different reasons why Vietnamese who are not Communist are with the Vietcong, and a further hundred reasons why Vietnamese who are not pro-western rally to the Saigon government and the Americans. Look at me, with all my children spread all over the board. What do I think of all these Americans?' he laughed softly and threw up his hands. 'I cannot tell even my own family. Do you expect me to tell you?'

The push-button nomenclature of loyalties which demands that an Asian be unambiguously for or against a lot of foreigners and their alien ideologies compounds the incomprehension between West and East. The American is not automatically loved for his big eyes or hated for his big mouth. The most important thing about him is that he is a stranger, to be weighed cold in the sensitive balance of Asian self-interest. 'Pro-American' Thais talk of his presence as a 'necessary evil'. In Vietnam 'anti-Communist' Vice-President Nguyen Cao Ky makes it known that he has more regard for Ho Chi Minh than for any 'foreigners'. But no 'pro-American' better expressed the Asian's severely pragmatic approach to rich benefactors than Diem and his brother Nhu.

Nhu defined the Americans not as friends but as 'material allies'. 'I want their money, arms and equipment,' he said shortly before his murder, 'but not them.' 'They have done everything to push me into the arms of Ho Chi Minh,' he later complained, and like much that is veiled, this threat was not idle. One night in September 1963 he slipped down to a rendez-vous in a Cholon hotel, taking only a bodyguard to stand outside one of the rooms. There he conferred until three o'clock in the morning with two go-betweens from Hanoi and several members of the Polish Delegation to the International Control Commission. Within a few days Diem summoned Colonel Thao and asked him a little diffidently whether he thought Ho Chi Minh really wanted to carry on with the struggle when their two systems now had 'so much in common'. (Ho was soon to describe a dead Diem as 'a patriot in his own way'.)

Even in that moment of dubious glory when 'pro-American' Phoumi had seized Vientiane with the indiscreet assistance of the CIA, he was already a very questionable all in the cause of anti-Communism, for the simple reason that he was not an American, he was a Lao. Ministers to whom I spoke privately in Vientiane at that time emphasized that Phoumi's government wanted to practise a neutralist policy, and some prophesied that he would wait for the right moment and then negotiate with the Communists. There is no paradox here. 'Do you think only Souvanna Phouma is a neutralist?' one asked me with a light Lao chuckle. 'We are all neutralists – only we are in competition with one another.' He was Ngon Sananikone, a tagged 'rightist' who had held fourteen different ministries in a colourful variety of governments, and was to sign the peace agreement with the Pathet Lao that officially ended the fighting in September 1973.

Neutralism means keeping out of other people's fights, and it appeals to Asians who are less anxious than the big powers might think to find out which of them is the paper tiger. If there was an awkward moment for Singapore when a trade mission from Hanoi arrived in the republic in the middle of the Vietcong's Tet Offensive in February 1968, it could easily be argued away. For only a few months before, American purchasing agents in the island had bought steel from Communist China for building bunkers in Vietnam against Vietcong attacks, and they were also believed to have ordered North Vietnamese cement through Singapore merchants for the same purpose.

Although the Singapore army was trained by Israelis, Lee Kuan Yew was a friend of President Nasser. When Israel knocked out the UAR in the blitzkreig of 1967, I therefore asked Rajaratnam how the Government could take it dispassionately. He looked at me with wide open eyes, shaking his head slightly as if I had unfairly accused him of murder. 'Nasser did not consult us before moving against Israel, so we are not required to take a stand,' he replied. They were the words of the immaculate neutral.

Singapore must be politically acrobatic, for it is a predominantly Chinese chip of an enclave in a predominantly

Malay region. 'Heaven help us if Peking offers to recognize us,' Goh Keng Swee shuddered over his bowl of 'drunken chicken' at dinner one night, 'the Malaysians and the Indonesians will think we are being converted into some sort of Maoist detonator to blow up the whole area.' 'A good thing President Johnson did not include Singapore in his recent tour,' another minister said to me at the end of 1966, 'it would have compromised us badly with Peking.'

In Malaysia Doctor Ismail bin Dato Abdul Rahman stood up in parliament and proposed that his country explore the possibility of neutralizing the whole of South-east Asia behind a screen of international guarantees from all the great powers, including Communist China. 'Many people agree with me that neutralization is the answer, but they won't speak up because the Tengku is not in favour of it,' Ismail told me afterwards in an air-conditioned study furnished like the cabin of a somewhat bookish sea-captain. He was on sick leave between two bouts of being Minister for Home Affairs, but he was not a man to mince his words. 'We could start, in fact, with the neutralization of Malaya.'

'Of course it would not mean anything unless the Chinese also accepted it,' he agreed before I had opened my mouth. 'But China need not make a positive move : it would be a beginning if Peking tacitly refrained from supporting terrorists and sowing subversion on our soil. We might make a gesture by legalizing the Malayan Communist Party. We are well placed to take the initiative in all this. We have a large Chinese population and we could make our first approach unofficially, through a suitable Malaysian Chinese businessman with standing enough to be able to meet Premier Chou En-lai.' It was bold talk, but it was to have its echoes in Bangkok and Manila and in Laos, where a minister neatly fixed the timing with six words of French : 'Once Mao is dead.' Doctor Ismail died in August 1973, and by that time not only was the subcontinent moving hesitantly towards a handshake with China, but the Association of South-east Asian Nations (ASEAN) that included Malaysia, Singapore, Indonesia, Thailand and the Philippines had issued a joint declaration that the region should be a 'zone of peace, freedom and neutrality', which the big powers would be asked to underwrite.

When anti-Communist counter-insurgency is discussed in Asia, a kind of hopelessness afflicts the infirm of spirit, for they at once point out that for years the rare achievements of half a million Americans in Vietnam were all too rare. They forget that by 1954 the country was divided into two, the North was already in independent Communist state, and the South spongy with the subversion that seeped through it during eight years of anti-colonial guerrilla war against the French. No other South-east Asian state was in this irremediably polluted condition.

It is equally fashionable for hawks to claim that neutrality is not a practical solution for Asian agonies, for the neutrality of Laos was guaranteed by all the powers concerned in 1962, yet seven years later the country was still an international battlefield. But Laos was neutralized just because it had already been carved up by warring Communist and anti-Communist forces, and this was not true of other South-east Asian states. The foundering of Vietnam does not prove that Thailand cannot be kept afloat, and the dismemberment of Laos does not convince Asians that neutrality is necessarily an illusion. It appeals to many of them as a cushion on which the great bulk of China (and Russia, and America) may be supported, the lining that could keep Communists and anti-Communists from direct, abrasive contact.

Extreme breeds extreme, and neutrality may be a safer defence against Communism than anti-Communism itself. In a world of opposites, leaders like Prince Norodom Sihanouk of Cambodia have been comforted by the belief that it is the thickness of the coin that holds head and tail apart, yet is committed to neither. For they do not forget that when the coin is spun, one side or the other must fall flat on its face.

'I am extremely moved,' Sihanouk wrote to Chou En-lai in 1968, 'by the tin of Chinese lichees of an exceptional flavour which you kindly sent me. May I convey to you my warm thanks for this token of your tactful solicitude and constant friendship. I take once again this opportunity of voicing our firm solidarity with the brotherly Chinese people in the anti-American imperialist struggle ...'

The delectable taste of the lichee is widely lauded, and more than 1200 years ago a doting Chinese Emperor arranged for this egregious food to be brought to the breakfast table of his beloved from the far south of the Middle Kingdom by special relays of horsemen. But although Sihanouk was giving syrop for syrop, he was not to be bought into the anti-American imperialist struggle with a can of fruit.

A few months later he was urging the Americans not to abandon the region. 'I need some cards in my hands to maintain a balance,' he protested. 'If the United States leaves Asia completely, it would be the end of my independence.' He would rather have American tourists than American troops in Cambodia itself, he said ('their dollars do not smell of policy'), but he hoped that the GIs would stay behind in Thailand and the Philippines after they had left Vietnam, so that he could 'manipulate' between Communism and Imperialism.

To his detractors, this Sihanouk of the sixties may have seemed a windsock of a man, but his problems were not simple, for there were evils within evils. In the past Cambodia had been ravaged not by China but by her vigorous neighbours. It was the Thais and the Vietnamese, for the most part, who chopped up the great kingdom of the Khmers and cut it down to the Cambodia we know today. 'If the French had arrived here twenty years later than they did during their period of colonial expansion in the nineteenth century,' Monseigneur once told me, 'there would not have been any Cambodia left for them to occupy.'

Sihanouk also needed China, therefore, as a guarantee against the further greed of Bangkok and Saigon. Nothing perhaps worried him more than a secret assurance from Chou En-lai that even if he started fighting the South Vietnamese, he had nothing to fear from the Thais at his back – he was at once assailed by the horrid thought that Bangkok might have done a deal with Peking while he himself was still hovering between East and West. Moreover, the Vietnamese threat was two-pronged, and for some years he had been obliged to use China and the United States not only to neutralize each other but also to discourage the predatory instincts of North and South Vietnam respectively.

If this tangle of hazards leaves the reader frowning and mumbling, let it be remembered that Sihanouk had to live with it. The Prince had one unwavering purpose: the survival of the Kingdom of Cambodia. This could be assured, he felt, if the frontiers and the neutrality of Cambodia were internationally guaranteed and respected. All who agreed were Sihanouk's friends, all who obstructed were his foes. These were the simple ground rules of an excessively complicated game, which did not end when Monseigneur was exiled in 1970.

At the coronation of King Suramarit in 1956 I stood on the high, floodlit balcony of the royal palace in Phnom Penh and gazed down with spurious condescension on the crowd of patient and humble Khmers who waited in the darkness below to see their glittering rulers and the promised fireworks. The place was full of princes, and close to the monarch himself stood the American and British ambassadors in full fig. It was one of those moments when you feel very expensive indeed.

Eight years later the patient and humble Khmers were back again, waiting for their rulers and the fireworks in the persistent rain. But the high, floodlit balcony under its upcurling roof this time held Prince Norodom Sihanouk flanked by Marshal Chen Yi of China and Mr Ignatov of the Soviet Presidium. The Anglo-Saxon presence was reduced to a knot of wet journalists with me in the mob below. The West had come a long way since 1956, and all of it downhill.

Out on the Vietnamese frontier it was easy to understand Sihanouk's displeasure. What was left of the little village of Anlong Kres lay baking on the floor of the vivid green Cambodian plain, just half a mile from the border. Deserted by half of its sixty families, who had peaceably grown rice and fruit and snoozed away the oven-like afternoons until disaster struck them, the village seemed to hold only a few men armed with old French and British bolt-action rifles, a surly home guard who stared at us without love.

That was not surprising. Over a wide area the bamboo houses

on stilts had collapsed completely, or stood at new, crazy angles, their legs broken and their wigs of palm-thatch askew. Among them were deep bomb craters filled with scummy rain-water, and amid the rubble, twisted slivers of exploded rockets. Vietnamese air force Skyraiders had bombed, rocketed or machine-gunned Anlong Kres twice within five days, and long-nosed American F-101s had repeatedly reconnoitred the village. Nine people had been killed, including four children. The Vietnamese claimed that they had made a map-reading error, but in fact they attacked Anlong Kres because they suspected it of harbouring Vietcong guerrillas, just as they had attacked other Cambodian villages along the frontier before it.

Yet there was no doubt about the impartiality of Cambodian detestation for Vietnamese of all colours. 'We distrust the lot of them,' a Cambodian captain told me down on the border, with a melodramatic sneer not uncommon among Indochinese when they speak of their neighbours. 'If they cross this frontier armed, we shoot them whether they are wearing the green uniforms of Saigon or the black pyjamas of the Vietcong.' The captain's headquarters were tactfully located well back from the Vietnamese border, and so were his troops. In the frontier area there were only militia and village home guards who could offer little resistance to well-armed intruders.

Nevertheless, to depict Sihanouk as a willing sleeping-partner of the Vietcong, as many diplomats did, was to carry out psychological surgery on the Prince and leave all his instincts screaming. For ideally he wanted everyone out of Cambodia and Cambodia out of everything. If half a million American troops could not stop the North Vietnamese from infiltrating into South Vietnam, how could his army of 35,000 men stop them from infiltrating into Cambodia across a 500-mile-long border of tousled hill and swamp, he asked reasonably enough. In 1973 he admitted that in order to replace the American aid he had rejected, he had been obliged to allow supplies to be transported through Cambodia to the Vietcong, but his dis-taste for this operation was almost palpable – 'two thirds for them, one third for us – like that one sells oneself,' he com-mented bitterly.

Characteristically, he still wanted an American counter-poise in South-east Asia, but he had no affection for the Americans. As allies of hostile anti-Communist states on Cambodia's doorstep – 'these vultures which are the eternal swallowers of Khmer soil' – the Americans introduced a new dimension into historical hatreds. In modern dress, old-fashioned enemies became 'pro-American' nations threatening to overrun the 'neutral' Khmers jammed between them. Furthermore, in supporting the Thais and Vietnamese, the Americans were supporting 'the Khmer Serei', the right-wing Cambodian insurgents who were engaged in armed conspiracy against the Prince and whose insulting and belittling radio broadcasts so outraged his immodesty.

'Drink some more champagne,' he cried at the end of 1963, looking around his conference table. 'Steward, bring the last bottles.' It came, slightly warm but of excellent vintage, and we sipped it sitting among the plush fixtures of his residence – the chandeliers, the gold-edged glass doors, the obsequious flunkeys. This was a luxurious introduction to austerity, however, for Monseigneur had suddenly announced that Cambodia would henceforth reject all American aid, cutting off in mid-stream economic and military assistance which was financing about twenty major national projects and generating the funds that paid for nearly 40 per cent of the Cambodian army. Sihanouk was cold-shouldering the West and turning for his devotions, as many do, to the East. But at the same time he warned the Soviet Bloc that before his country was converted into a Communist satellite, he would either go to gaol or become a simple citizen.

Monseigneur's passions and personal caprices should never have blinded foreign diplomatic observers to the essence of Sihanouk the statesman as against Sihanouk the prince. In matters affecting the sovereignty of Cambodia he was as calculating as a stockjobber balancing his prices and making sure of his turn, and he expected others to be the same. 'Of course I understand that the Americans help countries like Vietnam and Thailand that are committed to the cause of anti-Communism before they will help a neutral like me,' he once told me with refreshing candour and a small shrug. 'But that means they fob me off with rifles dating back to the War of Secession and helicopters which are only safe when firmly on the ground. So in the circumstances, I am naturally more inclined to trust the Chinese.'

He had no illusions that Mao was interested in propping up tropical monarchies, but the better the relations between Peking and Phnom Penh, the longer the Kingdom of Cambodia would exist. 'And fortunately we can be friends,' he said with simple irony, 'since we do not share a common frontier.' Long on American goodwill, short on Chinese love, he lowered the price of the first, raised the price of the second. China was a long-term investment, America a short-term hedge.

When in 1963 the Americans refused to attend a new Geneva Conference on the neutrality of Cambodia, the Prince threatened to sever relations with Washington and sign a military pact with Peking and Hanoi. And when in 1964 North Vietnam quibbled over recognizing Cambodia's frontiers, he damned the Vietnamese Communists for being 'as vague as the Anglo-Saxons' and threatened to negotiate with anti-Communist Saigon. In 1965 he broke with the United States, and so brightened the faces of the Chinese, but in 1967 he promised to break with Peking also if they did not at once stop trying to export revolution to Cambodia. In mid-1969 he accused the Thais of helping the dissident 'Khmer Serei' movement to set up a rebel Cambodian government, but reprieve was at hand, for the 'Khmer Serei' menace was now mirrored by a 'Khmer Rouge' menace of Cambodian Communist guerrillas. By the end of the year Sihanouk had re-established diplomatic relations with Washington and was warning Hanoi that he would break with North Vietnam and the Liberation Front if the Communists did not stop violating his borders.

The neutral leader is not a contemptible sycophant imbued with that slavish philosophy of certain dogs, 'If you can't lick 'em, lick 'em.' He is nobody's ally and therefore nobody's ward, and in the last analysis he must have the brazen cheek needed to flatter today where he insulted yesterday, impersonally, as part of the tasteless theatricals that pass for the defence of national interests.

'Logic demands,' wrote Sihanouk in 1965, 'that our independence and neutrality should be preserved always by playing off rival external influences against one another in such a fashion that they cancel each other out.' If one bloc attacked Cambodia, Sihanouk had to be able to turn to the other for protection. His tiffs and scenes and flirtations with both were merely the jerky arm-wavings of the tightrope-walker advancing steadily towards his objective – until adversaries overthrew him and so cast him into the hands of the Communists, much as Prince Souvanna Phouma had been forced to make common cause with the Laotian Left at Khang Khay by General Phoumi and the CIA.

Nothing could more strikingly vindicate the almost boneless tactical flexibility that concealed the steady strategic aim of the Prince than the fate of Cambodia once it was out of his hands. Until then a haven of relative tranquillity (despite furtive conflict and collusion between red and anti-red in a formally 'neutral' state), Cambodia was agonizingly tortured and torn open by the same forces that had eviscerated Vietnam – the Communist terrorists, the B-52 bomber, the callous South Vietnamese, the cold-blooded North Vietnamese, fire, butchery and ruin.

Sihanouk did not change when he set up his government-in-exile in Peking. He calmly allied himself with the Cambodian guerrillas he had hounded down, victimized and gaoled in his royal heyday, including three members of his present cabinet whom he was once reported to have liquidated. He did not pretend that they loved him, or he loved them. He made it clear that he collaborated with the Communists – Chinese, Vietnamese or Cambodian – for the same reason that Churchill collaborated with Stalin, or Mao with Chiang Kai-shek. It was a simple matter of expediency. He knew that he could count on Chinese support if he made his own unique contribution to a purely Cambodian revolutionary front, for the prospect that the Chinese found repugnant almost above all others was that Phnom Penh might otherwise become a dependency of Hanoi.

As a guest, Sihanouk behaved publicly with due, even deferential decorum, and when I attended a banquet given in the Great Hall of the People in Peking in October 1972 to celebrate his fiftieth birthday, he was as fulsome in his praise of the Chinese as he was interminable in his denunciations of the Americans, until the food grew cold and the champagne warm.

One year later, however, it seemed that he might yet be sacrificed for the sake of the *détente* between Peking and Washington, Communist and anti-Communist. And he did not hesitate to speak out, coldly analysing the situation. China was faithful, he said, but China was 'playing the big power-game with America now, and so cannot help as much as it would like'. As for the North Vietnamese, 'we have had to do without their active support since June 1972. They are not even helping us get any supplies any more. They want us to negotiate with the Americans and Lon Nol'. Well, they would find that neither he nor the Cambodian Communists would compromise with Washington and the right-wing president who had seized power from him in Phnom Penh – just so that Peking and Hanoi could 'get along with America'.

But like Souvanna Phouma, Sihanouk might nonetheless return to his capital, the indispensable waverer to whom the ideologically mulish of both extremes must turn for a middleman.

Moreover, the iron logic of Monseigneur's inconstancy was sometimes a refreshing change in a region that has given the world two four-letter words for its unchallenged performances in individual and collective irrationalism – *amok* and *koro*.

27

Cock and Bull

In the National Museum in Kuala Lumpur you may see displayed what looks like a finely-made, long-handled pitch-fork, the prongs judiciously set far enough apart to fit either side of a man's neck and pin him down. This is an amok-fork, but it cannot have been used very often. For when the *amok* rushes out among his fellows, *kris* or *parang* in hand, and frenziedly cuts down all in his path in a fit of homicidal mania, the circumspect rarely seek to capture him alive.

'Amok,' notes the *Encyclopaedia Britannica*, 'is the Malay equivalent of suicide.' But there is also an element in it of sheer frustration, of locked brakes that provoke a mental skid. Too often the Malay can only release his pent-up resentment with a *parang*, and the intrepid Isabella Bird has remarked that if an insult is offered by a man of high rank and out of reach, the injured party will seize his knife and 'slay all he can lay hands on'.

Nations do not run amok, but the new countries of South-east Asia – jealous of their often slender repute and conscious of condescension in others – will sometimes fling themselves into a seemingly senseless fury which bewilders the calculating West and introduces an x-factor into Far Eastern affairs that confounds all the computers. Irrational emotionalism, that ugly yet endearing quality which justifies the self-explanatory epitaph 'he was only human', did not die in Indonesia with the eclipse of Sukarno.

In 1968 the Minister for Information in Djakarta announced that if two Indonesian saboteurs were executed in Singapore for killing three innocent people, the Indonesians 'would have to review their friendly relations' with the island. Yet these are the facts: in 1965, two Indonesians smuggled a twenty-five-pound bomb into an office block in a busy Singapore street. The bomb exploded, killing a father of eight, a mother of six, and one other woman. The killers were dressed in civilian clothes, and although this meaningless act of murder was committed during Sukarno's Confrontation of Malaysia, no state of war existed. They were therefore tried and sentenced to be hanged, and the Privy Council upheld the judgement.

However, the Minister for Information in Djakarta was not the only man afflicted with moral strabismus. His Government claimed that the two gaoled bombers were marines, and should be treated as prisoners of war. President Suharto made a personal appeal for clemency, and when this was rejected, a twin-engined Ilyushin bomber flew into Singapore to take the bodies back to Djakarta, accompanied by a special presidential envoy of general officer rank.

In the Indonesian capital the killers were given a hero's burial after a lying-in-state attended by thousands. Muslim imams chanted from the Koran, flags flew at half mast. General Abdul Haris Nasution, Chairman of the People's Congress, swore that Singapore had insulted his country's honour. The press described the small republic as 'a colony of bloodsuckers' and demanded retribution, and the commander of the Indonesian Marines cried that he was ready to lead an invasion against the island. The Singapore Embassy and the private homes of five of its diplomats in Djakarta were sacked. Indonesian freighters on their way to Singapore were recalled, Singapore freighters in Indonesian ports were boycotted and left unloaded. Trade between the two states slowed to a stop.

This was vengeance with a vengeance, and it was going to sting. For about 65 per cent of Djakarta's exports normally passed through Singapore, the world's fourth busiest port and one for which backward Indonesia had no substitute. Furthermore, Indonesia was jeopardizing her chances of winning urgently-needed financial support worth half a billion American dollars from a nine-nation consortium. For the offer was conditional upon 'signs of decided improvement' in the national economy, which a second Confrontation now threatened to wreck once again. In the end, the counsel of men in Djakarta who did not believe that the nation should be destroyed as a memorial to two terrorists supervened. The fit lingered but finally passed, so that in 1973 Lee Kuan Yew was able to pay an official visit to Djakarta. But it was not so everywhere.

A slightly blasphemous Philippine legend has it that when God first tried to make man, he baked the first batch for too long so that it came out black, and the second batch for too short a time, so that it came out white. Only at the third attempt did he achieve perfection – the golden-brown Filipino, crisp as they come. This pretentious version of God's last job before the first week-end may explain the rather haughty lack of logic which Manila has displayed over the Philippine claim to the North Borneo state of Sabah.

In the Public Record Office in London the Lord Chancellor has under his care a document which opens picturesquely : 'We, Sri Paduka Maulana Al Sultan Mohamet Jamal Al Alam, Sultan of Sulu and the dependencies thereof, on behalf of ourselves, our heirs and successors, grant and cede of our own free and sovereign will to Baron de Overbeck of Hong Kong and Alfred Dent of London, their heirs, associates, successors and assigns forever and in perpetuity all the rights and powers belonging to us over all the territories and lands being tributary to us on the mainland of the island of Borneo . . .' Under the terms of this agreement, the 'successors and assigns' must pay the Sultan's heirs five thousand dollars a year, and the grant must never be transferred to any nation other than Britain without the sanction of the British Government. It is dated 22 January 1878, and is an object lesson in the importance of keeping correspondence.

The territory in question became a British protectorate in 1888 and in 1946 was ceded to the Crown. The Spanish and American masters of the Philippines successively recognized Britain's right to the north-eastern shoulder of the island of Borneo, and international law does not concede that a change of régime invalidates an agreed frontier. Then in 1962 the British, who were liquidating their empire in the East, proposed to appoint the new independent Federation of Malaya as their 'successor and assign' and to incorporate it into a wider Federation of Malaysia.

It stood to reason (unfortunately) that the Philippine Republic would accept the change with equanimity, even pleasure. The white colonial power was ebbing from Manila's doorstep. In its place would come a young Asian state of fraternal Malay stock. Yet although Manila had laid no previous claim with the British, the Filipinos now began to insist that the Sultan of Sulu had only leased the territory to Overbeck and Dent. Since Sulu was part of the modern Philippine Republic, it should be ceded without further ado to Manila, or the case be taken to the International Court. The British ignored this peremptory demand, however. The dependency was signed over to Malaysia, and was renamed Sabah. The Philippines then joined Indonesia in boycotting the formation of Malaysia and diplomatic ties with Kuala Lumpur were suspended.

The Philippine Republic was chipping away at its own favourite image of the Philippine Republic as a truly anti-colonial Asian state, keen to develop friendly regional cooperation with its neighbours. For it was ogling with unsuitably imperialistic acquisitiveness a territory whose people had been granted self-determination, and whose wish to join Malaysia had been established both by United Nations investigators and in free general elections. These considerations, other Asians felt, should override any historical claims based on dubious nineteenth-century deals in real estate. But although Indonesia's Confrontation of Malaysia died a natural and therefore lingering death in 1966, the Filipinos were still in oral action three years later, for any one Manila lawyer can talk the hind-leg off another.

There was to be more than talk, however. In 1968 details of a secret training camp for Filipino terrorists, who were being groomed on Corregidor for military operations against Malaysian Sabah, were suddenly exposed when harsh conditions on the island provoked a mutiny and a minor massacre, and a lone escapee told all. Faced with an international scandal, officials in Manila produced a quick flurry of contradictory explanations – that the men were training for an offensive against the Huks in Central Luzon, that they were to combat Indonesian infiltrators in the Southern Philippines – and the astonished Malaysians were then told sharply that anyway it was all a 'purely internal affair'. Filipinos were caught illegally ashore in Sabah, some of them with arms, Filipino jets buzzed ships in Malaysian waters, and an influential Muslim congressman in Manila demanded a holy war against the new Federation. The National Security Council was given a comparative evaluation of Philippine and Malaysian armed services, and a somewhat optimistic intelligence officer was quoted as saying that Sabah could be taken in two weeks.

Filipino fantasy was far from exhausted, however. In September of that year President Marcos signed a Bill which referred to Sabah as territory 'over which the Republic of the Philippines has acquired dominion and sovereignty'. Western reasoning might suggest that if, by way of a casual subordinate clause, Britain were to record the annexation of Calais in a Bill solemnly passed into law, France might have grounds for complaint. But when Malaysia sought further clarification, Manila's official reply read : 'This unwarranted interference of the Malaysian Government on a matter which is essentially within the domestic jurisdiction of the Philippines Government constitutes a flagrant violation of the United Nations Charter.' Three days later the Philippines demanded an immediate explanation from Britain because five RAF Hunter jets had flown over the state capital of Sabah and so had notionally violated 'Philippine' airspace. But when Malaysia suspended diplomatic relations again in protest over the new Bill, Mr Narciso Ramos, the Philippine Foreign Secretary, wailed in New York : 'What hurts is that we considered Malaysia a friend and neighbour and did not expect her to act contrary to the rules of fair play.'

Soundly based on human characteristics of monetary greed and political ambition, the entire script was nonetheless a masterly piece of unreason. Relations between the 'anti-Communist' powers – Malaysia, the Philippines, the United States, and Britain – were curdled by the squabble, and the strain thrown upon ASEAN, the new five-nation partnership in regional co-operation to which Malaysia and the Philippines both belonged, was threatening to break its back. Overzealous Filipino interception of Malaysian patrol boats meanwhile sabotaged their joint anti-smuggling agreement, which had been particularly welcome to Manila since the illegal cigarette traffic profited the Malaysians but grievously pained the Philippine Treasury.

The Filipinos had protested that Sabah was only eighteen miles from the nearest of their own islands and that they must be responsible for seeing that it did not 'go Communist', yet they explained the guerrillas training on Corregidor in terms of their own inability to control illegal armed insurrection, subversion or aggression by Marxist Huks or Muslim hotheads at home. Unquestionably the most irrational aspect of all to the humdrum western mind, however, was the exotic proposition that people of a state which was safely outside the frontiers of the Philippine Republic might actually want to join it. By 1973, however, the Sabah claim was still alive.

But then collective delusion can take peculiar forms.

In the fine autumn of 1967 strange, hallucinatory scenes are enacted in Singapore, noteworthy even in the days of the psychedelic happening and the general release of blue films. In a coffee-shop lavatory a small crowd, drawn by cries of anguish, gapes helplessly while a middle-aged soap-boiler clamps a pair of chopsticks over his exposed male organ to stop it from retreating into his body. The chopsticks snap. Some quick thinker substitutes a pair of market-stall steelyards, but these prove too unwieldy. Panic! One bystander seizes the reticent gender and starts pulling; another rushes off to dial 999; a third runs for a Chinese doctor.

This is no isolated event. Similar little dramas are being played in hundreds of homes, and sometimes in public. A young fellow is hastily carried down a village main street in his bed while his father jogs alongside, clutching the prostrate youth's masculine member. Another trots down a lane, his retiring nature in the firm grasp of a friendly pacemaker. Men arrive at the out-patients' entrance of hospitals with their sex stretched downwards by dangling weights, or held in an improvised wooden vice, or captive on the end of a piece of string or a loop of wire. For Singapore is in the grip of an epidemic of fear – the fear induced by *koro*, a condition whose principal symptom is a sudden, disconcerting shrinkage of the penis (which the Chinese somewhat pretentiously call the 'Sun-tool').

Western medicine regards this as a purely psychological affliction, a hysterical condition producing a real or imagined contraction of the male organ. But since worry can cause shrinking and the shrinking in turn causes worry, Singapore has been caught on a spiral of alarm. The Medical Association therefore sets out to allay public fright by making a few interesting disclosures, if in somewhat monumental English. 'The physiological causes,' a press conference is told, 'are cold weather, getting into bed, and anxiety. Those afflicted are beset with the great fear that should the retraction be permitted to proceed, the male organ would eventually be drawn into the abdomen, with a fatal outcome [*sic*]. The Medical Association wish to reassure the public that the condition of koro leading to death is definitely unknown. Medical science indicates this retraction is not possible, as the male organ is fundamentally an external appendage,' the doctors conclude comfortingly.

The rumour flies around that the koro comes from the meat of pigs vaccinated against swine-fever, and although assured that the phenomenon is illusory and could not possibly be produced by pork, many still cling to their old-fashioned fallacies, and slaughter in the abattoirs falls from 1,300 pigs a day to one hundred. Even at a banquet thrown for doctors in a smart downtown restaurant, pork is – symbolically – conspicuous by its absence. We give a buffet supper and Ping decides to label the boiled ham 'Ladies only'. For ten days of pandemonium, Singapore is the Land of the Shrinking Sun.

Mysterious epidemics are not unknown in the West, it may be protested. In 1968 men all over the United States complained that when they ate *won ton* soup in a Chinese restaurant, they began to feel giddy and numb, their necks ached, their heads throbbed, and their hearts palpitated. 'Chinese Restaurant Syndrome' was traced to a chemical flavouring, however. The narrow-minded westerner insisted that there must be a reason – and so he duly found it. But *amok* and *koro* are freakish embroideries upon a psychological pattern which has been sewn with a freer hand than the stencils of western rationalism usually allow.

Since Asians do not regard life as a theorem of Euclid, there is no Q.E.D. and in consequence their reasoning and their objectives are sometimes mysterious. In 1961 U Nu, then Prime Minister of Burma, revealed that Buddhist candidate-monks preparing themselves for holy orders not only cheated and cribbed their way to the cloth, but ostentatiously pulled out daggers and coshes in the examination hall to intimidate their invigilators. All men are prone to syllogism, but the Asian often deals in rope-trick logic. He likes his argument open-ended. One day when I returned from lunch to the Hotel Indonesia in Djakarta I found myself double-locked out of my room. The reception clerk refused to give me my key, and referred me to a Javanese assistant manager. 'But you are no longer staying at this hotel,' this dignitary told me. 'You checked out a week ago. So, of course, you cannot go into the room.'

'And who do you think has been living in it ever since?' I demanded. 'Who has been sleeping in the bed, sending out laundry, ordering breakfast, putting through telephone calls, picking up and depositing the key, asking for mail, signing chits? Whose possessions are in there right now?' He shrugged: 'You paid your bill a week ago,' he reiterated, 'You are not on our books.' 'That was last week's bill,' I protested, but the rope of reason had come to an end in mid-air, and it was half an hour before I was back in my room. '*Will* you get off this phone!' yelled an infuriated woman who had mistakenly called our number in Singapore three times in succession under the impression that it was that of a friend.

All is flexible in a flowing cosmos, many Asians contend. Truth, if left-handed, must be made to conform to changing circumstances, and history can if necessary be rewritten. The Minister of Information in Vientiane, importuned by correspondents who complained that they were receiving conflicting reports of what was happening to the Laotian war, remarked with asperity: 'If you *will* talk to different officials, naturally you get different answers.' Another minister, asked if it were really true that seven North Vietnamese battalions were attacking Phou Khoun as officially announced, replied readily enough, 'Well, it's only *partly* propaganda.'

The Vietcong twisted the malleable truth of Asia into their

own form of folk art. Doubtless anxious to please their superiors, they submitted statistics of such slaughter to higher echelons that their general staff claimed that 162,000 Americans had been killed in the first half of 1966 – nearly ten times the real number. Two years later I learned in Saigon that Vietcong units were being further encouraged to file false returns by instructions from above which laid down minimal killing quotas: 'In February the division will eliminate one thousand of the enemy, shoot down fifty American helicopters . . .' History was being written in advance this time, for back came the same figures from below at the end of the month, proving that all quotas had been fulfilled.

It is Asian to tell a man what he wants to hear, or to refrain from telling him what he does not want to hear. Dr Dooley wrote of a Lao assistant: 'He was not a liar, he was just congenitally unable to say no.' The courteous Malay who does not want to answer your inconvenient request with a brusque and final negative replies 'belum', and it is understood that this vague and elastic euphemism spans all future time, from 'not just yet' to 'never'.

The white man who accuses the Asian of double-talk is simply failing to understand what he is being told in plain, straightforward innuendo. South-east Asia is a polite subcontinent in which you say a man has short legs by calling him tall in the saddle. 'How many members do you have?' I asked the leader of a moderate political party in Brunei once, as we sat barefoot in his bungalow. 'About twenty thousand,' he replied. 'All staunch supporters?' I pressed on, in my brutal Caucasian fashion. 'Let me put it this way,' he answered with a plump smile, 'about eight hundred of them would probably have the sense not to join the extremists if there were another insurrection.' 'And how many pay party dues?' 'We do not levy dues,' he said loftily. 'We rely on well-wishers for our funds.' It was a painless way of saying that the party was being bribed from behind but if it came to the crunch about 95 per cent of its members would desert it.

In the East words are often uttered only because without them it would be more difficult to read between them, whereas in the West one is actually expected to take them at their face value. What is a subtle guide at one end of the world, therefore, may become an unsubtle disguise at the other. Unlike the Asians, the Americans do not spell out their fantasies in words of four letters, but pad out their truths with the polysyllabic falsies in which their national language is so rich. At their distorted five o'clock shadow of the Vietnam war known in Saigon as the daily press briefing, a helicopter attack became a 'vertical envelopment', failure to catch the enemy was a 'pursuit operation terminated with negative results', and raining five-hundred-pound bombs and napalm on Vietnamese peasants by mistake was an 'accidental delivery of ordnance which impacted on an inhabited area'. A communiqué dated 16 March 1968 read : 'In an action today American divisional forces have killed 128 enemy near Quangngai City.' That's the massacre at My Lai, that was. The unpleasant realities of war were often carved down to a set of deceivingly manly clichés until the name of the game became the name of the game.

'Joint project.' The words fall through from six years back, uttered in the lazy-river voice of Barry Zorthian, who chairs the daily briefing in his Saigon office. It is November 1964, and Zorthian reveals that the Vietcong have smashed or damaged at least twenty-seven American aircraft in a mortar attack on Bien Hoa air base. He hopes to get away with a deceptively candid statement of losses, but he is not to be left in peace, for now Joe Fried cross-examines for the *New York Daily News* (Joe Fried, veteran of a thousand briefings, has the long, sad face of a deadpan comedian into which some careless smoker has burned two angry eyes, but he writes his own patter. Zorthian is a hostile witness, and Fried is ready to tear him apart.)

Prosecution :	Weren't there any bays or revetments to protect these aircraft?
Witness :	There were some revetments, but not where the planes were.
Prosecution :	You're saying there were not enough revetments for every plane?
Witness :	That is correct.
Prosecution :	Was there a shortage of sandbags then?

Witness:	No, they had enough sandbags up there, and they were being filled as fast as labour and other commitments permitted.
Prosecution:	But the B-57 jets have been at Bien Hoa three months, how do you account for the fact that no revetments were built for them?
Witness:	There was no time with the labour available.
Prosecution:	What's the labour problem?
Witness:	Well, this is a joint project ...
Prosecution (pounces):	A *joint project*? What's 'joint project'? You mean an American holds a sandbag while a Vietnamese pours in the sand, or a Vietnamese holds the ... (leading question: objection sustained. Fried retires and a recess is declared).

Even with Fried present, the Public Affairs staff can refuse to answer questions on the grounds that they may incriminate someone, and too often the court scene turns into a commercial. There has always been a strong Javanese element in all this: reports should be 'appropriate'. On his departure after more than four years in Saigon, Barry Zorthian said straightforwardly that American officials had made mistakes in dealing with the press. They should have admitted, for example, that the air strikes against North Vietnam had sometimes hit civilian houses. This changed little, however. The department still worked with the precision and aplomb of a cuckoo clock, and the Javanese could look to their laurels. Their former Foreign Minister, Dr Subandrio, might have personified the heroic Indonesian struggle with truth. But others could be subandroid too.

28

The Tortoise and the Terrapin

ASIANS are not like or unlike Europeans. They are both. They are possessed of the human conscience, the sex urge, five senses or so, and forty-six chromosomes per cell-nucleus. They are hard-wearing, edible, combustible, and they float when inflated. But their programmers – history, environment, belief, tradition, prejudice – have not been the same. Since, therefore, magnanimous man is quickly convinced that his neighbour is mad when he is shown evidence that the fellow's morals and customs are different from his own, oriental and occidental are vulnerable to each other, and as the first superficial similarities give way to hidden surprises, narrow eyes may grow round, and round eyes narrow.

The Javanese with his Leyden degree, talking fluent English and Dutch, Russian ballet and vintage cars, may slowly reveal himself a man of rigid principles who does not, however, believe in any universal moral excellence, and whose regard for Lady Macbeth is increased by the fact that she stabbed Duncan in his sleep (for Macbeth he has only contempt). Nothing is more futile than to try to impose the West's standards upon the East, for the Asian has his own knife-sharp sense of what is fitting. A young Indonesian has himself buried alive 'to save his country'. A young Malaysian Chinese, sentenced to prison for armed robbery, earnestly begs the judge to have him whipped as well. In North Borneo a Sea-Dyak labourer indignantly accuses an army unit of paying him for a day's work he did not do. (In a less disordered world he would still be in his jungle longhouse, planning to decapitate some unsuspecting stranger at night from behind and hang up the head as an honourable trophy.)

Since culture wags the tongue, and not the other way around, languages of East and West often refuse to fit. In Burma 'jewellery' is not an optional adornment but 'apparel for the arms', a lack of which would be shameful. The westerner recoils quite unfairly, therefore, from the vision of the overdecorated eastern seductress up to her elbows in bangles. Each end of the world is quick to suspect the other of the worst and the dirtiest. The Christian lingers aghast before the sacred pornography in stone which Hinduism seems to inspire, and listens with pursed lips to accounts of sexual orgies in Buddhist temples. But sex with a 'spiritual wife' was once part of the strenuous ritual of certain forms of *yoga*, one of many religious exercises designed to bring the devotee to Nirvana.

The Asian, on the other hand, is often puzzled by what appear to be subtle distinctions in the Mysterious West that make Botticelli's *Birth of Venus* Art but girlie-magazine cheesecake Filth. On one occasion the Postmaster-General of Manila raised a storm in the press when he warned off a local newspaper for reproducing the *Venus*, and banned as 'obscene' an issue of *Time* magazine that carried a colour print of Goya's *Naked Maja*. Those who defended these works he described as 'public enemies of civilized society who simply want to cater to the animal instincts of the lascivious'.

But nothing separates men from men faster than money. 'It is no good,' said Ping, sinking back in her window seat with a sigh after vainly attempting to wade through the free champagne cocktails, the caviare and strasbourg paté and smoked oyster snacks, the five-course menu and the wines and liqueurs served at the front end of a jet liner across five hundred miles of South China Sea. 'It is nice to try once. But we Asians are *reary* born economy class.' A minority of orients may be wealthy, but in the East any westerner is the poor man's rich man. He lives in the dream world of that contradiction, the instant age, surrounded with enough plug-in gimmickry and gadgetry to blow a minor power station. His house could accommodate fifteen Malays, twenty Vietnamese, and his car is as big as many an Asian home. His cornucopia economy can shower him with all his heart may desire, from machine-stitched Bayeux tapestry to a prefabricated swimming pool.

The militant Vietnamese Buddhist leader Thich Tri Quang

had his own quaint image for this abundance: 'The Americans are giants who will become bloated and die if they eat but do not defecate. This defecation is their aid. If they cannot find ways of granting aid they will have no place to sell the goods they produce. If they cannot sell the goods the plants will have to shut down. If plants shut down, hundreds of thousands will be out of work. America will then be in danger. That is why we can insult the Americans as much as we please, and they must still do our bidding and grant us aid.'

Yet sadly, 'Green Imperialism' – the influx of the American dollar with the American soldier – has tended to make the rich of the subcontinent richer, the poor poorer. By the end of 1965 rents in Saigon had risen by as much as 400 per cent. Landlords refused to let premises to haggling Vietnamese, and taxis refused to stop for them, for they could charge Americans five times the correct fare. United States agencies overpaid the labour they hired, inflation took wings, and Vietnamese on fixed salaries found themselves angrily tightening their seat belts. By 1968 the cost of living in Saigon had nearly doubled in three years, and Thailand was also beginning to feel the windy discomforts of financial flatulence. The Americans had descended on the subcontinent like the north-east monsoon, but their fantastic torrents of goods and gold seemed to wash away more than they irrigated in terms of human life and happiness, and the unimaginable wealth and wastage alike confirmed the more uncharitable Asian in his bitter, often supercilious belief that the westerner was not Superman, but Supermonkey.

The overbearing occidental who struts through the subcontinent as if it were a condemned slum is balanced by his humble and unctuous brother who is forever prostrating himself before all things oriental, and apologizing for the unpardonable existence of the billion or so barbarians to the West. If he does it for kicks, he can expect them. For the Far East is full of pretentious arrogance and pretty conceits.

In a Japanese garden, we read, we may find in summer 'a tinkling contraption to listen to because only the Japanese can believe that a special sound can be cooling'. This is typical of the simpering school of Asian writers that lends to the Japanese a vocabulary of sensibilities which the crude westerner cannot be expected to understand. The pin-table parlour in Tottenham Court Road is dismissed, of course, as typical of the trash-can period in western culture, but it seems that the *pachinko* parlour in Tokyo, crammed like its European counterpart with idle, vacuous youth, is only one remove from a Zen school of archery, and should be treated with due reverence. The vertical pinball machine, notes one writer loftily, 'perhaps appeals only to the Japanese mind' because 'the great game is a test of manual dexterity, a trait the Japanese attach great value to', and it offers an entertainment suitable for 'the Japanese virtue of quiet concentration'.

There are many occasions on which I feel constrained to remark loudly that some of my best friends are British. 'You cannot possibly understand us,' Asians have told me woundingly. 'But with us it is different. We know you Europeans only too well.' This is frequently a ludicrously unjustified boast. The older Asian tends to see the white as a rather simple piece of apparatus for grasping, destroying and building, like one of his own mechanical grabs, the strictly materialistic product of a two-dimensional television culture thrown up by broad civilizing influences ranging from cowboys to Coca Cola. Christianity, with its improbable tales of mystery and imagination, seems to fall ignominiously into the category of the pop Asian religions so disdained by the Confucian intellectual or the Buddhist ascetic. The mystics and the philosophers, the awesome and virginal conceptions of Greece and Rome and Nazareth that made men free, the swelling paean of European art and life, are often ignored.

The East cheerfully murders the muses of the West without even knowing it. It is, for example, always instructive to listen to the background music for television programmes in Southeast Asia, and compare it with the subject. Among my specimens are: Liszt's *Liebestraum* for an announcement warning the public to lock their cars and houses against thieves, *Humoresque* for a newsreel of a motor-cycle race, Mussorgsky's *Night on the Bare Mountain* for a fashion parade of fur-coats, Gilbert and Sullivan for a Catholic funeral procession.

But it is only too easy for a westerner to offend. A Cambodian or a Burmese, a Chinese or a Lao will be loyal to the polite hypocrisies of an outwardly imperturbable society, and the first thing you learn when treating with Malays is to smile, damn you, smile. The Anglo-Saxon only puts himself in baulk if he becomes irritated by Asian obliqueness, by the habit of the Indonesian of hiding behind much tittering and the dark glasses that are his modern substitute for the traditional impassive face – 'the hangman's hood of the common man' as Ping puts it. It follows that a rush of blood to the head and a display of true feelings and temper must be looked upon by the educated Asian as evidence of a contemptible lack of self-control. Passions that slop over into the watching world are for animals, small children, ignorant peasants and white men. His is a society that deals uneasily with invasions of Anglo-Saxon sailors raised on roaring traditions of rum and Pensacola, or of great bony Australasians, their powerful vocal chords twanging like banjo strings as the beer flows faster.

Even the most sober and circumspect can fall into error, and ignorance of the lore is no excuse. In many parts of South-east Asia it is offensive to pat a child's head, for the head is the repository of Buddha-hood. Backslapping and pointing with the index finger are resented, shoes must be taken off on entering Japanese and Malay houses, and it is widely regarded as impolite for a man to sit with one leg over the other so that the sole of his foot faces his host, to sip the coffee or tea or lime juice that is set in front of him before he has been invited to do so. Among the Faithful, the quicksands are even more treacherous. The Koran must always be treated with a special reverence, and it is sacrilege not only to smoke or drink while it is being read, but to put another book or anything else on top of it at any time. And it must not be touched with the left hand which is, of course, unclean.

There is more to this matter of cleanliness. Strangers attributed the many cases of leprosy to be seen among the people in Angkor during the thirteenth century to 'their excessive passion and their habit of taking too many baths'. Marco Polo, returning to the West at about this time, writes with astonishment of the

Indians: 'Another of their customs is that all of them, male and female, wash their whole body in cold water twice a day. One who did not wash twice a day would be thought an ascetic.' A strict obligation to wash before praying is imposed on every Muslim, and upon this the finicky Mohammed commented: 'Were it not for fear of troubling disciples, verily I would order them to clean their teeth also before every prayer' (which would have meant five times a day).

The Buddhists are believers in the bath, and at New Year throw themselves into an orgy of drenching, for all must be purged of impurity at this time. As the week washes by, the siphons, pumps, buckets and syringes come out, the children enter into the spirit of the *Thingyan* (as it is called in Rangoon), a war of water develops and everyone gets a daily dousing. On two occasions that Chou En-lai conferred with Premier U Nu of Burma, the Chinese Prime Minister needed all his well-developed self-control to keep his temper, for since they coincided with the water festival in Burma and neighbouring Yun-nan respectively, he emerged from both experiences soaking wet.

Asia is an insanitary continent, reeking with ineradicable dirt and poverty, but famous for its laundering and inhabited by different peoples who wash thoroughly before getting into a hot bath, or who bathe in running streams, dance under a shower (if in public, fully clothed), or throw bucketfuls of water over themselves from great vats or jars. To them, the white man is disgusting, for he sits in a tub of water and rinses himself in his own filth. As to left-handed cleansing operations, the Chinese used paper before the West, but preferred goosefeathers in the heyday of the hedonists, and many orientals claim that water, sand or even stones are more hygienic.

If the westerner is unclean, he is also ugly, and his customs sometimes take much explaining away. American soldiers are no more brutal or licentious than others, but when they were unleashed on Taipei or Bangkok or Tokyo for five days of leave from the Vietcong, they were quite naturally less concerned with national manners than country matters, and since the evil that men do lives after them, by 1968 they had fathered more than 2,000 'red-haired' Thais alone.

It is useless to protest that while the Americans were increasing the mixed population of Thailand, the Thai 'Queen Cobra' Regiment was doing the same in Vietnam at the average rate of one baby for every thirteen men, or that in a given year seven unlucky Americans out of ten in some units had caught the 'Vietnam Rose' (which, by any other name, may be identified as a particularly stubborn form of clap). Asian prejudices have been hardened by scenes of public necking and drunkenness and brawling, and by the insults offered to their wives by white men for whom every pretty girl was a prostitute. Even the best-behaved American serviceman, walking sedately down a Bangkok street arm in arm with some permissive little piece, is a shameless *farang* who fans hidden fires of cultural indignation. For, strictly speaking, it is inadmissible for boy to touch girl in public in Thailand, even if the girl faints.

Little credit goes to thousands of westerners who set out to please. Yet if the British can be courteous and accommodating to local custom, to the point of letting the natives hack each other to bits, a really conscientious American behaves as if he had majored in manners. The Peace Corps, above all, presents in principle a new western visage – bland, smiling, helpful and understanding sometimes beyond all understanding as far as the bewildered Asian is concerned. In 1964 a Peace Corps volunteer invigilating a high-school class in Thailand politely began eating his way through nearly three dozen plates of food which the students, one by one, presented to him with a note in Siamese. He was finally saved by a Thai teacher who explained that they were not gifts from the girls, but their examination entries in the finals of a food-preparation course.

His behaviour contrasted agreeably with that of the late Marshal Sarit, who sipped his carefully chosen wine as guest of honour at a severely protocolaire dinner given by the British Ambassador in Bangkok, screwed up his face in disgust, flung his glass down on the table, and called for a bottle of brandy. Too often the touchy, thin-skinned Asian behaves as if everyone else had the hide of a rhinoceros.

Moreover the westerner cannot be blamed for the suspicion that in some countries oriental etiquette is overrated as a mechanical substitute for common consideration. I remember no better example of this habit of stifling courtesy with too many courtesies than an occasion in Hongkong when Ping and I waited patiently in a lift with four American ladies of indiscreet age, while two Japanese men bowed at each other a dozen times before one would be good enough to get in and allow us to go up. The itch to leave them bowing for another three or four minutes simply by pressing the button was almost irresistible.

However, the vices of the inventive white, yesterday damned for poisoning the wells of wise living in the orient, are adopted by Asian governments today provided they show a profit. The anti-colonial urge to fulminate against the foreigner as if he were the sole purveyor of all pot, sex, booze and gambling is giving way gently to a tacit admission that he is not the only man who is vile, after all. But there is still much room for misunderstanding in all matters of morality.

Like most of his Asian neighbours, the Lao lacks the Christian's sense of guilt. In his philosophy Man did not first come on stage against the setting of the Garden of Eden to perform Act One Sin One, for to him good and evil are inseparable. In consequence, as long as a man's actions are not motivated by a possessive urge, he may accept all opposites – the pleasure that is defined by pain, as well as the pain that is defined by pleasure, since they are all one and the same. This is the middle way between the *guru* and the *gourmand*. The Lord Buddha himself condemned excessive asceticism. The enlightenment that eluded him for six long years of self-denial and meditation embraced him finally after he had disgusted five fellow-sages by eating a square meal and taking a bath. That inspired the outlook which gives to millions of Asians their sense of perspective today.

But as at least one devout Lao commentator has plaintively remarked, Buddhism can easily become the doctrine of lethargy and self-indulgence. If to reason is to destroy the true vision of the Cosmos, don't think. If to strive is to bind yourself to this deplorable world of illusion, then don't strive. Moreover, as all Buddhists wish to 'gain merit' by performing charitable acts, and so edge nearer to Nirvana, it may be kinder to take than to give.

The Buddhist bonze who holds out his begging bowl to the Thai housewife and lets her fill it with food is doing her a favour, for she is gaining merit. The pagodas bless the community by allowing themselves to be showered with candles and flowers and fruit and children. How many times westerners have embarrassed or bewildered Asians by thrusting things upon them and expecting gratitude in return it is hideous to contemplate. Asian leaders who have taken the dollar aid and damned Washington afterwards have also assumed that in the unsentimental commerce of international relations the donor in any case gives because he needs the recipient. The recipient, therefore, renders service twice over.

The orient produces its own fine strain of hypocrisy, however, and while the Muslims and Buddhists of South-east Asia may remain strictly loyal to their faiths, they will argue that to cut corners is to take the straightest path. 'Fish?' an old peasant in Thailand once echoed, grinning toothlessly. 'No, I don't fish. I am old and will die soon. Why should I risk losing merit by killing living creatures? I leave fishing to my son. He's still young.' An angler caught in the act protested, 'But I only take the fish out of the water. If they die, that is not my doing.' In Malaya, Chinese Buddhists will happily eat the bird that has been decapitated out of sight by some other unfortunate. In Burma the rule that monks may not touch money was sidestepped long ago when people began giving the bonzes cylinders of silver coins contained in long nets. The Theravada Buddhist usually wears his hair shirt open at the neck, as it were.

The rigid morality designed for use in a western universe of fixed ethics is often replaced in Asia by a flexible casuistry more suitable for an eastern Cosmos in a constant state of change, just as the tortoise has legs for two-dimensional land, the terrapin flippers for three-dimensional water. They are cousins under the carapace, but the westerner on his solid philosophical ground believes he can manage his universe, while the oriental knows he must give way to tides and currents. He is more resigned to the liquid factors beyond his control, and therefore often more happy-go-lucky. To him, the white man with his feverish determination to measure and master everything always seems to be letting his nerves get on his nerves.

Gliding and eluding the disagreeable in what the West often regards as deceitful fashion, a Malay would rather say 'belum' than refuse or contradict, while with Indonesians one always seems to be surrounded by much nonchalant shrugging and self-deprecatory laughter. Yet behind this is the discipline of blandness which they believe leads to spiritual enlightenment. It is not weakness but a way of life, as the hippies discovered in Laos.

'The Third Eye' on the outskirts of Vientiane was a barn of a hippiedrome whose circling psychedelic lights flashed through rotating Chinese umbrellas of torn paper suspended from the ceiling, while the current throbbed through the guitars and the cats gave out their weary ectoplasm of song. But by 1968 it was living on borrowed time. The Laos had not taken to the western hippies who had flocked into their lotus land unbidden and unwashed. They saw nothing transcendental in filthy Europeans dressed in matted hair and jingling beads, and when these appeared with blackened faces and danced at the Laotian fertility rites, the Prime Minister took it as an offence to his people and their religion. The chagrined hippies had quite mistakenly assumed that they would find the Buddhist Laos as feckless and sloppy and permissive as themselves. The Laos regarded them coldly as a case of too many kooks.

The legend of laziness in South-east Asia must be examined, like all legends, for its inner meaning. 'How slothful they are,' sighs the newcomer to the East, watching gardeners listlessly cropping the grass or a cook sitting in a cane chair, fanning herself in slow motion. The simple cure for this sense of superiority is for the energetic westerner to try hanging a picture on a wall on a fine Sunday in Singapore or Saigon. Long before he has rammed his Rawlplug home he is soaked to the skin, his sweat has made a puddle on the floor, and he needs a long drink and a shower and a change.

It is quite unjust to imagine that oriental idleness is the same as the dishonest scrimshanking of the British worker who slacks on the job while the foreman has his back turned. The white man is a thief who steals paid time, but the indolent Asian would rather have the time than the money. Slowness and the siesta are his secrets of survival in the steamy tropics, and his philosophy leaves him with simple demands and a preference for leisure over lucre.

Buddhism has taught the Lao that he must cast off ambition, that nothing fails like success, and this suits him down to the ground. When provided by solicitous Americans with new strains of seeds that would double his rice crop, he remarked with pleasure that now he need sow only half his usual acreage. 'What would I do if I worked harder and earned more money?' repeated a Cambodian farmer, when told he, too, could double his yield. 'I don't know. I already have a bicycle and a radio. Get another wife, perhaps?' It was obvious he did not think that it was worth the effort. Furthermore, the Hindu sages have preached that life is divided into four phases, and in the last a man should grow old gracefully, indulge in the quiet contemplation that leads to release from material existence. By forty-five he may already be in the third state and loosening his worldly collar. He is not lazy, but he simply declines to lead the life of Reilly or Richard Nixon any more.

If there is work to be done, the Asian will do it. The Lao peasant must sharpen his plough, mend his harrow, repair his cart. He must plait his own ropes, thatch his own roof, weave walls of palm and split bamboo for his house. He must make fish traps, kitchen utensils, spinning wheels and looms for the cotton he grows and dyes. He must look after his buffalo, raise poultry and herbs, plant and reap and help his neighbour, for this is a do-it-yourself economy demanding diligence from all. But to ask the Lao for 'urgent' will raise a laugh, for that is another matter. The sensible man sees that straining to solve one problem only creates another, and may entangle him inextricably in the web of this world. It is not surprising if many Laos look askance at modernization and miracle rice, for instinct tells them correctly what will next come to pass : the bumper crops will demand more fertilizer and insecticides, then more roads and carts and trucks, then more mills and silos, more credits, more consumers at home and buyers abroad, more human involvement, and so, of course, more metempsychosis.

Man should not meddle. The West applies this principle to science fiction, postulating that the fool who takes a time-machine back to the Upper Jurassic and massacres all the megalosaurs may come back to the present to find Mao Tse-tung in the Vatican and Nixon King of England. But the East applies it to life: it may be dangerous to save a drowning child, for then you will certainly be responsible for changing not only its destiny, but also the *karma* of all others as its every move during the rest of its existence makes the ripples shudder outward to the ends of the earth and forward to eternity. It is better, therefore, to avoid fiddling with the fate of strangers. Who ran to catch little Adolf Schicklgruber when he fell? Whoever did has much to answer for, many Asians would say.

Most Muslims believe that all is decreed in advance, and the Buddhist sees the world of illusion rolling blindly forward beyond his control. Man's illness is terminal from birth, and the patient must accept with mild resignation all the funny and unfunny things that happen to him on his way to the cemetery. 'Now it is wet, now it is fine,' say the Malays. Fate, like England, does not have climate, but weather.

29

The Numbers Game

NAPOLEON was only just born a Frenchman, Mohammed only just founded Islam, and it is accidents like these that persuade so many Asians that it is better to accept destiny than to try to change it, to consult an astrologer rather than a computer. True, Asia has had its own enthusiasts for programming Fate and manipulating history mathematically, and it was the fudged calculations inspired by a preparatory war-game in Tokyo that persuaded the Japanese to attack Midway in 1942. 'The battle cost the Japanese two-thirds of their big carriers; it also cost them the war,' as Andrew Wilson noted with curt finality in *The Bomb and the Computer*.

But for the West, cold logic and the mechanical calculation seem to dictate increasingly today that sheer weight of men and money and machines can simply crush the elusive imponderables of life. Nowhere has this been more clearly applied than in western military response to eastern military mischief during the recent past, and an observer in the Straits of Malacca on one searing day in 1965 might have concluded that in defending Malaysia against Indonesian Confrontation, the British were emulating the eagle-beats-ants philosophy of their American cousins in Vietnam.

It is high noon. The whole universe seems to screech in agony when the Sea Vixens, each wrapped in its own wicked glimmer of condensation, rip viciously over the flight deck as H.M.S. *Eagle* sails like a matronly monarch through the heat haze, her foaming train falling carefully into place, her retinue of three more aircraft carriers in line astern. Up on top the world is flat. But prise open this ingenious metal container for fifty aircraft and three thousand men, drop a few decks, and pass through a steel door. The big Ops Room is in sepulchral darkness except for the glowing moon-faced dials of thirty different radar sets and other automatic registers, their revolving traces watched by mute shadows of men. Near one gloomy corner stands SINS (Ship's Inertial Navigation System), a fancy-looking tilt-machine that automatically plots the ship's course and position.

In the control room directly below this nightmare pin-table parlour are more rows of radar and, within a gyroscopically balanced solid steel cell, the masterminds themselves, the computers of ADA – Action Data Automation. ADA sifts all the information pouring in through these round electronic pupils, distinguishing friend from foe, identifying the type of approaching enemy and his speed and position. It then automatically selects the correct combination of weapons from the whole floating armoury to kill the threat at a comfortable distance, perhaps 200 miles away. The giant has not only its brains but all its sixty-odd blinking, cataracted eyes in its stomach. We are guided not by the stars above, but by our SINS below. Nobody looks at the sea.

I photograph the great beast as we rattle back to the palm-fringed Malaysian coastline in a Whirlwind helicopter. It has the doomed look of the stegosaur, the armour-plated monster with brains in its bottom as well as its head whose world the small, scurrying subversive little mammals inherited several ages ago. For the threat to Malaysia comes from guerrillas in the jungles of North Borneo – a motley mix of Indonesian regulars disguised as 'volunteers', Chinese Communist terrorists, and Malaysian rebels in jungle green or shirts and slacks. It comes from agents smuggled into Singapore with bombs and booby-traps, and from sneak-troops sealanded or parachuted into West Malaysia to set up revolutionary bases, panic the population with acts of savagery, or foment internal rebellion with false rumours and undercover political agitation.

I first saw *Eagle* from the bridge of H.M.S. *Maryton* as she sailed majestically towards us down the Straits of Malacca, decked out in all her man-killing finery, and swept by with a condescending wink from a signal lamp. But it was the wooden-walled 470-ton minesweeper and not the sophisticated 50,000-

ton flat-top that was the queen of the seas in this furtive battle. More than seventy British naval units were deployed to screen the long, vulnerable Malaysian coast from intruders, and *Maryton*, like all other minesweepers in the slender chain of patrols, was equipped for a strange guerrilla war on water with armed junks and prahus that tried to cross the narrow gulch separating the Indonesian archipelago from the shores of Singapore and the Malayan Peninsula. The crew soon discovered that their most useful ironware consisted of four Vickers machine-guns that were about to be thrown on to the scrap-heap when Sukarno first threatened to 'crush Malaysia'. *Eagle* could keep her science-fiction strike potential.

January 1965. It is deep night. Behind the blackout curtain of the tiny chartroom a bespectacled midshipman, motionless and unblinking in the dim light, watches the radar screen as a small white blob crawls across its surface like some obscene, sun-shy bug. This is a contact. The ever-swivelling scanner atop the bridge has picked up something out in the starlit Straits that is trying to move *across* the overcrowded channel, instead of up or down it, and is therefore suspect. Diesels whine, and a perilous game of blind man's buff begins for the fragile mine-sweeper as she cuts through the treacherous waters of this slit of an international sea-lane at maximum speed and with no lights showing, amid a flurry of small islands and a stream of freighters and giant tankers oblivious of the war at their skirts.

The trace on the radar screen suddenly shows another white blob scuttling between *Maryton* and the first suspicious pinhead. Uneasy, I step back on to the bridge, and my eyes at once cling to the towering shadow of a freighter ahead, the wide, fixed grin of its bridge windows seemingly half-way up the sky as it bears down on us at speed. Bells ring urgently. The blacked-out minesweeper heels over on a sharp turn, swerves around the freighter on the blind side with feet to spare, and comes up neatly upon the unsuspecting quarry. The captain calls 'Board-ing Stations!' A hollow explosion shakes the deck and there is an airburst to port as an old two-inch mortar filched from the army fires a starshell that casts a reddish glow over the onyx waters – and, like an apparition, a long, rakish Indonesian

prahu, powered by big outboard motors. Abruptly, the twin
Vickers on the bridge smash the momentary silence with two
sharp bursts across the intruder's prow, searchlights snap on,
and men move to the rail to cover the boarding party, Stirling
sub-machine-guns at the hip. No chances are taken. It is not
long since a similar raider met the challenge of H.M.S. *Ajax* with
a bouquet of hand-grenades. But there is no unpleasantness this
time. A police boat materializes out of the Stygian swell around
us. The Indonesian infiltrators are handed over to the Malaysian
security authorities. The minesweeper pulls away tactfully,
back on to her beat.

The night is not through with us, however. Another bug
crawls across the radar screen, the mortar slams a flare into the
sky and binoculars snap on to the suspect. It is a log of wood.
And this very Indonesian log of wood is the essence of Confrontation. In its own inert way it abets Sukarno's policy of making
warless war, of putting the defence to a maximum of trouble,
danger and expense with a bare minimum of prompts and
feints. But if the shadow-fighting is far removed from the hypothetical hell of a computerized conflict, it is characterized by its
own precise military niceties, as I first saw at some anonymous
point in Borneo in September 1963.

On the map it was reassuringly marked 'Landing Zone'. On
the ground it was a twenty-yard ledge above a dark river, a
tiny clearing of brushwood and tree stumps backed by a high
wall of tangled hill. The Wessex helicopter skimmed over the
rolling sea of treetops at 90 knots and dropped hesitantly on to
this uninviting shelf like some fastidious insect, the tips of its
whirling blades almost slashing the foliage. It was a place without a name, a mere map reference along more than 600 miles of
border between Sarawak and Indonesian Borneo where preci-
pitous, jungle-covered mountains alternated with deep, river-
seamed ravines in insanely repetitious waves. But a few days
before a group of armed terrorists from Indonesia had asked
the chief of the near-by Iban longhouse for rice, whereupon the
chief had paddled downriver for five hours to warn the Gurkhas
of the enemy's presence. Patrols now went out, ambushes were
laid, and the guerrillas were duly flushed. In the immensity of

this wilderness where troops can move only on rivers and over-grown jungle tracks, the Gurkhas had struck with almost un-canny accuracy.

It was the helicopter, the ubiquitous chopper, that made such operations possible. From the nearest battalion headquarters in the village of Song, the iron fans clattered out over the frontier area like hands moving over a chessboard, picking up a patrol here, putting down an ambush party there, sometimes hovering low over the screen of trees while troops slid down the fifty-foot rope from which they could drop to the ground for the next phase of the hunt. In three minutes a helicopter could fly a patrol to a position that it would have taken men up to three days' march to reach through the thick underbrush.

British officers nevertheless said that they were resigned to 'losing slowly', and one day in June 1964 I saw what they meant. Dominating the uneasy ocean of Sarawak jungle, the last and highest crest loomed above the transparent bubble of the diminutive Hiller helicopter and the pilot beside me suddenly pulled it into a tight turn. For up there, shimmering in the damp tropical haze, was the border of Indonesian Borneo. No more than five miles beyond the watershed lay the safe jungle camps from which the terrorists launched their raids into Malaysian Sarawak and Sabah. British, Gurkha and Malaysian troops were responsible for defending nearly one thousand miles of frontier to stop this enemy ahead of them from linking up with the enemy behind them – the Chinese Communist guerrillas along the coastal strip – but they were not allowed to cross that border and destroy him in his tantalizingly close bases. Frus-trated commanders therefore prophesied that they would have to go on parrying his attacks with their elbows until a political solution ended Confrontation – perhaps in ten years' time. The prospect was grim.

Only in theory, however. Sukarno had sworn that he would 'crush Malaysia' before the cock crew on 1 January 1965, and as the day when his bluff would be called came closer, Djakarta escalated the war with cold-blooded inefficiency. Indonesian regulars in jungle green or paratroop mottle and armed with mortars and machine-guns hit the beaches of the south-west coast of the Malayan peninsula itself in a series of seaborne assaults. They were soon eliminated. In September 1964, accordingly, blacked-out Hercules transports (for which Americans had recently delivered much-needed spare parts) flew a crack force of Indonesian paratroops with renegade Malaysian guides into South Malaya, dropping them some 95 miles north of Singapore. At Labis, focus of the operation, I found small Malay and Chinese children clinging like flies on a meat cover to the fence around the police station. On a patch of grass inside was a neat row of Indonesians in camouflaged uniforms. They were flat on their backs, their wrists and ankles trussed to carrying-poles, their Javanese faces discoloured in death. Concise killers from a Gurkha battalion had shot them down with surgical precision a few miles north of the town. They had been among the last to be liquidated.

The cock crew on 1 January 1965. The Indonesians had failed miserably. The whole untidy business of Confrontation had cost the Commonwealth forces 114 men killed in action before it whimpered to its own ignominious end. In a war whose potential hardly bore thinking about, most of the dangers proved hypothetical. The crewman on a chopper skimming over green waves of Sarawak jungle hooked a safety strap on me, and I sat beside him on the edge of the floor to photograph the long-houses beneath, legs dangling in the cool slipstream outside. More than one thousand American helicopters were to be shot down in South Vietnam, but here there was scarcely a chance in a million that anyone would fire at us. And when H.M.S. *Maryton* loomed unfairly over the low Indonesian prahu, I was reminded suddenly of the last years of the anti-Communist Emergency in Malaya, and the Operations Room of the South Wales Borderers in Johore.

'We've half a battalion working this area,' the second-in-command had told me, pointing to a vast expanse of rubber and scrub on the map, 'but the terrorists are devilishly elusive.' 'How strong is the enemy then?' I asked. 'Oh, just him and her. They're a married couple, you see,' and he pointed to two snapshots of a Chinese man and woman pinned to a board above their names, their full descriptions, and their biographies. 'That's all that's left. We've put paid to the rest. Pink gin?' Ten years later the Americans were still struggling against a quarter of a million unfriendly Vietnamese. Why did the British always seem to come off lightly?

Some British make facile and invidious comparisons between their own success against the Communist terrorists during the Malayan Emergency and Washington's predicament in Vietnam which first interest, then irritate, and finally just bore the Americans. For as the real experts know, the two problems may have been similar, but the attendant circumstances were certainly not.

Malaya was inhabited by two principal communities, Malay and Chinese, and as nearly all the Communist terrorists were Chinese, the British could automatically count on the loyalty of most of the Malays; but the Vietnamese Communists and the Vietnamese people were of one race, and anyone else was a foreigner. The Communists in Malaya with experience of guerrilla warfare numbered a few thousand, and they had no friendly base across the frontier; but the Communists of Vietnam had provided the hardened spearhead of a vast nationalist movement which had fought the French colonial power for eight years, the Vietcong had North Vietnam behind them, and North Vietnam had China behind her.

The British started on firm ground and all square with their enemy; the Americans inherited a battlefield already soft with years of subversion. The British could undermine the resistance by offering Malaya independence; the Vietnamese had already won independence for themselves from the reluctant French, and owed it in large measure to the Communists. Even so, the Malayan Emergency lasted for twelve long and gruelling years.

To compare Indonesian Confrontation with the war in Vietnam would be equally ludicrous. Had the roles been reversed, the Americans would probably have succeeded in suppressing the Malayan terrorists and the incongruous ambitions of Sukarno, and the British would probably have failed to suppress the Communists in Vietnam. All three situations nevertheless held similar seeds of disaster, and the scenario and the final fade-out in each case might have been very different. For the

British, afflicted with the national change of life from imperial past to parochial future, are perhaps less confident of their own righteousness than the Americans, and recognize more readily that the peoples of the East are pragmatists concerned with their own immediate interests who do not love Indonesians or Americans or democracy or the Queen as such. And this unromantic approach may make for a sounder relationship than one based on ideological breast-beating. It certainly did in North Borneo.

As helicopters whirred over the undulating mat of trees deep in the interior, long black holes would appear here and there, like cigar burns in an ill-used green rug. In these slots were the great, raised longhouses of the Ibans and Sea Dyaks, accommodating twenty-five or thirty families under a headman in a G-string and much elaborate blue tattooing. The Ibans drew comfort from the British presence, and pinned up Union Jacks next to their sometimes gruesome trophies, having snicked the heads off any dead Indonesians they could lay their hands upon when the troops turned their backs.

In remote jungle along the Indonesian border I once found two different tribes living amicably enough in adjacent, almost identical settlements of tin-roofed houses built of rough-cut logs and raised on stilts. The inhabitants were also similar in many ways. They loved good guns and good liquor. They were in excellent physical shape despite the over-simple, over-heated conditions of the Borneo back-of-beyond. Both groups were in many cases heavily tattooed and both stuck feathers in their headdress for formal occasions. But while the Ibans had their wives with them, the 1st Battalion the Royal Ulster Rifles did not.

The grinning Ibans were queueing up at a busy little dispensary of bamboo where the RUR company medical orderly handled thirty native cases a day, dispensing anything from aspirin to eye drops. He had made a name for himself by saving the life of an Iban with a bad spear wound, chopping out the blade and then remaining with him far out in the rain forest until they were both picked up by helicopter. There were similar stories to be heard everywhere. An RAF medical orderly delivered an Iban baby during the flight of a light single-engined

Pioneer, and a hovercraft saved a woman's life after a difficult birth in a midnight dash up the 'M1' – the great Rejang river that is the only highway in an anarchy of peaks and jungle completely devoid of road or rail. Inevitably the helicopters provided the main shuttle service of this welfare system, and in 1965 No. 845 squadron RN took the unusual step of asking the army to train two men as midwives. By that time the squadron had already carried more than 500 civilian emergency cases out of the jungle to the nearest town and hospital, including about 300 direly pregnant females many of whom had given birth within minutes of landing, and the odds were growing uncomfortably short.

The maid-of-all-work choppers evacuated longhouses on the border, lifting pigs and chickens and jars and gongs, carried water tanks into villages in the interior, brought out cholera victims. One pilot was adopted by a longhouse, renamed Booboo, and only allowed to go on leave after much lamentation among the locals (there was a scurrilous rumour that he used his machine not only for moving men, rations, ammunition and the wounded, but for taking 'Ma', the headman's wife, to market in the nearest town every week). At another isolated village a Scots corporal became the virtual chief of one hundred gentle, primitive Punans and taught them not to wash in the same water into which they relieved themselves.

All this casual neighbourliness was as nothing when set beside the highly-organized American charity drives in Vietnam. But it was subtly different. In Borneo the hearts-and-minds campaign was not something for the specialists. Doing-good was not a profession, but the hobby of half the servicemen in the forward areas, and some pilots passed almost as much time playing ambulance and postman and errand-boy for the people as they did dropping off and picking up patrols. Their superiors thought it well spent. Furthermore the population was never tempted to feel that it was playing host to a Jekyll-and-Hyde general staff that dealt out candy with one hand and catastrophe with the other. The Director of Operations, General Sir Walter Walker, made certain that all took extreme precautions to avoid shelling or bombing ordinary people. 'It was indelibly inscribed on our mind that one civilian killed by us would do more harm than ten killed by the enemy,' he has since written. Nevertheless, 'every time we defeated the enemy we took every precaution to ensure that he could not exact retribution on the nearest village'.

The British had the advantage of poverty. If you do not have a hundred heavy bombers to spare to hit 'suspect' hamlets, or a computer to work out how to be human by numbers, or a billion pounds to do the job of brains, it may be easier to preserve a sense of proportion and flesh-and-blood values. Riches in resources, on the other hand, can encourage a wild spending spree on gadgets and facts and figures that only obscure reality and create their own world of illusion. Too often the conviction that truth is a *deus ex machina*, born of the punchcard and the programmed computer, misleads to false and over-optimistic conclusions that deceive planners in war as in peace. In short, the desire to tidy up unkempt reality and express it in neat mathematical terms produces so much *pi*-in-the-sky.

In the villages of Vietnam the charts of statistics multiply, recording local loyalty in terms of the number of tons of fertilizer distributed by the Americans, and political prejudice expressed as medical aid received by the peasants, until even '1,505 haircuts offered free of charge since 1963' are weighed in the balance. But the enemy remains obstinately lethal, and this prompts another spoonful of polysyllabic slush : 'Much more must be known of the behavioural and attitudinal responses of the villagers to externally imposed changes.' How ? One American answer was AGILE, a computerized war-game to measure the factors governing the 'loyalty rating' of Vietnamese villages. Hearts-and-minds were fed into the machine, so to speak, and converted into tape.

In 1967 the 12,722 hamlets scattered over the war-ravaged face of South Vietnam were reduced by HES (Hamlet Evaluation System) to a security index of figures and percentages. In January 1968 this index was released, and it showed that by December 1967, 5,340 hamlets (42 per cent) were 'relatively secure' from the Vietcong, 3,500 (27·5 per cent) were 'contested', and 3,882 (30·5 per cent) were dominated by the Vietcong. Therefore 11·5 million people out of a total population of 17·2 million were living in secure towns or under 'reasonably good security conditions' in the country. This was an increase of 4·8 per cent over the previous eleven months, thanks to the work of pacification and the expenditure of 350,000,000 dollars. 'Let me say briefly I don't see how we can fail to do somewhat better in 1968 than we've done in 1967,' added Robert Komer, adviser on the South Vietnamese pacification programme in Saigon on 24 January 1968. The Communists launched their 'Tet Offensive' just a few days later, and soon any new-found sense of security the peasant had enjoyed was shattered. For all the figuring, the confidence trick had failed again.

But even without the Tet Offensive, the adding-machine evaluation system was suspect, for while it could measure the number of sheets of corrugated iron roofing supplied to pleasantly surprised villagers, and translate this into love, it took no account of all the secret personal factors that influenced the infinitely more complex human computers in their own heads. The impact of material aid on political allegiance cannot be sold by weight as a winner of wars, for the minds of rich donor and poor beneficiary so often do not meet anyway. In some parts of Vietnam American-inspired farming techniques proved so profitable that landowners started evicting their tenants in order to cultivate the land themselves, and the main byproduct of 'technical assistance' turned out to be a growing army of discontented and landless labourers. Elsewhere United States aid officials distributed gifts of rice and salt and cloth to needy refugees on one day, and South Vietnamese officials moved in and carted them all away on the next. In Thailand local administrators not only 'requisitioned' American largesse, but told peasants that American volunteers who gave them free injections were in reality selling them, and then furtively demanded cash in payment for the shots once the white nurses were out of sight.

As the supersonic jets from giant computerized carriers rained bombs on Tonking, yet small, skinny Vietnamese Communists fought on doggedly in the South, the war in Vietnam began to symbolize a wider contest between western invention and eastern intention. And in the hearts and minds of Asia, every day that the might of modern America failed to annihilate her diminutive enemy was a licking for the West. No intelligent Asian underestimates the enormous value and potential of the electronic brain, but many have become increasingly suspicious of the electronic blunder. They distrust a slide-rule civilization that will ask its gadgets anything from the name of the greatest heavyweight champion in history to the political and military alliances to be expected among forty-two countries with 'space capability' in a notional nuclear crisis in 1985. And they are waiting to see if the computers have got the second one wrong too.

30

Small Brother is Watching You

BY 1968 the affluent world of the white appeared to many Asians to have acquired the character of one of their own traditional despots – it was remote and rich and powerful, calculating but incalculable, often callously indifferent to poverty and suffering yet given to unpredictable, sometimes misguided gestures of generosity.

Parsimonious aid and timid investment from the haves accounted for only about 20 per cent of the foreign exchange of which the have-not countries disposed to buy the machines and the know-how that should one day enable them to 'take off'. But they were often unable to do so because the export drives upon which they depended to earn the other 80 per cent were cold-bloodedly blocked by protective tariffs in the West. Backward South-east Asia merited a little charity, it seemed, but not a fair chance. A censorious occident pointed to the evils and idiocies of the undeserving continent, to the repellent spectacle of impoverished millions being sacrificed to the political and pecuniary ambitions of corrupt or incompetent bosses, to the ugly tangle of chauvinism and violence within which this corner of the market seemed inextricably caught. Yet who were the white men to talk?

On television Singaporeans watched documentaries about destitute Londoners living in grimy tenements with leaking roofs and broken windows, surrounded by broods of nine or ten unwashed children and sleeping four to a bed. Newspapers told literate Asians that one person in five in the United States was a poverty-stricken squatter sunk without trace in some filthy slum, and that ten million Americans went hungry on the day Apollo Eleven hit the moon.

The West might write off Sukarno as a chauvinistic megalomaniac who had missed several good opportunities to die, but the East observed how Charles de Gaulle strove to put the *gloire* back into Gaul, demanding a hundred million Frenchmen by the year 2,000 (while Asians were being urged to keep their copulation counter-productive if they wanted to eat), and be-having in Quebec and Montreal as if Canada were some sort of transatlantic Malaysia whose creation had cheated him per-sonally of his rights. Had Sukarno denounced jeans and Beatle-cuts as Unindonesian? In 1968 the French solemnly removed the Mona Lisa from its place of honour in the Louvre because in future the whole of the Grand Gallery was to be reserved exclusively for French painters, and the works of mere foreigners were relegated to lesser rooms.

Vietnamese read of America's other dirty war at home be-tween black and white, and Malaysians opened their news-papers to find stories from Britain with headlines like 'Landlord Hired Dogs to Evict Negro Tenants' ('I am having no niggers in this house,' he said). Indians in Singapore heard with dis-gust that when Sikh bus-drivers and conductors were finally allowed to wear turbans as their religion stipulates, 200 ill-mannered English morons of the London Transport Board turned up for work sporting sarcastic headgear that ranged from dirty towels to deer-stalker hats with feathers on the side.

As rival Protestant and Catholic killers attacked each other in Belfast, backed up by their own parsons and priests, the brown and yellow men took note that intolerance of colour, race and creed in the patronizing West yielded in nothing to exacting standards set by the East. And the same held true of violence itself. In 1967 there were some forty million guns in private hands in the United States, 8,000 murders, 70,000 armed robberies, and a shooting every half hour. The following year bitter argument within the Democrat Party over the war in Vietnam led to the Battle of Chicago, in which the police struck out blindly at demonstrators and innocent on-lookers alike, clubbing and gassing with egalitarian impartiality and yelling, 'Kill 'em, kill 'em.' And then, in 1973, came Water-gate.

Other aspects of occidental political philosophy also repelled. In Britain industrial relations based on demands for unfair shares for all encouraged workers in a Northamptonshire factory to down tools because one of them had been asked to have his hair cut for his own safety, and the Ford Motor Company disclosed that it had enjoyed only twenty-three days free of strike threats during 1968 (which was a leap year). Under the British parliamentary system, the nation was the prisoner of the ruling party, and the ruling party was the prisoner of any group of parliamentary rebels that could threaten its majority, for its first concern was to stay in power. The caucus came before the country – and certainly, therefore, before any other country, as Lee Kuan Yew was to discover.

It was noon on a fine sweaty Saturday in January 1968. Upon the lawn in front of the Prime Minister's official residence in Singapore two men in white shirts and shorts sat at a table, gazing speculatively at me as I walked towards them. Lee Kuan Yew greeted me with a small, freezing grin, while Goh Keng Swee ordered more beer. The Prime Minister was obviously in an ominous temper and elated by his own fury. He had told his people that they would be safe from aggression 'with our British friends remaining until 1977', and now word was out that they were aiming to close all their military bases on the island and abscond by the end of 1971.

Goh Keng Swee, who habitually submitted all British promises anyway to the cold, impersonal appraisal of a pawnbroker conning a seed pearl through his jeweller's glass, rumbled gently from time to time but seemed to take it all as a matter of course. Lee, on the other hand, was brimming over with pugnacious arithmetic, totting up the stiff bill that he was going to make Britain pay for this treachery if the story proved true. He would take the republic's 200 million pounds' worth of reserves straight out of the sterling area, and the British would also lose the seventy million pounds a year that they earned from their industrial and commercial enterprises on the island. No new British business would be allowed into the country. The Singapore Government would not pay one cent for the bases, no one would buy the land, and Whitehall could bloody well abandon it, what? Moreover, he was not sure that he would be able to promise to protect British subjects from the fury of the people once they learned ...

'Hey,' protested Goh, suddenly less somnolent, 'Don't talk like that. They'll think we are a bunch of gangsters.' Lee stopped and smiled thinly, looking about as abashed as Eddie 'Dutch' Schultz. 'I am not saying anything against Britain,' he went on. 'I am talking about a small group of Labour leaders who are ready to jettison everyone's interests, England's as well as ours, because the left wing of their party wants them to pull out all their forces east of Suez, and they need the support of that left wing if they are to be re-elected. But don't quote me,' he added, his eyes like fine slivers of obsidian and his syntax shaking with anger. 'We don't know if it's true yet, isn't it?' Next day he did. After much rough and ready discussion, however, tempers slowly subsided, and if Singapore's sterling reserves started sidling off into other currencies, it was not because Lee had a tough spleen, but because Goh had a hard head.

That was not the first time that the Far East had had occasion to sweep broken British promises into the rest of the litter of shattered illusions about the excellences of western civilization, as everyone in Singapore knew from the Cabinet to our cook. Just two months earlier, her eyes watchful but sorry, Ah Fu had unlocked a drawer, pulled out a battered purse, and emptied its contents on to her dresser. Twenty slightly flattering pictures of Her Gracious Majesty Queen Elizabeth II fell out – 1,000 old Malayan dollars. Ah Fu was not the only one to have been caught by British devaluation. As Prime Minister, Mr Harold Wilson had said on thirty-three different occasions that the pound would not be unpegged, but this had inexplicably failed to arouse suspicion in the minds of many. Now the value of the old colonial dollar, which had been freely convertible at par into the new national currencies of Singapore and Malaysia up to that moment, was cut to eighty-five cents because it had been pinned to the pound.

The ghastly irony of it was that many uncomplicated Asians had put their faith in old bills stamped with the illustrious imprimatur of the great British Raj, spurning all later issues. Fifty-dollar notes bearing the crowned heads of the United Kingdom had actually commanded a higher price than their face value and had been sold for profit. Now they were emerging all over the area like dishonoured promissory notes, and Britons had much to blush for on that day. Those slightly crumpled royal faces symbolized a wider devaluation of the white which nevertheless gave pleasure to many. For some Asians are incurably colour conscious and compulsive racists themselves.

The compulsive racist is that poisonous animal, the man who will read racial discrimination into any fact or fiction, innocent or ugly, on the flimsiest pretext. In Singapore people have protested against westerns because they 'glorify the white man', and in Sukarno's Indonesia, 'Tarzan' was banned as propaganda deliberately designed to prove that one illiterate Caucasian was a match for 10,000 black Africans. An Indian publication closely associated with Krishna Menon has found that the most significant thing about the destruction of Hiroshima was that the Americans did not try out their atom-bomb on their blond German enemies. They dropped it on the yellow Japanese. It escapes the attention of self-righteous Asians that racists – whether white, black, brown or yellow – are the same trash under the skin.

The prism of colour prejudice east of Suez refracts tints more subtle than the black-and-white contrasts of the West, however. For where the white man is resented for his race, he may be envied for his whiteness, and where the black man earns sympathy as the victim of white oppression, he may be despised for his blackness. The negro in Asia can find a landlady's door slammed in his face as surely as if he were in Notting Hill or Little Rock, and in 1968 a Committee of the Concerned for Equal Housing was set up to fight discrimination – not in either of the Birminghams, but in Bangkok. The Asians sympathize with the black man's struggle for civil rights in the United States, as long as he stays there.

In the East caste and colour became confused with the passage of centuries, but the Sanskrit word *varna* in fact meant both, and the great Hindu epic, the *Mahabharata*, told the men

of India long before the birth of Christ: 'Brahmins are fair –
and Sudras are black.' Brahmins are the teachers and priests of
the highest caste, sudras are peasants and servants. An Asian
country is a land of many hues, in which the basic principle
of prestige is the lighter the better. Dark Indians, dark Cambodians, dark Indonesians suffer silently the disdain of their
paler compatriots. In Singapore and Malaysia Eurasians come
in all shades from ivory to ebony and yet will make cruel distinctions among themselves, off-white denying his mixed-blood
brotherhood with dark-oak. Many struggle purposefully up
the colour chart towards an alabaster Nirvana, deliberately
seeking wives fairer than themselves so that their children –
the next incarnation – will be a shade closer to the ultimate
bliss. Moreover, in a multicoloured subcontinent difference of
pigmentation sharpens the sense of racial superiority, and as
the tide of western colonialism ebbed in Asia, it left exposed
the Herrenvolk instincts of those who had been quickest to
complain of oppression by their former European masters. And
none felt this more promptly than the minority hill-tribes.

I first saw them in June 1955, when Ngo Dinh Diem accepted
the oath of fealty in Central Vietnam from the human remnants of ancient cultures that had been driven up the dishevelled mountains as successive waves of conquering Thais
and Vietnamese rolled into the fertile valleys and plains below. M'nong, Nung, Rhade, Djarai, Tho, Curu, the Vietnamese
lumped them together contemptuously under the generic term
Moi – 'savage'. They had dressed for the occasion in a riot
of native silver and copper, beads, belts and bangles, embroidered turbans and blouses and woven blankets of flaming
orange and red and black. As undulating girls, each shining poll
supporting a single tall black feather, beat a soft, liquid flow
of caressing notes out of five gongs, the main ceremony began
in a grassy clearing on the edge of the Annamese jungle,
framed by skeletal buttress trees and feathery tamarinds.

Diem – immaculate, shy, somewhat pink of face – sat on a
wooden elephant-head in a small open-sided pavilion and moved
his arms and legs like a reluctant marionette in accordance
with the whispered instructions of a ritual expert. Five menials

threaded their way through the watching crowd and placed
before him the bloody severed heads of a male and female
buffalo freshly sacrificed, together with selected parts of their
bodies. The eyes of the female were closed in quiet resignation.
Those of the male leered emptily into the middle distance. At
Diem's feet was a large banana leaf on which had been placed
an axe head and a cup of blood. The arch-sorcerer took up
Diem's well-shod right foot and placed it on this leaf (the gesture of a victorious and supreme chief). He then dipped a
thick wick into the cup of blood and touched Diem's shoes
with it. Chanting in Rhade, he next passed a thin gold bangle
over Diem's wrist and swore allegiance to him. He was followed
by a long line of tribal chiefs, more oaths, more blood and
bracelets.

After the tribal chiefs came the elephants, prized possessions
whose act of loyalty would symbolize the sincerity of their
Moi owners. Two hundred and sixteen of the great grey beasts,
piggy little eyes peering, trunks sweeping the grass, passed the
pavilion in majestic Indian file. As each drew level with the
new master of Vietnam, its mahout, perched barelegged on the
vast wrinkled cranium, pounded it with a heavy goad to make
it kneel before the man in the white sharkskin suit. Thirty
minutes nearer death and just as this repetitive procedure
began to pall, one vast fellow evidently suffering either from
stage fright or decided views started to turn towards Diem
obediently but suddenly swung about and knelt in the opposite
direction, presenting the startled Vietnamese leader with an
enormous expanse of uplifted pachydermatous rump which he
then declined to remove. The gesture was unmistakable : 'Thine
impudence,' remarks the Caliph in Flecker's *Hassan*, 'hath a
monstrous beauty, like the hind-quarters of an elephant.' The
old beast seemed to express the feelings of all the minorities
of South-east Asia.

The Mois hated and distrusted the Vietnamese, and the Vietnamese too often treated them arrogantly as expendable sub-
humans whose sufferings and privations were irrelevant. In the
middle sixties the hill peoples mounted two armed revolts, demanding that the upland tiger-country in which they lived

should be granted regional autonomy. In 1969 *montagnard* villagers were still complaining bitterly that when schools, food, and title to land were handed out, they were conveniently forgotten by Saigon. On their side, the Vietcong plundered villages and shot tribesmen in Central Vietnam in an attempt to frighten them into fighting for them, and kidnapped them at gunpoint to make them act as their porters.

Shans, Kachins, Karens, Mois, Thais, Meos, Nagas, Sakkais, Papuans, Dyaks, Dusuns, Muruts, Igorots, ranging from primitive aborigines to early settlers of a distinctive civilization, the minorities straddle the neat national boundaries that others have drawn straight through the troughs and crests of their mountainous territories, and ignore the borders that ignore them. And in most cases they have until recently been cheated, bullied, and sometimes enslaved by new Asian masters for whom 'Freedom' is a warcry when used against the West, but a dirty word when directed against their own brown or yellow power.

During the war against the Communist terrorists in Malaya it was the New Zealanders who were filtered into deep jungle to win over the Sakkais, the aborigines whom the Communists recruited as farmers, guides and spies, for it had been found that the Kiwis had the knack of winning their confidence and friendship. The Australians were trusted next, then the British, then the Gurkhas. Inevitably, the last on the list were the Malays, the new Asian overlords of the land. But the Malays have been models of magnanimity compared with the Burmese.

Most Burmese live in the lower reaches of the Irrawaddy valley and its delta; the great uplands in the north and the coastal area to the south are the domains of big minorities. But when in 1947 the country stood on the threshold of independence from British colonial rule, nearly all of these peoples agreed to join a sovereign Union of Burma governed from Rangoon, provided they enjoyed certain autonomous rights Separate Shan, Kachin, and Karen States were duly created, each with a minister in the Central Government and representation in the two Houses. The senior Shan ruler, Sao Shwe Taik, became first President of Burma.

Almost in a matter of months, however, the Burmese were showing that they were determined to dominate the entire country – by force if necessary – and militants among the minorities took to the hills in open armed rebellion. The Burmese then tossed out the constitutional right of the Shans and Karens to secede, and their trigger-happy troops moved into the mountains, sacking villages and brutally shooting or man-handling the hill-people in their homes.

When he was not up in his Shan capital of Taunggyi, Sao Shwe Taik lived in a rambling old house in Rangoon, and here I first met this good and gentle old man, who was dividing his time between translating Buddhist texts and feeling his way like some political osteopath towards a quick and painless con-stitutional twist that could end Burma's racial agony. But in February 1962 General Ne Win seized power. Soldiers sur-rounded the ex-President's house after dark, shot his son dead when he opened the front door to see who was outside, and then arrested the father. Sao Shwe Taik died years later in lonely custody and his widow lives in exile.

In 1966 a British television team was able to spend five months with the Shan rebels without being challenged by the Burmese military authorities, who could maintain only a tenuous hold on towns and roads in the north. Seven years later the fight that need never have started was still flickering over the fissured and splintered land whose title – the Union of Burma – was now nothing more than a sour joke. And the joke was all the more sour because U Nu – the former premier whom Ne Win had unceremoniously arrested in 1962 and only released in 1968 – had meanwhile renounced his plans to lead a concerted rebellion against his enemy in Rangoon, rather than promise the hill-peoples the autonomy they demanded as the price of their support.

In Thailand, where 300,000 restive Meos live astride the northern border, the Government reacted to the depredations of fewer than 200 armed tribesmen in 1968 by ordering air strikes on 'suspect' villages and by treating all who did not subsequently come out of the hills to be resettled in the plains as Communists. The Communists were indeed wheedling their way into the hearts of some Meos, enticing them for guerrilla training across the border in Laos with promises not only of all manner of good things from guns to girls, but – most significantly – of autonomy and of revenge against the Thais. But it was only after the Thais had bombed, burned and evicted the Meos that the Communist recruiting programme began to show really satisfactory results.

Meanwhile, like the dark side of the moon, the western half of the vast tropical island of New Guinea consistently shunned exposure to the light after it became the Indonesian province of West Irian in 1963. There were muffled reports of sudden armed uprisings by discontented Papuan natives in this territory which Sukarno had 'liberated' from the Dutch, but in that huge enigmatic wilderness the truth was not easy to determine. However, I remember how Lieutenant-General Djatikusomo – Javanese soldier, diplomat, prince and presumably gentleman – had spoken of Indonesia's compassionate task of freeing the oppressed Papuans from their colonial fetters as civilizing the dirty natives 'if necessary at the point of the bayonet'.

The New York agreement, concluded between Holland and Indonesia in 1962 through the good offices of the United Nations, permitted Djakarta to take over the territory provisionally but stipulated that in 1969 the Papuans must be allowed their own 'act of free choice' between independence and permanent incorporation in the Republic of Indonesia. But in 1969 Djakarta refused to organize a referendum, and instead only consulted members of the appointed councils in West Irian's eight regencies. In the best traditions of *Musjawarah*, this carefully-chosen selectorate voted unanimously for West Irian to remain in the republic, one servile delegate claiming a little boldly : 'since the time of Adam and Eve we have been part of Indonesia'. Djakarta had had no intention of ceding the territory from the outset, whatever the natives thought about it. President Suharto had declared that he would regard any decision by the people to leave the republic as 'treason against Indonesia'.

The betrayal of trusting tribesmen has become a cliché of

modern Asian history. The British handed their loyal friends over to the incoming brown or yellow sahib, and the French and the Dutch did the same. It was expedient to sacrifice them in order to keep on friendly terms with the new emerging master-races in the capitals of South-east Asia. The corollary of this, however, was that the minority peoples spread untidily across the high frontier lands of the subcontinent became prime prey for the Communists, until each of the new states began to fray and discolour at the edges.

The Wandering Chinese

UNDETERRED by the sometimes sad results of arbitrarily chopping up and combining the pieces and populations of Asia in new surrealistic patterns – a head severed down the middle here, an ear attached to a navel there – the British invented 'Malaysia'.

The existing Federation of Malaya was a drooping finger of peninsula on the mainland of South-east Asia peopled principally by indigenous Malays and by immigrant Chinese and Indians. Dangling from it by a 1,200-yard causeway, however, was the island mini-state of Singapore, in which the Chinese dominated and Malays were in the minority. And along the northern strip of the otherwise Indonesian island of Borneo, several hundred miles away across the South China Sea, Britain had other dependencies which she was also anxious to shed – two great undulating carpets of jungle and coastal mush, now known as Sarawak and Sabah, whose native inhabitants were upriver tribes like the Dyaks and the Dusuns. As their empire came under the hammer, the main problem before the British was how to unload this ill-assorted geographical bric-à-brac. The only answer was to lump it together as a single job lot, and knock it down to the one obvious buyer. And in this they succeeded.

Sitting next to him at a public lunch on 27 May 1961, I asked Tengku Abdul Rahman of Malaya whether his recent trip to the North Borneo territories had persuaded him to move into them politically. He cut cautiously into his gaudy sweet with a small spoon and replied: 'I was very touched. Everywhere I went, people who felt that the British were going soon seemed to be looking towards Malaya for leadership. But I shall have to think more about it first.'

Apparently it did not require too much thought, however, for as coffee was served, he rose to address the Foreign Correspondents' Association of South-east Asia and spoke for the first time of a possible political 'association' which would include Malaya, Singapore, and the North Borneo states. Two years later, after much acrimonious last-minute bargaining, this new expanded 'Federation of Malaysia' came into being under a predominantly Malay Central Government in Kuala Lumpur. But in Sarawak only one man in five was a Malay, in Sabah one man in twenty-five, and although the upcountry Dyaks and Ibans and Dusuns and Muruts had voted for union with Malaya (since they could not go it alone), they viewed their change of chiefs with some foreboding. They had unpleasant racial memories of the days when they had been administered by the callous minions of the Sultan of Brunei, and they imagined that all Malays were much the same. The take-over was quiet enough, but the surface smoothness was as deceptive as a Dyak longhouse on its high stilts, which looks clean because all the rubbish and ordure fall between the polished slats of the bamboo floor to the midden beneath.

A venomous stream of whispers fled zig-zag through the apprehensive valleys of North Borneo. The Muslim Malays were going to force the people to give up eating pork and to submit to circumcision. They were going to make Malay the compulsory national language for all by 1967, and only those who spoke it would be accepted into the police and administration. They were going to take over all key posts, exclude the natives, strip the country, and put nothing into it.

These spurious rumours lent a long shadow to any small incident that seemed to confirm them, and the Malays did on occasion give cause for a certain uneasiness. In 1963 an angry general privately complained to me of the insolence of Malay troops who contemptuously slapped and kicked the Dyaks and insulted their women, and later there were to be scattered skirmishes between soldiers and civilians. By 1967 the Dyak paramount chief who had become Malaysian Minister for Sarawak Affairs was openly accusing Malay ministers of favouring Malays and completely neglecting the Dyaks. 'I don't care if anybody kills me, but I have to say the truth,' he declared defiantly. Between 1970 and 1973 no fewer than 75,000 people were converted somewhat suddenly to Islam in the neighbouring state of Sabah, thanks (as the Tengku put it) to the 'untiring efforts' of the Malay Chief Minister, Tun Mustapha, who held the power to confer numerous concessions, licences and benefits upon the pliant – and withhold them from the stiff-necked.

When the third new state of Singapore proved intractable, the Tengku cut it loose from Malaysia. But he did not deign to consult the elected state governments of Sarawak and Sabah beforehand, although they had only joined the Federation on the understanding that Singapore would also be part of it. Non-Malay political leaders in North Borneo were outraged, for given the autocratic attitude that the princely Prime Minister had instinctively adopted towards the Constitution over the matter, they themselves might be stripped of their autonomous rights at twenty-four hours' notice if it ever suited Kuala Lumpur.

It was fair to say, however, that if discontented natives were suspicious of the Tengku's Government, the Tengku was equally unhappy. Already in 1964 he had spoken to me sorrowfully about the ungrateful Borneo states as we took tea in his old residence in Kuala Lumpur. 'The British did not train up an efficient local civil service there before they handed over to us,' he grumbled gently over the biscuits. 'These people are not always easy to deal with, and some of their politicians will not keep their mouths shut. The trouble is, you see, they are a rather primitive lot.'

Once again a good man had been fooled by figures. It had been accepted that Malaya and Singapore, split apart by the British colonial power during the nineteenth century in the unnatural course of events, should be reunited. But this meant that in their combined territories there would be more 'immigrant' Chinese than indigenous Malays, which was unthinkable. However, by adding all the 'proto-Malay' natives in Sarawak and Sabah to the ingredients (said the British slyly), the balance would be redressed, leaving the Malays with a comfortable lead of 407,000 head of population (4 per cent) over other races. In reality, only a minority of the natives of North

Borneo were Muslim and most of them should have been counted among the non-Malays, but at the time the price seemed right to the Tengku : the important thing was that the Overseas Chinese, the 'Jews of Asia', would be safely outnumbered.

The Chinese called it Nanyang, the South Seas, this exotic subcontinent of aromatic spices and healing herbs along the tropical sea-route to the Buddhist shrines of India, and their pilgrims trickled through its narrow waters and ancient cities at least 1,500 years ago. They were followed by enterprising traders who oversold things Chinese so successfully that in the thirteenth century the Dragon Throne decreed that the commerce must be cut back, and some celestial exports (notably grain and girls) were forbidden altogether.

But as the acquisitive European conquistadores sailed into these tepid seas and overran their coasts, Chinese mercantile communities sprang up in counter-point in the Spanish Philippines, the Dutch Indies, Portuguese Malacca, and when the British settled Singapore and Penang, it was the immigrant Chinese who flooded in to become the main inhabitants. Later many brought their own womenfolk from China and preserved the clannish customs of their homeland, until the entire demographic map of South-east Asia was mottled with alien, unabsorbed Chinese life.

In 1830 the tin mines of Malaya began drawing immigrant peasant labour from the impoverished villages of South China, and the soulless 'pig trade' in indentured workers, shipped out like so much merchandise, brought thousands of penniless contract coolies into Nanyang to join the Chinese carpenters and goldsmiths, the market gardeners and merchants who had already settled abroad – 'yellow, lean, smooth-shaven, keen, industrious, self-reliant, opium-smoking, gambling, hugging clan ties, forming no others, and managing their own matters even to the post and money order offices,' as Isabella Bird puts it.

Forbidden by Imperial edict to leave their own country, the Chinese had not travelled for love of the trip. Hard-working, thrifty, astute, they were driven by a desire for the security of wealth that frequently manifested itself in unscrupulous avarice and sharp practice. They became the village shop-keepers and money-lenders, the pawnbrokers and the bankers, and eventually the bosses of trucking services on which local farmers and fishermen depended for the distribution of their crops or catch. They were sullenly envied by their less business-like hosts, but they privately despised the indolent native and distrusted the white overlord.

Their domination of the retail trade in Indonesia dates from the eighteenth century when the Dutch East India Company used them as managers and middlemen, and the Malay mercan-tile class was edged out of business altogether. The Chinese ran and rigged the markets, bought up cheap the local rubber, tobacco, coffee, kapok and rice, and sold them dear. They gave the impecunious Indonesian producer credit, but slapped on interest at the rate of up to 25 per cent a month. By the time the archipelago had become an independent republic, some two and a half million Chinese controlled two thirds of all trade, nearly all inter-island commerce, and up to 90 per cent of all small and medium industry.

To resentment of this rich alien infusion that had filtered into the finest capillaries of the subcontinent was now added angry suspicion. The peoples of South-east Asia began to fear that the strong sense of brotherhood among the 14,000,000 Chinese scattered like fertile seed over their soil might most admirably suit the purposes of Mao Tse-tung.

Communist China sedulously cossetted her errant sons, for their remittances through Hongkong alone to relatives still living in the home country contributed £50,000,000 a year to foreign-exchange reserves. Local branches of the Bank of China in South-east Asia extended generous credit to merchants buy-ing goods from the mainland, and Peking accorded to selected Overseas Chinese traders in Singapore and elsewhere the ex-clusive right to handle this or that Chinese product on highly advantageous terms. A trellis of Chinese merchants and shop-keepers dependent upon the favour of Peking was built up – to carry the vine of subversion, many bitterly declared.

Chinese operations knew no frontiers. The Chinese in Cam-bodia smuggled Communist Chinese goods to Chinese mer-

chants in Southern Laos, and the Chinese in North Malaysia
smuggled Communist goods to Chinese dealers in South-west
Thailand. Money talked Maoism. Until 1965, every time a
Chinese living in Indonesia remitted money to needy parents
on the Communist mainland, the counterpart which he paid
in Djakarta went into a special fund held by the Chinese Embassy. The fund accumulated about £6,000,000 a year (at the
official rate of exchange) for financing 'revolutionary movements' in Indonesia itself, and it was swollen by voluntary
contributions exacted from rich businessmen. Peking actively
encouraged violence, and in 1967 militant young Overseas
Chinese could look back on weeks of riotous living inspired
by Mao's Cultural Revolution in China, where Juvenal's bread-
and-circus formula for keeping the masses happy had been
translated into a modern combination of rice-and-rampage.
Emulating the Red Guards on the mainland, they had fought
off police and beaten up bystanders in the streets of Hongkong,
Djakarta, Malaysia and Singapore, amid showers of brickbats
and burning debris, bottles and rotten eggs, hosepiping and
dustbin lids.

Ardour is always a matter of age, however. The disorderly
behaviour of an impetuous minority of students may have
suggested that the 'Great Cultural Revolution' was a danger
wherever two or three Chinese were gathered together. But it
would be wrong to mistake the froth for the beer. The un-
assimilated Chinese may champion their national culture, but
to identify Chinese culture with Communism is absurd, for
nowhere is it more fiercely defended than in Chiang Kai-shek's
Nationalist stronghold of Formosa. Most Overseas Chinese in
South-east Asia are not revolutionary animals. They are pragmatic fauna who want peace and quiet.

In 1967 the Indonesians revealed that out of a million and a
half 'People's Chinese' in Indonesia who theoretically owed
allegiance to Peking, only 20,000 had registered for repatria-
tion to China. Thousands were applying for Indonesian citizenship and were ready to buy it if they could – the Supreme
Court had already been obliged to sack four judges for 'irregu-
larities' in dealing with naturalization demands. In Bangkok

their new readiness to be assimilated is demonstrated by the fact that few Chinese under twenty-five years old speak Chinese or have Chinese names any more. At least fifteen Thais in every hundred have Chinese blood in their veins, on the other hand, and they include the King and most of the Cabinet.

When Norodom Sihanouk was still master of Cambodia, the Chinese showed how steady an eye they kept on the main chance rather than Mao Tse-tung by crowding the Chinese Embassy at receptions when Peking was popular with the Prince, but tactfully forgetting its existence when he talked darkly of Communist conspiracies against him. The majority of Overseas Chinese wanted a relationship with China that would be profitable, apolitical, and free of friction. So did the British, the Americans, the Canadians, the Australians and most of the rest of the world besides, and it was not long before their presidents and prime ministers were queueing for the flight to Peking, the smile of Premier Chou En-lai, and a glimpse of the book-lined study of Chairman Mao.

But as the new nations of postwar South-east Asia took their first, uncertain steps in sovereign rule, it was inevitable that they should turn censorious eyes upon the Chinese among them, with their hideous economic strength and their dubious political loyalties. The flamboyant shop signs with their dancing ideograms disappeared from the streets of Saigon–Cholon in 1957 to be replaced by neat notices in Roman-lettered Vietnamese, and the old air of faintly guilty gaiety was gone. President Ngo Dinh Diem had decreed that all Chinese born in Vietnam must become Vietnamese citizens and adopt Vietnamese names. Those who did not were barred from engaging in eleven of the most profitable and important trades, including the milling and distribution of rice. Chinese schools were allocated Vietnamese supervisors, who made sure that classes were taught in the Vietnamese language for sixteen hours a week. Chinese wives applying for their new identity cards were firmly advised to present themselves at registration bureaux wearing Vietnamese costume. It was the first attempt to convert one race into another at short notice by putting another language into its mouth, a sheaf of new identity documents into its pocket, and a strange if admittedly fetching new costume on to the backs of its women.

In Thailand and Burma and the Philippines the Chinese were the victims of similar measures, but Indonesia enjoyed the blackest record. When Djakarta ordered the Chinese to abandon their village stores in 1959 in an abortive attempt to break their hold on the economy, troops were called out to herd them into the crowded towns, and thousands of their homes and shops were burned down or wrecked by vengeful Javanese (many of whom seized this golden opportunity to set fire to all the IOUs in the hands of these alien money-lenders). Vicious anti-Chinese rioting flickered over the republic in 1963 and 1965, and in the grim autumn of 1967 Dyaks went berserk in Indonesian Borneo, butchering or burning entire Chinese families in their beds and forcing more than 50,000 to flee to the coastal towns, abandoning everything they owned (but exports from the island dropped by 40 per cent. Cash flows out with the blood when the Chinese are attacked.) Six years later Javanese on the rampage in Bandung killed one Chinese, injured scores of others, set fire to hundreds of cars and lorries, and ransacked houses and shops after hearing a completely unfounded rumour that an Indonesian had been killed by a Chinese in a traffic incident.

By 1968 it was illegal to use Chinese characters on shop signs, to celebrate Chinese festivals publicly, or to have a Chinese name. Parliament then passed a law prohibiting Chinese without Indonesian nationality from putting capital into any form of trade. The law was designed to encourage assimilation and to end Chinese domination of the Indonesian economy once and for all. But it will only come into effect after 1977. For if the business acumen of shrewd and grasping Chinese has been their downfall, it has also been their salvation : like most of the flabby countries in the South Seas, Indonesia cannot do without them yet, any more than man can do without muscle. In 1973 Chou En-lai once more stressed that emigrants should be loyal citizens of the country of their adoption, and the Bureau for Overseas Chinese Affairs in Peking was ostensibly dissolved. But the allegiance of those Chinese who were not citizens of the land they lived in still disturbed the sleep of Asian leaders. For China could not regard them as stateless, and had to claim them as her own responsibility – if only to prevent them from turning towards Taiwan.

In Malaya, the different races had long since learned to live side by side amicably enough on an ordinary day, but embers of distrust and enmity smouldered and flared from time to time, and after the Second World War the overbearing behaviour of 'victorious' Chinese who regarded the Malays as stooges of the hated Japanese prompted some savage fighting.

This was the unwinding brown-and-yellow scroll of past insult and injury in the region against which a predominantly Malay Malaya and a predominantly Chinese Singapore were merged in 1963, amid much public shaking of hands, and private shaking of heads.

32

The Mythical Malaysians

THE merger was strictly a marriage of convenience that ended
in a divorce on grounds of incompatibility of temperament. In
Singapore the Malays were outnumbered six-to-one by tiresomely vigorous Chinese who overshadowed them in government and administration. For the most part they were the
philosophical poor – fishermen, gardeners, postmen and mes-
sengers living in combustible *kampongs* – as they were on the
mainland. In Malaya, however, the king was a Malay Sultan,
the Prime Minister a Malay prince, all political portfolios in
the government were held by Malays, and the Constitution
recognized their 'special position' as the 'sons of the soil'.
Within the Malayan Alliance, the coalition that administered
the Federation, harmony between Malays and Chinese depended upon their prince-and-merchant relationship. The privi-
leged Malays dispensed favour, the rich Chinese funds; the
Malays held the power, the Chinese merely the purse-strings.

But while the Alliance was a troika of three separate racial
political groups – Malay, Chinese, and Indian – the ruling
People's Action Party in Singapore was an integrated organization of all races. The Alliance was conservative, the PAP
socialist; the Alliance was bent upon defending Malay privilege, the PAP demanded a 'Malaysian Malaysia' in which all
races would have a seat in the sun; in Malaya the Alliance
governed and the PAP was in opposition; in Singapore the
PAP governed, and the Alliance was in opposition. Within six
months of the merger the hostile PAP had advanced into
Malaya to put up candidates against the Alliance in the
general elections of April 1964. The Alliance, fearful that Lee
Kuan Yew planned to become the first Chinese Prime Minister
of the entire Federation, damned him for 'a hungry dog' whose

'itching hands' were bent on 'pulling down Malaysia', and whose party was 'ready to collaborate with the devil'. The brief, frigid honeymoon was already over.

The PAP called the Alliance leaders racists for protecting Malay rights at the expense of all others; the Alliance called the PAP leaders racists for calling them racists. Everybody was in the right, as usual, and so everybody was in the wrong. 'I have warned Tengku that there can be no Malaysian nation until all men are treated equally as Malaysians, and that otherwise there will be trouble,' Lee Kuan Yew told me in June 1964. 'But the old boy simply pooh-poohs the idea, tells me I don't understand Malaya properly and it will never happen.'

Within the two incompatible states were two incompatible prime ministers. Tengku Abdul Rahman was born an oriental Edwardian, a Muslim prince from a royal family that was a thousand years old even on paper, who spent his years at Cambridge avoiding study in the expensive company of girls and horses and flashy cars. By now over sixty, he was the master of Malaysia, a quasi-feudal father-figure of partly Siamese origin with the face of an elderly sealpoint who believed in the inalienable right of a man to pursue happiness (for which his personal recipe included poker and golf and football and the turf and adopting children of different races). He moved through the world of politics with the casual aplomb of an aristocratic amateur, taking life at an easy, patrician pace like a man wilfully avoiding a coronary.

Relying on rank, the Tengku remained aloof from the scramble for success, had no pretensions to arid intellectual brilliance ('I don't understand all this cultural stuff,' he once remarked of the new National Art Gallery in Kuala Lumpur, 'but if it makes people happy, let 'em have it.') He had the bluff common-sense manner of a plain prince, urbane but not suave, and there was something magnificent about the careless impartiality with which, a few years ago, he described Lee Kuan Yew as 'that bloody Communist Lee' and the Muslim Secretary of his own party who was Lee's bitterest enemy as 'that bloody fellow Albar' – all in one sentence. He could turn

the tables on an adversary as gently as another might turn
his cheek. 'Malays lazy? But all the nicest people are lazy,' he
once remarked. It was his philosophy. When an English journalist aroused wrath by writing that the Malays had no culture, 'no literature, no history except piracy', the Tengku
waited until the angry hubbub subsided and then asked:
'What's all the fuss about? The British are proud of all their
pirates, and we should be proud of ours.'

Like all the best with blue blood, the Prince–Premier had
the common touch, the air of a benevolent uncle who filled his
pockets with sweets for the kiddies and was ready to throw
any Communist suspect into gaol at the drop of an 'h'. But he
avoided acrimonious discussion, for it was beneath his dignity
to raise his voice, and he was always ready to let the past
bury the past. He also allowed it to bury all his enemies, and
he was to chop out of political power in Malaysia not only
Lee and 'that bloody fellow Albar', but half a dozen other
leaders who were so disloyal as to challenge his paternalistic
rule, displaying on these occasions all the characteristic Malay
indolence of a whiplash. He would then set off for Penang or
Singapore amid much tremulous speculation as to what these
further moves meant. But he was only going to watch his
horses run.

The Tengku was known as a firm enemy of racialism, and
although in 1964 he remarked, 'Wherever there are Chinese,
there are Communists', the assessment was correct. He got on
famously with them all provided they kept their place. But
Lee was another matter.

The Prime Minister of Singapore was the son of a moder-
ately successful merchant and just forty years old when their
two territories were joined. A brilliant, pugnacious lawyer and
politician with an absorbent memory and a mind like a cheese-
wire, he was feared for his incisive, often ironical argument
in the Legislative Assembly, but for mass meetings and alfresco
hecklers he reserved an open shirt, a closed fist, and a fiery
I'll-fix-you delivery. He was a socialist, yet no easy mixer, a
man of sudden, arrogant tempers who suffered fools badly.
Within Lee the intellectual was always at war with the tough,

the democrat with the political bronco-buster. Born to politics, he had the ability to rationalize questionable decisions that successful members of this disagreeable profession must acquire. His detractors called him ruthless and dictatorial, his admirers the very epitome of a Chinese hero (who must almost by definition be a bit of a thug). His cold intelligence and hot furies threatened to combine to destroy him, but with the disciplined tenacity with which he did everything, he applied himself conscientiously to the task of learning to be tactful and tolerant with the slow and the stupid. It was a long, painful business.

The Tengku liked an informal understanding as between men of honour. Lee preferred agreements in black and white. The Tengku was intuitive, Lee cerebral and pragmatic. 'They play poker up there in Kuala Lumpur,' Lee used to say. 'Down here we prefer bridge' (he did not realize that in that one sentence he had revealed that he might never have made a successful premier of a federation held together by flair and not logic). The Tengku thought Lee blunt and indiscreet, prone to dissect nasty little problems that he felt should have been left in the woodwork, a leftist, a twister, and no gentleman. Lee found the Tengku permissive, feudal, politically superannuated, and there was no sympathy between them. Lee reacted to the 'treatment' of girls, gambling and big balloon glasses he found awaiting him in Kuala Lumpur in certain houses like a purse-lipped twentieth-century Savonarola threatened with seduction. 'I'm not throwing in my hand just so's I can go to bed with a Thai actress,' he glowered after one visit, back in Singapore and doubtless intact.

Yet to Lee the Tengku was the only man in sight who could keep the peace between Singapore and Malaya. 'If Tengku went and someone like Albar became Prime Minister, there would be nothing left for us,' he said to me in August 1964. 'We would have to take to the jungle, and Malaysia would become another Vietnam.'

This Syed Ja'afar Albar showed what he thought of the concept that a man must be a 'Malaysian' whatever his race by declaring, 'Wherever I am, I am a Malay,' and the boast was all the more curious since he was not only 'that bloody fellow Albar', but an Arab, and indeed descended from the family of the Prophet himself. It should not be thought, however, that Albar was a Muslim fanatic to whom the presence of the pork-eating infidel was an intolerable affront. He has since been profitably associated, in fact, with a millionaire who in theory is everything he has been said to detest – a Chinese chauvinist and a left-wing champion of Chinese culture.

In 1963 Albar was a slightly corpulent gentleman with all the hallmarks of aristocratic distinction – a greying moustache, a fine sloping forehead, a long cigarette-holder, a plausible, quick-witted charm – and as Secretary-General of the Tengku's party, he made his philosophy clear to me in a reasonable, let's-face-it voice on two occasions. The Tengku was weak. The native peoples of North Borneo were ignorant and unreliable and no friends of the Malays as he had been fooled into thinking. The trouble with the Chinese leaders in the Alliance was that they were incapable of keeping their people 'under proper control'. As for 'that Communist bugger, Lee Kuan Yew', he ought to be put in gaol out of harm's way. Something would have to be done about all this.

Ten days after our second meeting Albar organized and addressed a Malay and Muslim Convention in Singapore headed by a 'Malay National Action Committee' whose object was to make more demands for special privileges for Malays on the island, and to prepare for a mass rally to protest against their 'victimization' by the P A P state government. The Malays must unite, Albar stressed, 'then not even a thousand Lee Kuan Yews can break us'. Those Malays who had accepted Lee's invitation to thrash out their problems with him peacefully were condemned as 'traitors'.

Lee had already been accused of brutal discrimination in favour of the island's 1,200,000 Chinese, of evicting Malays from their homes to make way for new blocks of cheap flats, of neglecting to build schools for them, and of failing to respect their 'special rights'. The Singapore Government in vain retorted that under current housing development plans, eight Chinese were being evicted for every one Malay, and that only the Malays enjoyed free education in the state up to and including university studies. Many Malays wanted more, for they felt unable to stand up to the dynamic Chinese man to man unless they were given false heels – an assured quota of jobs, free schoolbooks, subsidized rents, reserved lands. I picked up a leaflet headed 'Singapore Malay National Action Committee' and addressed to 'Malay brothers and sisters' which urged: 'Let us unite to resist the Chinese who want to kill us Malays. Before Malay blood flows in Singapore, it is better to flood the State with Chinese blood.'

One week later I stood at the end of a long, silent Singapore street covered with a glittering carpet of shattered bottles. Knots of sullen youths watched from the shadow of the arcaded sidewalks. A car burned quietly. The knives and the machetes had been out. Near by, hooligans had gouged a man's eyes from his head and then disembowelled him. Night in the critical district of Geylang was punctuated by screams and the alarm-beat of mosque drums as white, Sikh, Chinese and Malay officers of a mixed Singapore battalion led their men through the *kampongs* of wrecked or half-burned shacks to stop Malays from killing Chinese, and Chinese from killing Malays. The worst race riots in Singapore since the war had broken out on Mohammed's birthday. I cabled the story of Albar's convention and the leaflet to London and the *Observer* ran it under the headline 'Malaysia Premier's Party extremists inflame killings'.

Albar composed an open 'Letter to Dennis Bloodworth' and sent copies to the *Observer*, to a number of interested parties, and even to me. It was, of course, typed and unsigned. Relevant sections read:

I was amazed and utterly shocked when I read the heading of your article. I did not believe that I still live in the world that has been contaminated with falsehood and full of lies that have been spread by people like you.

In the Party that is led by the Tengku there are no extremists ... Moreover I do not believe that there is a single sane person who would say that there are extremists among the Malays who want to kill the Chinese.

The riots over, I was summoned to Kuala Lumpur by Tun Abdul Razak, the Deputy Premier who would succeed the Tengku when the old paterfamilias finally retired from the scene. Razak was no colourful personality, but his pale, owlish gaze and tenderized handshake concealed an able administrator and a formidable fixer. He complained about my article and hinted that Malaysia might have to start 'treating correspondents as they do in Ghana' if they published inaccurate and unfair reports. There had been no racial incitement in Singapore. 'The trouble began when someone threw a bottle at the procession on Mohammed's birthday, that's all,' he said, the light glinting blindly on his round glasses and the words implying that the culprit was not a Malay. He was sorry to see me writing this way. I said I was sorry he was sorry, but we parted without regret.

In an earlier interview Razak had told me that Albar was 'the greatest friend of the Chinese'. His appointment as Secretary-General of the ruling party in Malaysia was 'a good thing' because it meant that 'a firm front will be preserved against Lee'. If Lee Kuan Yew did not cooperate fully with Kuala Lumpur in future, he would be 'put in his place'. Later, he quietly gave the Communists in Singapore an assurance that they could come out and vote against the PAP in an important by-election without fear of arrest. One of the political bosses of the Chinese party within the Alliance then went behind the wire to see Lim Chin Siong, the young Chinese detainee whom the left-wing students and workers on the island regarded as their private Mao Tse-tung. A former senior police officer who had found politics infinitely more rewarding, this prison visitor with admirable professionalism extracted from Lim a written promise that he would fight Lee Kuan Yew for control of Singapore if Kuala Lumpur sprung him.

But nothing was being left to chance. As the police prepared to shelve the old dossier on Lim, they received orders to open a new one on Lee, and the 'ultras' in the Alliance began to press for his arrest. Contingency plans for dispatching more Malay troops to the state to overthrow his régime had already been drawn up in the Federal capital. At the beginning of

August 1965 the Tengku told Lee that pressure groups within the Alliance were insisting that he use 'totalitarian methods to force the rebellious state of Singapore into submission'. 'Things had gone so much out of hand,' the Malaysian Premier said afterwards, 'that my colleagues and I were left with no alternative but to legislate Singapore out of the Federation.' If it had remained part of Malaysia violence would inevitably have ensued, he explained.

The paternalistic Tengku did not deem it necessary to consult Parliament about snapping the Federation in two at the Causeway, however, and he deliberately avoided discussing his intentions with the British, who had confided Singapore, Sarawak and Sabah to the care of Kuala Lumpur in the first place and were defending them at that very moment from the ire of the Indonesians. Harold Wilson sent a message through the British High Commission in the Malaysian capital, strongly urging the Tengku to delay the ejection of Singapore from Malaysia, at least for twenty-four hours. Lord Head, the High Commissioner whose blunt talking sometimes dismayed the Malays ('Real plush nineteenth-century feudalism here,' he remarked to me once as we watched his pet gibbons at play, 'they've even got a racecourse that makes Newmarket look like a chicken run') was deflected so that he only ran Razak to earth at a reception on the evening of the last, crucial day, and the Tengku then refused to wait. On 9 August 1965 Singapore became an independent republic.

Albar, furious that the Tengku had made the terrible mistake of giving freedom to his enemies, began a round of private, silver-tongued little talks with prominent men in the Alliance in Kuala Lumpur whose general burden was that it was time the 'Father of Malaysia' retired. The benevolent eyes of the old prince went suddenly still when he heard this, it seems, and Albar was duly sacked.

The mud-slinging between Malaysia and Singapore that followed was accompanied by an economic slogging match with much wild hitting on both sides. This reached a point at which a Malaysian state minister solemnly suggested that the sale of sand to Singapore should be stopped in order to sabotage the island's housing programme, and the Singapore Government began talking of taxing lorries from Malaysia to pay for wear and tear on the roads of the republic. The common currency shared by Malaysia and Singapore was split into separate issues, to the enormous inconvenience of everyone.

No morphine muffled the agonies of amputation. The Singapore police force was full of Malaysians, and more than 500 had to be dismissed and sent home if the republic was not to open for business with a built-in fifth column. 'That's nothing,' Goh Keng Swee told me. 'Not only are half the men in our two regular army battalions Malaysians, but the battalions are under command of a Malaysian brigade with headquarters still on this island. And you heard about the Fleet? Well, we have this one ship, but of course it has been under command of the Malaysians. We don't even know where it is at present. So we've lost the whole damned Singapore Navy before we start.'

Matters were not to rest there, however. The Jews of Asia were to push the analogy to its illogical conclusion, and in the minds of many Singapore was to become 'Little Israel', a diminutive, bellicose, indigestible socialist state bracketed by the bigger, predominantly Muslim sister-nations of Malaysia and Indonesia. The basic suspicions which made these neighbours see eyeball to eyeball rather than eye to eye remained. A secret appreciation ordered by the Malaysian Government in 1968 described Singapore as a potential base for Chinese Communist activity and the subversion of Malaysia. In the same year officials in Djakarta, angered by the execution in Singapore of two Indonesian terrorists captured during Confrontation, attributed the act to 'the influence of Peking'.

Moreover, Lee had not only to lead a nation, he had to create one out of an ex-colonial immigrant community with about as much corporate sense as a mob of women commuters at a downtown remnant sale. The hostile-seas-around-us, every-man-a-soldier philosophy suited his purpose admirably. Israeli military instructors were brought in to train a tough citizen army, but were referred to in polite circles as 'Mexicans' in order to abate alarm and anger in Muslim capitals from Djakarta to

Cairo. The Israeli victory in the six-day war of 1967 was greeted with ill-concealed satisfaction and relief. 'We'd have looked a proper bunch of Charlies if the Jews had lost,' as one Singapore minister put it in his refined way.

All eighteen-year-olds and all those who joined government service were drafted, and the cream of the call-up, the 10 per cent off the top, was allocated to the regular army for two years of intensive battle training and ten years on special reserve. When the island celebrated the 150th anniversary of the foundation of the settlement in August 1969, its pocket army had grown to seven regular battalions and the tanks of its first armoured regiment grumbled their way past the saluting base. Jet pilots were back at school in Britain, a mosquito navy of fast patrol craft was in the making, the first munitions plant had opened, and Singaporeans were learning to operate sophisticated radar and Bloodhound missiles. Two hard-worked Scotswomen had converted half a hundred petite Asians into a kilted pipe band, and Dr Goh had only just been dissuaded from raising a squadron of ceremonial cavalry when the Indians tempted him with an offer of eighty horses.

Fortunately, however, hard self-interest had meanwhile worn hatred a little smoother, as both parties began to realize the extent of their economic and military interdependence. There followed a delicate exercise in gamesmanship whose object was to prove that neither needed the other. The Singaporeans stood off with raised eyebrows and played hard to get, while the Malaysians pretended that an impoverished and chastened Singapore was begging for readmittance into the Federation and the Tengku visited the island-republic as if it were a vassal state. But gradually they shook down into a wary, tacit truce, as the worst of good neighbours will. Immigration cards and car passes were introduced, Malaysia imposed restrictions on trade with Singapore, their joint airline split into two, and in the course of five action-packed months during 1973, so did their joint stock exchange, their joint rubber exchange, and their joint dollar. But the verbal crockery was not flying any more, for divorce is a more genteel state than marriage.

Racial relations continued to be frail, sometimes febrile,

however. Having failed to mix a Malaysian Malaysia, Lee was now concocting a Singaporean Singapore, and although some Malays responded capably to the challenge, for too many the trouble with this society seemed to be that all men were most unfairly being given an equal chance. In Malaysia it was otherwise, for the 'Bumiputra' or 'son of the soil' enjoyed preference and privilege – and for the purposes of the exercise 'Bumiputra' was simply a euphemism for Muslim Malay.

Four out of every five posts in public service had to be given to Malays (unless none qualified for them). In Kuala Lumpur taxi licences were issued only to Malays. For a new industrial company to obtain the tax-exemption that went with 'pioneer status', 30 per cent of employees had to be Malays, and the Public Works Department automatically favoured Malay contractors. The state of Pahang adopted a report recommending that 50 per cent of all scholarships should be given to Malays, irrespective of performance, and mining licences should only be granted to firms with Malay capital and staff. Private companies throughout the country were obliged to keep up to 20 per cent of their shares for Malays. In 1967 Malay became the national language of Malaysia.

The indignant westerner is prone to see in all this a conspiracy to cheat the non-Malays of their birthright. This is to fall into the error of egalitarianism. Each man has his place in the hierarchy and his particular role to play, Malays argue. And if this can be true of the individual, it can be true of the race. The Chinese nevertheless felt themselves treated as second-class citizens. The older businessmen might accept their inferior merchant status, buy themselves an 'Ali Baba', a Bumiputra with a trading licence (Malays make marvellous sleeping partners) and pile up a million dollars behind this legal if listless front. But many young Chinese-educated Chinese were lured by the siren voices of left-wing subversives, eager to smash a society which seemed to present them with nothing but open doors to dead ends.

Some enlightened Bumiputras felt humiliated by their self-inflicted wound, the admission implicit in their privileges that they could only qualify to compete with the rest in a handicap.

But frustrated non-Malays were nonetheless matched by frustrated Malays, the anachronistic products of Muslim schools and colleges more devoted to Koran-reading than calculus, misfits incapable of challenging the Chinese and Indians or of qualifying for jobs in a modern, secular administration. 'The Malays complain, but this year six Malays have been appointed to Government jobs for every one non-Malay,' a Chinese objected to me in 1967, when I made this point. 'The Chinese complain, yet today they hold at least half of the senior posts in the civil service,' retorted a Malay. And they were both right. If the frustrated Chinese became the recruits of left-wing extremism inspired by the Thoughts of Mao, the frustrated Malays became the recruits of right-wing extremism theoretically inspired by the Thoughts of Mohammed.

In May 1969 Malaysia felt the sudden jolt of a political gearchange when the Alliance, which had ruled the Federation since its leaders negotiated independence from the British twelve years before, was returned in the general elections with a severely reduced majority. Even the Tengku only scraped by in his own home state with a lead of 3,500 votes, against 11,600 in 1964, and three ministers lost their seats. More than 50 per cent of the voters supported the opposition, and the real winners were the mixed parties in which Chinese candidates predominated.

These jubilant opponents held a provocative victory parade in Kuala Lumpur, the Chinese sometimes obscenely insulting the Malays but offering them no violence. On the next day busloads of Malays armed with well-sharpened *parangs* rode into the capital for a counter-demonstration. This rapidly turned into a ghastly orgy of killing and burning in which young schoolchildren were brutally cut down while waiting for their after-school buses, and families were incinerated in their own shop-houses. The Chinese secret societies rallied, carrying the war to the Malays, whereupon troops were called out to restore order. Some of these blatantly ignored illegally armed Malays, but fired with alacrity into Chinese houses if anyone so much as showed his face at a window.

The tragedy was complete. Five years before I had asked

the Chief of Staff in Kuala Lumpur whether the Ministry of Defence would 'multiracialize' his almost exclusively Malay infantry by recruiting Chinese and Indians. 'That is impossible,' he replied briefly. 'The security risk would be too great.' Now, however unfairly, up to one half of the people in the Malayan peninsula might well regard their own national armed forces, in which Malays outnumbered non-Malays by two to one, much as the Irish had regarded the British Black-and-Tans in 1920. According to miniaturized official figures 196 people were known to have died hideously in the riots. Of these 143 were Chinese and only twenty-five were Malays.

But the election results had panicked Malays who saw their political mastery thrown into hazard. Democracy had turned nasty, and had to be curbed. Parliament was therefore suspended and an overwhelmingly Malay 'National Operations Council' took over control of public order and security as the curfew crept across the map like a black blight. Malay leaders of the Alliance lashed out nervously at their rivals. The violence had been the work of 'disloyal' Chinese. The opposition parties were racist groups financed with secret funds from Singapore and from Communist agents who used them as a cover for terrorist tactics. The electorate had been 'threatened and intimidated' into voting for tainted traitors who had provoked the rioting 'to overthrow the Government by force of arms and spread terror and panic throughout the country'. This fascinating farrago of inaccuracies was disproved by the known fact that the Communists had tried to bully the public into boycotting the elections altogether, and therefore all who voted for the opposition parties had not abetted the Maoists by doing so : they had defied them.

For the Malays, however, truth had to be 'appropriate'. In a hierarchical world, furthermore, truth went with rank. After the riots Malaysian ministers angrily dismissed reports of foreign correspondents who wrote that Malay troops had victimized innocent and defenceless Chinese civilians as ignorant, malicious and irresponsible lies, and conscientious police reports that seemed to confirm these hideous stories were rigorously edited. The fact that the correspondents and the police officers had been eyewitnesses, while the ministers had scarcely ventured outside their doors, was irrelevant. Accuracy must be in direct ratio to the importance of the speaker. Having cast the island out of Malaysia four years before, therefore, the moderate Tengku was able to claim with a straight face in 1969 that it was he and not the British who 'gave Singapore its independence'. But there is an unhappy parallel here. The Tengku's hand had been forced by Malay extremists on that occasion, and now reasonable men had once again felt compelled to echo the ravings of the racists in order not to lose the confidence of the mob – just as the sane feel compelled to humour the mad, but never the other way around.

Did the Malays ever intend to abolish their split-level society and bring into being that legendary creature, a true 'Malaysian' irrespective of ancestry? 'Not for a hundred years,' one Malay politician subsequently assured me. As a fabulous animal, he could already be said to exist. Why make more trouble by creating him? But the trouble was there, and the future looked forbidding. The phrases filtered back from the innocent past to the guilty present. I heard Lee's voice saying, '*I have warned the Tengku there will be trouble. But the old boy simply pooh-poohs the idea, tells me I don't understand Malaya properly and it will never happen.*' And Albar: '*In the party that is led by the Tengku there are no extremists ... Moreover I do not believe that there is a single sane person who would say that there are extremists among the Malays who want to kill the Chinese.*'

Pontius Pilate might have laughed but he was, after all, just another uncomprehending Caucasian. The entire Malaysian Dream itself had depended on the readiness of local politicians and local press to tell it the way it wasn't.

Razak became Premier, parliament reopened, and it was to the credit of the moderate Malay and Chinese leaders that although they were tied to their own struggling extremists in a three-legged race towards racial concord, no accountable blood was spilled in the four years that followed. Nonetheless, a Malay senator who righteously damned the British immigration laws as racist at the Commonwealth parliamentary conference in September 1973 was able to protest, hand on metaphorical heart, that the policy of his own country was beyond reproach, since Malaysia simply did not want immigrants of any colour. 'We have enough problems with what has been left to us by the British,' he explained characteristically.

'The problems' he was referring to were the immigrant Chinese of Malaysia – including a quarter of a million of them who were still not Malaysians sixteen years after the Federation had become independent.

The Seventies: Adults Only

FACTS rarely flatter the national *figura* and usually only fit where they touch. They have therefore quite understandably been trimmed to suit the self-styled image of many new independent countries in South-east Asia. Britain and the Commonwealth fielded 80 per cent of the regular troops that fought the twelve-year jungle war to cleanse Malaya of Communist guerrillas and drive the last remnants of them across the Thai border, but the Tengku later declared that a handful of Malay battalions dealt the terrorists the final, decisive blow after 'the might of the British army had not succeeded'. His party newspaper added that the Anglo-Saxons had run helter-skelter from Malaya, but the 'sons of the soil' had then heroically defended the plantations and tin mines of 'foreigners like the Australians and British'.

This twistory was to repeat itself. The Malaysian army was still a pocket force when Sukarno launched his Confrontation in 1963, for Kuala Lumpur had a military agreement with London which threw the burden of defending the Federation on to Britain, and when he was asked whether there would be a general call-up of Malaysians to serve their country, the Tengku said no, he did not think the time had yet come to 'deprive the chaps of their pleasures'. The Commonwealth soldier was spared the embarrassment of any effusive gratitude or false bonhomie from those he shielded, however. Relations were unhypocritical, and towards the end of 1965, Malaysian national trade union leaders proposed a general boycott of British military, so that troops returning to mainland Malaya for rest from the Borneo jungle would be refused service in bars, restaurants and shops, and prevented from using public transport.

Once Sukarno's star was safely on the wane and Confronta-

tion faded into peace, the wretched British caused grave offence
by declining to grant the Federation additional military aid
worth £75,000,000. Mr Tan Siew Sin, Malaysia's pragmatic
Finance Minister, compared them with the tottering, imperialistic playboy that they had just been defending him
against, and added rather unamiably that Britain was nothing
more than a 'toothless old lion'. His first peacetime gestures
were to switch the parity of his currency from sterling to gold
and then abolish Commonwealth preference on a large number
of imports. The British had only been guarding their own investments in Malaysia, he said.

The arithmetic of this argument was the subject of much
fudging on all sides, but it was undeniably weakened when the
Labour Government decided to close all military bases east of
Suez by 1971. The failure of the British to continue protecting
their interests was only seen as more treachery, however. The
Federation had 'gloriously fought for its independence' but it
was still Britain's duty to defend it and to uphold the Alliance
Government.

In 1965 the parsimonious attitude of the United States also
hurt those thoughtful Malaysians who felt that Britain was poor
and played-out, and that in the national interest their country
should now turn to a richer patron. For when Kuala Lumpur
appealed to Washington for additional defence aid, the Americans answered with an offer of a seven-year loan on standard
terms at 5 per cent interest. The press enlarged sarcastically on
Malaysia's '5 per cent friends', and an outraged Government
party leader accused the United States of making a profit out
of the fight against Communism.

The mistake of the West has been to imagine for some reason
inexplicable to most Asian leaders that there should not be one
law for the poor and another for the rich. The principle applies
in the exacting world of the income tax assessment, where the
poor get preference and the rich are cut down to size. And it
can apply outside, they say. It was therefore quite seemly in the
eyes of South Koreans that although the dollar was worth 1,450
hwan on the open market in Seoul in 1960, the long-suffering
Americans, who still had 50,000 troops committed to the defence

of their country, should make all local military purchases at the official rate of 650 *hwan* to the dollar. The Thais may tell the Yankee dogs to go home in most insulting terms, but will attack with almost serpentine sibilance any western slights upon their own godliness, girls, cleanliness or clear soup as slanderous and scandalous distortions of the truth. The Filipinos demand an end to the special privileges enjoyed by the Americans in their republic, yet stress that the special preferences accorded to Philippine produce in the American market should be maintained.

If alms or investment are not forthcoming Asian finance ministers are quick to cry shrinking fisc, and to threaten the niggling occident with the spectre of Communism. In 1966 Razak told the western powers that if Malaysia was not given £220 million pounds in loans and aid, it might go red, and in rare harmony Singapore chimed in with a similar warning. Although hands were raised in horror at the massive deployment of American troops in Vietnam, the massive deployment of the American dollar has not always come amiss, and the delicate moral decision taken by disapproving Asian governments is best expressed in the sad old music-hall song about the girl gone bad in the wicked city :

> For her parents in the country
> She buys cases of champagne.
> They may curse the hand that sends them
> But they drink it just the same.

Why not? The western colonialists had outraged and exploited the tender and defenceless states of the East. The world owed them a living.

Professional anti-colonialists are cheap and abundant in Asia, for any fool can flog a dead horse, and it was typical of the breed that when Singapore celebrated its 150th anniversary in 1969, voices should be raised against homage to the founder of the settlement, for he was a white man. Malay sociologist and Chinese editorialist alike protested that Sir Stamford Raffles had not settled the island 'for the benefit of the indigenous people', and that it owed its success and prosperity not to the colonialists but to the 'sweat, blood and tears' of its Asian settlers. As these human anachronisms well knew, Singapore had become precisely what Raffles had intended it to be – one of the greatest ports in the world. Had the white man stayed away, it might have dozed through the future, as it had dozed through the past.

However, Rajaratnam retorted with a short and pithy paragraph of miniaturized philosophy which left the dust to bury the dust and contained the precious seed of all Asia's salvation : 'When our People's Action Party first came into power,' he said, 'It was so anti-colonial that the statue of Raffles was earmarked for removal. But now we have polished him up. He has an honourable place, and we are celebrating the 150th anniversary of the founding of Singapore by him. To pretend that he did not found Singapore would be the first sign of a dishonest society.'

It was no accident that it should have been Rajaratnam who so promptly laid the ghosts of the past, for he is a new Asian with a new look. His words can be as hard as his voice is soft, and they reprove the old invertebrates whose political life has consisted almost exclusively of whining and dining. Those who rummage amid the myths of history to justify the glorification of their race or land or religion he calls 'political archaeologists'. 'Neo-colonialism' is a fiction, an intellectual subterfuge of incompetent outmoded nationalists. What these superannuated patriots do not realize is that 'the younger generation never experienced western colonial oppression, but they are acutely conscious of the oppression, corruption and ineptitude prevailing among their own indigenous rulers'. Empty nationalist braggadocio has only given youth 'disintegration, decadence and misery'.

Rajaratnam's formula for the future is to stop blaming the evils of the white past for the ills of the polychromatic present. 'Instead of concentrating on concrete problems,' he told the Algiers Conference of non-aligned nations in 1973 sardonically 'members have been more interested in highlighting their grievances against the developed world. Perhaps leaders find it easier to blame imperialists and Communists for their troubles, instead of recognizing their own wrongs.' There must be a new philosophy of 'development nationalism' that builds instead of destroying, inspiring people to accept responsibility for their own shortcomings, he had said at the turn of the decade. 'Anti-Communist postures, and alarmist cries about a Communist take-over will not in future bring western money and western troops rushing to our side,' he warned. These would only be made available to help a South-east Asia that was already strong, stable, and prosperous and did not look to others to fight its battles for it.

In Kuala Lumpur, Tan Siew Sin gazed at me through gold-rimmed spectacles and produced his rueful, almost imperceptible auditor's smile. 'Cooperation with Singapore is now a must,' he said. 'It seems a pity that Lee Kuan Yew and the Tengku are hardly on speaking terms.' In February 1969, however, Lee promised to send a detachment of Singapore infantry to Malaysia if the need ever arose, and the Tengku described this offer as 'a gesture of friendship on his part, which I appreciate very much'. While the British danced with impatience on the sidelines, the two sister-states edged tentatively and suspiciously towards the military *gotong royong* without which any regional defence system would simply fall apart at the Straits of Johore.

What had happened? At the beginning of 1968 the Labour Government announced that it would withdraw all troops from Singapore and Malaysia by the end of 1971. If these Commonwealth partners were attacked thereafter, Britain would fly in fire-brigade forces from Europe. VC-10 troop transports, 'Nuclear bat' V-bombers and supersonic fighters practised dry runs to show just how quickly they could be back in their old Asian bases in an emergency. But although the British might go through the martial motions, they would never fight again in the Far East, it was objected. 'They may come back for exercises, but they won't come back for a war,' said one minister. A demonstration drill of their technical ability to deploy men from Europe, therefore, promised no more protection than a pistol in the hand of a pacifist parson.

Tan Siew Sin had words of comfort: 'The British won't die

for South-east Asia, but the Americans will.' One year later, however, it became evident that the Americans felt that they had died quite enough for South-east Asia already. The South-east Asians must learn to do more of their own dying in future. The Americans would help them. After years of frantic bailing and pumping and damming and blasting, Washington was at last preparing to give the subcontinent a chance to find its own level. But as Thanat Khoman of Thailand had warned, peace must be underwritten by the big powers, and while the first US Marines to leave Vietnam in 1969 happily packed their kitbags for home, the frail states of South-east Asia were finding that a new dimension had been added to the problem of survival. Like men juggling two spirit-levels simultaneously on a slope, they now had to calculate their position of maximum stability not only between the western and Communist camps, but also between the Soviet Union and China.

The Russians, determined to ensure that if the Americans followed the British out of the subcontinent, Peking should not fill the vacuum, were feeling their way artfully into the area. They had already appointed as ambassador to Malaysia a genial, well-dressed shoulder-patter who could play golf with princes and talk nicely to the peasantry, and within months were to dispatch another ambassador to Singapore. By now the Soviet Union was the biggest single buyer of Malaysian rubber, and its ships were calling at Singapore at the rate of forty a month. As Russian commercial missions and shipping offices moved into position in the two territories, Thailand and the Philippines began practising in the mirror those conciliatory speeches and taut little smiles that might later establish for them a new relationship with the white Communist world. Later Soviet diplomats insinuated themselves into the hearts of certain leaders in Kuala Lumpur as the 'best friends' of the Federation by telling them not only that they hated the Chinese, but that the Soviet Union would always back a Malay Malaysia against a Chinese Singapore.

Moscow must nevertheless fight an uphill battle. The Russian invasion of Czechoslovakia reminded the wiser men in the

East that a bear whose muzzle was dripping with honey was still a bear. Others have baulked at the idea of repeating Indonesia's unfortunate mistake of buying naval and air power and industries and irrigation wholesale from the Soviet Union, and thereafter being dependent upon Moscow's political goodwill for everything from mechanical replacements to the rescheduling of debts. The Russians are caught at the intersection of two lines of prejudice – one because they are white and the other because they are red. Moreover when Mr Leonid Brezhnev, the Soviet Party Secretary, spoke of 'the task of creating a system of collective security in Asia', Asia reacted cautiously, anxious not to be dragged into any confrontation with China. The Russians had feared that the countries of the region wanted to stay neutral. And they were right. The small states were becoming increasingly suspicious of big brothers who flew monster kites, even if the strings attached to them were longer. Asked in 1972 whether Malaysia would consider signing a treaty of friendship with the USSR, Razak replied briefly that he did not think it necessary. The relationships between the two countries should always be within 'the context of a neutral South-east Asia'. Moscow might want to be the *grand patron* behind a wide-screen security system that would also include Japan, India, Pakistan, Afghanistan and Bangladesh, but South-east Asia would settle for South-east Asia. 'If we bring in the big nations,' Razak commented with typical understatement, they in turn 'will bring in problems we will find difficult to resolve.'

The emergence of a thinly-smiling China from sulky isolation was provoking another double-take, for while Chairman Mao might receive President Nixon and Chou En-lai practise ping-pong diplomacy, there was no sign of a softening in Peking's attitude towards world revolution. The Chinese merely separated state-to-state diplomacy with America from their party-to-party policy of active support for all right-thinking, left-leaning comrades engaged in the ungentle art of armed insurrection against the governments that China courted. And by 1972 the graphs of subversion and terrorism were on the upcurve.

The conviction was growing that the patterns of international policy were traced in water, and it was not surprising that all powers began to feel their way towards the future like men in a moving maze of glass, for amiable enemies might at any moment prove preferable to dubious friends as the situation revolved. Which way were they to look? Should they be relieved that Washington seemed to be developing a new relationship of cold-blooded cordiality with both Moscow and Peking? After all, 'when the buffaloes fight, it is the grass that gets trampled'.

If they flirted the effect was the same, retorted Lee Kuan Yew. This was a new South-east Asia from which the United States was being accused of withdrawing with unseemly haste, abandoning its allies to their anachronistic anti-Communism and the mercy of Peking and Hanoi, while paradoxically the Chinese discreetly encouraged a continued if diminished American presence in order to dampen the ambitions of others. For as the American and Chinese arch-enemies drew closer together, the rivalry between red powers – exemplified by Chinese support for Sihanouk and Russian recognition of Lon Nol in Cambodia – correspondingly sharpened.

The Russians feared that their influence on Hanoi would be submerged beneath a flood of reconstruction aid from Washington and Peking. On their side, the Chinese needed the Americans not only to counterbalance the Russians, but to dissuade their 'younger brothers' in North Vietnam – by 1973 the strongest military power on the subcontinent – from cherishing dreams of regional hegemony on China's sensitive southern border. When Lee Kuan Yew told the British that he would be 'seriously alarmed' if the American air bases in Thailand were closed down, therefore, he may have vexed Bangkok and Hanoi, but not necessarily Peking.

Lee's anxiety was understandable. The solid British presence in Malaysia and Singapore, which had included 50,000 men and some seventy naval units in the mid sixties, had shrunk to ANZUK, a miniforce fewer than 7,000-strong, contributed after much haggling by Britain, Australia and New Zealand to the joint five-power Commonwealth defence of the two Asian partners. But Australia teetered uncertainly on the edge of the rowdy South-east Asian playground like a new boy of the wrong colour who wants to be loved by all adversaries simultaneously. Although Canberra had promised to keep troops and jet fighters in Singapore and Malaysia after the British pulled out, the Tengku disgustedly wrote these arrangements off as 'useless', for twice in six years enemies had threatened the North Borneo states of Malaysia, and twice in six years the Australians had refused to commit combat troops to their defence – in 1963 for fear of angering the Indonesians, in 1969 for fear of angering the Filipinos. Nothing had been more consistent than this Antipodean hedging. The Australians were ready to station battalions in Singapore provided they never became involved in a fight, it appeared. 'If our neighbours attacked us, the first thing they would do would be to pull out,' as one minister put it to me.

In the event they did not wait to be attacked, for in 1973 the new Labour Prime Minister, Gough Whitlam, announced that he would withdraw his 1,500-odd ground troops from Singapore by early 1974, leaving the British and the New Zealanders to sweep the remains of ANZUK together into an even smaller heap.

At the other end of this tangle of nations lay Mother India, but it was unlikely that the states of South-east Asia would turn with much confidence towards New Delhi for either military support or economic cooperation. The patronizing airs and loquacious arrogance of many Indian politicians and diplomats hardly appeared to be justified by events in their own country, where every sordid problem of the East from starvation to sticky palms seemed to be magnified a hundred times, and China's ability to invade India with impunity in 1962 increased the impression that the Indians might be good for gods, but not for guns.

The earlier withdrawal of the main British forces from Malaysia and Singapore, and President Nixon's dismaying doctrine of disengagement, were meanwhile cutting small lines of worry on faces in Japan, the world's biggest importer of oil. For 90 per cent of this oil came through the narrow gullet of the Malacca Straits and across the South China Sea. In 1969 and for the first time since the Second World War, accordingly, a destroyer squadron of the Maritime Self-Defence Force (exquisitely polite Japanese for the ocean-going navy which the postwar constitution expressly forbids) sailed out of Tokyo to make a 24,000-mile 'goodwill' tour of the entire region. This had American blessing, for Tokyo's economic power and military potential seemed to offer a pair of long Asian tongs with which Washington might one day be able to manipulate the critical mass of the orient from a distance. The Japanese already had more than 250,000 men under arms, an air force of nearly 600 combat aircraft, a navy of ten submarines and about fifty destroyers and frigates. Moreover, bigger and better weapons were on the way to enable them to play policeman in Asian waters – to help keep the peace stable and the traffic moving.

However, in spite of the obvious reluctance of the Japanese Government to assume any form of international responsibility that did not show a clear margin of profit, and the power of the peacemongers in a land that had both sown and reaped so much death and destruction only a quarter of a century before, South-east Asians watched Tokyo through narrowed eyes. The new concern about the Straits of Malacca brought to Singapore a curious succession of inquisitive Japanese journalists and 'journalists', their cameras as eager as their questions, who visited the naval base and assiduously interviewed officials. Many were middle-aged men with somewhat middle-aged ideas. One of them deplored the mood of the Japanese young who were so careless of their country's 'national interests'. The peoples of Singapore and Malaysia might not like to see Japanese troops on their soil again, but surely a few Japanese warships on the skyline would be acceptable? After all, had it not been for the atomic bomb . . .

Throughout the region memory dies hard. A tall, stiff, bone-white pylon of stone in the centre of Singapore, paid for out of a £6,000,000 'blood debt' grudgingly conceded by Tokyo, reminds citizens of the 50,000 victims of the 'Greater East Asia Coprosperity Sphere' whom the Japanese massacred on the island. More significantly, perhaps, no one in the region has forgotten the *kaishas*, the big Japanese combines that moved into South-east Asia during the Second World War to set up protected monopolies, and whose shamurais ruthlessly fleeced the subcontinent until it was red and raw.

By 1969 there were faintly unhappy faces among finance ministers as the Japanese economic invasion began to look to many like the beginnings of a second take-over bid. The airborne army of investors that now descended on Asian capitals from Tokyo was polite, sometimes apologetic. 'But we must watch them like hawks to make sure that they are not turning us all into industrial satellites', one senior official told me. It was already established that the Japanese aimed to harness the subcontinent to their own economy as a cheap workhorse, investing money in labour-intensive industries in countries where wages were lower while reserving highly-sophisticated production for Japan itself. In Manila the Filipinos voiced a thinly-veiled suspicion that Tokyo only wanted to mine the area for raw materials and ready buyers of cheap Japanese goods, and when at an international conference in Singapore the Japanese Foreign Minister suggested that a permanent committee be set up for the development of South-east Asia, the idea was at once thrown out as a possible ruse to get the wolf in among the sheep. Instead, the Philippines proposed that the underdeveloped countries should work to create a South-east Asian Common Market from which Japan would be rigorously excluded.

Dr Adam Malik, the Indonesian Foreign Minister, prophesied that in the seventies Japan might be 'more of a vexing problem than China' and an object of 'envy, suspicion and fear among its Asian neighbours'. The Japanese, he added, 'have themselves to blame for this'. 'When they first came back to South-east Asia,' another minister told me, 'they bowed low. Now they merely nod. God help us the day they don't even nod.' In 1969 the Japanese promised to double their aid to Asia in five years. But responsible political leaders share a healthy determination not to allow Japan to reconquer with bank drafts what she could not hold with bayonets.

This was the problem picture that Asian politicians were

still studying in 1973 when the Vietnam cease-fire proved
paper-thin, and it may be the making of the subcontinent, for
while it has evoked much inflated prose from those who believe
in talk, it has also evoked sound pragmatic thinking from those
who believe in action.

By the late sixties already, the more perceptive local leaders
had begun to realize that salvation could lie only in social
revolution and regional solidarity among themselves. Their
peoples had squabbled and cheated and sulked behind a nursery-
wall of western defence, but the wall was coming down and
they were going to be exposed to the world outside. It suddenly
seemed as if in holding them together, their white protectors
had in fact been holding them apart. In a new and chilly age
of nuclear superpowers, Europe had been compelled to bury
its innumerable hatchets and start creating 'Europe'. However
wild the idea, South-east Asia must now start to create 'South-
east Asia'.

The emphasis was placed increasingly on self-reliance. 'Aid
has not only corrupted the small nations, but absolute aid has
corrupted them absolutely,' Rajaratnam said unhappily in 1972,
and went on to delineate the new outlook. The United States
had given up crusading, and from now on must be expected
to be swayed only by its own national interests. The naïve,
emotional, committed American would give way to a hard-
headed rational being with whom, however, it should be much
easier to cope, for he would be more predictable. Meanwhile
the main menace to the region in the future would most probably come from left-wing subversives capitalizing on the just
grievances of the people. Governments must therefore concentrate on building a fair and prosperous society, for 'peace begins
at home'.

Adam Malik of Indonesia urged the countries of the subcontinent to make sure that they were not used as expendable
pawns by superpowers that were themselves not 'willing any
more to be dragged into conflicts between small nations' and
would only be pursuing their own 'paramount' national interests. The small nations must remain impartial in any competition between the major powers, and strengthen their own

position by settling existing disputes among themselves and preventing any new ones from arising.

Like the first ice of winter, regional cooperation had begun to crystallize almost imperceptibly into unmatching fragments that had so far only broken the surface tension here and there. New sets of initials in an acronymic age sprawled over the maps of the Far East – ASPAC, covering nine Pacific countries bent on 'greater cooperation and solidarity'; ASEAN, covering five bent on 'accelerating economic growth, social progress and cultural development through joint endeavour and partnership'; ADB, the Asian Development Bank 'to promote investment, finance regional, sub-regional and national development projects ...' These were the Asian civilian sons of the older soldiers – ANZUS, ANZAM, SEATO – whose business had hitherto been with 'armed attack' and whose colour was more Anglo-Saxon than oriental.

As the peripheral lands to her south edged towards 'normal' relations with China, the anti-Communist regional pacts had to be cannibalized if they were not to become obsolete. A moulting SEATO, already shedding members ominously, ceased to be a device for legalizing American military intervention in the area, and started to provide funds for building village schools and digging irrigation ditches and other civic action projects drawn up for the fight against local Communist insurgency. Weighed down by the membership of Taiwan, ASPAC foundered in 1973, when it proved impossible to persuade other partners to hold the overdue eighth ministerial meeting of its Council in such embarrassing company.

Within ASEAN, talk slowly coagulated into joint action on scholarships, fishery promotion, airlines, coordination of tourism, standardized spelling, but it soon became obvious that many years would pass before the surface would be solid enough to take any real strain. At the fifth ministerial meeting in April 1972 Lee Kuan Yew pointed out that ASEAN had above all a fine record for inaction. Out of nearly 700 recommendations on regional cooperation that its Foreign Ministers had adopted since 1967, it had implemented precisely eighty. It was nonetheless the only existing syndicate that could translate small-nation diplomacy into concerted international action, and by 1973 it had made the incontrovertible progress that one recognizes more easily in the path of the plodding tortoise than that of the capricious hare. The five partners – Singapore, Indonesia, Malaysia, the Philippines, Thailand – had agreed to declare South-east Asia a 'zone for peace, freedom and neutrality', to set up permanent machinery to make the declaration a reality guaranteed by the big powers, and to consult each other before recognizing Peking.

They were aware that China would not guarantee the neutrality of the subcontinent until all foreign bases defending it were closed down, but although any suggestion that their economic, cultural and political association could ever be given sharp teeth as a military alliance was consistently pooh-poohed, bilateral military cooperation between member states was already a fact of life – and sometimes death. The Indonesians and Malaysians ran joint operations against Communist terrorists along their common border on the island of Borneo, and the Thais and the Malaysians did the same along their common border on the mainland. The Philippines and Indonesia mounted joint sea patrols, and the Malaysians still had their naval base in the Republic of Singapore.

Yet this may be less relevant than the ultimate capability of the non-Communist states of South-east Asia to develop a thriving common market and coordinate a new diplomacy. They are nine undermuscled nations, each of which has individually had to hold in balance four huge powers – China, Russia, America, Japan – while simultaneously enduring the shooting pains of armed Communist insurgency throughout its limbs. However, any semi-literate piano-lifter knows how to ease his own burden in such circumstances, and willing cooperation could save the subcontinent – even if its problem is not one of furniture-moving, but foreign policy. It may all take a very long time, but time is relative, and it will still be worth while if it is achieved when the old men who dreamed the dream are dead, but the young men who saw the vision live.

34
The Adhocracy

IN accordance with the inexorable law that the better you learn to build, the better you learn to break, the older Japanese have outstripped the rest of Asia in establishing a modern state and therefore the younger Japanese have mounted the most spectacular of rebellions against it. But the war of the generations hit the Far East long before student guerrillas seized sixty universities in Japan in 1969.

The spectrum of the postwar generation was as multi-coloured in Asia as it was in Europe, and ranged from Trotskyist to teddy-boy in Saigon as in Southampton. But there was a broad band of young men and women for whom the colonial era and its 'democratic' aftermath seemed all part of the same pattern of degradation. Ashamed of their parents for their preoccupation with money and its glossy, wax-like fruits, they wanted to purge themselves spiritually by proving their capacity for honesty, industry, thrift and self-sacrifice, and they were inevitably attracted by the demands and disciplines of Communism (although most of them could not have told the Theory of Value from Capitalist Encirclement). These were only prototypes, however, and by 1968 their successors were swinging left or right according to circumstance.

Like spontaneous fire from rotting hay, student power in Asia kindled from corruption – the corruption of a dream. In the eyes of cheated youth, the bright postwar promise of a brave new world for men born free was translated at best into government by middle-aged nationalists still steeped in the discreditable conventions of the past. At worst it yielded a mess of crooked or sick-in-the-head dictators and military juntas with barrack-square answers to the problems left by abortive experiments in democracy. The reaction of many students to the constraint imposed upon them by those so sardonically referred to as their elders and betters was therefore characteristically savage. 'Make Love' is the motto of disillusioned youth repelled by the deceits of overstuffed western societies, for a hippy is a child of an affluence that the young Asian did not know. The Asian was square, politically-minded, still imbued with old-fashioned ideas about fair shares and social justice and morality.

In their self-appointed role of national conscience, umpire and scandal-breaker, the students of Asia have proved salutary, sometimes infuriating watchdogs, and their methods have often been picturesque. In 1968 they distributed a manifesto in Manila condemning the 'lavish display of wealth' put on by the Vice-President of the Philippines for his fortieth wedding anniversary and listing some impressive statistics – 1,000 guests, a fifteen-piece orchestra imported from America, a twenty-five-foot-high fountain of champagne, ten buffets, eight bars. In Indonesia they have published details of the luxurious villas and limousines owned by high-ranking officials on the principle that by definition upright men, like upright pianos, take up little space.

In the fight against speculation and profiteering they have jammed telephones, seized rice stores, appropriated the keys of fuel depots, and in 1970 they plastered official cars with notices asking 'Where does the foreign aid go?' Attacking decadence and immorality, they have raided brothels, closing fourteen at the port of Belawan in East Sumatra in spite of the furious objections of local authorities that foreign ships would no longer call there and the entire province would suffer a severe loss of revenue. By 1969 they had obliged a reluctant Attorney-General in Djakarta to set up an anti-corruption task force, and they were demanding a louder voice in a legislature in which their appointed representatives already sat as a 'functional group'.

The young are sometimes exploited as political pawns, or misled by megalomaniacs, but in a subcontinent in which too often the elected legislature has been faked, bought, suspended or ignored, the irreverent barracking of schoolboys in the gallery is frequently the only effective protest that can limit flagrant abuse of authority. Americans who resigned themselves

too early to financing the unedifying capers of potentates disguised as popular government, like monkeys in mink, were
isolating themselves on the wrong side of the generation gap.
Student power put the cutting edge on the axes that felled
three of the strongest dictators in the Far East – Syngman Rhee
in South Korea, Sukarno in Indonesia, and (with other forces)
Ngo Dinh Diem in South Vietnam. Then, in October 1973,
200,000 Thai students demanding a democratic constitution and
free elections mounted gigantic demonstrations in Bangkok
which led to bloody clashes with the army, and forced the
military bosses of the kingdom to abdicate and flee.

The young are not entirely alone, for new values are emerging among their fathers. Hallowed traditions of official extor-
tion and graft are under attack, and although the diehard
opposition to the newfangled morality is naturally stiff, there
are at least some small signs that South-east Asia may be jerking
awake instead of nodding off soporifically into another permissive decade of pocket-lining. In Vietnam special anti-
corruption committees have been created, and in Thailand
graft was the main campaign issue in the 1969 elections. In
Malaysia civil servants are forbidden to receive gifts, may be
arrested for accepting complimentary tickets to a cinema, have
been warned to think twice before taking even a cigarette from
a member of the public. By 1973 Filipino officials had also been
warned against accepting presents in any circumstances whatever, and Thai officers caught taking bribes from youths anxious
to avoid military service were being thrown into prison. In
Singapore Rajaratnam attacked the 'kleptocracy' – the society
of the corrupt – and Lee Kuan Yew told a Commonwealth
conference pointedly that Afro-Asian administrations should
take a look at themselves 'when instead of dams and power
stations, roads and railways, we have Rolls-Royces and executive mansions, not to mention golden bedsteads'.

Do these censorious islanders have the right formula for the
future? In their little laboratory-state they have been carrying
out a bold experiment, which could prove to be the pilot scheme
for immunizing Asia from the grosser attractions of Marxist
materialism and Mao Tse-tung. Lee Kuan Yew and his People's

Action Party have taken the unusual step of regarding government as hard work, and public money as something to be spent on the public. Capital and confidence pour in, but Lee lives in the same old rambling family house in which I met him a dozen years ago, and Rajaratnam lives in the same three-and-a-half-room bungalow that he bought when he was a journalist.

Another modest fellow who has not moved house is my neighbour Dr Lee Siew Choh, Chairman of the left-wing Barisan Sosialis, or Socialist Front. 'You British are here to suppress our people and to sabotage democracy,' he tells me at our first meeting, 'and the PAP Government of Singapore is merely the stooge of the Anglo-American colonialists.' We are sitting together on his small lawn, drinking Tiger beer from his battered old refrigerator, and Dr Lee is being his usual affable self. Friendly but frank, a western-trained doctor with an all-wool bedside voice, he produces the strip-language of Communism as effortlessly as a conjurer pulling yards of ribbon from between his teeth. But Dr Lee is not a happy politician. It is not easy to play the militant in Singapore.

He complains that the twenty-nine left-wing unions that support the Barisan Sosialis are split. Some of them are ready to fight it out in the streets, but the others believe that the Prime Minister will keep his promises of a bright future. How many unionists can he trust at a pinch? 'Your guess is as good as mine,' he answers gloomily, putting his head in his glass, 'perhaps little more than half of them. It looks as if what we'll have to do is simply be patient and let time prove that the Government is not really sincere.' But the Government does not suddenly stop building Singapore and abscond with the funds, and this is Dr Lee's problem.

His frustration is understandable. The relationship between Premier Lee Kuan Yew and these left-wing extremists, who also started public life within the PAP, was for years like one of those energetic *pas de deux* during which it is hard to tell whether the partners are supposed to be fighting or fornicating. But whichever way you look at it, Lee Kuan Yew emerged on top. The break-away came when the pro-Communists walked out of the PAP and formed the Barisan Sosialis, after which

most of their leaders were thrown into gaol without trial as
security risks. His detractors are quick to point out, therefore,
that Lee did not beat the Communists in a straight contest for
the minds of the masses.

However, six out of every ten men in Singapore were Chinese-
educated Chinese, chauvinists proud of Mao's achievements in
their homeland, many of them as red and ripe for trouble as
Eve's apple. But when the Barisan Sosialis put up ten candidates
in the general elections of September 1972, the PAP won all
the seats and the Barisan won none of them. Balancing his
special security powers against his special security problem,
Lee Kuan Yew can still claim to have proved that Asian Communism can be killed with Asian kindness. For his Government
has done more than lock up the left wing. It has swept away
slums and given the people towering blocks of low-rental flats,
new networks of roads, a new port, a new industrial complex,
nearly one hundred new schools, a new social security system,
a new face and a new future. In the summer of 1969 Lim Chin
Siong, the darling of the Singapore Maoists whom the
Malaysians had tried to use against Lee Kuan Yew in 1965, became the latest of a long line of left-wing detainees to capitulate
and recant. (He was then released and dispatched to England
to study law, for ex-colonial Singapore is taking poetic revenge
upon its former masters. In the days of empire, Britain's black
sheep were bundled off to distant tropical dependencies to live
useful lives, but now the tropical dependencies get rid of their
red sheep by bundling them off to Britain.)

It says much for Lee Kuan Yew that bold and outspoken
men have accused him of being a Fascist, a Communist, even
a democrat at different times, and at those different times all
of them have ostensibly been right. For Lee, ideology is not
contained in sacred books: it is written by a moving finger in
the shifting sands of the political arena. English democracy,
like the English language, grew up naturally in a changing
cosmos – untidy, flexible and durable because it was spared
the otiose attentions of pedants and academics. In a changing
cosmos Lee Kuan Yew's democracy also twists and evolves
with the passage of years, assuming unorthodox new shapes as

he and his political partners adapt and tropicalize this alien northern concept on an *ad hoc* basis.

In 1965 Lee and his team began trying to knock their small island and its two million miscellaneous inhabitants into a serviceable and coherent nation. The raw material was 225 square miles of low-lying equatorial estate and an ex-colonial mince of money-minded Asian immigrants to whom 'home' was not Singapore, but the land of their respective forefathers – distant India, unfriendly Malaysia, Mao's China.

In the early stages, the drive for a new, unaccustomed civic and national pride produced some elegant planning, for the Prime Minister promised the people 'a garden city with flowers and trees, tidy and litterless', and he set about providing it. But one must suffer to be beautiful. He also promised them compulsory standardized dustbins whose rental would be added to their electricity bills, and fines ranging from £17 to £120 for shopkeepers who flung their refuse into the streets. The courts started ordering citizens to pay a painful price for dropping even an empty peanut packet out of a car, and tenants of the new government flats were warned that they would be evicted if they proved incorrigible litterbugs.

'Keep Singapore Clean' was followed by 'Keep Singapore Fit'. Morning physical jerks for all were introduced, and 1,000 teachers were specially trained to supervise compulsory tooth-brushing after meals for the pocket-state's 400,000 primary school children. The watchwords of the government were 'discipline', 'survival', the 'rugged society'. On TV Singapura pretty little speakerines with sanitized voices warned the public weekly against dirt, dodging the draft, bad driving, too many babies. Determined that the young state should be lovely and therefore loved, the administration created an all-year-round cleansing organization under an act that also abolished week-end overtime pay for employees in essential services of this type. The public was not going to be made to carry the can for the night-soil worker.

In 'Socialist' Singapore the trade unions might no longer negotiate about the dismissal or retrenchment of staff. Workers must do a forty-four-hour week and retire at fifty-five, and they were allowed an annual holiday of only seven days until they had been ten years at the job. Four public holidays were struck from the calendar, and the tight labour laws left a man little purchase with which to lever himself more pay for less work in the fatally luxurious traditions of the British trade union movement. Workers who rebelled were accused of 'high treason', and Lee warned troublemakers that they would be sacked, kicked out of their houses, possibly deprived of citizenship and deported back to those 'homes' abroad from which their forebears had originally come. Strikes whimpered out. The employer was made master in his own house, so that Singapore could attract much-needed foreign capital, and as fast as it won private investment, the government paradoxically advanced a policy of 'Creeping Socialism' by going into business on its own account and also becoming a partner in more and more joint industrial ventures.

In 'Democratic' Singapore, the PAP held all the seats in the parliament, the Communist Party was outlawed, a Security Ordinance allowed the Government to detain political 'undesirables' indefinitely without trial, and students entering university were screened for reliability. Daintier democrats might understandably wince, but men like Lee pointed out that they were manhandling the muck of Asian social realities, not teaching political theory in an aseptic classroom.

Singapore had first become a one-party state simply because the Barisan Sosialis had boycotted the general elections of 1968, and the PAP had won a landslide victory against the rest of the opposition. But party leaders were still faintly uneasy, like men improperly dressed for democracy. Back-benchers, exhorted to political self-flagellation, began to strike out heavily at their own government. Contingency plans were drafted for splitting the party into two so that it might fight itself more effectively if the need arose. A Presidential Council of nominated members was fabricated to protect the citizen against the parliament he had elected. Sacred beliefs were nevertheless held up to scrutiny and flouted. Abortion and voluntary sterilization were introduced, and juries were abolished. A man on trial for his life must now appear before two judges of the High

Court, and his fate depends upon their unanimous verdict.

This new law was attacked with characteristic ferocity by David Marshall, ex-Chief Minister of Singapore and a brilliant criminal defence counsel who might well have been invented by Erle Stanley Gardner had he not already existed. He argued that a venal government could more easily put pressure upon the judges it appointed than upon a random jury of independent citizens who, given their practical common sense and knowledge of the world outside, were in any case better qualified to weigh the truthfulness of testimony affecting the conduct of the ordinary mankiller-in-the-street. But Lee objected that the English of Asian jurors was frequently unequal to the rigours of legal jargon, and that they were often confused or intimidated and over-reluctant to convict. He had his way, of course – and then invited David Marshall to become a member of the Presidential Council.

No one mentions words like 'nationalization' in polite society in Singapore today, and even 'equality' is on the way out. For Lee and his ministers are determined to place the destiny of the island in the hands of a politically pure élite with a pride and stake in the republic. In 1969 the Government opened its first Junior National College, a character-forming super-school that accepted 'loyal and dedicated' students chosen for their sense of social discipline, their initiative and physical fitness, as well as for their academic ability. These institutions – of which a second was to be inaugurated in 1974 – have the specific task of moulding the best of each generation into the bilingual all-round leaders Singapore needs. Some enter the civil service and the army, but many become key cadres in the nationwide youth movement. Their function is to keep the young fit and free from the sins that stretch from prurience to pink-think in a new, brash society nearly 60 per cent of whose citizens are under twenty-one. Socialist Singapore is creating its own indoctrinated aristocracy, but there is more than that to the subtle machinery that gears the government and the party to the masses.

The PAP has conventional party branches in all districts of the island, but these are far outnumbered by the 186 com-

munity centres of the 'People's Association', which ostensibly
has little to do with politics and is partly financed by the people
themselves. However, the overwhelming majority of the 1,000
full-time organizers of these centres are PAP members in regular if discreet contact with the local party branch. The main
business of the centres is to draw and hold the public within
a light and attractive web of welfare services. They organize
sports and gymnastics for the young, run some 600 courses
in everything from sewing to soldering, and had opened 400
kindergartens and crèches in outlying rural areas by 1969.
They provide cheap fertilizer for the farmer, arrange for the
free inoculations for his livestock. But every community centre
is also fitted with the square cyclopean eye of a television set,
the voice and view of the state-run broadcasting division which
comes under the political direction of the Ministry of Culture.

This exotic, liberty-gibbet synthesis of capitalism and socialism, authoritarianism and freedom, is the product of Lee's urge
to create a tightly-organized, dynamic and disciplined community in a diminutive cockleshell of a country that must
somehow ride the uncertain seas of the seventies. Almost inevitably, he is at his unhappiest with the students. He has
chastised them humiliatingly for 'lacking guts' when they
have stayed out of the political arena, yet arrested or banished
them if they have then entered the lists but ill-advisedly shown
their left hand in attacking his administration. Of the curious
social quagmire to the West, he has said bluntly : 'We cannot
and will not allow this permissive, escapist, drug-taking, self-
indulgent, promiscuous society to infect our young.'

The universities must be assets to the republic, he insists
angrily. Graduates must link their interests to those of Singapore. 'You mean the interests of *your* Singapore,' reply rebellious students, for every turn of the screw drives the iron
deeper into the soul, and they turn huffily to Law or Philosophy,
dreaming of post-graduate years in England and Australia where
they will not be cheek by jowl with this domineering, exasperated juggernaut of a man.

Lee's Singapore is a success story, nonetheless. If the republic's leaders are imaginative manipulators of the democratic

system, they are also energetic and uncorrupt, and they deliver the goods. By 1969 the small Singaporean seemed to be enjoying a prosperity and security he had never before known, on an island that was being transformed so fast that it was as if the cake of mud had miraculously come alive. By 1972 it was almost literally buoyant, for it was rising out of the tepid waters around it at the rate of an acre a day, thanks to a vigorous land reclamation programme. Its annual economic growth continued to top 10 per cent, and its cargo-handling port was by then believed to have displaced Yokohama as the third largest in the world. The Government disposed of foreign reserves and assets estimated to be worth a thousand million American dollars – $500 or £200 per head of population.

The symptoms of affluence were unmistakable. Rapid urban development would put four people out of five into modern flats before the end of the decade; with more than 160,000 private cars for two million people and 225 square miles of territory, the island had the shortest distance between two bumpers of any state in South-east Asia. Prawns cost 60p a pound in the fish market, and a semi-detached house £60,000 and more. Per capita income had passed the $1,000 mark. Singapore was officially a 'developed' country, and no longer a 'developing' one. Detractors complain not only that the PAP régime is undemocratic, but that it is opportunistic and 'has no ideological basis whatever'. This probably means that it will stand an excellent chance of survival in a world painfully stiff with political pedantry and prejudice. If Lee can show that he has achieved a miracle and not just a mirage, his 'rugged society' may be the working model for other modernizing Asian states in a world made safe for Adhocracy.

Dangerous Liaison

ACROSS developing South-east Asia tall shoots of concrete and glass thrust skyward like some alien crop, while new ribbons of road unfurl, smooth six-lane streamers laced with petrol stations and soft-drink cafés, shacks, shops and saloons. The neon signs flicker and multiply and the sparse, spiky hedges of television aerials thicken with the passing years. In Bangkok a great temple with golden spires takes on the dignified but defensive air of a dowager in a discothèque as the old city of canals is relentlessly rebuilt into a series of deep grooves for deafening traffic jams. Hongkong appears to sink beneath the weight of its new stone colossi, and in low-lying Singapore rain brings flash floods as the spreading cement encases more and more of the absorbent soil beneath.

Ah Fu, the old amah who cooked with a pair of chopsticks and a couple of blackened pots, disdaining to use even an egg-whisk, has been replaced by young Ah Yook whose small hands play with professional competence upon electric cooker, washing machine, refrigerator and deep freeze, waffle-iron and toaster and coffee percolator and floor-polisher, as if they were all related percussion instruments and she the star drummer doing her daily solo.

The accelerating tempo of a West agonizingly caught up in the breath-taking age of the blast-off is beginning to subject Asia also to the first incipient moral and material strains. The young Chinese flock out of the schools looking vainly for work worthy of their literacy, the Malays move from the *kampongs* to the big towns and the bright lights, and fall into feckless delinquency. But a new middle class pushes its way forward, greedy for gadgetry and gracious living, and in highly organized cities the worker is not far behind. Asia is taking its first steps down the dead-end to the junk-yard of accumulated wealth, possessions and prestige so well symbolized by the mountain-ranges of rusting, abandoned cars that characterize the land-scaping of the affluent age in America.

It follows that, as in the West, faith is in retreat. Fewer Muslims make the pilgrimage to Mecca from South Thailand (you can buy a second-hand car for the same money), and many young Malays cut mosque. 'How can we compete if we have to stop everything and pray five times a day?' one expostulated to me. Buddhists are also sidling slowly away from their earlier piety, neglecting the rites and slaughtering ancient images of the Lord Buddha, chopping off sacred heads and hands for sale to collectors and curio-dealers.

For the more the Asian learns to want scooters and stereo, sex and similar status symbols, the greater becomes his devotion to the dollar. And this inspires reverence for new gods of wealth like Tourism, whose manifestations as Creator, Preserver and Destroyer are today enslaving South-east Asia. The demand for a handy mock-world for the package-tour pilgrim is slowly but inexorably transforming the Far East into the Exotic Orient, since the fascinating if sometimes grisly reality is not good enough for him and he must be presented, rather, with a deodorized technicolor dream, all kimonos and Kleenex and Quaint Old Customs.

Change Alley, the long, narrow slip of a street market running down to the Singapore waterfront and choked with a mass of struggling humanity haggling over a few cents, was for long a raw, pungent slice of Asia. But in 1965 men put up illuminated arches at each end of it 'to give it an oriental atmosphere', as one well-meaning Chinese solemnly explained. Stallholders were asked to arrange their goods tidily, to be polite, to turn Change Alley into 'Change-Alley-World-Famous-Shopping-Centre', part of the modern mirage that could be purchased with a round-trip air-ticket and a sheaf of travellers' cheques. The island's ramshackle trishaws, pedalled by gaunt, mahogany-faced Chinese with calves like veined iron, ceased to be painful anachronisms due for the scrapheap and were re-classified as Genuine Tourist Attractions.

Singapore called itself 'Instant Asia' and began assembling all the marvels of the East in convenient clumps for the harassed holidaymaker. Not to be outdone, Malaysia started constructing a 200-acre Far East of its own with Chinese and Japanese gardens and traditional houses and kampongs and temples, with a sample rubber estate, rice farm, and tin mine, and an orchard full of all the fruit-trees of Malaysia, plus genuine jungle (no plastic), equatorial lake, waterfalls and many other extras, the whole to be served by monorail and cable car .

There are air-conditioned hotels in Hongkong so crammed with chinoiserie that by the time you have had a drink at the long bar designed like a red and gold dragon-boat, unloaded your cigarette ash into a fake Chou dynasty bronze sacrificial vessel as big as a beer barrel, eaten in a grill hung with Chinese paintings and silk lanterns and strolled through a disinfected foyer decorated to resemble the tomb of a Han Emperor, the Chinese town beyond the glass doors looks like the less inspiring end of Tottenham Court Road.

Not all prefer the palm-studded lobbies to the palm-studded beaches of the orient, however, and the energetic are being systematically relieved of their surplus on Bali, at Borobodur, and at the Great Temple of the Cao Dai in South Vietnam where even in wartime, Vietcong permitting, the priests were ready to switch on the lights, open up all doors, and advise the three-eyed invader not only about the best angles for his pictures but what exposures to use.

All over Asia, the pagoda is becoming a tourist trap, for festivals and faith can be big business. Hundreds of camera-shutters blink impersonally as the Hindu penitents of Singapore dance down the streets at Thaipusam, chest and back pincushioned by the fifty sharp needles of the metal arches of atonement they carry on their shoulders, and the event is listed in the local tourist guide. The canny globe-trotter who times his moves correctly may then snap the Christian penitents in Manila on Good Friday as they, in their turn, whip themselves through the city or are flogged by obliging friends until the blood flows.

Some Asians object, but others show much ingenuity in satisfying the morbid urges of the mob. Indonesia, justly famed for its many volcanic disasters, now has a 7,000-foot drive-in crater for the curious. In 1973 tribesmen in New Guinea offered to revert to cannibalism and eat a corpse selected from the nearest morgue as a special summer attraction. As early as 1960 Panmunjom in the demilitarized zone between North and South Korea, scene of permanent tension and sporadic violence, was taking nearly 20,000 visitors a year. When Sukarno dropped his crack paratroops into South Malaya during Confrontation, Australian trippers with box lunches were almost breathing down the back of my neck as I tried to reach the fighting. Now that the Vietnam war is officially over, however, properly organized package tours are available to those eager to soak up the atmosphere of the bloodiest battlefields in Southeast Asia. And then there is Quemoy.

A Chinese colonel leans over the dazzling concrete wall of the sty to poke a large and exceptionally ugly pig with his sunshade. 'A countryman of yours,' he murmurs to me slyly. 'He's come from England for cross-breeding with our local hogs.' The pig and I look at each other with the barely-concealed antipathy of fellow-Britons meeting abroad. He is used to strangers, however. Quemoy may be the Gibraltar of the East, an embattled, shell-raked Nationalist fortress in the mouth of the Communist mainland. But Quemoy in the sixties is also an island of Riviera-like beaches, golf courses and tennis courts, seven cinemas, five faintly girlie teahouses and five jive bands. There is a punctual bus service, and two private taxi companies run comfortable American cars.

Courteous officers conduct the visitor around the sights – the underground tunnels leading to the big coastal guns, the nearest point to the mainland, the ceremony of releasing gas-filled balloons carrying propaganda to the Communists across the way. Quemoy is famous for its excellent pork and its kaoliang wine, a small glass of which will burn brightly for five minutes if lighted instead of drunk, and bottles may be bought duty-free in the underground waiting room at the heavily-bunkered airport on departure. A black Dakota from Formosa, almost skimming the choppy sea to flummox the enemy radar, drops on to the airstrip, its windows blocked by steel shutters. It is the daily bus that will take you back to Taipei. And you are still not sure which is uppermost in your mind – the picture of the grim offshore bastion, or 'Come to Sunny Quemoy'.

One day I find that selected pretty girls are being paid to walk about in Singapore in cheongsams and sarongs and saris because, although there are thousands of other pretty girls walking about in cheongsams, sarongs and saris, they are doing it naturally and not as colour-slide models for tourists. In a Hongkong hotel I ask for the menu and a Chinese waitress offers me 'Ye Olde English Breakfast Piping Hot from the Skillet: Crispy Toast and Choice Marmalade, Two Fresh Country Eggs with Slice of Hickory-Smoked Ham, a Good Old Cup of Tea or Coffee, and Newly-Squeezed Orange Juice.' The whole world is nothing but illusion, say the Buddhists. If that is not already a fact, it may well turn out to be an accurate prophecy.

It might be thought that the last citadel of oriental culture must be the stomach. The Burmese use the phrase 'I grew up eating rice' to mean 'I wasn't born yesterday', for rice is the basis of all the delicate, subtle or brutally hot cuisines that overlap across a continent in which a cook is still prepared to spend an afternoon crushing chillies in a stone mortar or subjecting a duck to the full treatment for females – to be massaged and bathed, perfumed and dressed, and stuffed and finally served. The Chinese can prepare anything delectably from bird's nest to fish lips, the Laos like chicken stuffed with peanuts and cooked in coconut milk, ant's eggs, and placenta from the mother-cow, the Thais work wonders with red-hot peppers and lemon-grass, the Burmese make cocktail crisps out of deep-fried buffalo-skin. The poorer Vietnamese survives on rice and *nuoc mam*, a vivid sauce made by packing salted fish in a jar and leaving them to rot, and the Korean loves *kimchi*, three-month-buried pickled vegetables which can give him a breath that takes everyone else's away.

A six-month-long publicity campaign in Singapore to persuade families to change from rice to cheaper wheat in 1968 converted less than one in fifty, and even these turncoats only ate bread for breakfast or tea. But this stubborn defence of rice is essentially a rearguard action. Switch on the television and Ironside with Malay subtitles is interrupted by clattering Cantonese voices urging hitherto happy islanders to buy American fruit juice and British baby foods, bottled essence of chicken and extracts of beef, deep-frozen fish fingers and tinned Scotch broth. Children brimming with blackcurrant juice are shown diving into sparkling pools, tired husbands sip their reconstituted mushroom soup and assume slow, lecherous smiles.

The Asian audience is unsuitably impressed, and eating habits begin to alter. The supermarkets of Singapore, originally opened for white men raised on bottles and cans, paper packets and similar unrewarding fodder, are full of eager yellow and brown faces and hands. As the edibility gap closes, peoples who thought that one of the most sinister aspects of the westerner was the way he went on drinking milk long after he should have been weaned now have cream and butter in their own refrigerators at home.

Japan, farthest of all to the East, leads the way towards the West in all things. Japanese are forgetting tea and taking to coffee, and there are about 100,000 coffee-houses today in their narrow islands. They are also less faithful to rice and taking to noodles and meat and milk and even cheese – by early 1969 more than 500 rice-dealers in Tokyo alone had put up their shutters. The Japanese are importing mutton and lamb and beef, for they are consuming ten times as much meat a head as they did in 1930, and their own magnificent ale-fed herds could no longer meet domestic demand even when the price of eight ounces of home-grown sirloin rose to £4 in 1972. But in order to eat gross western foods it is necessary to use gross western methods, and among the white-collar workers of Tokyo chopsticks are going out, and the knife and fork are coming in. *O tempura, o mores!*

Not only the food of the screwtop civilization, but its science and sport, its dress, and its culture are increasingly tempting eastern appetites. The West is building its biggest empire after the colonial era has slipped into history. In 1968 a Malaysian minister suggested that television had helped to reduce the birth-rate for it had given the masses something else to think about after dark. But more often than not, what it gave them to think about in between commercials would be Perry Mason and the Wild West, the problems of Peyton Place and the FBI, the vicissitudes of the Avengers and Coronation Street.

In South-east Asia the arts are drawn from rich and varied cultures, for Islam and India and China are all foster-fathers of the subcontinent. Like early Celts and Saxons, the ancient Buddhists carved geometrical designs rather than the living form, and built their holy shrines of stone but their homes of wood. From these beginnings came the magnificence of Angkor and Borobodur, intricately wrought giants that dwarf the temples of the West. And out of the past flowed the liquid music of the gong and *gamelan* – 'the sound very strange, but pleasant and delightful', noted Sir Francis Drake – the statuesque dances of Bali and Thailand and Cambodia, the love-courts of Laos and Malaya at which girl and boy nimbly toss impromptu verse to and fro.

But in Laos there is no literature of note, in Thailand intellectual life is at low ebb, and a Malay remarks sadly but truly that almost everything written about Asia has been the work of people who were not Asians. This constitutes a puny barrier against the onslaught of an industrialized, mass-producing occident that can pour out culture as easily as it pours out cars. The graceful, touchless dancing accompanied by antique songs that was common to most countries of the region has today been adulterated with soul music, miniskirts and the mini-thoughts of modern lyrics. The cinema heavily influences the traditional Indonesian shadow play, breaking down its classical philosophy into the trite idiom of western romance and violence. And the choice of films is narrow. Spreading out the entertainment page of a Singapore newspaper a few years ago, I found the following fare: 'The Devil's Brigade', 'The Brain Stealers', 'Killers Five', 'Coffin for a Gunfighter' and 'The Tramplers'.

Western rape or eastern urge? It is always difficult to place the responsibility for seduction. Chinese boxing and sword-fighting films have since become so popular outside Asia that

in March 1973 Hongkong studios were planning to link up with
European and American companies in order to be able to make
them all over the world. But then they are the only authentic
eastern westerns. As the more striking manifestations of modern
occidental culture from muckbooks to beatlecuts first streamed
into the area, governments nonetheless hit back. Singapore
banned the juke box, Korea the pin-table. In Indonesia rock 'n
roll records and tapes were burned, youngsters were arrested
for wearing winkle-pickers and bandleaders for playing Beatle-
music, while troops armed with scissors chopped off overlong
hair and slashed overstretched jeans. By 1973 South Koreans
could be jailed for wearing hot-pants or secretly teaching dancing, while in Thailand women could be detained for wearing
backless dresses and men for not wearing shirts.

Indonesia was perhaps the only country in the world in
which the tight skirt was elaborately defined – in terms which
reflected rather curiously on the customs and pastimes of Indonesian women. The elders of Makassar ruled that it was a skirt
in which the lady could not run when chased by a dog, could
not pick up a fallen handkerchief, could not step into a jeep
without help, and could not have a beerbottle placed between
her knees. Miniskirts were frowned on in both Bangkok and
Djakarta. Formosa, Indonesia, and Laos all cracked down on
the flower people, native or imported, and Thailand banned
hippies from the country until they shaved off their beards and
cut their hair. The way-out was on the way out from the start.

However, the West was also giving of its best, and the undiscriminating Asian housewife who today opens a can of
stew instead of cooking her own curry is paralleled by the discriminating Asian intellectual who opens a can of Scriabin
rather than make his own music. And he is matched in turn
by the man who would rather deal in a modern international
language than his own inadequate mother-tongue. In consequence, one of the greatest imperialists of the post-colonial
era has been English.

Nearly 100 years ago King Mongkut of Siam hired a certain Mrs Leonowens (thereafter to be known as Anna) in a
letter which ran :

We wish the School Mastress to be with us in this place or nearest vicinity hereof to save us from trouble of conveying such the lady to and fro almost every day also it is not pleasant to us if the School Mastress much morely endeavour to convert the scholars to Christianity than teaching language and literature etc. etc. like American Missionaries here because our proposed expense is for knowledge of the important language and literature which will be useful for affairs of country not for the religion which is yet disbelieved by Siamese scholars in general sense.

The King's reservations expressed with the eccentric elegance of a smooth linguistic skid the feelings of generations of orientals to come who wanted English to be a simple harmless tool, not the sharp end of an insidious alien culture. But it advanced steadily in spite of all opposition from local postwar chauvinists imbued with new-found national pride, and by 1969 seven countries had set up a regional language centre in Singapore to improve the teaching of English as a second (or first foreign) tongue in nearly all the states of the subcontinent.

It could be argued that the centre met a long-felt want. In 1960 Air Vietnam advertised itself as 'The Most Experimental Airline in the East' (the French for 'experienced' being, rather unfairly, '*experimenté*'), and when the former President of South Korea visited Saigon a felicitous banner read 'Welcome Syngman Rhee, Fighter of Freedom'. Even more subtly, a Singapore telegraph clerk made me pay extra for a quick query to the *Observer* which began 'Canst cable soonest weekend requirements ...' despite all my expostulations. ' "Canst" is two words,' he declared firmly, 'and so is "soonest".'

It remains to be seen who laughs last. The invader who strikes boldly across strange territory inevitably risks being cut off and mauled piecemeal, and English, like Latin before it, has been no exception. The impeccable thin red line of language was first broken by *pidgin*, the speech of nineteenth-century Chinese who somehow found it easier to understand 'Makee fire here chopchop number one' than 'Make a good fire here quickly'. The Chinese have abandoned this extreme case of spastic syntax as hopeless, but it survives nonetheless, and is the talk of New Guinea.

A copy before me of the newspaper *Nu Gini Tok Tok* announces 'Nu Ailan Transport Sasaiti Ltd istap long Kavieng i-bin baiim wanpela sip i-kosim ol olsem $140,000, kamap pinis long Pot Mosbi long las wik.' My guess is: 'New Island Transport Society Ltd at Kavieng been buy-him one-fellow ship cost-him all all-same $140,000, come-up finish along Port Moresby along last week.' *Nu Gini Tok Tok*, which sold 'Fo Tausan kopi' and 'i-kos 5 sen tasol' (that's-all), also carried an item about tinned 'pusikat bilong Australia' (which happily turns out to be Neomelanesian for rabbit). It is to be noted that the Asians played their variations on the English tongue back on the white man, who found himself gabbling in turn about 'Catchee one piecey manee' or writing 'Sekretari-Jeneral U Thant bilong Yunaited Nesin'.

The Japanese are masters at swallowing English and regurgitating it as a poor thing but their own. Consider the unlikely man in a suit and overcoat drinking a cocktail while watching a sex film on television in his hotel at Christmas. He becomes an even more unlikely man in a Saburo (Savile Row= suit) and Oba drinking a Kakateru and watching an Ero on Terebi in his Hoteru at Kerisumasu. And what of the Japlish for cross-eyed – 'Lonpali' (one eye on London, the other on Paris)? Some Asians are beginning to ask why they should speak English this way or that. What is English, anyway? There is English English and American English and Australian English – in 1973 the University of New South Wales ran a four-week course for foreign students in Australian colloquial obscenities. Why not Malaysian English, and even more pronounced mutants like Vietlish, Thailish, Angloporean?

However, most not only want to learn conventional English, but may bring a fresh, tropical taste to a tongue jaded with stale jargon. In a Burmese newspaper an indignant letter-writer described an accident in 1959 like this: 'Then, bang, one car coming to city hit the poor woman with mudguard and the woman fell spinning in the middle of the road. We stop, but the other dirty dog he's only small red light fading into distance. The woman make no sound and no more.' With a mistake in every line, it compares well with an example of contemporary English literature that was received on the same day from a local European publicity writer: 'Hi folks. This is B.H. and with a big new piece of news. Under the aegis of the old scribe now comes that fabulous territory, the Federation of Malaya ...' Ten years later an American told me seedily that there were 'all kindsa things we haven't got which I don't know why'. This somehow seemed to sanction Ping's sprightlier references to dieting: 'You are not allowed to lose more than too much,' and to bad laundering: 'Why the people wash the shirt so dirty?' And to libraries: 'Rows and rows of books up to the floor.'

Who, in fact, is doing what and to whom? One hundred years ago the Duke of Beaufort played a novel game that derived its name from his seat in Gloucestershire – Badminton. Today the world champions are drawn with almost monotonous regularity from Indonesia. The Chinese are the acknowledged masters of ping-pong, and the Japanese swarm over the golf courses of the entire world. On the other hand great was the consternation in Tokyo when a Dutchman won the international judo championship in 1961 and the French won the world karate tournament twelve years later. Singapore painters show the influence of European techniques and European clichés. Beethoven becomes the uncrowned king of music in Japan. But on their side the British experiment with the Japanese Susuki system for teaching the violin, Australian companies engage Japanese and Chinese singers for the operas of Puccini and Poulenc and a Japanese is commissioned to produce the designs for a production of *King Lear*. White audiences acclaim Chinese pianists and Chinese conductors devoted entirely to serious western compositions, while in England records of Indian classical music sell like hot discs. The East opens a can of stew but the West crowds into thousands of Chinese restaurants to eat the chop suey that is its oriental equivalent, and if the Asian earnestly dismembers English, the Anglo-Saxon has taken to butchering Chinese.

Yet the young are not just cultural transvestites, borrowing each other's clothing and parading in their oriental or occidental drag. For there is the beginning of a new and deeper understanding that like all else the *yin* and *yang* of East and West are part of the universal Oneness. The impoverished little materialist from the spiritual East turns eagerly to the West for the good things of life. The heavily beaded and bearded and besandalled Buddhist from the suffocatingly affluent society of the West turns to the East for the good things of death. But the young West also learns slowly that the Orient can be practical as well as pious, and the young East learns that the Occident has not only riches, but values.

The youthful Asian wants freedom, perhaps an Asian democracy like his Asian English. He is being drawn into the rat-race away from his traditional philosophy that problems are hydra-headed, and since to dispose of one is simply to create two others it may be better to do nothing. This is a triumph for the West. But the Asian is not the only one learning and adapting. When I flew into South-east Asia nineteen years ago, the Americans were just taking their first confident steps into the quagmire of Vietnam, and the British in Singapore were debating just how they could rid themselves without revolution of a turbulent left-wing menace elected to the Legislative Assembly called Lee Kuan Yew. Ngo Dinh Diem faced Ho Chi Minh across the Seventeenth Parallel in Indochina, Sukarno strutted in Djakarta, Syngman Rhee dictated in Seoul, Dulles dictated in Washington, and power came out of the barrels of guns pointed in all directions simultaneously.

A generation, fortunately, is an elusive, transitory affair, and the elder statesmen of the era are on the edge of eternity, if they have not already disappeared into the silence. In East and West the demagogues of yesteryear are deadweight today, the times call for bureaucrats more than barricades, and 'hero' is in danger of joining all the other four-letter words. Despite setbacks, freedom has been scoring points, if below the line. It is 1973. The Filipinos are under martial law, and in South Korea President Park is not unduly disturbed by the failure of his party to win a clear majority at the recent polls, for under the new constitution he has imposed on his country only two thirds of the 219 members of the National Assembly are elected – he nominates the other seventy-three himself. But

Malaysia has reverted to parliamentary democracy after the shock of the 1969 riots, popular government will replace rule by Revolutionary Council in Burma by March 1974, Thailand is to have a new constitution, and in Indonesia the dominant 'Golkar' group is being gradually transformed from an instrument of the Government and the generals into something more like a plain-clothes political party. We have, moreover, witnessed the twilight of the god-kings.

Whether the East will go Communist, or fall among despots, or work its own elaborate variation on the simple one-finger-one-note theme of democracy will depend on many things – above all, perhaps, on the yawning sociological gap between the highrise, Hiltonizing cities and the hungry villages. In South-east Asia Bangkok may begin to look like Broadway, but many a Muslim in South-west Thailand still lives in primitive squalor and earns no more than £60 a year. In consequence, as one Asian minister told the United Nations in September 1973, 'Third World cities are becoming refugee camps for the rural poor'.

Even modern Japan's gimcrack structure is like a sad skit on the century, for it suffers simultaneously from a ridiculous glut of gadgetry and a lamentable shortage of elementary plumbing (in 1969 only nine homes in a hundred had a flush toilet, against ninety-eight in Britain and thirty-seven even in France). In the early seventies about forty major Japanese cities were being progressively poisoned by a thickening pall of pollution and recurrent smog that in Tokyo alone could take 10,000 victims to hospital with eye, skin and chest troubles in a single month.

Successful disciples of the material-minded occident, the Japanese should in theory have been delirious with joy, nonetheless. Their gross national product was the third highest in the world. In the towns, most families had a refrigerator, a washing machine, and a television set, and there were 16,000,000 cars on the road. But in 1972 a new index that itemized not only housing, cars, food and medical care, but pollution, prices and other social evils, disclosed that the Japanese were in fact twice as miserable as most of their Anglo-Saxon fellow-

sufferers in the West. Suicide was popular, neuroses and im-
potence were on the increase, and the high pitch of nervous
frustration evoked by the insane jumble of competitive man
with his competitive dirt and his competitive toys was almost
audible.

Not surprisingly, a watchful South-east Asia is edgy about
the white from the wicked West whose baggage can be equally
dangerous, whether it contains spiritual decadence or dollars.
Even investment is suspect, for many fear a neo-colonial take-
over – economic, cultural, perhaps political – by the same
people who have made a miserable mess of Indochina, built up
multinational corporations that could buy and sell the economies of many small states in this region before breakfast, and
developed in the hippy cult a psychosomatic ulcer that betrays
their own sick condition.

Nonetheless, the destiny of the whole world may depend
upon the greater understanding that must grow between its
two halves. In this context the flirting and prying and filching
and cannibalizing that make up the latest, slightly obscene
chapter in the long, brutal story of interplay between East
and West must be welcomed. It may be the prelude to a
respectable and responsible relationship. For the most dangerous liaisons of the past often lead to the safest marriages of
the future.

Synopsis of Events

Definitions

Kachins, Karens, Shans – minority peoples of non-Burman stock, mainly living in the mountainous north.

The Events

January 1948 – Burma becomes an independent, sovereign state following postwar negotiations with British. U Nu is the first Prime Minister. The Constitution provides for autonomous Shan, Kachin and (subject to referendum) Karen states with their own local government and own civil service.

1948–51 – There are Communist – and Muslim – uprisings, followed by an insurrection of the Karen minority.

October 1958 – General Ne Win, Army Chief of Staff, compels U Nu to relinquish power and establishes rule by military junta.

1959–61 – Active Shan rebels increase from 800 to 3,000. Karens and Kachins are also still in revolt.

February 1960 – General elections: General Ne Win steps down, U Nu becomes premier again.

October 1960 – The Sino-Burmese frontier agreement and Treaty of Friendship are signed.

January 1961 – Premier Chou En-lai of China visits Burma, and offers a £30,000,000 credit.

1961 – Buddhism is made the State Religion.

March 1962 – Ne Win seizes power by coup d'état and sets up a military government under a 'Revolutionary Council' with himself as Chairman. U Nu and other political leaders are arrested.

1963 – The Burma Socialist Programme Party is formed to implement Ne Win's 'Burmese Way to Socialism', which includes progressive nationalization of all capitalist enterprises and eradication of foreign investment and economic power.

All rebel groups are invited to negotiate a peace, but the Shans demand a federal state with the right of secession, the Kachins want to leave the Union of Burma, and talks break down in November.

Mid-1967 – Provocative acts of local Chinese 'Red Guards' in Rangoon lead to anti-Chinese rioting. Peking attacks Ne Win's 'Fascist régime'.

1968 – 40 per cent of Burma is troubled by armed insurgency. Ne Win releases U Nu and other political leaders and asks thirty-three of them to advise him on a new constitution.

1969 – Ne Win rejects the suggestions of these political leaders for a return to a multi-party system. U Nu goes abroad and declares that the Ne Win régime will be overthrown, by force if necessary.

November 1969 – Ne Win reveals 500 men have been killed in major clashes between the Burmese army and rebels in the north near the China border.

Ne Win announces his decision to transform his Burma Socialist Programme Party (BSPP) into a popular mass organization.

1970 – U Nu is reported to have entered into an anti-Ne Win alliance with Mon and Karen minority rebels, and to have set up his headquarters inside Burma. Diplomatic relations between Burma and China are restored after a break of thirty-one months.

May 1971 – Rangoon reveals that a 350-strong 'patriotic army' loyal to U Nu has been operating in South Burma since February. In general, insurgency throughout the Union is weakening, however, and the Burmese army dislodges a main force of 1,500 Communist rebels near the Chinese border, killing 500.

July 1973 – U Nu refuses to promise the minorities autonomy in exchange for their help in overthrowing Ne Win by force, and says that he will withdraw into exile in the United States.

October 1973 – Ne Win announces a twenty-year economic plan, and the drafting of a new constitution. The constitution will be submitted to a public referendum, general elections to a National Assembly will then be held, and Burma will have a democratic government by March 1974.

INDOCHINA

French Indochina consisted of the three regions of Vietnam known as Tonking, Annam and Cochinchina, and the kingdoms of Cambodia and Laos :

CAMBODIA

Definitions

Cambodia – successor of the earlier Khmer Kingdoms of Chen-la (sixth to ninth century) and Angkor or Kambuja (ninth to fifteenth century).

Khmer – the Cambodian people, their language, etc.

The Events

1941 – Prince Norodom Sihanouk becomes King of Cambodia.

November 1953 – Cambodia becomes independent of the French.

March 1955 – Sihanouk abdicates in favour of his father and becomes Prime Minister. He creates the Sangkum Reastr Niyum (Popular Socialist Community).

May 1955 – Cambodia enters into a military aid agreement with the United States.

September 1955 – The Sangkum wins all seats in the National Assembly in general elections. Sihanouk announces a policy of neutralism.

March 1956 – Sihanouk's father, Norodom Suramarit, is crowned King.

July 1957 – Cambodia recognizes Communist China.

April 1960 – King Suramarit dies. There is no successor. Sihanouk is Head of State.

November 1963 – Sihanouk announces rejection of all further American economic and military aid.

1965 – Sihanouk breaks off diplomatic relations with the United States.

September 1966 – General elections are held, with candidates from the Sangkum only.

April 1967 – Khmers Rouges (Cambodian Communist guerrillas) launch armed attacks in Battambang province. As Maoist subversive activity intensifies, Sihanouk turns on Peking and threatens to recall the Cambodian ambassador. Premier Chou En-lai smoothes matters over with a reassuring response.

1968–9 – The Khmer Rouge threat to Cambodia increases, and Sihanouk also estimates that up to 40,000 Vietcong have violated his frontiers.

Sihanouk re-establishes diplomatic relations with the US. He is nevertheless the only non-Communist leader to attend the funeral of President Ho Chi Minh in Hanoi in September 1969.

March–May 1970 – Sihanouk is deposed by rightists during his absence in France. Cheng Heng becomes head of state, Lon Nol remains prime minister. Sihanouk sets up a 'Royal Government of National Union' in exile in Peking under the aegis of the Chinese, and in collaboration with Khmer Rouge leaders. American and South Vietnamese forces cross into Cambodia from South Vietnam to destroy North Vietnamese sanctuaries on Cambodian soil.

April 1970 – Sihanouk calls a summit conference of Indochinese leaders to establish a common front. Prince Souphannouvong of Laos, Pham Van Dong of North Vietnam, and Nguyen Huu Tho of the Vietcong attend, and Chou En-lai hosts a banquet for them.

July–October 1970 – The Cambodian Government declares martial law and condemns Sihanouk to death in absentia. The National Assembly votes in favour of replacing the monarchy with a republic.

1971 – The insurgents of Sihanouk and the Khmers Rouges set up numerous training camps inside Cambodia and organize political support in the villages. The Government in Phnom Penh controls no more than 30 per cent of the country.

October 1971 – Lon Nol dissolves the Senate and the National Assembly.

March–July 1972 – Cheng Heng relinquishes power to Lon Nol, who wins the first Cambodian presidential election and proclaims himself first president of the new Republic.

September–October 1972 – The first general elections since 1966 are held, the Lower House is opened, and Lon Nol also swears in the first Cambodian Senate.

August–September 1973 – American bombing of insurgent targets, running at fifty B-52 strikes a day, is halted. The insurgents are estimated to number 50,000, but Sihanouk says they cannot take Phnom Penh as the Chinese and North Vietnamese are no longer giving them aid.

LAOS

Definitions

Lao – the dominant race in Laos, their language, etc. Plural: Laos.
Laos – the country. Adjective: Laotian.
Pathet Lao ('The Lao State') – the Communist-directed guerrilla movement under Prince Souphannouvong.

The Events

July 1949–50 – The French accord partial sovereignty to Laos. Of the

leaders of the Laotian independence movement, Prince Souvanna Phouma therefore accepts a ministry in Vientiane, but Prince Souphannouvong forms the Pathet Lao with the help of the Vietminh and takes up arms against the Royal Government and the French.

1953 – Laos becomes independent.

July 1954–1957 – The Geneva Agreement ends the Indochina War. Souvanna Phouma becomes Prime Minister and forms a Government of National Union with Pathet Lao participation in Vientiane.

1958 – The Pathet Lao score heavily in supplementary elections. Alarmed, the Laotian right wing force Souvanna Phouma to resign. A new Government is formed without Pathet Lao ministers.

1959 – Vientiane announces Communist North Vietnamese troops are moving into Laos. The new right-wing Prime Minister is given 'special powers' to deal with the Communist threat. The Laotian Government asks United States to provide military technicians to train the army. Souphannouvong and other Pathet Lao leaders are arrested.

January–June 1960 – Rigged general elections. The right wing scores a heavy victory and all Pathet Lao candidates are defeated. A new Government is formed with General Phoumi Nosavan as Minister for Defence. Prince Souphannouvong and other arrested Pathet Lao leaders escape and rejoin their guerrillas upcountry.

August 1960 – The neutralist paratroop Captain Kong Le seizes Vientiane by coup d'état, Souvanna Phouma becomes Prime Minister, announces that he will negotiate with the Pathet Lao again and asks for Soviet aid.

December 1960 – Right-wing troops of General Phoumi throw Kong Le out of Vientiane. Boun Oum becomes new Prime Minister, with General Phoumi as Defence Minister and the real 'strong man'.

March 1961 – Souvanna Phouma, still recognized as Prime Minister by Communist powers and supported by Soviet airlifts, sets up headquarters with the neutralists of Kong Le and the Pathet Lao under Prince Souphannouvong at Khang Khay on the Plain of Jars.

1961–2 – A second Geneva Conference is held, and guarantees the neutrality of Laos. Boun Oum, Souvanna Phouma and Souphannouvong agree to form a provisional government of national union. Souphannouvong and Phoumi Nosavan are vice-premiers under Souvanna Phouma, holding Finance and Economy portfolios respectively.

1962–4 – There is no true reconciliation. Fighting resumes. Souphannouvong leaves Vientiane and returns to his headquarters on the Plain of Jars, and later withdraws the remaining Pathet Lao ministers from Vientiane.

January 1965 – Abortive right-wing coup in Vientiane. General Phoumi flees to Thailand.

January 1967 – General elections are held without the Pathet Lao, and a new Souvanna Phouma Cabinet takes office in Vientiane without Pathet Lao participation.

1968–9 – Intensified military action between the Royal Lao Army and the combination of Pathet Lao and North Vietnamese troops in Laos, who are now estimated to number 40–50,000. Heavy American bombing helps Government forces to recapture much of the Plain of Jars. The Communists nevertheless dominate most of the territory.

February–April 1970 – Pathet Lao and North Vietnamese forces over-run the Plain of Jars, advance beyond the 1962 cease-fire line for the first time, and take Attopeu in Southern Laos. Increased American bombing inhibits tentative peace talks. Refugees now total 700,000 – about one Laotian in four.

February 1971 – South Vietnamese troops cross into Laos in order to attack the Ho Chi Minh trail. Thai volunteers are already fight-ing with the Royal Laotian army.

May 1971 – North Vietnamese forces in Laos overrun the Bolovens Plateau in the south.

July 1971 – In a major military shake-up, General Oudone Sananikone ceases to be Chief of Staff and is appointed Director-General of National Defence.

August 1973 – Former air force general Thao Ma mounts an abortive right-wing coup d'état.

September 1973 – The Royal Government and the Pathet Lao sign a peace accord in Vientiane, and agree to form a joint government.

VIETNAM

Definitions

Annam – the central region of Vietnam, the former centre of the Empire.

Tonking – the northern region of Vietnam, now Communist.

Vietcong and Vietminh – apart from their precise meanings ('Viet-namese Communist' and 'League for the Independence of Viet-nam' respectively), these terms have been used loosely for the Communist-led Vietnamese insurgents. The 'Vietminh' fought the French; the 'Vietcong' the Americans.

The Events

1946–54 – The Indochina War. The Vietminh defeat the French at Dien Bien Phu in May 1954.

June 1954 – Ngo Dinh Diem becomes the Prime Minister of Vietnam with the reluctant consent of the Emperor Bao Dai.

July 1954 – The Geneva Agreement divides Vietnam into North and South zones at the 17th Parallel, pending joint general elections in 1956 and reunification.

November 1954 – The Vietminh take over Hanoi from the French. The North becomes the 'Democratic Republic of Vietnam' under President Ho Chi Minh.

March–May 1955 – A Sect rebellion under the leadership of the Binh Xuyen is mounted against the Diem régime in Saigon. Diem crushes it. The Emperor makes an abortive attempt to appoint General Nguyen Van Vy as Commander-in-Chief and to remove Diem.

October 1955 – Diem organizes a referendum and South Vietnam becomes an independent republic with himself as President; the Emperor is deposed. The Americans start reorganizing the South Vietnamese army.

1956 – South Vietnam refuses to hold joint general elections with North Vietnam in order to unify the two halves of the country.

1959–60 – The first major acts of terrorism are committed by the Vietcong. 'Agrovilles' are created to protect the peasants from the guerrillas (they will be followed by 'Strategic Hamlets' and 'New Life Hamlets' as the struggle intensifies).

November 1960 – An abortive military coup is organized against Diem.

January 1961 – Hanoi Radio announces the formation of the 'National Liberation Front' in South Vietnam.

February 1962 – The US Military Aid Command is set up in South Vietnam. Rebel Vietnamese Air Force pilots bomb Diem's palace in Saigon as the first move in a second abortive coup against him.

May–August 1963 – Buddhist demonstrations in Hue are brutally suppressed by the Diem régime. More demonstrations follow. The first Buddhist monk publicly burns himself to death in Saigon. The Government carries out numerous arrests of Buddhist monks and students. Tension mounts.

November 1963 – Army generals organize a successful coup d'état. Diem and his brother, Ngo Dinh Nhu, are assassinated. General Duong Van Minh ('Big Minh') heads the country as the leader of a new 'Military Revolutionary Council'.

January 1964 – Major-General Nguyen Khanh seizes power.

August 1964 – North Vietnamese torpedo boats attack American destroyers. The Americans bomb North Vietnamese naval bases. Khanh attempts to make himself President of South Vietnam, but is discouraged by Buddhist and student riots.

October–November 1964 – Mr Tran Van Huong forms a new government. Khanh remains Commander-in-Chief.

The Vietcong attack Bien Hoa air base, twelve miles from Saigon.

December 1964 – Khanh acquires the real power again at the head of an 'Armed Forces Command'.

February 1965 – The repercussions of a coup against Khanh mounted by Colonel Pham Ngoc Thao force him to resign as Commander-in-Chief and to leave the country. The Americans begin regular bombing of North Vietnam.

June 1965 – The military take over again from the civilians. Air Marshal Nguyen Cao Ky becomes Prime Minister. Major-General Nguyen Van Thieu becomes Chief of State at the head of a 'Council for the Leadership of the Nation'.

July 1965 – There are now 75,000 American troops in South Vietnam. Colonel Thao is caught and shot on government orders.

September 1967 – Thieu and Ky are returned as President and Vice-President in general elections.

February 1968 – The Vietcong launch a major 'Tet Offensive' at Vietnamese New Year against fifty-four towns of South Vietnam.

May 1968 – The Americans open negotiations with the North Vietnamese in Paris.

Tran Van Huong becomes Prime Minister of South Vietnam for the second time.

November 1968 – The Americans stop bombing North Vietnam.

February 1969 – There are 543,054 American troops in South Vietnam.

June 1969 – The Americans start to withdraw their troops.

August–September 1969 – Huong is replaced as Prime Minister of South Vietnam by General Tran Thien Khiem.

President Ho Chi Minh of North Vietnam dies. He is succeeded by a collective leadership headed by Le Duan, pragmatic party chief, and Truong Chinh, sectarian Chairman of the National Assembly.

April–June 1971 – North Vietnam holds elections to the National Assembly for the first time for seven years, and the Assembly confirms the appointment of Ton Duc Thang as head of state in succession to Ho Chi Minh.

July–October 1971 – In South Vietnam, Air Marshal Nguyen Cao Ky breaks with Nguyen Van Thieu, who is elected President for a second term unopposed with Tran Van Huong as Vice-President.

March–April 1972 – The Americans resume the bombing of North

June–September 1966 – Confrontation is ended by signed agreement. Indonesia rejoins the UN.

February–March 1967 – Suharto officially becomes Acting President.

August 1969 – After consulting only 1,000 appointed representatives, the Indonesians announce that West Irian has opted for permanent incorporation in the republic.

October 1969 – The army is reorganized into six territorial defence commands. Authority is concentrated at the top and at the centre, and the powers of regional commanders are severely curtailed.

June 1970 – Ex-President Sukarno dies.

July 1971 – The first general elections held since 1956 are won by the government-backed Sekber Golkar (organization of functional groups). There are 360 elected seats in parliament, and 100 nominated seats, of which seventy-five are reserved for the armed forces.

August 1971 – President Suharto announces a twenty-five-year programme for economic development. During this year the Government is partly 'demilitarized', and only five out of twenty-four ministers are now soldiers. Nearly 50,000 suspects arrested after the abortive left-wing coup in 1965 are still detained.

October 1972 – Suharto installs a new, elected People's Consultative Assembly of 920 members.

March–April 1973 – In a major military reshuffle, revolutionary generals of the older generation are relieved of key commands, and centralized control of the command structure further strengthened.

August 1973 – One Chinese is killed and scores are injured by anti-Chinese rioters in Bandung, who do damage estimated at one million pounds.

September 1973 – Golkar holds its first national congress, and initial moves are made towards converting it from an instrument of the army and government into a political party. The number of soldiers on the board is reduced from seven to five.

MALAYSIA

Definitions

Dyaks – natives of Borneo, divisible into Land Dyaks and Sea Dyaks or Ibans (who are in reality upriver people).

Malay – the dominant race in the Malayan Peninsula and Indonesia, their language, etc.

Malaya – the Malayan Peninsula whose eleven states formed the independent Federation of Malaya from 1957 to 1963. Adjective: Malayan.

Malaysia – the wider Federation created in 1963, taking in not only Malaya, but Singapore and the North Borneo states of Sarawak and Sabah. Adjective: Malaysian.

The Events

September 1945 – The British return to Malaya following the Japanese surrender.

June 1948 – Communist terrorists murder three British planters, and a State of Emergency is declared. The campaign against guerrillas of the Malayan Communist Party (MCP) continues until 1960.

1955 – The Alliance Party of Tengku Abdul Rahman wins all but one of fifty-two elected seats in parliament under a new constitution.

August 1957 – The 'Federation of Malaya' becomes an independent, sovereign state. The Tengku is Prime Minister.

1960 – The Emergency is declared over. The remnants of the MCP terrorists are now hiding on the Thai side of the Thai–Malaysian frontier.

1961–2 – The British intend to liquidate their colonial dependencies in North Borneo (Sarawak and – as it is to be called – Sabah), and discuss with Tengku Abdul Rahman the possibility of his incorporating them with Singapore into a larger 'Federation of Malaysia'.

Mid-1962 – President Macapagal of the Philippines lays claim to Sabah.

1962–August 1963 – UN delegations satisfy themselves on the ground that the peoples of the North Borneo dependencies think their best course is to join the proposed 'Federation of Malaysia'. Pro-Malaysia parties are returned in local elections in both territories.

Mid-September 1963 – The Federation of Malaysia comes into being. The Philippines and Indonesia withhold recognition, and Indonesia launches economic and military 'Confrontation' against Malaysia as a 'neocolonialist' invention.

April 1964 – General elections: the Alliance wins eighty-nine out of 104 seats.

August 1965 – Deteriorating relations lead to the expulsion of Singapore from Malaysia.

June 1966 – Confrontation is ended by a signed agreement between Indonesia and Malaysia. But Communist terrorists are again active on the Thai–Malaysian border.

August 1967 – Malay becomes the sole official language.

1968 – Malaysia learns that Filipinos have been undergoing training on Corregidor Island for terrorist operations in Sabah.

Manila enacts a law to include Sabah constitutionally in the Philippines. Malaysia suspends diplomatic relations.

May 1969 – The Alliance suffers a severe setback in general elections. Fierce race-riots between Malays and non-Malays follow, a State of Emergency is declared, Parliament is suspended, and a National Operations Council takes over control under Deputy Premier Tun Abdul Razak.

December 1969 – Malaysia and the Philippines agree to resume diplomatic relations.

March 1970 – Malaysia and Thailand allow each other's armed forces 'right of pursuit' across their common frontier when hunting down Communist terrorists.

April–June 1970 – Five-power Commonwealth defence exercises are held. Britain demonstrates her capacity to fly forces from Europe to Malaysia in an emergency.

June–July 1970 – Postponed elections are finally held in Sarawak and Sabah, giving the Alliance a total of ninety-three seats out of 141 in the Federal Parliament.

July–September 1970 – The Sedition Act is amended to include any questioning of the special position of the Malays, the establishment of Malay as the national language, or of citizenship laws.

September 1970 – Tun Abdul Razak succeeds Tengku Abdul Rahman as Prime Minister. A 'national ideology' is proclaimed, providing for a united, democratic, just, liberal and progressive Malaysia.

February 1971 – The constitution is amended to forbid the discussion of 'sensitive issues' (e.g. race relations) even in Parliament. Parliament is reconvened for the first time since the May 1969 riots.

April 1971 – Britain, Australia, New Zealand, Malaysia and Singapore form a new defence alliance, providing for an integrated air defence system and ANZUK – a small Commonwealth force to be stationed in Singapore. This alliance replaces the old Anglo-Malaysian Defence Agreement.

April 1972 – Malaysia and Indonesia form a border committee at ministerial level to cooperate in the fight against Communist insurgency along their common frontier in Borneo.

August 1973 – Tun Doctor Ismail, protagonist of a neutral South-east Asia, dies.

September 1973 – Tengku Abdul Rahman, now Secretary-General of an international Islamic Secretariat, claims that 75,000 people in Sabah have been converted to Islam since 1970.

THE PHILIPPINES

Definitions
Moros – Muslims of the Southern Philippines.
Tagalog – the dominant ethnic group of the Philippines, their language, etc.

The Events
1942 – The 'Hukbalahap' (People's Anti-Japanese Army) is formed, and its strength is subsequently built up to 30,000.

July 1946 – The Independent Republic of the Philippines is inaugurated. Manuel Roxas is first President. The Bell Act provides for preferential trade between the Philippines and the United States, and Americans are granted equal rights with Filipinos within the republic.

1947 – An agreement is concluded whereby the United States may maintain bases in the Philippines for 99 years.

1950 – Ramon Magsaysay is appointed Secretary of Defence in view of the increasing Communist Huk menace, and rapidly destroys its central organization.

1953 – Magsaysay is elected President (Nacionalista Party). He attacks the Huks effectively, reducing their fighting strength to about 650, and introduces reforms to abate discontent.

March 1957 – Magsaysay is killed in an air crash. He is succeeded by Vice-President Carlos Garcia.

November 1961 – Presidential elections.

January 1962 – Diosdado Macapagal (Liberal Party) becomes President, with Emmanuel Pelaez as Vice-President.

1962–3 – Macapagal officially advances the Philippine claim to British North Borneo (Sabah). Manila refuses to recognize the new Federation of Malaysia, which includes Sabah, and diplomatic ties are suspended.

November–December 1965 – Presidential elections. Ferdinand Marcos becomes President (Nacionalista Party).

1966 – Relations with the Federation of Malaysia (formerly Malaya) are restored.
President Marcos visits Washington. The lease of the US military bases in the Philippines is cut from ninety-nine to twenty-five years.

1968 – The Philippine Congress passes an Act constitutionally including Sabah within the frontiers of the republic. Malaysia suspends relations with Manila.

November 1969 – Presidential elections. Marcos is re-elected after a violent campaign.

December 1969 – Malaysia still does not agree to submit the Philippine claim to Sabah to the World Court, but tension eases and the two countries agree to resume diplomatic relations.

January 1970 – Five die in violent demonstrations against President Marcos mounted by students calling for clean elections and a non-partisan constitutional convention in 1971. Marcos blames the Communists.

August 1971 – Two fragmentation grenades thrown at a political rally in Manila kill ten and wound or maim the entire opposition Liberal Party leadership. Marcos blames the Communists, and suspends Habeas Corpus. There are widespread arrests. The year generally is marked by student demonstrations, strikes, and political rallies.

September 1971 – Sporadic fighting in the Southern Philippines leads to pitched battles between Christians and Muslims in which scores are killed.

January 1972 – Marcos restores Habeas Corpus and normal constitutional rights. District and rural elections are held.

September 1972 – As unrest mounts and the Maoist 'New People's Army' that now spearheads the Communist insurgency grows in strength, Marcos proclaims martial law.

October 1972 – Marcos signs a land reform decree under which 700,000 farmers will each be given twelve acres of land. Fighting between rebels and security forces breaks out in the Southern Philippines.

November 1972 – The Constitutional Convention approves a new constitution, which provides that Marcos can head an interim government during an indefinite period of transition to the new parliamentary system.

January 1973 – The new constitution is ratified by a national plebiscite.

March–April 1973 – A government spokesman declares 8–9,000 Muslims are defying the security forces in the Southern Philippines. Marcos puts total number of rebels at 14–16,000, but the situation is said to have stabilized.

July 1973 – A national referendum gives Marcos the right to stay in office after 1973 (when his presidential term normally expires), so that he can continue to build the 'New Society' he has started to create during ten months of martial law.

August 1973 – Some 523,000 firearms have been surrendered or seized during the President's war on crime.

SINGAPORE

The Events

May 1959 – The People's Action Party (PAP) of Lee Kuan Yew wins forty-three out of fifty-one seats in the first fully-elected Singapore Legislative Assembly under a new constitution granting the island internal self-government.

February 1963 – Lim Chin Siong, Secretary-General of the pro-Communist Barisan Sosialis, is detained with some other party leaders.

September 1963 – The PAP wins thirty-seven seats in general elections, the Barisan Sosialis thirteen.

Singapore merges with Malaya and becomes part of the new Federation of Malaysia.

July 1964 – Race riots between Chinese and Malays break out on Mohammed's birthday.

August 1965 – After an increasingly abrasive relationship, Malaysia expels Singapore from the Federation. Singapore becomes an independent republic.

October 1966 – Under the chairmanship of Dr Lee Siew Choh, the Barisan Sosialis boycotts parliament and 'takes the struggle on to the streets'.

April–May 1967 – The Barisan Sosialis calls for a general strike and for a mammoth demonstration on Labour Day. Both are failures.

November 1967 – The old British Straits dollar is devalued, following devaluation of the pound.

January 1968 – The British disclose that they intend to withdraw their forces and close their military bases in Singapore and Malaysia by the end of 1971.

April 1968 – Snap elections are held in Singapore. The Barisan Sosialis boycotts them, and the PAP wins all fifty-eight seats in the Legislative Assembly.

July 1968 – A stringent Industrial Relations Bill is introduced, stipulating a forty-four-hour week for all.

1969 – Bills are introduced to legalize abortion and to abolish juries.

July 1969 – Lim Chin Siong, detained Secretary-General of the Barisan Sosialis, recants, is freed, and goes to the UK.

August 1969 – Singapore celebrates 150th anniversary of the founding of the settlement by Sir Stamford Raffles.

March 1970 – Tengku Abdul Rahman visits Singapore.

January 1971 – The Conference of Commonwealth Heads of State is held in Singapore.

April 1971 – Singapore forms a new defence alliance with Malaysia, Britain, Australia and New Zealand which provides for a reduced Commonwealth force (ANZUK) to be based permanently in the republic.

March 1972 – Premier Lee Kuan Yew visits Malaysia.

September 1972 – The PAP wins 70 per cent of votes and all sixty-five seats in general elections.

May 1973 – Lee Kuan Yew visits Indonesia.

THAILAND
(formerly Siam)

The Events

January 1942 – Marshal Pibul Songgram, the Thai Premier, declares war on the Allies.

1944–6 – As the Japanese begin losing the war, Pibul resigns, and is later gaoled for one year as a war criminal.

November 1947–April 1948 – Pibul seizes power again in a military coup, and becomes Prime Minister.

1950 – United States military assistance begins.

1951 – Pibul suspends the constitution and the fully elected parliament in view of the 'Communist threat'.

1954 – The headquarters of the South-east Asia Treaty Organization is established in Bangkok.

September 1957 – Marshal Sarit Thanarat, Commander-in-Chief of the Army, overthrows Pibul. Elections are held.

October 1958 – Sarit assumes direct power in his own name, dissolves the new National Assembly and cabinet, imposes martial law, abrogates the constitution, and bans political parties.

December 1963 – Sarit dies. Field Marshal Thanom Kittikachorn becomes Prime Minister.

1964 – The Communists announce the existence of a 'Thai Patriotic Front' fighting for 'liberation' in North-east Thailand.

1965 – The decision is taken to establish a joint Thai–Malaysian headquarters in South Thailand in view of the increasing terrorist activity of the Malayan Communist Party guerrillas on the border.

1966–7 – The United States builds up its forces in Thailand and its bases for bombing Vietnam.

Thailand sends the Queen Cobra regiment to fight in Vietnam.

Foreign Minister Thanat Khoman urges relentless bombing of North Vietnam.

Communist-trained Meo guerrillas become active in Northern Thailand.

June 1968 – A new constitution is promulgated. Political parties are legalized.

September 1968 – Municipal elections are held. Only 20 per cent of voters go to polls.

February 1969 – General elections. Marshal Thanom forms a new government.

Thanat Khoman, the Foreign Minister, expresses readiness to hold talks with Peking.

September 1969 – Thai–US discussions on the future withdrawal of 48,000 American servicemen in Thailand begin.

June 1971 – Thanom visits Malaysia. The Thais release Muslim Malays arrested under the régime of Marshal Sarit for allegedly plotting the secession of Southern Thailand.

November 1971 – Thanom mounts a bloodless coup, dissolves his cabinet, abolishes parliament, suspends the constitution, and proclaims martial law. He himself becomes chairman of a new National Executive Council.

December 1972 – An interim constitution is promulgated replacing the National Executive Council with a cabinet. A National Assembly of 299 appointed members is created – 200 of them drawn from the police and armed services.

August 1973 – The United States begins withdrawing 3,500 men and 100 aircraft from Thailand, leaving some 41,000 men and 500 aircraft.

October 1973 – Thanom takes refuge in the United States, following massive student demonstrations in Bangkok involving several hundred deaths. A new civilian government under Sanya Thammasak promises a new constitution within six months, and general elections.

Bibliography

SOUTH-EAST ASIA GENERAL

A History of Modern South-east Asia by John Bastin and Harry J. Benda. Federal Publications, Kuala Lumpur.

Communism in South-east Asia by J. H. Brimmell. Oxford University Press.

People and Progress in East Asia by Eli Ginzberg. Columbia University, New York.

A History of South-east Asia by D. G. E. Hall. Macmillan & Co., London.

Asian Drama, Vols. I–III by Gunnar Myrdal. Pantheon, Random House, New York.

East Asia in Old Maps by Hiroshi Nakamura. East West Center Press, Honolulu.

The Revolution in South-east Asia by Victor Purcell. Thames & Hudson, London.

Time out of Hand by Robert Shaplen. André Deutsch, London.

INDOCHINA GENERAL

The Struggle for Indochina by Ellen J. Hammer. Stanford University Press, Stanford, California.

The Emancipation of French Indochina by Donald Lancaster. Oxford University Press.

(see also 'Cambodia', 'Laos' and 'Vietnam' under their own headings).

PHILOSOPHY AND RELIGION

The Sayings of Muhammed by Allama Sir Abdullah Al-Mamun Al-Suhrawardy. John Murray, London.

Buddhist Scriptures translated by Edward Conze. Penguin Books, Harmondsworth.

Islam by Alfred Guillaume. Penguin Books, Harmondsworth.

Buddhism by Christmas Humphreys. Penguin Books, Harmondsworth.

The Wisdom of China and India by Lin Yutang. Random House, New York.

Buddhism: an Introduction by Luang Suriyabongs, M.D. The Buddhist Council of Ceylon, Colombo.

Hinduism by K. M. Sen. Penguin Books, Harmondsworth.

Malayan Buddhism by Teng Eng Soon. Eastern Universities Press, Singapore.

The Way of Zen by Alan W. Watts, Penguin Books, Harmondsworth.

BURMA

The Union of Burma by Hugh Tinker. Oxford University Press.

Outline of Burmese History by G. E. Harvey. Orient Longmans, Calcutta.

Burmese Family by Mi Mi Khaing. Orient Longmans, Calcutta.

CAMBODIA

Angkor: an Introduction by George Coedes. Oxford University Press.

A History of Cambodia by Manomohan Ghosh. J. K. Gupta, Saigon.

Angkor: Art and Civilization by Bernard Groslier and Jacques Arthaud, translated by Eric Ernshaw Smith. Thames & Hudson, London.

Cambodia: The Search for Security by Michael Leifer. Frederick A. Praeger, New York.

Cambodge compiled by Charles Meyer, published by the Ministry of Information of Cambodia, Phnom Penh.

Cambodia: Country Survey Series by David J. Steinberg and collaborators. Human Relations Area Files, New Haven.

INDONESIA

Sukarno: an Autobiography as told to Cindy Adams. Gunung Agung, Djakarta.

The Mythology and the Tolerance of the Javanese by Benedict R. O'G. Anderson. Monograph Series, Cornell University, New York.

Indonesian Communism by Arnold C. Brackman. Frederick A. Praeger, New York.

Indonesia by G. A. Chatfield. Eastern Universities Press, Singapore.

Indonesia by Bruce Grant. Melbourne University Press, Melbourne.

Indonesian Upheaval by John Hughes. David McKay Company, New York.

Indonesia by J. D. Legge. Prentice-Hall, New Jersey.

Indonesia: a Profile by Jeanne Mintz. D. Van Nostrand Company, Princeton, New Jersey.

Rebels in Paradise by James Mossman. Jonathan Cape, London.

The Smiling General by O. G. Roeder. Gunung Agung, Djakarta.

The Fall of Sukarno by Tarzie Vittachi. André Deutsch, London.

The Republic of Indonesia by Dorothy Woodman. The Cresset Press, London.

LAOS

Aspects du Pays Lao by Nhouy Abhay. Éditions Comité Littéraire Lao, Vientiane.

Kingdom of Laos by René de Berval. France-Asie, Saigon.

Conflict in Laos by Arthur J. Dommen. Frederick A. Praeger, New York.

The Edge of Tomorrow by Thomas A. Dooley, M.D. Berkley Publishing Corpn, New York.

MALAYA

Malay Customs and Traditions by Alwi bin Sheikh Alhady. Eastern Universities Press, Singapore.

Essays on Indonesian and Malayan History by John Bastin. Eastern Universities Press, Singapore.

The Golden Chersonese by Isabella L. Bird. Oxford University Press.

Malaya's Eurasians – an Opinion by C. H. Crabbe. Eastern Universities Press, Singapore.

Sarawak, Brunei and North Borneo by Nigel Heyward. Eastern Universities Press, Singapore.

Land Below the Wind by Agnes Keith. Michael Joseph, London.

A History of Malaya by J. Kennedy, M.A. Macmillan & Co., Kuala Lumpur.

Menace in Malaya by Harry Miller. George G. Harrap & Co., London.

Prince and Premier by Harry Miller. George G. Harrap & Co., London.

Costumes of Malaya by Katharine Sim. Eastern Universities Press, Singapore.

Piracy and Politics in the Malay World by Nicholas Tarling. Donald Moore Gallery, Singapore.

Malaysia and Singapore by K. G. Tregonning. Donald Moore Press, Singapore.

THE PHILIPPINES

The Philippines by G. A. Chatfield. Eastern Universities Press, Singapore.

The Philippines by Albert Ravenholt. D. Van Nostrand Company, Princeton, New Jersey.

SINGAPORE

The Singapore Story by Kenneth Attiwill. Frederick Muller, London.

Sinister Twilight by Noel Barber. Collins, London.

Lee Kuan Yew by Alex Josey. Donald Moore Press, Singapore.

The First 150 Years of Singapore by Donald and Joanna Moore. Donald Moore Press, Singapore.

Singapore: A Popular History by H. F. Pearson, Eastern Universities Press, Singapore.

Raffles of the Eastern Isles by C. E. Wurtzburg. Hodder & Stoughton, London.

THAILAND

Thailand by Noel F. Busch. D. Van Nostrand Company, Princeton, New Jersey.

The Rice Bowl of Asia by David M. Davies. Robert Hale, London.

Thailand by M. Palmer. Eastern Universities Press, Singapore.

My Country Thailand by Phra Sarasas. Mazusen, Tokyo. Reprinted privately in Bangkok.

Politics in Thailand by David A. Wilson. Cornell University Press, New York.

VIETNAM

Histoire du Viet-Nam by Philippe Devillers. Éditions du Seuil, Paris.

Ho Chi Minh on Revolution by Bernard B. Fall. Pall Mall Press, London.

The Two Viet-Nams by Bernard B. Fall.

The Making of a Quagmire by David Halberstam. Bodley Head, London.

Ho Chi Minh by Jean Lacouture. Allen Lane The Penguin Press, London.

Vietnam between Two Truces by Jean Lacouture. Secker & Warburg, London.

Vietnam: the Lotus in the Sea of Fire by Thich Nhat Hanh. SCM Press, London.

Visages et Images du Sud Viet-Nam by A. M. Savani, Saigon.

The Lost Revolution by Robert Shaplen. André Deutsch, London.

The Road from War by Robert Shaplen. Harper & Row, New York.

Trip to Hanoi by Susan Sontag. Farrar, Straus & Giroux, New York.

The Last Confucian by Denis Warner. Penguin Books, Harmondsworth.

GENERAL

A History of the Chinese in California. Chinese Historical Society of America, San Francisco.

The Travels of Marco Polo translated by Ronald Latham. Penguin Books, Harmondsworth.

The Bomb and the Computer by Andrew Wilson. The Cresset Press, London.

The Asia Magazine, Hongkong.

The Far Eastern Economic Review, Hongkong.

Glossary

(Note : Definitions of peoples and places – 'Lao', 'Laotian', 'Malaya', 'Malaysia', 'Vietcong', 'Vietminh', etc.– are given under the respective countries in the 'Synopsis of Events'.

Ao-dai – Vietnamese woman's dress of a long, high-collared silk coatee and trousers.

Barong Tagalog – Filipino man's national dress : usually a cream-coloured embroidered shirt, worn loose.

Barrio – a Filipino village.

Batak – a minority people of Sumatra.

Bomoh – a Malay medicine-man.

Bonze – a Buddhist monk.

Bung – an Indonesian word for 'Brother'.

Confrontation – Indonesia's undeclared war against Malaysia : 1963–6.

Cyclopousse – in Francophone territories, a trishaw or tricycle rickshaw.

Daimyo – Japanese feudal lord.

Dong – Vietnamese piastre : the rate of exchange of the North Vietnamese dong in Hanoi in 1955 was 10,000 to the pound.

Dukun – Malay medicine-man (cf. *Bomoh*).

Gamelan – an Indonesian orchestra in which the most important instruments are drums and xylophones.

Kampong – Malay village or homestead.

Karma – according to Hindu belief, our destiny as it evolves from the sum of all our actions, good and bad, in all previous lives, and the impact of the karma of others upon it.

Kempetai – Japanese secret police.

Kris – the Malay dagger, often with a twisted winding blade like a snake.

Longgyi – Burmese equivalent of a sarong (see *Sarong*).

Mahayana Buddhism – 'Great Vehicle' Buddhism from North India whose canon is in Sanskrit, and whose sects postulate saints, Heaven, and the power of faith. (See *Theravada Buddhism*.)

Parang – a Malay chopping knife, or machete.

Pitji – a short Indonesian velvet cap, usually black. (See *Songkok*.)

Prahu – a Malay boat.

Sampot – Cambodian equivalent of the sarong.

Sarong – a long, voluminous Malay step-in skirt, whose slack is folded across the body and tucked in to give a tight, sheath-like effect.

Stengah (satengah) – a Malay word literally meaning 'half'. In colonial drinking terms, a small whisky.

Songkok – the Malay black velvet cap. (See *Pitji*.)

Theravada Buddhism – sometimes known as Hinayana (Little Vehicle) Buddhism. It originated in South India, its canon is in Pali, and it promises only the bliss of extinction if after many incarnations a man achieves enlightenment.

Trishaw – tricycle rickshaw.

Index

Index

visits Djakarta, 289; Malayan
Alliance on, 342–3; and race
relations, 343, 346, 352;
Rahman on, 343; background
and character, 344–5; Albar
on, 346; Razak on, 348;
Malaysian Alliance and, 348–9;
problems facing, 350; quoted,
355; and American presence in
Thailand, 364; and ASEAN,
369; integrity of, 373–4; and
Communism, 374–5; and
democracy, 375–6; and the
law, 378; and students, 379;
on Western society, 379
Lee Siew Choh, Dr, 374
Leonowens, Anna, 388
Liberation Front, Vietnam, 198,
240–41, 242, 247
Lim Chin Siong, 348, 375
Lukman, M. H., 76

Macapagal, Diosdado, President
of the Philippines, 39, 55, 94,
127
MacArthur, General Douglas, 38
Macnamara, Robert S., 230, 232
Madjapahit empire, 24, 26, 27
Malacca, Straits of, 31, 171, 366
Malaya : Britain and, 32, 149;
Japanese in North, 34; politics,
65; guerrilla warfare in, 68,
69–70; Independence
ceremony, 70; Communist
terrorism in, 72; ethics, 122,
123; head-dress, 128; *belum*,
295, 307; customs, 302; Malays
and Sakkais, 329; and
Federation of Malaysia, 334,
335, 341; Chinese in, 341
Malayan Alliance, 65, 342–3, 348,
353

Malayan Emergency, 67, 315,
316–18, 357
Malays : and Chinese, 342, 347,
353; Rahman on, 344; in
Singapore, 346–7; preferential
treatment in Malaysia, 352–3,
354
Malaysia, Federation of, 342–56;
language in, 44; remarkable
behaviour of politician in, 62;
political prisoners in, 65–6;
Communism and, 72–3; birth
rate, 91; Britain and, 149, 310,
312, 333, 364, 365; and
Indonesia, 150, 259; and
corruption, 164, 373; bribery
in, 168; smuggling in, 172, 338;
superstition in, 177–9; magic
healers of, 179; Islamic laws
in, 191; and religious unrest,
201; equality of women in,
210, 212; Indonesian
Confrontation of, 260–61, 290,
310, 311, 313–15, 357; and USA,
261, 358; and China, 275; and
neutralization of South-east
Asia, 278; ASEAN, 278, 370;
Sabah incorporated in, 289–90;
and Philippines, 290–92; mixed
population of, 333; early days
of Federation, 334; Singapore
and, 334, 335, 341, 349–50, 351;
Albar and, 348; Chinese
immigrants, 356; and USSR,
362, 363; Australia and, 365;
and tourist trade, 383;
parliamentary democracy in,
393; synopsis of events in,
405–7
Malik, Dr Adam, 367, 368
Manalo, Felix, 185
Manila : Catholicism in, 48, 184,

Manila (*contd*)
383; Uncle Sam burned in
effigy, 49; American influence
in, 50–51; violence in, 51–2, 57;
Police Department, 52–3;
democracy in, 54–5; parties
given in, 94–5; Clark Air Base,
96; Indonesian trade with, 152;
new mosque promised for,
201; lawyers of, 290; and
tourist trade, 383
Manners and customs, 298–309
Mao Tse-tung, 285; his ambitions
in South-east Asia, 72; and the
peasants, 73; 'Quotations from
Mao', 73; and 'Cultural
Revolution', 75; early allies,
98; Pham Van Dong and, 104;
and Ho Chi Minh, 105; and
Vietnam, 105; Sukarno and,
143; and unity of China, 274;
South-east Asians fear, 337;
and Malaysian Chinese, 353;
and Nixon, 363
Maoists, 180, 191, 196, 375
Marco Polo : on Cham marriage
customs, 22; on unicorns, 26;
on Indian habit of washing,
302–3
Marcos, Ferdinand, President of
the Philippines : and USA, 49,
50; tries to suppress crime and
violence, 52; imposes martial
law, 57; attacks Communism,
57; creates 'new society', 57–8;
'New People's Army' and, 98;
and Muslim–Christian conflict,
201; and China, 275; and
Filipino claim to Sabah, 291
Marshall, David, 378
Martin, Robert Pepper, 153
Marxism, 130, 197

Mecca, 190
Mekong Delta, 90, 187, 236
Menander, King, 188
Meos, 329, 330–31
Meyer, Charles, 197, 221, 222,
224
Midway, 310
Mikoyan, Anastas, 113–14, 115
Minority groups, 327–32, 334
Mohammed, 27, 122, 143, 204–5,
303, 310
Mois, 327–9
Mongkut, King of Siam, 388–9
Mongols, 25
Moros, 27
Muruts, 60, 329, 334
Muslims, *see* Islam
Mustapha, Tun, 201, 334

Nagas, 329
Nasser, Gamal, Abdul, President
of UAR, 277
Nasution, General Abdul Haris,
77, 182, 288
Nationalism, 45; colonialism and,
41–2; language and, 44; and
Communism, 66, 68, 71; and
Indonesia, 141, 142;
Vietnamese Liberation Front
and, 242
Ne Win, General, President of
Burma, in power, 129, 130–31,
161, 330; and Buddhists, 202;
and China, 275; and U Nu, 330
Netherlands, 46, 147, 149, 331
Neutrality, 278–86
New Guinea, 149, 384, 389
New Zealand, ANZUK, 364, 365;
New Zealanders, 329
Nhu, Ngo Dinh, 132, 160–61, 244,
276
Nhu, Ngo Dinh, Madame,

Subandrio, Dr, 182, 297
Suharto, President of Indonesia:
postpones elections, 65;
anti-Communist, 77; his
cabinet, 89; his astuteness, 158;
on his wife, 168; attempted
assassination of, 180; and
Djojobojo's prophecy, 181;
and superstition, 181, 182; and
marriage laws, 200; and affair
of terrorists in Singapore, 288;
and West Irian, 331
Sukarnapura, 143
Sukarno, Achmad, President of
Indonesia, 141–6; and Japan,
37; Western influence on, 39;
Madiun uprising, 68; and
Communism, 76–7, 259; out of
office, 77, 89; and Khrushchev,
79, 80, 81, 86; appearance, 79;
and foreign visitors, 81–2; and
Indonesia, 83, 149–50; on
Khrushchev, 84; in dept to
USSR, 88, 259; social position
of, 127; Rahman and, 128–9;
and Netherlands, 147–8, 331;
and Malaysia, 148, 150, 259,
314, 357; Western opinion of,
148, 180, 322–3; and civil war,
156, 158, 193; and Tjikini
Affair, 159, 193; corruption,
167, 168; and superstition, 180,
181, 182; and Djojobojo's
prophecy, 180–81; Darul Islam
against, 193; and USA, 260; his
style of making war, 313; and
West Irian, 331; student
power and, 373
Sullivan, William, 74
Sulu, Sultan of, 289, 290
Sulu Sea, 172
Sumarit, King of Cambodia, 281

Sumatra: rhinoceros from, 26;
Japanese invasion of, 34; civil
war in, 151, 155–8, 267;
resentment against Java, 151,
156; Darul Islam, 152, 193;
American small arms for, 153;
author and foreign
correspondents in, 153–7;
trade, 158; Minangkabau
houses in, 203; legend of
dispute with Java, 203–4;
student action in Belawan,
372
Sumitro, Dr Djojohadikusomo,
152, 158
Superstition, 176–83
Sutan Sjahrir, 45
Suzie, 221, 222

Taiwan, 369
Tan Siew Sin, 358, 361–2
Taruc, Luis, 97
Taylor, General Maxwell, 232
Tengku Abdul Rahman, Prime
Minister of Malaysia: Western
influence on, 39; and
Macapagal, 94; prince, 127;
and Sukarno, 128–9, 146; and
Minister of Education, 164; in
detention, 190; 'Turk' and, 193;
attitude to neutralization, 278;
and Malaysia, 333–4, 335; his
background, 343; character,
343–4, 345; attitude to
racialism, 344; and Lee Kuan
Yew, 345, 349, 361; Albar and,
346, 349; and Singapore, 349,
351, 355; his reduced majority,
353; and Malayan Emergency,
357; and Indonesian
Confrontation, 357; and
Australia, 365

MORE ABOUT PENGUINS
AND PELICANS

Penguinews, which appears every month, contains details of all the new books issued by Penguins as they are published. From time to time it is supplemented by *Penguins in Print*, which is a complete list of all titles available. (There are some five thousand of these.)

A specimen copy of *Penguinews* will be sent to you free on request. For a year's issues (including the complete lists) please send 50p if you live in the British Isles, or 75p if you live elsewhere. Just write to Dept EP, Penguin Books Ltd, Harmondsworth, Middlesex, enclosing a cheque or postal order, and your name will be added to the mailing list.

In the U.S.A.: For a complete list of books available from Penguin in the United States write to Dept CS, Penguin Books Inc., 7110 Ambassador Road, Baltimore, Maryland 21207.

In Canada: For a complete list of books available from Penguin in Canada write to Penguin Books Canada Ltd, 41 Steelcase Road West, Markham, Ontario.

SUKARNO

A POLITICAL BIOGRAPHY

J. D. Legge

Modern Indonesia – potentially one of the richest areas in the world – is largely the creation of Kusno Sosro Sukarno, who put Indonesia on the political map.

In this detailed and informative biography, Sukarno, who was often represented in the West as an absurd playboy, is considered as a serious political figure. Professor Legge examines Sukarno's policies and his conduct as a leader, and (taking into account the traditional Javanese attitudes towards the ruler) throws a new light on the more flamboyant aspects of his leadership. Falling victim to the conflicting elements of nationalism, separatism and the competing interests of the power blocs, Sukarno was finally ousted from power in 1966. Nevertheless, as Professor Legge points out, we must not underestimate the repercussions of his statecraft on South-East Asian Politics.

A Pelican Book

MY WAR WITH THE CIA

THE MEMOIRS OF PRINCE NORODOM SIHANOUK
AS RELATED TO WILFRED BURCHETT

These memoirs are an eloquent account of Prince Norodom Sihanouk's fight for Cambodian independence – first against France and then, for over twenty years, against the United States. Sihanouk shows that Cambodia's freedom from the French was only the beginning of an even more arduous struggle. Exposing American efforts to sabotage his neutralist policies, he describes the ever-present CIA involvement with his domestic opponents, the corrupting influence of dollar aid, the assassination attempts against him, and the coup that finally toppled his government in 1970. His book is thus a startling report on the tactics used by the world's strongest power to force smaller nations away from their chosen policies. As Professor Richard A. Falk, of Princeton University, has written, 'Even the most cynical reader will be shocked by Prince Sihanouk's remarkable account of what the CIA did over the years to his country'.

'Timely insights ... The Prince writes with the clarity of a brilliant politician'. – *Chicago Sun Times*

'Valuable and intriguing' – *Noam Chomsky*

A *Pelican Book*

THE DUTCH SEABORNE EMPIRE

1600—1800

C. R. Boxer

For Holland the 'Golden Century' was the seventeenth. Astonishing indeed was the Dutch nation's sudden rise to prosperity and power, in view of the country's smallness, its religious and political divisions and its recent oppression by Spain.

In this 'fascinating and vividly written book' (as Christopher Hill called it in the *New Statesman*) Professor Boxer makes their large, even fabulous trading empire the key to the Dutch explosion – an empire in which the Dutch East India and West India Companies played an important part. He shows the Dutch brushing aside political, religious and even racial differences in their pursuit of profit and devoting all their energies and resources to the construction of a 'burgher' nation, inspired by trade and commerce. But there were flaws in the story of success, and Professor Boxer records how too often sober merchants succumbed, in the hot climates, to the temptations of gin and dissipation.

The Dutch Seaborne Empire admirably portrays the early Dutch incursion into the modern world, to which Holland added its full quota in scientific and artistic achievement.

A Pelican Book

MAN'S ESTATE

André Malraux

As a member of the revolutionary committee, André Malraux witnessed the doomed Communist rising in Shanghai in 1927. *Man's Estate* (*La Condition humaine*) emerged from this experience.

Against a background of violence, betrayal and massacre, his characters are driven to try to transcend the 'human condition': Ferral, a French businessman, through sex, and Clappique, a bizarre arms-dealer, through gambling. Amongst the Communists, Chen chooses terrorism: Kyo Gisors, the intellect and old Gisors, opium ... reactions to the human situation now more general than when *Man's Estate* first appeared in 1933 – or, as a Penguin, in 1961.

Arguably the most influential figure of the enlightened militant European conscience in the thirties, Malraux derives his power 'from his genuine poetic creation ... his ruthless interpretation of reality in terms of his private myth of revolutionary tragic contemporary man' – J. B. Priestley

THE BIRTH OF COMMUNIST CHINA

C. P. Fitzgerald

This Pelican, which is a fully revised edition of the author's
Revolution in China, sets out to assess the significance of the
Chinese Revolution.

After sketching in the background of China's long history
and social structure C. P. Fitzgerald, who is now Professor
of Far Eastern History at Canberra, opens his main account
at the fall of the Manchu Emperors in 1911 and traces the
origins of revolution through the early republic of Sun Yat-
sen and the Nationalist dictatorship of Chiang Kai-shek to
the military campaigns of Mao Tse-tung. He assesses the
varying influences of Confucianism and Christianity, of East
and West, and of the Japanese and Russians on this massive
movement, and makes it abundantly clear that the China of
today is not an inexplicable freak but a logical development
of its immensely long past.

Professor Fitzgerald has a gift for fluent narrative and a
long experience of China, and his interpretation of one of
the central political events of this century is as readable as
it is reliable.

A Pelican Book